"Finding practical skill for living li [ ] produced a highly readable, text driven, and practical exposition of the book of Proverbs. This work is technical enough for the scholar, yet clear and relevant for the layman. Phillips' commentary will help anyone navigate the challenges of contemporary life by explaining God's ancient book of wisdom."

—Dr. Michael Rydelnik, professor of Jewish studies,
Moody Bible Institute, author, *The Messianic Hope*

"Dan Phillips is a first-rate exegete with the tracking skills of a bloodhound and the tenacity of a pit bull. He won't rest till he's thoroughly searched a matter out and once he's got a hold on the truth he won't let go. He delivers the goods, and he does so with nerve and verve, punch and panache. You'll find *God's Wisdom in Proverbs* to be both scholarly in its depth and sagacious in its insight and application."

—John A. Kitchen, senior pastor, Stow Alliance Fellowship,
Stow, OH, author, *The Pastoral Epistles for Pastors*

"The list of really useful literature on the book of Proverbs is rather short. *God's Wisdom in Proverbs* is a welcome and needed addition to that list. Proverbs is a book rich with insight and instruction, motivation and exhortation. However, for too many Christians it's a book of pithy sayings that make one either nod the head with feigned (but mystified) agreement or which are applied in ways that would have made even the wise Solomon scratch his head in bewilderment. Dan's book goes a long way to help clear one's head of mystery and misapplication. The reader of *God's Wisdom in Proverbs* will find, if not the key to Proverbs, at least a lamp to illumine and a guide to correct or confirm on the path to accurate interpretation. *God's Wisdom in Proverbs* offers an introduction to the wisdom of Proverbs for the beginning disciple as well insights for the seasoned scholar. Dan knows his stuff and it shows. Pastors who read this book will want to preach Proverbs; teachers will want to open the book's knowledge for students; all Christians will be delighted and challenged. After reading Dan's book, some will grow wiser, some will draw closer to the Lord, and some (after reading Dan's treatment of Proverbs 22:6) will have to take that old "cross-stitch verse" off the nursery wall."

—Kevin D. Zuber, PhD, professor of
Theology, Moody Bible Institute

"Though it is regularly read, Proverbs is seldom taught because it is, well, proverbial. Thankfully, Dan Phillips has gifted us with a new go-to resource in *God's Wisdom in Proverbs* that makes the task of expounding Proverbs slightly less intimidating. Dan's thorough treatment of the critical issues and his interaction with other literature not only equips, but his accessible model will actually excite pastors and teachers to again declare the wisdom of Proverbs in and to the church. The appendices alone are worth the price of the book! I expect to make frequent use of *God's Wisdom* in my public ministry and personal counseling. Moreover, Dan's eye for contemporary application and his personal humor make this a valuable resource for classes, Bible studies, and personal discipleship in our church. All Christians who are seeking godly wisdom in a world of folly would show great discernment by starting with this book."

—STEVE MEISTER, associate pastor, River City
Grace Community Church, Sacramento, CA

"*God's Wisdom in Proverbs* is a valuable resource for anybody who wants to study or teach the book of Proverbs. Dan Phillips does not merely spoon feed the meaning of each individual verse to the reader, but instead lays a foundation upon which one can effectively interpret the book on his own. This book will now be the first work I turn to the next time I have the privilege of teaching the book of Proverbs."

—CASEY LUTE, author, *But God...The Two
Words at the Heart of the Gospel*

"For those already familiar with the insightful, unapologetic writing of Dan Phillips from his web presence, this commentary will serve as a traveler's guide to the landscape of Proverbs from a familiar and trusted friend. And to the newcomer his book will serve as the first resource to consult when teaching, studying, or preaching from Solomon's sayings. Phillips knows how to write, and this text is filled with powerful yet practical interpretation and application. He has sat at the feet of some of the greatest expositors of Scripture and now we get to sit at his."

—DR. TODD S. BUCK, senior pastor, First Baptist Church, Clewiston,
FL, adjunct professor of Theology, Liberty Baptist Theological
Seminary and New Orleans Baptist Theological Seminary

"*God's Wisdom in Proverbs* is written brilliantly at a level that will challenge anyone who is interested enough in gaining wisdom and understanding to be serious in that quest. Readers will range from serious students of Scripture to casual lay readers on their way to a more serious approach to Scripture. It explains the wisdom of Proverbs (and the biblical nature of wisdom *per se*) in a clear, readable fashion that will be extremely helpful to everyone from students entering the academic world for the first time, to new parents seeking biblical insight into the process of child-rearing, to anyone in a position of responsibility or leadership. I recommend it for all who are tired of the superficial, self-centered themes that have filled evangelical pulpits and bookshelves for the past three decades (or more). If you are hungry for biblical material, *God's Wisdom in Proverbs* will feed your appetite."

—PHIL JOHNSON, executive director, Grace to You

"The writer of Proverbs promises to teach us wisdom so that we may know how to live. It is immediately obvious that our 21st century world, and the Western church in particular, lack such wisdom. It is tragic that Solomon's life work is so widely neglected and misunderstood today. Proverbs is a challenging book. You will find things in it that are hard to understand. It is a book to wrestle with. My friend Dan Phillips has loved and fought with the book of Proverbs for many years. His work deserves to be widely read. It will instruct you, provoke you, and at times you may find yourself disagreeing with him. But my prayer and his is that the message of Proverbs will challenge the values the world is trying to squeeze into you every day. A people truly exhibiting God's wisdom to the world will be the result."

—ADRIAN WARNOCK, author, *Raised with Christ:*
How the Resurrection Changes Everything

"This is a great work on Proverbs and its literature! Pastors will find it most useful for teaching their members to read and understand the literature of wisdom, and to tie wisdom to its parallels in the Old Testament historical literature. While making full use of recent scholarship on Proverbs, the work is very accessible to eager readers who desire to grow in their fear of the Lord. Philips has provided a work that will help the church grow wise before the Lord."

—ERIC C. REDMOND, senior pastor, Reformation Alive Baptist
Church, Temple Hills, MD, assistant professor of Bible and Theology,
Washington Bible College,author, *Where Are All the Brothers?*

"Though many know that the wisdom diamonds of Proverbs are worth more than the Crown Jewels, they feel unprepared to study this rich section of Scripture. Now Daniel Phillips has given us a resource that shows us how to mine Proverbs in order to build up a rich storehouse of wisdom. Indeed, Phillips puts the wisdom jewels of Proverbs on display. Building on decades of study and with meticulous attention to the biblical text and theological scholarship, *God's Wisdom in Proverbs* deserves a place on the shelf of every student of the Word of God."

—CHRIS BRAUNS, pastor, The Red Brick Church,
Stillman Valley, IL, author, *Unpacking Forgiveness*

"One of the great pleasures of life is puzzling through the book of Proverbs, and if you're looking to navigate life with Solomonic skill, Dan Phillips is ready to show you the ropes. This book's author is not too proud to learn from the Bible and he's not too scared to think for himself. This is the first book I would recommend for those wanting to study Proverbs."

—DR. JAMES M. HAMILTON JR., associate professor of Biblical
Theology, Southern Baptist Theological Seminary, Louisville,
Kentucky, author, *God's Glory in Salvation through Judgment:
A Biblical Theology*

GOD'S WISDOM

in

Proverbs

Hearing God's Voice in Scripture

DAN PHILLIPS

GOD'S WISDOM in Proverbs

Published by Kress Biblical Resources
PO Box 132228
The Woodlands, TX 77393

Unless otherwise indicated, all Scripture quotations are from The Holy Bible, English Standard Version® (ESV®), copyright © 2001 by Crossway, a publishing ministry of Good News Publishers. Used by permission. All rights reserved.

Scriptures cited as DJP are the author's translations for the purposes of this study only, usually to give a more literal rendering that makes poetic form more transparent. Italicized words have been added to smooth out or clarify the English.

Scriptures cited as GW are taken from *GOD'S WORD®*. Copyright 1995 God's Word to the Nations. Used by permission of Baker Publishing Group. All rights reserved. Scriptures cited as HCSB have been taken from the Holman Christian Standard Bible®. Copyright © 1999, 2000, 2002, 2003, 2009 by Holman Bible Publishers. Used by permission. Holman Christian Standard Bible®, Holman CSB®, and HCSB® are federally registered trademarks of Holman Bible Publishers. Scriptures cited as LBA are taken from the La Biblia de Las Americas ®, Copyright © 1986 by The Lockman Foundation Used by permission (www.Lockman.org). Scriptures cited as MLB have been taken from the Modern Language Bible, copyright 1945, 1959, 1969 by the Zondervan Publishing House. Used by permission. Scriptures cited as NAS are taken from the New American Standard Bible®, Copyright © 1960, 1962, 1963, 1968, 1971, 1972, 1973, 1975, 1977, 1995 by The Lockman Foundation Used by permission (www.Lockman.org). Scriptures cites as NET are taken from The NET Bible, Version 1.0 —Copyright © 2004, 2005 Biblical Studies Foundation. Quotations designated (NIV) are from THE HOLY BIBLE: NEW INTERNATIONAL VERSION®. NIV®. Copyright © 1973, 1978, 1984 by International Bible Society, www.ibs.org. All rights reserved worldwide. Scripture quotations marked (NLT) are from the Holy Bible, New Living Translation. Copyright © 1996. Used by permission of Tyndale House Publishers. Scriptures cited as NRSV are taken from the New Revised Standard Version Bible, copyright 1989, Division of Christian Education of the National Council of the Churches of Christ in the United States of America. Used by permission. All rights reserved. Scriptures cited as RSV are taken from the Revised Standard Version of the Bible, copyright 1952 [2nd edition, 1971] by the Division of Christian Education of the National Council of the Churches of Christ in the United States of America. Used by permission. All rights reserved. Scripture quotations marked (TNIV) are taken from the Holy Bible, Today's New International Version®. TNIV®. Copyright© 2001, 2005 by Biblica, Inc.™ Used by permission of Zondervan. All rights reserved worldwide. www.zondervan.com.

ISBN 978-1-934952-**36-8**

Interior design by Greg Wright (DiamondPointMedia.com)

Cover design by Mario Kushner

Printed in the United States of America
10 9 8 7 6 5 4 3 2 1

*To the glory and honor of Him who is the way, the truth,
and the life, who is the wisdom of God,
in whom are hidden all the treasures of wisdom and knowledge.*

Contents

BIBLE VERSION ABBREVIATIONS

ASV   American Standard Version

ESV   English Standard Version

MLB   Modern Language Version

NAS   New American Standard Version (1977)

NIV   New International Version

NKJV   New King James Version

RSV   Revised Standard Version

TNIV   Today's New International Version

ABBREVIATIONS and CITATION METHODS

BDB

Brown, Francis, Samuel Rolles Driver, and Charles Augustus Briggs. *Enhanced Brown-Driver-Briggs Hebrew and English Lexicon.* electronic ed. Oak Harbor, WA: Logos Research Systems, 2000. Because quoted from the electronic version, no pages will be given.

Delitzsch

Delitzsch, Franz. *Proverbs, Ecclesiastes, Song of Solomon.* Vol. 6, *Commentary on the Old Testament in Ten Volumes.* Grand Rapids: Eerdmans, 1973 [reprint of 1872 edition]. The commentary is in two volumes within vol. 6; hence, citations are by volume and page number (i.e. the first volume, page 47 will be 1:47, etc.).

Fox, *Proverbs*

Fox, Michael V. *Proverbs 1–9.* Vol. 18A, *The Anchor Bible.* New York: Doubleday, 2000; and *Proverbs 10–31.* Vol. 18B, *The Anchor Bible.* New York: Doubleday, 2009. Citations are by volume and page number (i.e. the first volume, page 47 will be 1:47, etc.).

HALOT

The Hebrew and Aramaic Lexicon of the Old Testament by Ludwig Koehler and Walter Baumgartner, subsequently revised by Walter Baumgartner and Johann Jakob Stamm with assistance from Benedikt Hartmann, Ze'ev Ben-Hayyim, Eduard Yechezkel Kutscher, Philippe Reymond, translated and edited under the supervision of M.E.J. Richardson © 1994–2000 Koninklijke Brill NV, Leiden, The Netherlands. BibleWorks 8 edition. Because quoted from the electronic version, no pages will be given.

ISBE

Bromiley, G. W., editor. *International Standard Bible Encyclopedia.* 4 vols. Grand Rapids: Eerdmans, 1988.

Kidner

Kidner, Derek. *Proverbs.* Tyndale Old Testament Commentaries series (InterVarsity Press: 1964).

Kitchen, *Proverbs*	Kitchen, John A. *Proverbs.* Mentor Commentaries (Christian Focus Publications: 2006).
Longmann, *Commentary*	*Proverbs.* Baker Commentary on the Old Testament Wisdom and Psalms. Grand Rapids: Baker, 2006.
NIDOTTE	VanGemeren, Willem A. *New International Dictionary of Old Testament Theology and Exegesis.* Five volumes. (Zondervan, 1997). Used by permission.
NT	New Testament
OT	Old Testament
TDNT	*Theological Dictionary of the New Testament.* 1964—(G. Kittel, G. W. Bromiley & G. Friedrich, ed.) (electronic ed.). Grand Rapids, MI: Eerdmans. Logos edition.
TLOT	Jenni, E., & Westermann, C. (1997). *Theological Lexicon of the Old Testament.* Peabody, Mass.: Hendrickson Publishers.
Toy	Toy, Crawford H. *A Critical and Exegetical Commentary on the Book of Proverbs. International Critical Commentary.* Edinburgh: T. & T. Clark, 1899.
TWOT	Harris, R. L., Archer, G. L., & Waltke, B. K. (1999). *Theological Wordbook of the Old Testament* (electronic ed.). Chicago: Moody Press. Logos edition
Waltke, *Proverbs*	*The Book of Proverbs,* in two volumes (Eerdmans Publishing Company: 2004 and 2005). Citations are by volume and page number (i.e. volume one, page 47 will be 1:47, etc.)
ZPEB	Tenney, Merrill C., editor. *Zondervan Pictorial Encyclopedia of the Bible.* 5 vols. Grand Rapids: Zondervan, 1975. Used by permission.

Preface

Invitation

I am so glad that you picked up this book.

Now it's my happy task to make you glad that you picked it up, and unwilling to put it down.

What Are We Doing?

We are about to dive into the Biblical book of Proverbs, a book that has suffered much at the hands of its friends. In Proverbs we confront a volume that deserves to sit on a shelf all its own.

Sticking with the literary metaphor, if the Bible is a library, then the Book of Proverbs is a library within that library. Proverbs is a kaleidoscopic microcosm of the wisdom of God. It will be our challenge and our joy to explore it together.

Under another image, we could envision a text for some course. In this case, however, Proverbs is not merely a lesson in a larger class. No, Proverbs is an entire curriculum in itself, devoted to the study of Wisdom.

Bruce K. Waltke, in his magisterial commentary on Proverbs, well observed that "the book of Proverbs remains the model of curriculum for humanity to learn how to live under God and before humankind."[1] How broad is that curriculum? Since "The earth is the LORD's and the fullness thereof, the world and those who dwell therein" (Psa. 24:1), all of life is God's concern. God does not honor secularism's upward-slanted "No Trespassing" signs.

That being the case, the book of Proverbs is as broad in scope as life itself, moving in and out of the home and the workshop, the field and the palace, the bedroom and the courtroom, the tombs and the Temple.

Who Is This For?

As we shall see, in writing Proverbs Solomon cast a wide net, both in subjects and objects addressed (1:2–6). The following studies do the same. Like Proverbs itself, they form a sort of smorgasbord. Whoever you are—with only one exception—this book has something just for you.

---

[1] Waltke, *Proverbs*, 1:xxi.

Feedback I've gotten on this book in the latter stages of preparation encourages me to hope that it will be used by all of the following:

- Pastors
- Bible study leaders
- Sunday School teachers
- Biblical counselors
- Discipleship trainers
- Seminary students
- College students (Bible college and/or otherwise)
- Parents (homeschooling, single and/or otherwise)
- Grandparents
- Serious-minded Christians
- …and basically all kinds of people from all walks of life.

My, that is a wide swath! Let's look at it another way. Who will profit from this book?

If you are a *beginning, growing Christian* who is new to Bible study, prepare for an adventure. No need to cringe or be intimidated by anything in these pages. Solomon wrote for all kinds of beginners:

> For giving to the gullible ones shrewdness,
>   To the youth knowledge and planning skill. (Prov. 1:4 DJP)

Here is my promise to you: stay with me, and you will not get lost. Some material may not reach you easily where you are right now, but never fear. Stick with it. All will be explained clearly. There will be "cookies" on every shelf, no matter what your reach is.

If you are a *maturing Christian* who has studied Scripture for years, you will find provocative, demanding material in these pages. In the Proverbs' introduction, Solomon calls out "Let a wise man listen and add learning, And let a discerning man acquire a knowledge of the ropes!" (Prov. 1:5 DJP). Proverbs provides more than enough material for seasoned believers to chew over.

The unique nature of a study on Proverbs necessarily adds to the "chewiness" factor. For one thing, Proverbs was written in Hebrew. Any in-depth study must interact with the Hebrew text. When I cite the Hebrew word, I will also provide an English transliteration. However, you needn't know Hebrew. Read on, and the word's meaning will be made clear.

The body of the text will provide information understandable to any English reader, while the footnotes (I have a massive aversion to endnotes) will both document our studies and point to further resources. Get out your fork and knife, tuck in your napkin, and get ready to sink your teeth in.

"But you said there was one exception," a reader might note. Indeed there is.

I know from the outset that I will utterly fail to reach some readers, no matter how Herculean my efforts. If anyone *thinks he has nothing to learn*, then I am afraid that I have nothing to offer—nothing, that is, that such a one would want to receive. After all, we are about to study a book that warns us, "Do not be *someone who is* wise in your *own* eyes" (Prov. 3:7a DJP). The chief writer, Solomon, knew the hopelessness of trying to teach someone who either already knows everything, or who has no desire to learn. He wrote,

> Do you see a man who is wise in his own eyes?
> There is more hope for a fool than for him. (Prov. 26:12)

This, Not That

Can we be so absolute? Solomon characteristically is. In his proverbs, Solomon depicts many truths in binary—in ones and zeroes, rights and wrongs, blacks and whites. The king knew that men and women basically fall into two categories: the *fools* and the *wise*, each progressing along well-worn paths. Solomon also knew that both categories have their own characteristic responses to teachers of God's truth: the former have no interest, whereas the latter will listen, learn and grow. Each can be seen in the respective lines of Proverbs 12:15—

> The way of a fool is right in his own eyes,
> but a wise man listens to advice.

We will see that there are different degrees and shades of folly, ranging from the still-reachable "naïve" or "gullible" person (1:4), to the hardened and hopeless "scoffer" (1:22). Of that latter sort, Solomon warns with the voice of long experience:

> Whoever corrects a scoffer gets himself abuse,
> and he who reproves a wicked man incurs injury.
>
> [8] Do not reprove a scoffer, or he will hate you... (Prov. 9:7–8a)

The Question to You

In which category do you find yourself? Only you and God can say, at this point. If you want to know of God and His ways, read on. If you are eager to learn your Lord's wisdom and counsel, you will find juicy, succulent meat in our studies to come. The number of candles on your birthday cake, or the presence or absence of letters after your name, make absolutely no difference.

However, perhaps you are someone who is resistant to God's wisdom, whether because you think you've already "arrived" or because you are unwilling to learn. If you are, and you are honest enough to admit it, I can only commend to you the wise man's counsel…

> Whoever conceals his transgressions will not prosper,
> but he who confesses and forsakes them will obtain mercy.
> (Prov. 28:13)

…and his warnings:

> When pride comes, then comes disgrace,
> but with the humble is wisdom. (Prov. 11:2)

> Pride goes before destruction,
> and a haughty spirit before a fall. (Prov. 16:18)

> He who is often reproved, yet stiffens his neck,
> will suddenly be broken beyond healing. (Prov. 29:1)

So, if we know who we are, and why we are here, then let's get going.

Explanation of "DJP" Renderings

I would encourage all readers to have a good translation such as the ESV, CSB, or NAS at hand. I count on you to look up passages I reference and discuss. When I quote a version without note, it is the ESV.

You will also notice that the passages I quote in full are often marked "DJP." These are my own translations of the Hebrew or Greek text of Scripture. Usually these are very literal renderings. My intent is not to supplant standard versions, but to provide a more literal and consistent representation for the basis of our study.

As I shall explain, Hebrew poetry is a distinctive style, and is not easily conveyed in English. The process of translation tends to iron out bumps and wrinkles in the necessary interests of smooth reading. Sometimes, however, those bumps and wrinkles give us clues to Solomon's intention. When they are lost in translation, it is a loss for the reader. For instance, many proverbs have a *chiastic* structure that is invisible in English.[2] Also, English versions almost invariably use one word to translate Solomon's several terms for "fool." By contrast, I adopt and stick to a specific term for each.

My point is not that such an overly literal translation is superior overall. For my aim in this study, however, something closer to word-for-word often serves best.

The reader will note as well that I use the old-school convention of *italicizing* words that I add in my translation so that it makes some kind of English sense.

All clear? We have a challenging, exciting journey ahead of us, and I'm eager to get going.

So let's launch—right after some absolutely necessary…

Literary Technique in reverse order
Chiastic - words repeated in reverse order
A-B-B'-A'

---

[2] I explain *chiasm* in Chapter 4.

Acknowledgments

This book has been many, many years in the making. Many, many thanks are owed.

Thanks first and foremost to the triune God, for loving me with an everlasting love. By grace alone, He transformed me forever. One day I was someone who thought the Bible in general (and the Old Testament in particular) to be boring, insulting, and offensive. The next day, I had been drawn to believe in and love Jesus Christ and, because of Him, believe and love the Old Testament as well as the New. Since then, I have found the heart and mind of the living God unveiled in its pages.

The deeper I've gone, the deeper it gets.

Thanks to my many (endlessly patient!) teachers through the years, in churches and classes and lectures and sermons and books. In particular, though we came to have very different convictions, I am still grateful to the late David Morsey for taking a just-converted, undisciplined, wobbly high-school graduate, patiently starting him off in Biblical Greek and a bit of Hebrew, and thus launching nearly four decades of delightful absorption in the original languages of Scripture. Many patient, patient men followed, and I thank them all.

Thanks to congregations in three states (and counting) who have given me the opportunity to open up Proverbs, in seminars and sermons.

Thanks to the readers of my blog (http://bibchr.blogspot.com) and of the team blog Pyromaniacs (http://teampyro.blogspot.com), for their gracious reception of the Proverbs studies I've presented over the years.

Thanks to my friend Phil Johnson, Executive Director of Grace to You (an incredibly sharp, wise, and hysterically funny man), for giving me such a platform; and to my friend, the ineffable Frank Turk, for being my partner in... uh, what's the opposite of "crime"? Is it... like ministry?

Thanks to Tom Lusby, for being my Proverbs 17:17 friend, and for his years and years of prayers and friendship.

Thanks to John A. Kitchen, pastor of Stow Alliance Fellowship (Stow, Ohio), himself the author of a number of books, including a solid commentary on Proverbs. John took sacrificial time from his busy schedule as a pastor, an international teacher, and an author, to go over this manuscript with a fine-toothed comb. The final text benefits from scores of John's amazingly detailed, helpful observations and comments.

Thanks to Dr. Randall McKinion, Associate Professor of Old Testament and Biblical Languages at Shepherds Theological Seminary, in Cary, North Carolina. Randy reviewed the entire manuscript, with particular attention to the work in the Hebrew text. His comments were fewer in number than John's, but many of them sent me fleeing back to the grammars, the lexicons, and/or my thinking-cap. *Tôdâ rabbâ!* Thank you very much in Hebrew

Both of these men have my gratitude for helping this book to be what it is. Blame for its shortcomings falls on me alone.

Thanks to Eric Kress and Brian Thomasson for their interest in this project, and for the very fact that it is seeing the light of day. Thanks to Garry Knussman of Grace to You for his careful reading and many valuable corrections.

Thanks in particular to the following for permission to quote:

> BASIC BOOKS, for permission to quote from Robert Alter's *The Art of Biblical Poetry* (New York: Basic Books, 1985).

> JOHNS HOPKINS UNIVERSITY PRESS, for permission to quote from James Kugel, *The Idea of Biblical Poetry: Parallelism and Its History* (Baltimore: Johns Hopkins, 1981).

All my children have taught me about parenting, and about a great many other things. Two remain at home: I thank my youngest, beloved sons, Josiah and Jonathan, for understanding why Dad had to be visited out in the office so much of the time.

Most of all the horizontals, I thank their mother, my dear wife and *'ēšet ḥayil,* Valerie, for so generously seeing to it that I had the time to work on this manuscript—work on it, then work some more, and then when that was all done, to do some *more work* on it! Valerie bore more than her share of household duties as I was at this labor of love, and the most fitting words to express my gratitude and love are those at the close of Proverbs—

> Many daughters have done excellently,
> But you—you have surpassed them all! (Prov. 31:29 DJP)

> Honey, the book's done. Time for a date!

Woman of Valor

xxi

CHAPTER ONE

Essentials for Understanding Proverbs

Exposition of Proverbs 1:1

> "Proverbs of Solomon, son of David, king of Israel" (DJP)

Authorship and Composition[1]

Let us dive right into the Biblical evidence, face it, and consider some options. After that, I will lay out what difference this understanding makes to us as readers of the text, and how it should help and influence the way we hear God speak to us through Proverbs.

What Does Proverbs Say?

Some Biblical books, such as Matthew and Job and Hebrews, offer no direct statement of authorship whatsoever. This is not at all the case in Proverbs. In fact, several verses provide us with specific assertions:

> The proverbs of Solomon,
>> son of David, king of Israel (1:1)

> The proverbs of Solomon. (10:1a)

---

[1] This section summarizes and assumes the case I develop and document at much greater length in Appendix One, "Who Wrote Proverbs, and What Difference Does It Make?"

Incline your ear, and hear the words of the wise,
    and apply your heart to my knowledge… (22:17)

These also are sayings of the wise. (24:23a)

These also are proverbs of Solomon
    which the men of Hezekiah king of Judah copied. (25:1)

The words of Agur son of Jakeh. The oracle. (30:1a)

The words of King Lemuel.
    An oracle that his mother taught him (31:1)

The *prima facie* evidence, then, only names three authors: Solomon, Agur, and King Lemuel. Some would add "the wise," from verses 22:17 and 24:23; I will explain my demurral in a moment.

To respect the text, we must build our understanding on its explicit statements. Unfortunately, there is no additional canonical book titled "On the Composition of Proverbs." Wouldn't that be nice? Without such a book we are left to engage in a degree of speculation. Our goal will be to speculate as minimally as possible and to anchor our thoughts to the text itself as closely as we can. This will pay rich dividends, as I mean to demonstrate.

Going back to 22:17 and 24:23, then, some scholars would add "the wise" as additional, unnamed authors, inserted by an editor or editors after the Solomonic material. However, in both cases, the author continues to speak in the first person ("my knowledge," 22:17; "I passed by," 24:30). There is no need to surmise an anonymous addition.

A more natural explanation lies close at hand: Solomon promised in 1:6b to give insight into "the words of the wise and their riddles." In fact, 22:17 uses that very expression: "words of the wise." Then 24:23 in Hebrew simply says, "These also are of the wise," so we could as easily supply "words" as the ESV's "sayings."

That being the case, why should these sections not be examples of just such selections, picked and presented by the only author presented by name in all of the first 29 chapters of the book? After all, both sections add echoes of Solomon's theme of the fear of Yahweh[2] (24:21; 28:14). It would be odd suddenly for

---

[2] "Yahweh" is God's personal name throughout the OT, usually hidden by translators behind

unnamed writers to elbow their way among the named authors, bringing their "I" and "my" but no further introduction. Therefore, we can discard these as indicators of unnamed authors and return to the direct statements of the text.

Relative to genuinely anonymous books, then, it would seem that Proverbs presents quite a bit of definite evidence. It names Solomon as the author, directly (1:1; 10:1) or by transcription (25:1), of the bulk of the book. That being the case, we may equally surmise that the appendices by Agur (30:1) and King Lemuel (31:1) may not be later additions at all, but could have been pieces selected and included by Solomon himself. That possibility is borne out by the nice textual bookends (*inclusio*) we have if we consider that Solomon himself framed his book with the thematic motto, at its start and its finish:

> The fear of Yahweh is the beginning of knowledge;
> Wisdom and discipline, dense people belittle. (1:7 DJP)

> Charm is deceitful and beauty is nothing;[3]
> A woman who fears Yahweh, it is she who shall be praised.
> (31:30 DJP)

What of 25:1, then, with its explicit statement that it commences a section of "proverbs of Solomon which the men of Hezekiah king of Judah copied"? Of course, it is possible that Solomon's original material ended with 24:34, and everything after was added by a later prophet/editor. This would fit the direct statements acceptably.

However, it would leave Proverbs' framing by 1:7 and 31:30, with their constant refrains within the book (1:29; 2:5; 3:7; 8:13; 9:10; 10:27; 14:2, 26–27; 15:16, 33; 16:6; 19:23; 22:4; 23:17; 24:21; 28:14; 29:25), more coincidental than I think warranted. Accept first and last chapters as edited by Solomon, and we then see Proverbs not as a book of wholly unrelated and untethered sayings adrift in the universe, but as a book composed by Solomon on the theme of the fear of Yahweh.[4]

Another option is to translate the verb in 25:1 not as "copied" but as "moved." Thus we have, "These also are proverbs of Solomon, which the men of Hezekiah,

---

"LORD" or "GOD." This will be further explained in Chapter 3.

[3] Or "vain"; the term means a vapor, a breath.

[4] Hamilton well says, "Proverbs shows that life in the fear of God leads to shalom [peace]; rebellion leads to misery" (James M. Hamilton Jr., *God's Glory in Salvation through Judgment* [Wheaton: Crossway, 2010], 290).

king of Judah, moved" (DJP). It raises the possibility of seeing Hezekiah's men (prophets?) as taking a body of Solomon's proverbs and moving them into the book. The collection fits Solomon's overall design nicely, as it contributes two more reverberations of the theme of the fear of Yahweh (28:14; 29:25). Naturally, Hezekiah's men insert the collection at the end of Solomon's proverbs and before the guest appendices.

Conclusion as to Authorship and Composition

I think the text *demands* that we see at least Proverbs 1:1–22:16, and chapters 25–29, as directly Solomonic. I also think the most natural reading of 22:17–24:34 includes them with Solomon's proverbs. The two appendices may either post-date the Solomonic collection, or they were part of Solomon's original book, with Hezekiah's men inserting chapters 25–29 between the Solomonic original and Solomon's own guest appendices. My preference is the latter. This makes all the book originally written during Solomon's reign in the 10th century BC, with only one verse (25:1) necessarily composed as late as Hezekiah's reign, in the late-eighth or early-seventh century BC.

What Difference Does This Make?

Briefly put, this knowledge is immensely important and helpful to us as readers of Proverbs. First, it is encouraging to know that words in Scripture mean what they seem to mean. God does not move Solomon to speak to us in code, or in impenetrable literary devices only scholars can understand. "Proverbs of Solomon" means what the plain sense of the words would indicate.

What is more, this understanding we've gained means that we have a known chronological framework for the book, and so we also have an intellectual and spiritual context for the proverbs.[5] We know a lot about Solomon, so we know a lot about the author's qualifications and his perspective. More than that, we have a background, because we have a pretty good idea of which Scriptures would or could have been in Solomon's mind, as a context for his thinking.

This puts us at a great advantage over those who reject or ignore the text's own assertions. They have to imagine scribal schools and wisdom movements with no

---

5   Hamilton correctly notes that Proverbs "results from Solomon's obedience to Deuteronomy 6, filtered through his obedience to Deuteronomy 17, as he creatively teaches the Torah to his son" (ibid.).

clear time-frame, and thus no clear context. Scripture has given us much better facts and information to aid us.

In some cases, as I will show, this actually assists us in interpreting an otherwise-isolated, ambiguous verse (e.g. on Prov. 22:5, in Chapter 3).

So now that we know who wrote most of the book, let us find out whether or not he had what it took to write such a lofty composition.

Solomon's Qualifications

Proverbs' Preface

Let us consider Solomon's preface to his own book, in Proverbs 1:1–6.

Proverbs of Solomon, son of David, king of Israel:

[2] For becoming acquainted with[6] wisdom and discipline,
    For discerning sayings of discernment.

[3] For receiving intelligent discipline[7]—
    Righteousness, and justice, and uprightness.

[4] For giving to the gullible ones shrewdness,
    To the youth knowledge and planning skill.

[5] Let a wise man listen and add learning,[8]
    And let a discerning man acquire a knowledge of the ropes![9]

[6] For discerning a proverb and a satire,
    The words of wise men and their enigmas. (DJP)

This section unfolds the *design* of the book as being quite simply comprehensive instruction in faith, righteousness, and intelligence. It is edifying to note that Solomon intends his writings to find a very broad audience. He insists that he

---

[6]   Or "knowing."

[7]   Or "discipline which produces intelligence"; literally "discipline of intelligence."

[8]   The noun is related to the verb translated "receive" in verse 3, and thus means his store, his accumulation, his acquisition of learning.

[9]   Or "guidance," or "leadership." The word comes from the noun meaning "cable" or "rope" (particularly such as was used in directing a boat), from which came the word meaning "sailor" (as one who uses the ropes to guide a ship). Felicitously, the English expression "to know the ropes" means to have an experienced grasp of the details, and is thought to have originated similarly, from sailors steering by managing the ropes that controlled the ship's sails (cf. NIDOTTE, 4:285; HALOT, art. תַּחְבֻּלוֹת).

has something for both the gullible, youthful novice (v. 4), and for the mature, accomplished fellow-sage as well (v. 5).

Heady claims such as these had better have some pretty solid backing. Discerning book-buyers always read the back flap of a book's dust jacket, to confirm the author's qualifications. This miracle diet—was it designed by a medical doctor? Or was it concocted by an actor (and his ghost-writer)? This book on the Holy Spirit—was it written by someone who's "paid his dues" by gaining the tools of the science of Bible study, or by some showy, crowd-gathering huckster?

So let us read the "back flap" together. Who was Solomon, that he should claim to be able to teach us the all-important wisdom which we need for life?

Solomon's Background

Our pronunciation "Solomon" sounds more like the Greek spelling of the king's name. If we were to say his name as David and Bathsheba pronounced it (2 Sam. 12:24), we would call him "King Shlomo." Do you notice that "Shlomo" sounds like one of the very few Hebrew words that most Gentiles know? Try saying it without the final "o" and you'll hear it: *Shlōm*. The root word is *šālôm* (often written in English as "shalom"), and it means *peace*. Shlomo (Solomon), then, means *peaceable*.

Why was this an appropriate and significant name for David's successor/son? It was meaningful because the bulk of Solomon's reign would differ starkly from his father's turbulent life. David was a man of bloodshed and war (1 Chron. 28:3), but God would bless Solomon with a peaceable, tranquil reign.

To the world at large, he was and is known as Solomon. But he had another name.

Do you have a nickname, like "Lefty," or "Slick," or "Smiley"? Solomon did. While you might have gotten your nickname from kids at school, or from your friends, Solomon's nickname actually came from God Himself. The prophet Nathan called Solomon "Jedidiah," which means *Beloved of Yah*[10] (2 Sam. 12:25). It was a token of Yahweh's love for Solomon (v. 24).

Solomon's Résumé

Solomon was King David's tenth son, Bathsheba's second.[11] Solomon's reign

---

[10] *Yah* is a short form of *Yahweh*, the personal name of God which occurs about 6,823 times in the Old Testament. We will discuss this name in Chapter 3.

[11] So G. H. Livingston, "Solomon," ZPEB, 5:470. David F. Payne says Solomon was the eighth ("Solomon," ISBE, 4:566).

started about 970 BC.[12] Solomon's life was changed shortly thereafter. We read of Solomon's opportunity and dilemma in 1 Kings 3:3–8.

As Solomon worshiped Yahweh earnestly in Gibeon one day, he received a vision of God in a dream in the night (v. 5). In this dream, God gave Solomon a choice that most of us…well, we could only dream of it. However, Solomon's "dream" was a reality. God said, "Ask what I shall give you" (v. 5). Breath-taking. A blank check, from God.

Solomon was clearly overwhelmed by the mammoth task of governing the nation of Israel, which at that time consisted of all twelve tribes united somewhat uneasily[13] into one nation. He felt himself to be but a little child, utterly unequal to such a task. And so Solomon made his request of God and got his answer, in 1 Kings 3:9–14.

Solomon asked for "an understanding mind" so that he could "govern" God's people and "discern between good and evil" (v. 9). God replied that He would give Solomon what he asked, *and* riches and honor besides (vv. 10–13).

The fact that Solomon had indeed received this gift is then illustrated in the famous story of 1 Kings 3:16–28.

How 1 Kings 3 Connects with Proverbs

The narrative of the entire chapter is of particular interest to us in helping us assess how and whether Solomon might have been fit to write Proverbs. Remember, Solomon asked for "an understanding mind" in verse 9. The phrase translated "understanding mind" is a לֵב שֹׁמֵעַ, a *lēḇ šōmēaʿ*, which very literally means a *listening* heart, or a *hearing* heart. The meaning of this expression is a heart that hears with a mind to obey. It is what a mother means when she tells her children, "Listen to me!"

Solomon says something reminiscent of this in Proverbs 20:12, when he writes,

> A hearing ear and a seeing eye,
> Yahweh has made even the both of them. (DJP)

---

[12] 1 Kings 6:1 says that Solomon began building the Temple in the fourth year of his reign, which would be the 480th year after the Exodus. This event is dated fairly firmly at 967/976 BC. Hence a starting date for Solomon's reign of c. 970 BC.

[13] See 2 Samuel 19:40–20:2.

And so indeed Solomon, who was given a "listening heart" by Yahweh, will tell us "Let a wise man listen and add learning" (Prov. 1:5 DJP).

Further, Solomon asked for and received the ability "to govern" God's people (v. 9). He wanted to be just and to administer justice. God gave him this ability to a supernatural degree. And so it is unsurprising to read that Solomon promises that his book is beneficial…

> …For receiving intelligent discipline—
> Righteousness, and justice, and uprightness. (Prov. 1:3 DJP)

Finally, Solomon requests the ability to "discern between good and evil." The phrase translated "to discern" is לְהָבִין (*l*ᵉ*hābîn*, from the root *bîn*). The verb *bîn* means to have penetrating insight, to understand, to distinguish. It serves well in contexts such as this to denote the ability to tell the difference between[14] good and evil, wisdom and folly.

In fact, this leads us to another fascinating little contact-point between the sacred history and Proverbs. The historian tells us in 1 Kings 4:29 that God gave Solomon gifts of wisdom in abundance: "And God gave Solomon wisdom and understanding beyond measure, and breadth of mind like the sand on the seashore." When the writer says that God gave Solomon "wisdom," he uses the common Hebrew word חָכְמָה (*hokmâ*).

Wisdom, of course, is a central, recurring theme of Proverbs. Solomon informs the reader right off the top that his book is intended "for becoming acquainted with wisdom and discipline" (1:2a). Solomon is qualified to acquaint the reader with wisdom, because God Himself gave Solomon wisdom.

Further, the narrator in Kings says that God gave Solomon "very great discernment," the word for "discernment" being תְּבוּנָה (*t*ᵉ*bûnâ*), which is a relative of *bîn*, our friend from a few paragraphs back. *Discernment* is a quality that recurs constantly in the book of Proverbs as well.[15]

So Solomon asks for wisdom and discernment, and God gives it to him in great abundance. In the book of Proverbs, we can all benefit from that gift.

Is that not precisely what we all need? God singularly gifted Solomon in just this area. If we listen and learn from Proverbs, we too shall gain discernment from

---

[14] In fact, the verb is written almost identically to the Hebrew preposition *bên*, which means "between."

[15] See Proverbs 2:2, 3, 6, 11; 3:13, 19; 5:1; 8:1; 10:23; 11:12; 14:29; 15:21; 17:27; 18:2; 19:8; 20:5; 21:30; 24:3; 28:16.

the Word of God through this uniquely qualified man.

When God gave these qualities of mind and heart to Solomon, the Golden Age of Israel was the result. This Golden Age is vividly painted out for us in 1 Kings 4, especially vv. 20ff. Prosperity, art, and literature abounded, all of them fruits of Solomon's God-given wisdom. In this period, Solomon himself produced some 3,000 proverbs and 1,005 songs on a wide array of topics, and he won the opportunity to tell kings from all over of the wisdom of Yahweh, God of Israel (1 Kings 4:32, 34).

The Center of Solomon's Wisdom

If you had the time (and dubious judgment) to wade about in the dry and dusty works of Old Testament scholarship on Proverbs, you would likely be taken aback by some broadly-held assumptions about these writings. Not long ago, it was a commonly-maintained notion of Old Testament scholarship that Proverbs is virtually in a different world from the rest of the Bible.[16] It was thought that Proverbs has nothing to do with any other book of the Old Testament.

An academic named James Crenshaw made bold to claim that Proverbs, Job, and Ecclesiastes were in a *"different thought world."*[17] Even the name "Yahweh" in 1:7 and elsewhere, the personal name of the God of Israel, wasn't thought to be particularly significant.[18]

But we have every reason to take the Bible more seriously, and to treat it at least as respectfully as we would treat an historical document of its caliber[19]— more than that, to regard it with reverence, as Jesus did (John 10:35). When we do, the pieces fit together like a beautiful mosaic.

The historical background provided in 1 Kings confirms and fills out what we find in Proverbs. The second chapter depicts King David's stirring final charge to Solomon. We read his words in 1 Kings 2:2–4. Here David is passionately urging

---

[16] For some more technical discussion and documentation of this, see Daniel J. Phillips, *The Sovereignty of Yahweh in the Book of Proverbs: an Exercise in Theological Exegesis* (Master of Divinity thesis, Talbot Theological Seminary, May 1983), pages 11–14. See also the discussion of and response to liberal critical theories in Archer, 518ff.

[17] James L. Crenshaw, *Old Testament Wisdom: an Introduction* (John Knox: 1981), 29.

[18] An example is J. Alberto Soggin, who thinks that we could just substitute "God" or "deity" for Yahweh, without any problem (*Introduction to the Old Testament*, translated by John Bowden [Philadelphia: Westminster, 1976], 379–380).

[19] This case is made at length by Phillips, 14–23.

Solomon to study and do the Word of God (v. 3).[20]

This command locks Solomon into the whole body of God-breathed books and writings that had been revealed up to his time. What would this library include? It would certainly contain the Pentateuch, and probably numerous other books such as Job, Joshua, Judges, Ruth, and the psalms of David, Solomon's father.

But we must also see that David is not "making up" this earnest exhortation. David is no innovator here, dreaming up the notion that King Solomon ought to stay in the Word on a regular basis. David learned the idea in the same place from which all wise parents get their very best ideas: from God. See the word of God, in Deuteronomy 17:18–19—

> "Now it shall come about when he [every Israelite king] sits on the throne of his kingdom, he shall write for himself a copy of this law on a scroll in the presence of the Levitical priests. [19]And it shall be with him, and he shall read it all the days of his life, that he may learn to fear the LORD his God, by carefully observing all the words of this law and these statutes,..." (NAS)

This passage is so crucial for our understanding of Proverbs that it would be difficult to overstress it. Notice how verse 19 says that the king will "learn to fear Yahweh his God, by carefully observing all the words of this law and these statutes." Does that not sound a familiar note, a refrain we find echoing throughout Proverbs? Indeed it does. It is the theme of "the fear of Yahweh," which forms the fundamental motto of the book.

> The fear of Yahweh is the beginning of knowledge;
> Wisdom and discipline, dense people belittle. (DJP)[21]

Solomon underscores the pivotal, foundational nature of the fear of Yahweh. But how did he learn about the fear of Yahweh? First Kings tells us: Solomon learned it by studying Scripture closely, as his father had done.

---

[20] Solomon similarly charges his son (i.e. 1:8; 2:1; etc.) and alludes to his own father's charge in 4:3ff.

[21] See also Proverbs 1:29; 2:5; 8:13; 9:10; 10:27; 14:26, 27; 15:16, 33; 16:6; 19:23; 22:4; 23:17; and 29:25.

And so, we have every reason to believe that Solomon, for as long as he walked with the Lord, held to his father's advice (cf. Prov. 13:13; 16:20). He was a sage, schooled in the regular study of the Word of God. This fact certainly cements Proverbs to the rest of the inspired literature of the Old Testament, giving us a larger context for understanding what the book teaches.[22]

God-given wisdom is not a free-wheeling entity, separated from the Word of God. Wisdom is (in part) the application of objective revelation to the details of life. Therefore, as we shall see, wisdom is *skill for living in the fear of Yahweh*.

> WISDOM: skill for living in the fear of Yahweh

The Basic Structure of Proverbs

Here is the simplest outline that I can design for the book of Proverbs:

> 1. Introduction and Motto (Prov. 1:1–7)
> 2. Proverb Discourses (Prov. 1:7–9:18)
> 3. Classic Proverbs (Prov. 10–29)
> 4. Guest Appendices (Prov. 30–31)

I did say "simplest." Of course, Proverbs displays much more complex structure.

Proverbs' Structural Complexities

Can Proverbs Be Outlined?

Often, a first step in teaching a book such as Romans or Genesis or Isaiah or Ephesians is the creation of an outline. The outline begins by sketching out the author's main thought-flow. Under the main headings, subtler developments can be detailed.

---

[22] Specifically, Walter Kaiser correctly observes that the "fear of Yahweh" weds wisdom literature to the OT as a whole (*Toward an Old Testament Theology* [Grand Rapids: Zondervan, 1978; used by permission]), 46. He develops how this central idea connects Solomon to preceding canonical literature, 168–171.

We want to understand Proverbs. Will it help us if we outline it more closely than the outline given above? Can it even be done? Let's see what we encounter as we wade in.

Chapters 1–9 clearly contain distinguishable discourses. However, a glance at the outlines in standard commentaries by Waltke, Fox, Clifford, Garrett, Kidner and others will find no unanimity in how to divide those sections. A simple read-through reveals the first chapter alone containing at least three distinct sections: the preface (1:1–7), a discourse focusing on a youth's heeding his parents' warnings in dealing with the wrong crowd (1:8–19), followed by an arresting portrayal of Lady Wisdom[23] as a street-preacher (1:20–33).

We also notice that the two discourses are of different kinds. The first is a parental exhortation. The second is an extended metaphor.

The following chapters display the same variation and are not as easily partitioned. For instance, where does the sentence begun at 2:1 end? By what thought-flow do we segue from the search for wisdom (2:1–11) to avoidance of evil influences (2:12–22)?

Similarly, in chapter 3 we have a neat alternation of exhortation and promise in vv. 1–12. But then Solomon waxes lyrical in praise of wisdom (vv. 13–20), after which he returns to exhorting his son to heed wisdom (vv. 21–26)… and then he gives some charges about how to treat one's neighbor (vv. 27–35). How does that all divide out?

In *chapters 10–29* any attempts to create outlines become immeasurably more complex, if not altogether futile.

At first glance, we see very little flow of thought. The King James Version served readers poorly by not dividing the form into two lines, as every modern translation does. The NIV, whatever its other weaknesses, merits particular praise in that it divides off the individual verses with an additional space. Thus the format indicates that each proverb should be savored on its own.

Groupings?

Yet a closer reading does show some sort of grouping here and there, at least. For instance, the vast majority of proverbs in chapters 10–15 are *antithetical*, where

---

[23] Feminine because qualities tend to be feminine in Hebrew, and because the noun translated "wisdom" is feminine.

Line B begins with "but" and introduces some form of contrast. Chapter 16 features a concentration of verses about Yahweh's sovereignty (vv. 1–5, 7, 9, 33).

Read Proverbs in Hebrew, and you will see even more clusters and clumps. Often *catchwords* link some kind of flow within sections, though the meaning of the flow is not always clear. For instance, similar words play around in the Hebrew of Proverbs 11:3, 5 and 6 (emphases added):

> "The *integrity* of the *upright*"
> "the *righteousness* of men of *integrity*"
> "the *righteousness* of the *upright*"

Yet verse 4, stuck right in the middle of this little cluster, has none of those terms. If we want to *make* a thought-flow, we may have to get out the hammer.

Again, the Hebrew word *nepeš* (often translated "soul") is found in 16:2–4. But in verses 2 and 4, *nepeš* means "desire," while in v. 3 it has a different sense (soul, or life). Is that a flow? How? Is it rather a case of one proverb about *nepeš* reminding Solomon of another, and then another?

There are other ways of binding sections together, such as 10:1–5, where verse 1 introduces the wise and foolish son, and v. 5 caps the topic. Then the thought of each Line B is taken up in the next verse's Line A, and virtue (+) and vice (-) alternate thus: +:-, -:+, +:-, -:+, +:-.[24]

> The proverbs of Solomon.
> A wise son makes a glad father,
> > but a foolish son is a sorrow to his mother.
>
> [2] Treasures gained by wickedness do not profit,
> > but *righteousness* delivers from death.
>
> [3] The LORD does not let the *righteous* go hungry,
> > but he thwarts the craving of the *wicked*.
>
> [4] A *slack hand* causes poverty,
> > but the hand of the *diligent* makes rich.
>
> [5] He who *gathers in summer* is a prudent son,
> > but he who sleeps in harvest is a son who brings shame
> > (emphases added)

---

[24] Cf. Waltke, *Proverbs*, 1:451.

Is it stream of consciousness?

Again, 11:9–14 all arguably deal with the impact of a man's *mouth* on his larger community. The *king* is the topic of Proverbs 16:10, 12–15. These are some of several groups and clusters may be discerned here and there.

Larger Groupings?

Some writers have seen larger structures throughout Proverbs. Writers such as Garrett[25] and Waltke[26] work hard to find groupings and structures through all of this portion of Proverbs, basing their cases on just such clues. Indeed, Garrett's commentary often seems to focus more on finding and defending such structures than on commenting on the verses themselves.

For my part, I think Michael V. Fox is right in observing that such an approach can make Proverbs into a sort of Rorschach test. One sees what he expects to see, even if it is not objectively there. Each proposed "structure" reflects the individual scholar's mind more than it does Solomon's.

What is more, the idea of such a master-design may itself be anachronistic. Fox poses it this way:

> It is far-fetched to imagine editors compiling proverbs according to grand and detailed designs. It is implausible that an editor would write down all the proverbs on little bits of papyrus or parchment and move them around until they fit into tidy, well-organized groupings and larger, well-designed structures, with certain repeated words and phrases—which were already present in the original sayings—being located in exactly the right places. It is even more implausible that the editor did all this in his head. Rhetorical effect is an unlikely motivation, seeing that very few commentators—who have studied the book far more intently than most readers—have uncovered the same patterns.[27]

Fox proposes rather that a "proverb is like a jewel, and the book of Proverbs is like a heap of jewels," and he asks, "Is it really such a loss if they are not all laid out in pretty, symmetric designs or divided into neat little piles?"[28]

---

[25] Garrett, 46–48, *et passim.*
[26] Waltke, *Proverbs*, 1:45–50.
[27] Fox, *Proverbs*, 2:481.
[28] Ibid.

How can we understand Solomon's method of arrangement? I think Fox makes a good case that the mechanism causing such structures as we observe is *associative thinking*. One thought simply leads to another. Proverbs 19:11–14 is an example.

> The importance of patience (v 11) calls to mind the king's wrath (v 12), which is the opposite of patience and a dangerous form of irritation. This leads into a proverb on an irritable wife (v 13), which in turn evokes a proverb on a virtuous one (v 14), which balances the negative picture.[29]

Conclusion

So is there a master-structure for all of Proverbs 10–29? None has convinced me. Some sections observably do play with a theme, but even then not in any way akin to an epistle or an extended poem. My approach is (A) neither to demand nor expect to see a grand, all-encompassing structure, and thus (B) not to assume that the surrounding verses form a thought-flow context such as one finds in epistles, prophecies, and poems, but (C) to keep my eyes open for hints and connections that bind groupings of verses together into thought-clusters.

How to Read Proverbs

Literary Style: Poetry

Yes, the rumors you have heard are all true: Proverbs is a book of *poetry*. Now maybe you, like me, are…well, let's say I am *not partial* to poetry, with its artificiality and pretense.

If you feel similarly, there is no need to panic. Hebrew poetry is delightfully free from pretentious puffery. It is earthy and vivid, while sharply communicating heavenly truth. Hebrew poetry is, as Robert Alter notes, "the best words in the best order."[30]

Hebrew poetry is the development of ideas in a creative, evocative way. It is not quite like an epistle, although James and parts of Colossians are quite Proverbial in their pointedness and brevity. It is not a narrative of some historical event, and so is different from the Law and the historical books.

---

[29] Ibid., 2:480.
[30] Robert Alter, *The Art Of Biblical Poetry* (New York: Basic Books, 1985), x.

Hebrew poetry is a literary genre unto itself and must be approached appropriately.

Characteristics of Hebrew Poetry

What characterizes Hebrew poetry? One may almost say it is the opposite of what one commonly thinks of as English poetry. In English poetry, lines commonly rhyme words, and parallelism is not much of a factor. Hebrew poetry is the opposite: lines seldom if ever deliberately rhyme words,[31] and parallelism is (almost) everything.

> *English* poetry tends to rhyme *words*,
> *Hebrew* poetry tends to rhyme/develop *thoughts*[32]

The simplest form of Hebrew poetry as we encounter it in Proverbs is the *two-liner*. Throughout this book, I refer to each as Line A and Line B. Proverbs 10:2 provides a fine example:

LINE A: Treasures gained by wickedness do not profit,
LINE B: but righteousness delivers from death.

You see an interplay of ideas between the two verses. "Treasures gained by wickedness" in Line A is contrasted with "righteousness" in Line B, while A's "do not profit" is answered by "delivers from death" in B. Put another way, Line A tells what unjust gain *does not* do, while B tells what righteousness *does* do. But these two parts unite to make one point: the vast superiority of godly living over against wicked gain.

It is not always as easy to identify Hebrew poetry as one might expect.[33] We mustn't think of the Biblical characters as twenty-first century Americans in

---

[31] There are some pretty nifty little sound-plays, though. Take the first line of Proverbs 10:9. To make a non-technical transliteration, it reads like this: "Ho-LAKE ba-TOM yay-LEK beh-TACH."

[32] As I shall develop shortly, this should not be taken to imply that Hebrew poetry "rhymes" words in the sense of simply echoing and repeating them. Each "rhyme" is a development of some sort.

[33] This is developed at length on a technical level in *Idea of Biblical Poetry* (Baltimore: Johns Hopkins, 1981). Kugel notes that "There is no [specific] word for 'poetry' in Biblical Hebrew" (69).

(1) Terseness

sandals. Their mode of thought and expression was different from ours, and in some cases even their common speech was more elevated, vivid and picturesque than our flat, utilitarian prose tends to be.

However "not easy" is far from "impossible." Hebrew poetry tends to be identifiable by its *terseness*, its use of *imagery*, and its employment of *parallelism*.[34]

Terseness is the *first* of the three indicators which characterize Hebrew poetry. In a proverb, the language is stripped down to its essentials for maximum impact and memorability. This is extremely important to remember, if we are going to read Proverbs as Solomon means us to:

> A *proverb* is a *saying*, not a *dissertation*

A proverb is (if I may say so) an *adage* without *"paddage."*

Ask yourself: Which of the following two ways of saying the same thing is the more memorable?

- "A bit of perceptive and proactive forethought, followed up with appropriate and prompt action, will head off the need to spend a great deal more time and effort in regretfully remedying the situation down the road"; or…

- "A stitch in time saves nine."

Proverbs are designed for lean economy of expression.

We do not see this trait in translation, though it is quite plain in Hebrew. Most of the proverbs in chapters 10 and following literally average around 7 or 8 words each, total. The English translations are much wordier.

For instance, the Hebrew text of Proverbs 10:6 is a mere 7 words long:

> Blessings for-head-of righteous,
> but-mouth-of wicked-men conceals violence.

---

[34] David L. Peterson and Kent H. Richards, *Interpreting Hebrew Poetry* (Mineapolis: Fortress Press, 1989), 1, 14; Raymond B. Dillard and Tremper Longman, *An Introduction to the Old Testament* (Grand Rapids: Zondervan, 1994; used by permission), 26–29; Waltke, *Proverbs*, 1:38–39. Of the three, Longman singles out *terseness* (Tremper Longman III, "Merism," *Dictionary of the Old Testament: Wisdom, Poetry & Writings* [ed. Tremper Longman III and Peter Enns (Downers Grove: InterVarsity, 2008)], 464).

To make smooth English, the ESV blows it up until the verse is *sixteen* words long—more than twice the length of the Hebrew verse.

> Blessings are on the head of the righteous,
>> but the mouth of the wicked conceals violence.[35]

This quality of terseness is both the genius and the challenge of Hebrew poetry. It is effective in the way the imagery or thought is embedded on the mind. But one feels the challenge in interpretation, as the writer expects the reader to use his familiarity with the imagery, and his imagination, to fill in the gaps. The challenge is particularly keen to twenty-first century English-speaking urbanites, who find the writer's terms tough to translate, and his imagery removed from our daily experience.

Imagery, the *second* of the three poetry indicators, refers to the abundance of picturesque, figurative language in Hebrew poetry. A few examples from Proverbs should suffice (emphases added):

> Hear, my son, your father's instruction,
>> and forsake not your mother's teaching,
> [9] for they are a *graceful garland* for your head   *sweet*
>> and *pendants* for your neck. (1:8–9)

> [3] yes, if you call out for insight
>> and raise your voice for understanding,
> [4] if you seek it like *silver*
>> and search for it as for *hidden treasures*. (2:3–4)

> A gentle tongue is a *tree of life*,
>> but perverseness in it breaks the spirit (15:4)

In reading Proverbs, you'll find word-pictures to your imagination's delight. You'll cringe from crucibles, flee from whirlwinds, wince at thorns, dodge arrows, shiver in snow, and sweat in the heat. You'll plunge your hands into gold and

---

[35] Another of many possible examples would be Proverbs 26:16 (6 words in Hebrew, 15 in ESV, nearly three times as long); or 12:4 (6 words in Hebrew, 20 in ESV, *over* three times as long). Hebrew readers will note that I count *maqqēf*-words, which one might think of as hyphenated words, as single words.

3. Parallelism

Call to book
Part 1 pics of
of Proverbs

silver and jewels. You'll drink (or run) from fountains and springs; pluck fruit off trees; and luxuriate in exotic fragrances and spices. You'll behold both feasts and famine, rooftops and deserts. You'll ponder ants and lions and coneys and roosters and snakes and eagles and vultures.

What a rich gallery Solomon has laid out—and every picture tells a story.

Third and finally, both the simplest and the most complex aspect of Hebrew poetry is *parallelism*. It is simple in that one can sum it up simply: in parallelism, one line is then developed in (at least) a second line that completes the thought in some way. But in saying that, one has said far too little. The ways in which that second line develops the thought of the first are complex and varied.

I shall return to parallelism shortly, but here let me just briefly illustrate the variety of parallels we find in Proverbs.

Some pairings are as obvious as a nursery-rhyme

> A soft answer turns away wrath,
>   but a harsh word stirs up anger. (Prov. 15:1)

Here each term in Line A is countered by an answering term in Line B, with one exception. It is clearer in the eight words of the Hebrew proverb, but the English is quite plain. "A soft answer" contrasts with "but a harsh word." The picture of "turns away" counters "stirs up." However, "wrath" and "anger" are synonyms, so here lies the unity of both lines. The whole proverb is about anger: how to provoke it, and how to avoid it.

See? Simple.

However, other pairings are far more opaque. Skip down to verse 3 of the same chapter:

> The eyes of the LORD are in every place,
>   keeping watch on the evil and the good

> B completes A

Line B does not open with a conjunction ("and," "but," etc.). The terms in A are not echoed in B. Yet the thought of A is extended and completed in B. In this parallel, then, B in no way echoes A; rather, it completes it.

In Line A of Proverbs 15:3, Solomon poses the thought of God's eyes, everywhere. But what are His eyes doing, everywhere? Line B answers: they are *watching* both evil and good. A verb (צָפָה, *ṣāpâ*) is employed that conveys the idea of an intent, attentive watch. It is a pregnant assertion, for the God of Proverbs (as of the larger Canon) does not merely "watch" forever.[36]

Proverbs 15:3 asserts Yahweh's moral government of the universe: nothing escapes his attention; and so, no good will go unrewarded, and no evil unpunished.

Interpreting Proverbs

The fact that Proverbs is a book of poetry is absolutely critical for interpretation. You may not need me to tell you (but I will, anyway) that we interpret different types of literature according to different rules.

You already apply this in your own life without needing to pause and reflect. Without special instructions, you will read a Dr. Seuss book differently from a software instruction manual. We pick up signals for this almost unconsciously. If a book begins, "Once upon a time, in a big, dark forest on the edge of good King Shakaboom's land…," we prepare for one sort of reading. However, "It was the best of times, it was the worst of times," prepares us for another kind of reading. "Many factors led to the American Revolution: among them are…" would announce yet a third style.

Biblical poetry is no different in this regard. The Bible is an entire library wedged between two covers. In that collection are several different literary genres, including narratives, letters, and our current genre: proverbial poetry.

Accordingly, if we are to read and understand Proverbs wisely, we must apply different interpretive rules from those we employ in reading and understanding (say) Philippians. The latter is a little letter, the former is a big book of pithy pointers. We could express the central principle this way:

> Proverbs convey pithy points and principles,
> not precious particular promises[37]

Remember that poetry by design is *terse*. If that is true of poetry in general, it is true of proverbs to the tenth power.

It is important that we grasp the fact that this is intentional. It is the nature of the genre.

---

[36] Cf. Prov. 12:2; 20:22; 22:23; 25:22; Eccl. 12:14, etc.
[37] See Bullock, 162.

A "knock-knock" joke is what it is. It is a *successful joke* (if it is a good one), not a *failed dictionary*. Similarly, Proverbs are wonderfully successful at being what they are: *proverbs*. They are not failed prophecies or systematic theologies. Proverbs by design lays out pointed observations, meant to be memorized and pondered, not always intended to be applied "across the board" to every situation without qualification.

The point was well-made by Derek Kidner:

> Naturally [proverbs] generalize, as a proverb must, and may therefore be charged with making life too tidy to be true. But nobody objects to this in secular sayings, for the very form demands a sweeping statement and looks for a hearer with his wits about him. We need no telling that a maxim like "Many hands make light work" is not the last word on the subject, since "Too many cooks spoil the broth."[38]

We can fairly easily think of illustrations from our own culture's proverbs. Take this pair:

Look before you leap

And yet...

He who hesitates is lost.

Do these two proverbs contradict? Formally, of course they do. So, which one is true? Both! One applies to some situations, the second comes to play in others. The first warns against haste, the second against dithery indecision. The first could apply (say) to a marriage-decision; the second (say) to responding to a terrific, limited-supply sale. The application requires wisdom on our part.

One obvious, intended example from Proverbs of this is found in Proverbs 26:4–5—

Answer not a fool according to his folly,
    lest you be like him yourself.

[5] Answer a fool according to his folly,
    lest he be wise in his own eyes.

---

[38] Kidner, *The Wisdom of Proverbs, Job & Ecclesiastes* (IVP: 1985), 26.

Do these two proverbs contradict each other? They do—but only formally. It is a case of one proverb applying in some situations, and the other applying in others. The first warns against adopting a fool's way of thinking, the second counsels disarming him with his own weapons.

Or again, we could think of Proverbs 16:7—

> When a man's ways please the LORD,
>> he makes even his enemies to be at peace with him.

The principle of this proverb is transparent: the vertical takes precedence over (and overrules) the horizontal. Our relationship with God is more important, and determinative, than our relationships with people.

Yet if we press the words into a promise for our here-and-now situations, we can run into tremendous grief...or cause it. Does the verse demand that we assume that we must be displeasing God, if anyone hates us? Should we counsel others who have relational conflict, who have lost a friend or a spouse because of their love for Christ, that they must have sin in their lives? Must we tell them that God's favor necessarily means that all relationships will be warm and trouble-free?

The rest of the Bible shouts out the answer. All we need do is think of Jesus. Did ever a man live who was more pleasing to God than His own dear Son, the Lord Jesus? Certainly not. Yet was ever a man more roundly and wrongfully hated and despised than He? No. His enemies did not come to peace with Him in His earthly ministry.[39]

It is for this reason that Proverbs may appeal in the wrong way to the dogmatically-minded, to people who compulsively pigeon-hole everything. Do you know folks like this? Are you one?

I have in mind Bible-believers who, like Job's three "friends," feel that every problem and every situation has a simple, quick explanation. Persons of this mindset would reason backwards from circumstances to causes, as did Job's "friends."

Nor are folks like this lacking superficial "proof-texts" from the Bible. Think of the use that could be made of Proverbs 12:21—

> No harm befalls the righteous,
>> But the wicked are filled with trouble. (NAS)

---

[39] We could say the same of most godly men in the Bible, from Moses to Paul (cf. 2 Tim. 3:12).

Taken on face value as if it were prose, this verse voices a sentiment that Job's friends could have heartily "Amen-ed, " and which they would have used further to club him over the head as with a frozen meat chub. Job's three wretched comforters reasoned that misery, "harm," is always caused by sin.[40] Then these men noted that "harm" had befallen Job. He was "filled with trouble." Conclusion: Job *could not* be "righteous," and his misery *must* have been caused by some personal sin.

Or, again, those ignoring the genre might seize upon Proverbs 22:4—"The reward for humility and fear of the LORD is riches and honor and life." Armed with that verse, they might observe: "You aren't rich…so that means you are arrogant and godless."

So we are learning that Proverbs both *teaches* wisdom, and *requires* wisdom for its correct interpretation and application. Proverbs itself makes this clear. A proverb is not a magical formula, bringing wisdom and blessing by incantation: "Like a lame man's legs, which hang useless, is a proverb in the mouth of fools" (Prov. 26:7). If not approached and applied with sound Biblical wisdom, a proverb won't get us any further than a pair of lame legs.

What is more, a misused proverb can cause much pain and harm: "Like a thorn that goes up into the hand of a drunkard is a proverb in the mouth of fools" (Prov. 26:9). One who hastily memorizes a few proverbs and begins flinging them about will be less like a master sage, and more like "The Sorcerer's Apprentice" in the old Disney cartoon.

"Proverb" Defined

Frustrated readers might have noted that I have been talking about "proverbs" as if we are all agreed on what they are. Let me offer my own definition of a *proverb,* by which I am referring to the briefer, usually two-line type of proverb.

> A proverb is a compressed statement of wisdom, artfully crafted to be striking, thought-provoking, memorable, and practical

---

[40] There is some truth in this thought, but not all truth. Sin is the ultimate root of all misery (Rom. 5:12). It is not, however, the immediate cause of each misery. For instance, sin is the reason why people die. But Abel (for instance) did not die as a punishment for a personal sin.

What is a proverb

Proverbs are brief, pithy, pointed, and memorable pointers for dealing with life's issues.

In this way, proverbs can squirm their way into the details of daily living in a way that other kinds of literature cannot. "Do not steal," "Do not commit adultery," "Do not bear false witness" are all clear, categorical commands. It is not difficult to understand what is prohibited, in general and virtually all-embracing terms. But what uses of my time are kinds of theft? What are the paths that lead to adultery? What behaviors cultivate a healthy marriage? What are the real-life fruits of God's frown upon those actions? What are the kinds and results of lying? The commands do not deal with these issues directly, but Proverbs does.

I enjoy the way Derek Kidner brings out the particular genius of the book of Proverbs:

> "Make the bad people good, and the good people nice", is supposed to have been a child's prayer: it makes the point, with proverbic brevity, that there are details of character small enough to escape the mesh of the law and the broadsides of the prophets, and yet decisive in personal dealings. Proverbs moves in this realm, asking what a person is like to live with, or to employ; how he manages his affairs, his time and himself. This good lady, for instance—does she talk too much? That cheerful soul—is he bearable in the early morning? And this friend who is always dropping in—here is some advice for him...and for that rather aimless lad...[41]

A proverb typically is *truth dressed to travel.* It is wisdom compressed, compacted, stripped down to its essentials, and ready to go. Proverbs are tailored in such a way as to snag and stay in the mind. Think of that ad jingle you can't get out of your head, that bumper-sticker so clever you can't wait to tell a friend, that T-shirt so sharp and on-target that you want to wear it to parties. Proverbs do not try to say everything. But what they do say, they say artfully and memorably.

"Proverb" Formation

It is safe to say, then, that in Proverbs we have a Wisdom book that requires wisdom for right handling. Some wisdom can be gained when we pause a moment to consider how proverbs were formed.

---

[41] Kidner, *Proverbs*, 13.

Henry Virkler provides helpful, stimulating insight in his *Hermeneutics: Principles and Processes of Biblical Interpretation* (Baker: 1981). In the course of discussing figures of speech such as similes, metaphors, proverbs, parables and allegories, Virkler brings out a sparkling insight into proverbs.

To receive full value, it will help if we briefly brush up on a pair of definitions. A *simile* is the comparison of A to B, and a *metaphor* says that A *is* B. Virkler describes the former as an expressed comparison, and the latter as an unexpressed comparison.[42] Handily enough, Proverbs 15:19 gives one example of each:

> The way of a sluggard is like a hedge of thorns [simile],
>   but the path of the upright is a level highway [metaphor].

Then Virkler constructs a positively brilliant observation. He first notes that a *simile*, if extended, becomes a *parable*; and a *metaphor*, if extended, becomes an *allegory*. Then Virkler goes on to observe that if the resultant parable or the allegory is compressed, it becomes a *proverb*.[43]

This compression factor highlights both the genius and the peril of the proverb. *Genius* in that it simply will not do to read the book of Proverbs in a hurry. Proverbs is not intellectual fast-food, though it may appear so at first glance. Instead, Proverbs are meant to be chewed over, savored, relished slowly and thoroughly. We have to see through a proverb's beguilingly brief statement, and unpack the larger story—the parable or the allegory—that lies behind it in the writer's thinking.

But this compression factor is *perilous* to the interpreter, too. If we try to force the compressed form to say everything, we miss its point. A proverb is not always intended to be a guarantee, or an exhaustive statement on any given subject. Rather, it is a pithy pointer, usually designed to drive one truth into the mind. Ryken says it well: "The aim of a proverb is to make an insight permanent."[44]

Note well: *an* insight; not *all* insight.

---

[42] Virkler, 158.
[43] See the chart in Virkler, 161.
[44] Leland Ryken, *How to Read the Bible as Literature* (Grand Rapids, Zondervan: 1984; used by permission), 122.

Verses are not cats

Major Types of Proverbs

As I observed earlier, "classic," two-line proverbs require a different reading approach than other books of the Bible.

Pastors and Bible teachers hammer into their hearers the fact that the most important principle in sound Bible interpretation is *context.* Verses are not cats, each on its own independent mission. We encounter verses in a literary setting nestled within a longer poem, a prophecy, a narrative, a letter.

That simple concept, *context,* is the bane of most Scripture-twisting cultists. Many of false teachers' "proof-texts" vanish like snowflakes on a hot summer day the moment we take in the surrounding verses. We must always read what precedes and follows, before we even begin to imagine that we understand a verse.

However, with most of the book of Proverbs, this golden principle has to be radically adjusted.

I have mentioned that most of the proverbs from chapters 10 on are stand-alone two-liners. Let me illustrate further what I mean, by contrasting two pairs of verses:

> Then what advantage has the Jew? Or what is the value of circumcision? ²Much in every way. To begin with, the Jews were entrusted with the oracles of God (Rom. 3:1–2)

> ¹ A wise son makes a glad father,
>   but a foolish son is a sorrow to his mother.

> ² Treasures gained by wickedness do not profit,
>   but righteousness delivers from death. (Prov. 10:1b-2)

The first pair is from the apostle Paul's letter to the Romans. "Then" in verse 1 signals that Paul is logically proceeding from something earlier. He is taking up a thought from chapter 2, and interacting with it. He poses two questions in verse 1, answers them in verse 2… then continues the discussion in the following verses. None of these verses makes complete sense, if plucked out and taken by itself.

Contrast the next pair, taken from Proverbs 10. The first verse is about what kind of sons gladden or sadden their parents. Although it is a very fitting hinge-verse from the introductory nine chapters, it contains no linking conjunction such as "Therefore" or "Accordingly." Then, the second verse is about theft versus righteousness. What is the relationship, the flow of thought, from the first to the second verse? None is evident; none may be intended.

That is the point: Proverbs is a collection of…well, proverbs! And proverbs by definition are short and pointed. They burst in the front door, bang a cup on the table, have their say, and then exit with a slam—leaving us blinking in amazement, and mulling over what they said.[45] We cannot read the two-liners as we would read Romans or Hebrews… or Genesis or Matthew.

Now let us classify some of the major types of proverbs, according to eight categories I have settled on and found helpful.[46] In so doing (with the exception of #8), I shall assume a two-line proverb. And so, with that in mind…[47]

#1—*Synonymous* Proverbs

In this, Line B *re-words the thought of* Line A. Consider some examples:

> Whoever brings blessing will be enriched,
>> and one who waters will himself be watered. (11:25)

> How much better to get wisdom than gold!
>> To get understanding is to be chosen rather than silver. (16:16)

> Before breaking—pride,
>> and before a fall—a haughty spirit. (16:18 DJP)

In these, the individual proverb provides its own context. For instance, "Whoever brings blessing" (Line A) thought-rhymes with "one who waters" (Line B) in 11:25. "Wisdom" (Line A) thought-rhymes with "understanding" (Line B) in 16:16. "Pride" (Line A) thought-rhymes with "a haughty spirit" (Line B) in 16:18.

---

[45] As noted, it is true that we can see some proverbs of similar subject-matter apparently grouped together (i.e. 10:3–5 [work]; 16:12–15 [kings], and so forth), but even in such collections, each verse tends to make its own two-line point, rather than building collectively to a conclusion.

[46] For some of these, see the studies in Delitzsch, 1:7–12; Bullock, 159–160; R. B. Y. Scott, *Proverbs, Ecclesiastes* (Anchor Bible series; Doubleday: 1965), 5–8; and Archer, 481–483.

[47] Also keep this in mind: unlike the proverbs themselves, these categories are not God-breathed. The categories overlap. A verse can be both antithetical and satirical, for instance (e.g. 15:19); or antithetical and consequence (10:27).

Let me hasten to reiterate, however, that the "rhyme" in Line B is far from a mere echo or synonym. In some way, Line B advances Line A.[48] Sometimes the specifics are not visible in English, as the Hebrew term chosen may well be the more literary term. But often the echo is more specific, more emphatic, more heightened, more picturesque.

#2—*Contrast* (or *Antithetical*) Proverbs

In this category, Line B *contrasts with* Line A. We could think of it as equivalent to saying "A, but B." The dead giveaway of this category is generally the antithetical conjunction "But" at the beginning of Line B. This grouping is probably the most common from 10:1 on. In these examples, the conjunction is italicized.

> A wise son makes a father glad,
> > *But* a foolish son is a grief to his mother. (10:1b NAS)
>
> Poor is he who works with a negligent hand,
> > *But* the hand of the diligent makes rich. (10:4 NAS)
>
> A sated man loathes honey,
> > *But* to a famished man any bitter thing is sweet. (27:7 NAS)

The effect of this kind of proverb is to make a point startlingly clear by holding up opposites. In 10:1 we have a wise boy versus a wiseacre, and a glad dad versus a glum mum. In 10:4 we have the idle poor verses the working rich. In 27:7 we have the stuffed snob verses the starving omnivore.

#3—*Comparison* Proverbs

In this sort of proverb, Line A is *like* Line B. One mark of this class is the use of the words "like" or "as." Consider these samples, emphases added:

---

[48] "…it is the dual nature of B both to come *after* A and thus to add to it, often particularizing, defining, or expanding the meaning, and yet also to harken [sic] back to A and in an obvious way to connect to it" (Kugel, *The Idea of Biblical Poetry*, 8). Waltke agrees that "B both corresponds in thought with A and in some way advances it, often specifying or intensifying it. The versets normally move from general to specific, from abstract to concrete, from ambiguous to less ambiguous, from usual to unusual vocabulary and/or from less intense to more intense" (*Commentary*, 1:43). Alter "notes that the characteristic movement of meaning [from Line A to Line B] is one of heightening or intensification (as in the paradigmatic case of numerals), of focusing, specification, concretization, even what could be called dramatization" (Alter, 19).

> *Like* vinegar to the teeth and smoke to the eyes,
> > so is the sluggard to those who send him. (10:26)

> *Like* cold water to a thirsty soul,
> > so is good news from a far country. (25:25)

> *Like* a madman who throws
> > firebrands, arrows, and death
> [19] is the man who deceives his neighbor
> > and says, "I am only joking!" (26:18–19 [a four-liner])

The idea may be clear even when the word is missing.

> A ring of gold in the snout of a pig,
> > A beautiful woman and yet turning away from *good* taste.
> (11:22 DJP)

Do we really need the "Like" and "so" that many standard translations supply? [49]

In these comparing proverbs, there is always *some* point of contact. Sometimes, Line A is symbolic, and Line B literal, as in 10:26 and 25:25 (see above). But the point is still clear: Line A of 10:26 is grating, annoying, and irritating—and so is Line B. Line A of 25:25 is refreshing and life-giving—and so is Line B. Lines A^1 and A^2 of 26:18 and 19 paint a picture of widespread destruction—and so do lines B^1 and B^2. Line A of 11:22 portrays an absurd and un-fitting picture—and so does Line B.

#4—*Satirical* Proverbs

These are striking, memorable little portrayals which use the humorous device of *satire* to penetrate and arrest our attention. Proverbs of this sort warn against a foolish, immoral, or destructive way of life by mocking either that behavior, or its practitioners.

Often the second line paints the opposite path, the way of wisdom. These proverbs amount to saying that "Mr. [or Ms.] Line A is *nothing like* Line B." Some examples will make this clear:

---

[49]   In a number of these proverbs, the Hebrew lacks "like" or "as," which are then supplied in the English versions—possibly blunting Solomon's stylistic intent (cf. 11:22; 25:12, 14, 18–20, 25, etc.).

Whoever is slothful will not roast his game,
   but the diligent man will get precious wealth. (12:27)

The soul of the sluggard craves and gets nothing,
   while the soul of the diligent is richly supplied. (13:4)

The simple believes everything,
   but the prudent gives thought to his steps. (14:15)

Sometimes the satire takes both lines:

The sluggard buries his hand in the dish
   and will not even bring it back to his mouth. (19:24)

Why is a fee in the hand of a stupid man
   to gain wisdom—but no brains? (17:16 DJP)

The first (19:24) is synthetic in form, and is the hysterically funny image of the man *so lazy* that he sticks his hand (say) into a bowl of peanuts… and then just can't muster the energy to bring the crunchy morsels up to his mouth. The second (17:16) is also synthetic, and depicts a young student who has brought his tuition-fee… but, oops! No brains!

Then there is the occasional extended satire, as in chapter 7, or in Proverbs 24:30–34.[50]

We should not be surprised to find biting satire in Proverbs. For one thing, satire and parody are common methods throughout the Bible, from Genesis to Revelation. But to be more specific, Solomon himself told us from the outset that one purpose of his book was "For discerning a proverb and a satire, The words of wise men and their enigmas" (Proverbs 1:6). It is, or should be, no great shock that Solomon provides us with some satire and parody of his own.

#5—*Evaluation* Proverbs

Evaluation proverbs amount to asserting that Line A is *better than* Line B. The use of the word "Better" can be a giveaway, but it is not the only clue. Here are some varying examples:

---

[50] The Alert Reader may note that the examples above are a type-within-a-type, in that the *form* of the whole verse may be antithetical, and may be made up of two satires. Categories overlap.

> Better is a little with the fear of the LORD
>> than great treasure and trouble with it. (15:16)

> Let a man meet a she-bear robbed of her cubs
>> rather than a fool in his folly. (17:12)

> A man of many companions may come to ruin,
>> but there is a friend who sticks closer than a brother. (18:24)

> To do righteousness and justice
>> is more choice to Yahweh than sacrifice. (21:3 DJP)

Some of these examples demonstrate that bright markers such as "rather," "more" and "than" are not always present in evaluation proverbs. The point of an evaluation proverb is that two concepts are being compared and contrasted, with the better standing out clearly.

Another example of an evaluation proverb that uses none of the "dead giveaway" terms would be Proverbs 10:2—"Ill-gotten gains do not profit, But righteousness delivers from death." In form, this appears to be a simple contrast, as indicated by the "But" that begins Line B.

However, when one reflects, one sees that the verse is a comparison between two lifestyles: that of gaining dishonestly, and that of living righteously. The first is said not to profit, but the second delivers from death. Which lifestyle, then, is the God-fearing choice? Clearly the latter. And so, almost without our feeling it, Solomon has slipped us an evaluation proverb.

Evaluation proverbs acknowledge that life is not always ideal, and choices are not always perfect and crystal-clear. They live where we live. They give us wisdom for making the most God-fearing (and thus wisest) choice when alternatives beckon.

#6—*Consequence* Proverbs

Proverbs of this category amount to saying that Line B is *what happens when you do* Line A. This is one of Solomon's brilliant contributions toward maturing us, and forcing us to "wise up." Our tendency when we are young, and our tendency as sinners, is rashly to throw ourselves into an action or choice without weighing the end results.

Consequence proverbs are of two general kinds. Some issue *warnings*. These force us to look coldly, clearly, and unromantically at what can or will come of a line of actions. They warn against a behavior, often, by showing where it leads.[51]

Other consequence proverbs *commend* a way of life, by showing where it leads. Do this (good thing), and these (good fruits) will result.

Consider an illustration of each kind:

> Everyone who is arrogant in heart is an abomination to the LORD;
>> be assured, he will not go unpunished. (16:5; others include
>> 19:27; 20:4; 22:6)

> Do you see a man skillful in his work?
>> He will stand before kings; he will not stand before obscure
>> men. (22:29)

Of course, there are variations here as well. For instance, each line may give us a deed-destiny snapshot, as in 20:13—

> Love not sleep, lest you come to poverty;
>> open your eyes, and you will have plenty of bread.

#7—*Synthetic* Proverbs

Here, Line B builds on or extends and completes the thought of Line A. It is "Line A—*and what's more*, Line B."

> Leave the presence of a fool,
>> for there you do not meet words of knowledge. (14:7)

> The eyes of the LORD are in every place,
>> keeping watch on the evil and the good. (15:3)

Other examples would include 16:29; 17:8; and 26:4–5.

#8—Proverbial *Discourse*

These are the protracted didactic poems we discussed earlier, found chiefly in chapters 1–9. They are longer lectures and discourses on selected topics,

---

[51] An example from our own culture would be "spare the rod, spoil the child"—although this is (A) Biblical in origin (cf. 13:24; 29:15, etc.), and (B) probably waning in popularity, given the Children's Rights movement.

introductory to the shorter proverbs which follow. Within this section there is the typical Hebrew parallelism (e.g. 1:20, among many others), and the varieties observed above (cf. 2:1–5).

Summary

Respect for the text of Proverbs will incline us to see the whole as from King Solomon's hand as author and editor, with 25:1 being the sole, sure exception. God uniquely qualified Solomon to write this book. We also have met some of the indispensable principles for understanding and categorizing Proverbs.

Now we are ready to dig into the text.

Questions for Thought or Discussion

1. What are the reasons for seeing Solomon as author or editor of the whole?

2. What difference does Solomonic authorship make in how we interpret the book?

3. How does Proverbs differ from Deuteronomy, or 1 Samuel, or Romans?

4. What is Hebrew poetry?

5. What is a proverb?

6. What are the pitfalls and dangers of failing to understand what a proverb is meant to be?

7. How have you heard Proverbs misapplied?

1) He tells us
2)
3) It's Poetry
4) Terse, Imagery + Parallelism, Thoughtfully Crafted.
5) a terse statement of wisdom,
6)
7)

CHAPTER TWO

The Stated Design of Proverbs

What Good Will This Book Do Us?

Translation of Proverbs 1:2–6[1] (DJP)

> 1:2 For becoming acquainted with wisdom and discipline,
>   For discerning sayings of discernment.
> 1:3 For receiving intelligent discipline—
>   Righteousness, and justice, and uprightness.
> 1:4 For giving to the gullible ones shrewdness,
>   To the youth knowledge and planning skill.
> 1:5 Let a wise man listen and add learning,
>   And let a discerning man acquire a knowledge of the ropes!
> 1:6 For discerning a proverb and a satire,
>   The words of wise men and their enigmas.

King Solomon wisely writes a preface to his book. As modern authors often do, the King tells us the good his book will do us if we will but study it. In these five verses Solomon spells out *seven* benefits which we will gain from the study of this book.[2] Let's see if we need any of them, shall we? (Hint: we shall.)

---

[1]   See translation footnotes for this section in Chapter 1.
[2]   Judging by the distinct verbs, Solomon promises seven benefits from his proverbs. (By strict

First Benefit (1:2a)

For becoming acquainted with wisdom and discipline,

This verse promises that this book will acquaint us with two assets for life: with *wisdom* and with *discipline*. Let us analyze the verb, and the two nouns.

The Verb: Pleased to Make Your *Acquaintance*

The phrase Solomon uses for "for becoming acquainted" is לָדַעַת (*lāda'at*), which any Hebrew student will (or should) tell you is a Qal infinitive construct from the word ידע (*yāda'*), meaning simply *to know*.

I say "simply," but actually it isn't that simple. The Hebrew verb *yāda'* generally suggests an involvement that we do not necessarily attach to "know" in English.[3] It is not as sheerly cerebral as we might assume, though it does require the exercise of mental powers. For instance, we would have no difficulty conceiving of a 600-pound doctor who "knows" all about diet and weight loss. But to the Hebrew mind, that doctor wouldn't really *know* much at all about the subject.

Solomon aims at more than the mere acquisition of facts. Information is indeed essential and invaluable. But it is not an end in itself. The facts lead to a "knowing" which is an encounter, a relationship with the truth. As Longman says, "knowledge was never an abstract proposition in the book of Proverbs; it always implied a relationship."[4]

Solomon's Goal

Since *wisdom and discipline* are two heavy-duty themes in Proverbs, we can be sure that Solomon desires more than merely a shallow, barren, sheerly-intellectual formal knowledge of what he has to say. We see this plainly in the only other identical occurrence of the Hebrew phrase translated "for becoming acquainted," in Proverbs 4:1 (DJP, italics for emphasis):

---

count, there are eight verbs, but the two in v. 5a are an essentially synonymous pair.)

[3] The classic example that every modern reader of the King James Version could cite is Genesis 4:1, where we read that Adam "knew" (*yāda'*) his wife. Since the result of this "knowing" was pregnancy, we are safe in assuming that this went well beyond acquaintance with some facts.

[4] Tremper Longman III, *Proverbs* (Grand Rapids: Baker, 2006), 97.

> Hear, sons, the discipline of a father,
> And give attention *so as to become acquainted with* discernment.[5]

This suits our real need. We must not merely become theoretically aware of some nice ideas; we must get involved with wisdom, we must become personally acquainted with it.

Nor can this be accomplished overnight. Aiken says that it is "not 'to know,' as this suggests the finished result rather than the process, which is 'to become acquainted with, to acquire.'"[6] Gaining this personal knowledge is a process, and King Solomon says that his book will begin that process for us. Solomon intends to initiate the reader into the life-long journey of wisdom.

But what, exactly, is "wisdom"?

The First Noun: *Wisdom*

By studying Proverbs, we can become personally acquainted with wisdom. In English, once again, we might tend to think of merely intellectual knowledge, or of primarily broad acquaintance with ideas and concepts. In Hebrew, the word is חָכְמָה (*hokmâ*),[7] a word truly rich in meaning.

A survey of some of the categorizations of *hokmâ* in the exhaustive BDB Hebrew lexicon is helpful. The Hebrew noun *hokmâ* is used of skill in war (Isa. 10:13), in technical work (Exod. 28:3; 31:3, 6), and in sailing (Psa. 107:27). It also refers to wisdom in administration (Deut. 34:9; Isa. 29:14). The corresponding adjective חָכָם (*hākām*) is used of skilled sailors (Ezek. 27:8), and skilled tabernacle workmen (Exod. 28:3; 31:6; 35:10). The adjective is used of Joseph (Gen. 41:33, 39), of judges (Deut. 16:19); of David (2 Sam. 14:20); of Solomon (1 Kings 2:9; 3:12); of the prince of Tyre (Ezek. 28:3); and even of four kinds of "wise" animals (Prov. 30:24ff.).[8] Clearly, the words have a wide range of possible uses.

---

[5] The Hebrew here is *lāda'at bînâ*.

[6] Aiken's remark is in Otto Zöckler, "The Proverbs of Solomon," translated and edited by Charles Aiken, in John Peter Lange's *Commentary on the Holy Scriptures* (Zondervan: 1978 [reprint]; used by permission), V:43.

[7] Pronunciation of *hokmâ* does not come easily to a native English-speaking tongue. If one is set on trying, he could take the *ch* from the Scottish word *loch*, and add "-okhmah" (the middle "k" is a little soft).

[8] BDB, article חָכָם.

> The ESV conservatively translates *ḥokmâ* by
> wisdom 143X, skill 7X, ability 2X, and wits' 1X.
> Among the ESV renderings of adjective
> *ḥākām* are *wise, wiser,* or *wisest* over 100X;
> *craftsman* or *craftsmen* 6X; *skilled* or *skillful* 15X.

Several of these uses are particularly fascinating, and helpful. I have long been struck by these verses from Exodus (uses of *ḥ-k-m italicized*):

> "And you are to speak unto all those who are *wise* of heart, whom I have filled with the spirit of[9] *wisdom*, and they shall make Aaron's garments to make him holy so as to serve as priest for Me." (Exod. 28:3 DJP)

> "…and I have filled him with the Spirit of God, with *ability* and intelligence, with knowledge and all craftsmanship." (Exod. 31:3)

> "And as for Me, look: I have given with him Oholiab, son of Ahisamach, belonging to the tribe of Dan, and in the heart of everyone who is *wise* of heart I have given *wisdom*,[10] and they will make all that I have commanded you." (Exod. 31:6 DJP)

What an interesting cluster of verses. They do not easily fit what we might have expected as Biblical descriptions of "wisdom," do they? Is it not what we would think of as a secular ability, the ability to do skillful work in craftsmanship? Yet the texts clearly state that these are abilities that qualify as being "wise of heart," expressly given by the Spirit of God. So what is "wisdom" in these verses, if it is not skill and expertise?

We must also see that these isolated verses. Psalm 107:27 refers to sailors in a terrible storm being "at their wits' end." The Hebrew text more literally says, "And all their wisdom was confused," or "swallowed itself up." The wisdom (*ḥokmâ*) referred to obviously is their skill as sailors; in other words, their skill was not sufficient to cope with the storm.

If one were to follow out the other references, he would soon find that the word *ḥokmâ*, wisdom, frequently refers to skill of one sort or another—often what

---

9   Or "Spirit who gives…" (cf. 31:3).
10 ESV: "… I have given to all able men ability…."

we would think of as sheerly secular skill and adeptness. There is no denying that "*ḥokmâ* [wisdom] can mean technical expertise and other professional capabilities of various types."[11] So, likewise, the חָכָם (*ḥākām*), the wise man, is the "man who has mastered something."[12]

It is not hard, then, to see that the elements of *skill, adeptness, expertise* and *savvy* are integral to the word. Wisdom is not primarily abstract. Wisdom is never merely a matter of knowing facts, but of knowing what to do with them—and doing it.

The Concept of Wisdom

Although the Bible values wisdom highly, we see from Jeremiah 9:23–24 (Hebrew 22–23) that human wisdom is not an end in itself.

> Thus says the LORD: "Let not the wise man boast in his wisdom, let not the mighty man boast in his might, let not the rich man boast in his riches, [24] but let him who boasts boast in this, that he understands and knows me, that I am the LORD who practices steadfast love, justice, and righteousness in the earth. For in these things I delight, declares the LORD."

One is not truly wise unless he knows the Lord personally. Solomon will make this very clear when he says, "The beginning of wisdom is the fear of Yahweh, And the knowledge of the Holy Ones[13] is discernment" (Prov. 9:10 DJP). Though Proverbs is much concerned with what we might call "horizontal success"—success in relationships, business, character-building—it is no less concerned with success in our vertical relationship with God. It is as Archer says: *ḥokmâ* "came to be applied to the art of getting along successfully with God and with men."[14]

The wisdom with which Solomon proposes to acquaint us, then, is *skill for living in the fear of Yahweh*. It subsumes all under the Godhood of God (Prov. 1:7;

---

[11] TLOT, 421. Cf. NIDOTTE, 2:132.

[12] TDNT, 7:483.

[13] The plural is not a typing error. However jarring, it is undeniably present in the Hebrew text. Although many Hebrew students call this a "plural of majesty," "honorific" (Waltke), or some suchlike, I see here and in numerous similar plurals a hint at the doctrine of the Trinity, of which I find evidence in both Testaments.

[14] Archer, 485.

9:10; 31:30), and casts every bit of life within that framework. This God-centered wisdom will encompass all our endeavors, including excellence in relationships, in personal pursuits, finances, child-rearing, "the whole shooting match." But the constant backdrop of these living skills will be the imperative of a life lived in reverence for God, in conscious application of His revealed wisdom, and dedicated to promoting His glory.

Put another way, the Biblical call to wisdom tells us two things. On the one hand, mere human how-to knowledge is not enough by a long shot. Fear of God must be foundational. This is our Square A.

On the other hand, lofty sentiments about God, coupled with a life carelessly lived, falls equally short of the mark. A healthy relationship with God will bear fruit in a life wisely lived, a path sagely walked. We must strive to live excellently for God, applying the revealed counsel of His Word to every area of our lives.

The Second Noun: *Discipline.*[15]

The term used here is the Hebrew מוּסָר (*mûsār*; translated in the LXX as *paideia*[16]). It is built from the root יָסַר (*yāsar*), which means to *discipline, chasten, admonish.*[17] The noun *mûsār* means *discipline, chastening, correction.*[18] This noun has the idea of "correction which results in education."[19]

> The ESV translates *mûsār* as instruction 25X,
> discipline 15X, correction 4X, warning 2X, censure 1X,
> chastisement 1X, punishment 1X, bonds 1X

Perhaps we can get a better "feel" for this verb by considering some occurrences. Specifically, if we want to get into Solomon's mind, we will focus on the word's use in the Scriptures that Solomon could have had in hand. So, for instance, *yāsar* is used in Leviticus 26:18 and 28 of God's *punishing* disobedient Israel by the dire, destructive providential blows with which He would strike her (cf. vv. 23–24).

---

[15] For a detailed (but more academic) discussion of this group of terms, see Appendix Two, "Words Related to Teaching in Proverbs."

[16] The "LXX" is the Septuagint, the Greek translation of the Old Testament. The Greek word *paideia* is the word from which we get "pedagogy"; it has in mind the training of children.

[17] BDB, article יָסַר.

[18] BDB, article מוּסָר.

[19] Paul R. Gilchrist, TWOT, 1:386.

> "And if in spite of this you will not listen to me, then I will
> *discipline* you again sevenfold for your sins, ...[23]And if by this
> *discipline* you are not turned to me[20] but walk contrary to me,
> [24]then I also will walk contrary to you, and I myself will strike
> you sevenfold for your sins. ...[28]then I will walk contrary to you
> in fury, and I myself will *discipline* you sevenfold for your sins.
> (Lev. 26:18, 23–24, 28; emphases added)

So God says that He will *punish* Israel, and He defines this punishment as
(if you will) spanking them seven times—whack, whack, whack, whack, whack,
whack and, of course, *whack*. This is "education" with oomph.

There is breadth, as well, to the use of this noun, as we can see in Deuteronomy
11:2–7. We can see that verse 2a states the *fact* of the discipline, whereas vv. 2b-7
expand on the *contents* of this discipline. Yahweh's discipline served to teach Israel
fundamental theology, the essential doctrines of God's nature. This discipline
included the revelation of His greatness and glory, the vengeance on Pharaoh
and Egypt, the provisions in the wilderness, the deaths of insubordinate Dathan
and Abiram, and basically all of His great work.

All of this was *discipline*. Discipline, therefore includes verbal instruction
enforced if need be by punishment, and much more besides.

In fact, the *aim* of discipline is shown clearly in Deuteronomy 4:35–36.

> To you it was shown, that you might know that the LORD is God;
> there is no other besides him. [36] Out of heaven he let you hear his
> voice, that he might *discipline* you. And on earth he let you see his
> great fire, and you heard his words out of the midst of the fire.

The intent of the discipline is to bring Israel to *know* that Yahweh is the sole
and supreme God. And to this end, they saw the theophanic fire that signified
His presence, and they heard His voice from afar. Once again, although *mûsār*
may include spanking and punishment, it is by no means limited to it.

---

[20] More literally, "If by these you are not *disciplined* to Me...."

The Concept

Kidner says delightfully that this term gives "notice at once that wisdom will be hard-won, a quality of character as much as of mind."[21] He adds that it usually conveys "a note of sternness, ranging from warning …to chastening."[22] Delitzsch translates the word as "instruction," and explains that the idea is "properly discipline, *i.e.* moral instruction, and in conformity with this, self-government, self-guidance."[23] Instruction may produce knowledge, but *discipline* produces *character.*

The Benefits

The benefits of Yahweh's discipline, however, are not enjoyed automatically. We do not grow and gain in wisdom without our own personal investment in the process. Parents cannot mechanically apply Methods A, B and C, and be assured of Result D.

For instance, the benefits can be canceled if we resist and are stubborn. Solomon would have known that fact from the history of Israel, who resisted Yahweh's discipline. We also see the truth in the following passages from Jeremiah, writing after Solomon:

> O LORD, do not your eyes look for truth?
>> You have struck them down,
>> but they felt no anguish;
> you have consumed them,
>> but they refused to take *correction.*
> They have made their faces harder than rock;
>> they have refused to repent. (Jer. 5:3; cf. 2:30; 7:28; 17:23)

We can see, in all these cases, that Yahweh corrected His people. But it is equally plain that this correction did them no good. Why not? Was it some defect in Yahweh, or a deficiency in His methods? Absurd thought! The defect was in the people. They did not listen, did not accept, did not take to heart God's correction. They stiffened their neck and refused to repent.

---

[21] Kidner, *Proverbs,* 36.
[22] Ibid., 34.
[23] Delitzsch, 1:54.

Consequently, the correction did not "take." A pill may be a literal wonder-drug, but if it is not swallowed, it will do no more good than watching a documentary.

This point is of great importance to you and to me. For God's discipline to do us any good, we must heed it. Hear God's words in Jeremiah 32:33:

> They have turned to me their back and not their face. And though I have taught them persistently, they have not listened to receive *instruction*.

We must listen, and we must receive instruction. There must be that "Hey—He's talking to me; I'd better listen up and get moving" moment.

Otherwise, God's discipline, even that which we have in the book of Proverbs, will not do us any good whatever. In fact, that discipline will stand in judgment over us (cf. the principle of Luke 12:47; John 5;45–47). God may teach and teach and teach, but unless we learn and repent and do, we not only make no progress—we actually *lose* ground (Jer. 8:5–6).

All parents will identify with this without any difficulty. Dads, moms: how many times have you told your child something again and again only to have your child repeat the same exact wrong action, sometimes within seconds? Was there something wrong in what you said, or in how you said it? Probably, but not necessarily. The problem is simply that the child heard, but did not listen. The eardrum vibrated, the malleus and incus and stapes were all doing their thing—but the heart was hard and motionless. The reproof, the discipline, was not accepted.

Summary: acquainted with wisdom and discipline

In Proverbs we will find the corrective education that we all need for skill in godly living. When we master its principles, we will be trained and corrected. However, we must be receptive to this discipline. We should begin our studies assuming that we need God's correction, and therefore we must pray that God help us remain wide-open to His correction through His Word.

Second Benefit (1:2b)

> For discerning sayings of discernment.

Discerning "Discerning"

We shook hands with this term in Chapter 1. It is the infinitive construct לְהָבִין (*l'hāḇîn*), from the root *bîn*, whence comes the preposition *bên*, meaning "between." The signification of *discerning, distinguishing, or discriminating* is seen in 1 Kings 3:9 ("Give your servant therefore an understanding mind to govern your people, that I may discern between [*l'hāḇîn bên*] good and evil, for who is able to govern this your great people?"), and brought out in the story of 3:16–28, where Solomon must do exactly that. Thus, the verb means to *discern* or *have insight, to show penetrating insight.*[24]

The Concept

Delitzsch explains the noun as "the understanding as the capability effective in the possession of the right criteria of distinguishing between the true and the false, the good and the bad (1 Kings iii. 9), the wholesome and the pernicious."[25]

Sometimes the object of this distinguishing insight is the Word of God itself, as we may observe in the following verses from the NAS, with the uses of this root *italicized*:

> And he read from it facing the square before the Water Gate from early morning until midday, in the presence of the men and the women and *those who could understand*. And the ears of all the people were attentive to the Book of the Law. (Neh. 8:3)

> *Give me understanding*, that I may keep your law
>   and observe it with my whole heart. (Psa. 119:34)

---

[24] The English word "discern" is from Latin roots meaning "to separate apart," and conveys the idea of perceiving clearly, distinguishing, being able to identify or to tell one object from another. "Insight" indicates a penetrating or deep knowledge. The two map out a good semantic range for representing the Hebrew words.

[25] Delitzsch, 1:54.

> Your hands have made and fashioned me;
>> *give me understanding* that I may learn your commandments.
> (Psa. 119:73)

In these cases, obviously, there is no thought of parting good from bad. Rather, the idea is that acute analysis which produces understanding. In other words, to understand God's Word, we must analyze it, and penetrate to the meaning of the words. This process is caught by the verb *bîn*.

Because God wants us to utilize His Word as our means of understanding, our own private *bînâ*[26] is ruled out, because it is insufficient. As God tells us through Solomon in Proverbs 3:5, "Trust unto Yahweh with all your heart, And unto your own discernment [*bînâ*] do not lean" (DJP). We are not to sort things out for ourselves without a thought to God's revealed, inscripturated wisdom (vv. 1–4). We are to learn and absorb His wisdom, and apply it in sorting out the details of our lives.

"Sayings of Discernment"

This phrase is אִמְרֵי בִינָה (*'imrê bînâ*), meaning sayings that are characterized by, or that communicate, discernment. These are sayings that will teach us discernment, insight. Archer well observes that the noun translated "discernment"

> connotes the ability to discern intelligently the difference between sham and reality, between truth and error, between the specious attraction of the moment and the long-range values that govern a truly successful life. … there is always an analytical or judgmental factor involved and the ability to distinguish between the valid and the invalid, the false and the true.[27]

The book of Proverbs is filled with such sayings, i.e., sayings characterized by the ability to analyze life-issues in accord with Divine viewpoint. For instance, we might think that a crooked business deal is just the thing that we need to set us up in life. We might even tell ourselves that it is "for the family." Everyone's doing it. It's expected.

Yet God warns us, "Treasures gained by wickedness do not profit, but righteousness delivers from death" (Prov. 10:2).

---

[26] This is the noun form, meaning *insight, perception, discernment*.

[27] Gleason L. Archer, Jr., *A Survey of Old Testament Introduction*, 3rd. ed. (Chicago: Moody Press, 1998), 517.

Or again, a young man might think that, once he finds a beautiful and affectionate young lady, he knows all he needs to know about her. She's pretty! Duh! Win!

Yet God warns, "A ring of gold in the snout of a pig, A beautiful woman and yet turning away from *good* taste" (Prov. 11:22 DJP).

Or a young lady might think that masculine assertiveness (i.e. pushy, self-centered rudeness) is her best path to self-fulfillment. It's modeled in movies and magazines. Anything else is to fail as a woman, to fall short of your full potential, to be a pathetic throwback.

Then she hears God saying, "A gracious woman[28] attains honor" (Prov. 11:16a).

These are all sayings of discernment. They all lead us to sort out the good from the bad, the worthwhile from the worthless. They help us to analyze, rather than merely emote. In fact, when we analyze these analytical sayings, *they* analyze *us*—and we gain insight into God's way of seeing things.

Third Benefit (1:3)

> For receiving intelligent discipline—[29]
> Righteousness, and justice, and uprightness.

The Action: *Receiving*

The Hebrew infinitive is לָקַחַת (*lāqaḥaṯ*), from a verb meaning to *take* (לָקַח, *lāqaḥ*). This bespeaks the fact that God gives this wisdom through His Word, and so we must take or receive it in this way. See Proverbs 2:6—"For Yahweh gives wisdom; From His mouth, knowledge and insight" (DJP).

How do we "receive" this education? Should we pray for God to give us wisdom, and then be open to "receive" it, directly? This is what the dominant mystical element in the church would have us believe today. "Just pray for wisdom, and then listen for that still, small voice within, as the Holy Spirit whispers in your spiritual inner ear," we are counseled, often by widely-respected Christian speakers and pastors.

---

[28] Literally "woman of grace."

[29] Or perhaps "education that produces intelligence." See Fox, *Proverbs*, 1:59–60, who discusses five alternate ways of taking the two Hebrew words.

But that literally cannot be what Solomon means. Remember, Solomon is saying that this is the purpose of his writing this book. Proverbs took a lot of effort and strain and sweat to write. It takes a lot of effort and strain and sweat to study, understand and apply.

So ask yourself this: Why would Solomon write a book to give us something we could get easier and better by mystical channels? If the formula for wisdom is "Just add prayer and mystical openness, and *pop!* wisdom!"—then why waste all the quills and papyrus? Just tell us to go mentally limp, and you will save a few trees… or, rather, reeds.

This "intelligent discipline" will not come to the intellectually lazy. Intelligent discipline becomes ours only as we diligently apply ourselves to obtaining what Yahweh has objectively given, once and for all time, in Scripture. To access it, we must open up, bear down, and accept instruction. Fox well says that the phrase here means "to take it to heart, to absorb it and change one's ways."[30]

The Benefit: Intelligent Discipline

"Intelligent discipline" is a translation of the Hebrew phrase מוּסַר הַשְׂכֵּל (*mûsar haśkēl*). As we have seen, the term *mûsār* signifies *corrective education*. The second term (*haśkēl*) denotes insight, cleverness.[31] Both Delitzsch[32] and Goldberg[33] say that *haśkēl* indicates the process of reasoning our way through a complex arrangement of thoughts, resulting in wise dealing and the use of good, practical common sense. The phrase translated "intelligent discipline" is

> such morality and good conduct as rest not on external inheritance, training, imitation, and custom, but is bound up with the intelligent knowledge of the Why and the Wherefore.[34]

This, then, is intelligent, disciplined strength of character. It is something that a book cannot give all by itself; but *this* book, Proverbs, can point out for us the way to acquire such intelligence.

---

[30] Fox, *Proverbs*, 1:59.
[31] HALOT, article שׂכל.
[32] Delitzsch, 1:55.
[33] Louis Goldberg, TWOT, II:877.
[34] Delitzsch, 1:55.

Solomon's Own Expanded Definition

Solomon himself defines "intelligent discipline" by the three words which follow: righteousness, justice, and uprightness. *Righteousness* (צֶדֶק, *ṣedeq*) is personal dealing which is in line with the standard of God's law. *Justice* (מִשְׁפָּט, *mišpāṭ*) is the character of a man who embraces the rulings[35] of Yahweh, the great Judge and moral Governor of all. And finally *uprightness* (מֵישָׁרִים, *mêšārîm*) is literally *straightness*. In Proverbs, it is a life built on the assumption of God's revealed way as the norm. It bespeaks staying right within the spiritually and morally straight path laid out by God's Word.

Solomon, *the* wise man, believed that any truly wise man would be a righteous, good man. Those qualities were necessary corollaries, or fruits, of wisdom. John Kitchen has it right:

> The wisest course of action in any circumstance is bringing your life into conformity with the character and actions of God. Insight is not given for the stuffy halls of academia, but for the trenches of daily life.[36]

Clearly, the King did not divorce intelligence from morality. The idea of "values-free education" would have been a contradiction in terms to him. To Solomon, education not grounded on the centrality of God as Lord was no education (cf. 1:7; 9:10). A truly educated man would be a truly good man, because he would be a truly godly man.

Fourth Benefit (1:4)

> For giving to the gullible ones shrewdness,
> To the youth knowledge and planning skill.

Who Will Be Helped?

Here Solomon lists two categories of people who will be helped by his book. The *first* class is the *gullible.* This translates a form of the Hebrew adjective

---

[35] Cf. Exodus 21:1; 24:3; Deuteronomy 4:1; 1 Chronicles 16:12; Psalm 105:5, all of which use this noun, though English versions render it variously.

[36] Kitchen, *Proverbs,* 39.

(here used as a noun) פֶּתִי (*peṯî*), which is from the verb פָּתָה (*pāṯâ*), which means "to open."[37]

The word *peṯî* indicates the person whose mind is dangerously open. He is gullible, he is naïve. He may have opinions, but he lacks deeply thought-through and field-tested convictions. He will believe anything (Prov. 14:15). He is specifically contrasted with the *'ārûm*, the shrewd, savvy man (14:15, 18; more on this contrast below).

Have you ever known someone like this? Have you ever been someone like this? This is the fellow whose mind is so "open" that it is open at both ends. His mind is thus open to evil influences. He is untrained, he is inexperienced, and he is unprincipled. "Sounds good to me" is his watchword, and his sign is the shrug.

This naïve soul badly needs to heed the call of Lady Wisdom (Prov. 9:4), but he is also precariously open to the enticement of Lady Folly (9:16). His danger is that he may love his naïve state (1:22), and thus be destroyed by the apostasy which that mindset spawns (1:32).[38] He must acquire savvy and brains by listening to the revealed wisdom of Yahweh (Prov. 8:5), which is built on fear for Him (Prov. 1:7), and which enables one to build a framework of convictions for thought and life.

The *second* class who will be helped is the נַעַר (*na'ar*), the *youth*. This term basically covers anyone from infancy to young adulthood. It is applied to baby Moses crying in the reeds, in Exodus 2:6. Equally, the full-grown Absalom is also called a *na'ar*, in 2 Samuel 14:21.[39]

Though this term refers primarily to chronologically young people, the main idea is immaturity.[40] Unfortunately, maturity and chronological age are not always linked, although they should be (Prov. 16:31; 20:29). Sadly, I have met all too many "big babies," men and women who may be old enough to drink, but not old enough to think; who may be old enough to vote, but not old enough to take note—at least judging by their thinking and behavior.

---

[37] Cf. NIDOTTE, 3:174.

[38] You can see a little moral cautionary short story of the *peṯî*, the gullible man, in Proverbs 7:7ff.

[39] Cf. Milton C. Fisher, TWOT, II:585, 586.

[40] The noun *na'ar* is found in six other passages in Proverbs, all of which describe a person who is not yet matured, not yet "done." In 7:7, the *youths* are synonymous with the gullible, from whose number steps out the one young man described as "short on brains." In 20:11 it is a *child* whose character is not known until expressed in deeds. In 22:6, it is the spoiled *youth* whose parents let him have his own way. In 22:15, it is the *child* whose heart is tangled up with folly that only discipline can expel. In 23:13, it is the *child* in need of discipline to correct his life's

These career-adolescents are still led by feelings and moods, not principles and convictions. They flit from this to that, going about with chips on their shoulders, and causing wreck and ruin wherever they go. They hang around others of their kind (Prov. 7:7). Their inborn folly has never been effectively driven out (22:15).

This lot has no "sense of self" *coram Deo*,[41] built on a relationship with God through Christ on the basis of His Word. Therefore they have no plan, no goal, no guiding principle to their lives that will stand God's judgment in time (cf. Matt. 7:24–27).

Proverbs has help to offer the immature. May God grant that more in this era of overgrown babies will take advantage of what He offers.

What Help Will They Receive?

We had two sorts of people needing help, the gullible and the young. Similarly, Solomon will provide two packages of help.[42]

First, what help does Solomon provide to the *gullible*? The gullible are given *shrewdness.* The Hebrew word is עָרְמָה, *'ormâ* (LXX *panourgia* [craftiness; cf. its use in Eph. 4:14]). It is from the root עָרֹם (*'ārōm*), to be shrewd, crafty.[43] The word means *cleverness, savvy, shrewdness.*

Words built on עָרֹם (*'-r-m*) have interesting associations, both positive and negative. Our word *'ormâ's* cousin, עָרוּם (*'ārûm*), has a decidedly shady history. Its first appearance is in Genesis 3:1, where the term is used to describe the serpent—

> Now the serpent was the most cunning [*'ārûm*] of all the wild animals that the LORD God had made. He said to the woman, "Did God really say, 'You can't eat from any tree in the garden'?" (CSB)

Here *'ārûm* describes a creature that is shrewd, and cunning; what Tolkien's Gollum might call "tricksy." The serpent hits right upon something that appears to have been bothering Eve. He maneuvers in just such a way to "close the sale"

---

path. In 29:15, it is the *child* who will shame his mother if deprived of the rod and reproof. See further discussion in Appendix Three.

[41] Latin, "before the face of God."

[42] It is possible that the paired words are a hendiadys, which means two words communicating one concept (so Fox, *Proverbs*, 1:61). I will treat them individually (as Waltke, *Proverbs*, 1:178).

[43] Cf. BDB, article עָרֹם.

with her in literally record time. He's *smart*—but not in a good way.

In spite of its ominous debut, the adjective *ʿārûm* is used in a good sense throughout Proverbs. One example is Proverbs 13:16—"Every shrewd man [*ʿārûm*] acts with knowledge, but a stupid man displays[44] denseness" (DJP). Additionally, Proverbs underlines the fact that the gullible needs this shrewdness several times. Consider Proverbs 8:5, where Lady Wisdom calls out,

> "Discern, you gullible men, shrewdness,
>   And, you stupid fellows, discern good thinking!"[45] (DJP).

The same contrast is seen in chapter 14, which paints the gullible man as the opposite of the shrewd man in the former's dopey credulity (v. 15), and in his natural trajectory (v. 18).

Why do the gullible so desperately need shrewdness? It is because of their lack of a God-centered conceptual matrix, a grid for looking at life and discerning right from wrong, worthwhile from worthless. Solomon touches on this in 14:15 when he observes that "The gullible believes everything, but the shrewd has discernment as to his steps" (DJP).

Second, what does the *young man* receive? He receives *knowledge and planning skill*. We have already seen that *knowledge* [*daʿat*] is personal and experiential in addition to being intellectual. What is *planning skill* (מְזִמָּה, *mᵉzimmâ*)? The common rendering "discretion" is not very helpful nor accurate, in my judgment. The inset box shows the wide variety of renderings in the ESV, as its translators struggled to capture the idea.

> The ESV translates *mᵉzimmâ* as *discretion* 5X, *evil devices* 3X, *schemes* 2X, *purpose* 2X, *intents* 2X, *thoughts* 1X, *malicious intent* 1X, *mischief* 1X, *schemer* 1X.

The word *mᵉzimmâ* is a feminine noun meaning variously *purpose, discretion, device*,[46] *project, plan, scheme, discretion, prudence*.[47] It comes from the root word זָמַם (*zāmam*), which means to *consider, purpose, devise*. The related feminine noun

---

[44] Or "spreads."

[45] The word is *lēḇ*, meaning *heart*, which in the Bible indicates the center of thinking and deciding.

[46] Cf. BDB, article מְזִמָּה.

[47] Cf. HALOT, article מזמה.

זִמָּה (*zimmâ*) means *plan* or *device*. The word *mᵉzimmâ*, then, signifies the power of making successful plans. It could also be translated "a plan," or "a purpose."

The concept of the word is that of planning skill. Crawford Toy translates the word as "insight,"[48] and explains it as "the power of forming plans or perceiving the best line of procedure for gaining an end, then the plan itself, good or bad."[49] McKane gives it the thought-provoking rendering of "resourcefulness."[50] Perhaps best, John A. Kitchen explains this as "the ability to form a practical plan of action and work to its end."[51]

Surely this aptitude is just what young people need—a purpose, a plan, the ability to make a plan. What does one observe in all too many young people? Orange and pink hair, paper clips in their noses, sharp objects deliberately poked through various parts of their bodies, carvings and markings, addiction to immoral sex and drugs and addictive behaviors, knee-jerk uniform viewpoints on virtually everything, and a sad, purposeless nihilism. One pictures the tattooed, pierced, disfigured young ignoramus at age 35 asking, "Mom, why can't I get a job?"

Perhaps one wonders, "What is these kids' plan?" The truth is, many of them have no plan. There is no "game plan," no "Big Picture," beyond finding a way to the next joyless thrill. To some of these aimless young folks, life is a big party hall, and their highest ethic is, "Don't let your issues harsh my mellow!"

Sadly, parents often fail such children. "Yes, sure, whatever, go on" they reply to each boneheaded fad, impulse and idea, eager to remain in the child's good graces. Why? Because they don't have a plan themselves. What they lack, they cannot impart.

Government school systems say that they will teach the kids about how to be good citizens, how to feel good about themselves, and how to think through ethics—a chilling thought, at best. Proverbs, by contrast to everything the world is trying to substitute (whether by godless liberalism or godless conservatism), points to a real overarching purpose.

Solomon will unveil the proper way to evaluate and place lesser goals and plans. What is that way? It is the way of putting God right in the throne at the center of our universe, and ourselves at His service (1:7—"The fear of Yahweh is the

---

[48] Toy, 4.

[49] Ibid., 7.

[50] William McKane, *Proverbs: a New Approach* (Old Testament Library; Philadelphia: Westminster, 1970), 211.

[51] Kitchen, *Proverbs*, 40.

beginning of knowledge; Wisdom and discipline, dense people belittle" [DJP]).

However, we should not imagine that it is only the irreligious who have not developed the ability to form and pursue plans. Among Christian young men, various false notions, social trends, and bad teaching have combined to produce vapor-lock. Grown men live at home with their mothers, waiting for God to reveal the next step—when God in His Word has already provided everything they need to know to get moving.[52]

As we shall see, this center, "the fear of Yahweh," provides worthwhile goals, it provides righteous values, and it tells us how to get there. Surely, this is just what young folks—of all ages—need.

Fifth Benefit (1:5a)

> Let a wise man listen and add learning,

Addressing Whom?

Here Solomon directs his remarks to the *wise man*. Who is the wise man? He is the man who has demonstrated some skill for living in the fear of Yahweh. What matters is not his IQ, but his "I do"—his wholehearted commitment to embracing and living God's revealed worldview. That is real wisdom.

"But," one might understandably object, "if he is wise, then what more does he need?" Excellent question! Here we encounter a bit of a paradox:

- Anyone who thinks he has "arrived" is a fool (cf. 3:7; 12:15; 18:2; 26:16; 1 Cor. 3:18).
- The truly wise know they need to learn more (cf. 9:8b-9; 12:1; 19:27; 25:12).

The wise man is not he who thinks he already knows everything. That man is a stubborn, dense, benighted fool.

Most pastors have met all too many such fools. I have often remarked that, by God's grace, I seem to be able to teach virtually anyone—except dead people, uninterested people, and people who think they already know everything. These

---

[52] It was out of pastoral concern for just such aimless Christians that Kevin De Young wrote the superb little book *Just Do Something* (Chicago: Moody, 2009). Pastor De Young's timely tome's apposite subtitle is *How to Make a Decision Without Dreams, Visions, Fleeces, Open Doors, Random Bible Verses, Casting Lots, Liver Shivers, Writing in the Sky, etc.*

folks are unteachable. I can't feel too bad about it: Jesus Himself couldn't teach them (John 8:43; 10:24–26); God Himself can't teach them by words alone (2 Chron. 24:19). No lowly pastor can do what God can't do.[53]

What is the attitude Solomon urges upon the wise man?

What the Wise Man Must Do

Solomon calls on the wise man, and bids him *listen*. The simple, common little word *listen* is a really, really big word in the Bible. Listen![54]

Warning clarification.

Let us be very clear on what we are considering here, though. Too many professing Christians would perk up here and say, "Ohh, yes. We must all learn to *listen* to God, to that still small voice of His Spirit in our hearts. It is so important to return to spiritual disciplines that help us hear God apart from His Word." I once actually heard a missionary in a doctrinally sound baptistic church say that the great need of the day is to wean Christians away from the Reformation truth of *sola Scriptura,* and teach them to use medieval, Roman Catholic disciplines to listen for the extra-Biblical voice of God.

In this way, the mysticism which has derailed so much of the professing Christian church might be read into this verse.

We must, as I said, be crystal-clear on this point. "Listen" does not mean, here or anywhere else in Scripture, to harken to a subjective, mystical, murmury, semi-revelatory inner voice of God. God has no intention of turning our attention within ourselves, of urging us to seek after holy hunches and vaporous mumblings inside of our own deluded hearts. He categorically condemns such orientation (Prov. 28:26; Jer. 17:9). God knows all too well that dense foolishness is "original factory equipment" in our fallen minds, thanks to Great-Great-Granddad Adam (Prov. 22:15)

No, God is not speaking of our listening to the inscrutable mumblings of some spirit, as if it were His Spirit. Rather, here and everywhere God is urging us to listen to the Word of God (cf. 1:23, 33; 16:20; contrast 28:9). The context makes this unavoidable: Solomon means the wise man to listen to *the words he is*

---

[53] God can however perform the one miracle that no pastor can: He can change the *heart* of a fool (cf. Ezek. 36:26, 27). When He does that, the spiritually blind see, the deaf hear, and what we once hated becomes unspeakably precious.

[54] Recall that Solomon literally prayed for a "listening heart" in 1 Kings 3:9. (It is hiding in the Hebrew text, behind the common paraphrase "understanding heart.")

writing. Internal, lowgrade, spiritual "sweet nothings" would have been far from the inspired king's mind.

The lesson to all

God commands us all to listen. He has no happy little "precious promises" for people who will not listen to the Word of God—unless we count Proverbs 29:1, which is indeed a promise:

> A man who hardens *his* neck after much reproof
> Will suddenly be broken beyond remedy. (NAS)

A related promise to those who refuse to hear may be found in Proverbs 28:9—

> If one turns away his ear from hearing the law,
> even his prayer is an abomination.

During my time as a pastor and afterward as well, I have encountered two major, crippling attitudes. First is the person who has absolutely no spiritual hunger, nor any interest in Bible teaching, whatsoever. No good plants grow from such soil.

Then again, I have met the person who is academically interested in doctrine, but who thinks that he has nothing to learn, no need to listen anymore. Amassing information and concepts and categories suits him. Hearing a word of God addressed to him, demanding transformation of life—not so much.

In either case, we have a person who *will not listen,* and thus *will not grow* in a vital relationship with Christ.

The only people who do not need to learn are corpses (for whom it is too late), fools (for whom it is of no interest), and glorified saints (who, I am confident, are not reading this book).

What the Wise Man Must Add

It is insufficient, however, for a wise man merely to listen, and leave it there. In his listening, he must *"add learning."*

This introduces us to an intriguing word. The wise man must add לֶקַח (*leqaḥ*).[55] The noun *leqaḥ* comes, unsurprisingly, from the verb לָקַח (*lāqaḥ*),

---

[55] ESV translates as "precepts," "seductive speech," "instruction," "teaching," "learning," "persuasiveness," and "doctrine"—seven different renderings for a word found only nine times!

which means to receive, to accept, to take. We met a form of the simple verb back in 1:3, where Solomon underscored the need for "receiving" (*lāqaḥaṯ*) discipline, education.

This noun, as used here, simply takes us a step further. Of itself it can denote *teaching*, as it does in Deuteronomy 32:2; Job 11:4; Proverbs 4:2; and Isaiah 29:24.[56] Here it is the object of the verb "add" (i.e., "let him add"). I think the picture is thus: a wise man receives education from God's Word, and then this wise man *hoards up* what he *receives*. He has, and he adds-to. As a result, he amasses a repository of learning that he has acquired. The instruction that he receives becomes his own personal store and possession.[57] For that reason, we might even translate this, "Let a wise man...add to his reserve," "to his acquisition," or "to his repository."

Getting Personal

Do you want to be a wise man, a wise woman? If you want to be a wise person, then you must be actively involved in building up a repository, a storehouse of Divine Wisdom that you are gleaning from His Word. Also, if you are a wise man or woman, you will heed the call to add to that repository, you will never regard it as "full enough."

As a pastor or a conference speaker (if the conference is small enough), I characteristically pass out outlines to the hearers of my sermons. I myself have not always loved outlines. When I was a young Christian, I thought outlines were usually artificial and distracting. One falls to guessing what the next two "C's" or "P's" will be, rather than listening attentively.

So I try to design outlines that would engage folks, help them keep what they're being given. I aim to maximize the hearers' opportunity to log information. The hope is that they will build their own personal repositories of information, ideas, and directives gained from our studies of the Word. If I thought it would catch on, I would call the outlines I give out "repository notes," because of Proverbs 1:5.

Many have taken advantage of this opportunity, and of the help provided by the outlines. In some places, the folks in the churches have responded with great delight. Still, through the years, there has been no lack of pew-sitters who have not seen note-taking as being anything that they personally need. Although they

---

[56] Later, the noun is used to denote doctrine in the Qumran writings (TLOT, 651).
[57] Cf. BDB, article לֶקַח.

are physically and mentally able to take notes, they do not do so, presumably because they do not think that they will ever desire or require them.

Then what happens? If you and I applied some Proverbs, we could readily guess. Do you remember what Solomon finds to be so instructive about the humble little ant? What made her a model of wisdom? Solomon points out that

> she prepares her bread in summer
> and gathers her food in harvest. (Prov. 6:8)

Solomon says that lazy folks should observe her ways, and wise up.

That same characteristic of the ant wins the admiration of Agur, who calls ants "exceedingly wise" because they "are a people not strong, yet they provide their food in the summer" (Prov. 30:25). Though a dumb, tiny insect, the ant does not wait until the colony is starving before going out in search of food. It is constantly on the lookout to locate, acquire, and store up provisions from the future.

But what of the lazy person who is not willing to learn from the ant, and who accordingly will not provide for the future? King Solomon addresses such a person, and warns:

> your poverty will come in like a vagabond,
> And your need like an armed man (Prov. 6:11 NAS)

In fact, Solomon later states plainly that "He who gathers in summer is a prudent son, but he who sleeps in harvest is a son who brings shame" (Prov. 10:5).

The application to Christ's students is clear. It relates to those who give no diligence to building a repository of divine wisdom. They are content to read a book and forget it. They are happy enough to hear a sermon and forget it. They have what they want just now. They're doing all right, right now.

But what will happen when their own personal "winter" comes, whether a personal crisis or a family calamity? They will have nothing left over from harvest-time, for they slept. Or again, what will happen when people about them have needs—a child, a spouse, a friend? I suppose that they will hope that the pastor, or some other growing Christian, takes care of the problem.[58]

Do we not desire to be wise men and women? Do church leaders want to

---

[58] This is clearly contrary to the design of God for the every-member ministry of the church, as spelled out in Ephesians 4:11ff. and elsewhere.

produce such wise men and women? Of course we do—or so we profess. Yet I think it safe to say that many churches have no overall "game plan," except perhaps to attract a lot of church members, and to pay bills. At a Bible-*teaching* church, however, you can personally and regularly build a structure of Biblical wisdom. You can literally build a *repository* of Biblical wisdom.

If we are to be Christ's genuine students and know His liberating truth, we must continue in His Word (John 8:31–32). Let us heed Solomon's exhortation, be wise, and apply ourselves to constructing a repository of divine wisdom.

Sixth Benefit (1:5b)

> And let a discerning man acquire a knowledge of the ropes.

We have discussed what *discernment* means in Proverbs. It refers to the ability to distinguish, to tell the right from the wrong, the good from the bad, the worthwhile from the worthless. A man who can do this is a *discerning* man.

What the Discerning Man Must Do

Solomon says that a discerning man must make a "knowledge of the ropes" his own. Let us begin by a brief consideration of the meaning of the *verb* translated "acquire." The Hebrew verb is יִקְנֶה (*yiqneh*), from the root קָנָה (*qānâ*). It means to acquire something, to possess it as one's own, sometimes by purchase. A familiar use is in Proverbs 8:22a, where Wisdom says, "Yahweh possessed me at[59] the beginning of His way" (DJP). Wisdom was Yahweh's personal possession. The related noun is *qinyān*, meaning a possession, a thing acquired for one's own.[60]

The discerning man makes "knowledge of the ropes" his own personal possession, his property, if you will. This contrasts with merely letting others appreciate wisdom, or being comforted by knowing that it is "around." It means making wisdom, "knowledge of the ropes," my own

Not all professed Christians share this attitude. One of the most extreme examples was a pastor I heard who actually thought and taught that a person can profit spiritually while literally sleeping through a church meeting. His idea was

---

[59] Or "as."
[60] Used in Genesis 34:23; Proverbs 4:7; Ezekiel 28:12, 13, and elsewhere. Interestingly, another related noun is *miqneh*, which can mean *cattle*—presumably as a prime purchasable possession (Gen. 13:2).

that the "spirit" can profit without the mind necessarily being engaged.

The Bible holds out no such model for spiritual growth. The book of Proverbs cries out against it, both in so many words and by its very existence. No one will gain understanding without fully engaging his mind so as to acquire wisdom, to lay hold of it and retain it. We must make the commitment, and must take the necessary action, to make wisdom our personal possession.

We should test ourselves. We should ask, "Am I doing this? If someone watched a film of my life as a silent movie, would he be able to discern clearly my commitment to making God's revealed wisdom my own personal possession?"

What the Discerning Man Must *Acquire*

The discerning man acquires a "knowledge of the ropes." The one Hebrew noun translated by this phrase is the feminine plural תַחְבֻּלוֹת (*taḥbulôt*; LXX *kubernēsis*). The older standard Hebrew lexicon BDB gave the root as חָבַל (*ḥābal*), which means *to bind, to pledge*.[61] From this root comes the noun חֶבֶל (*ḥebel*), meaning *cord, territory*,[62] *band*. The word we find here, תַחְבֻּלָה (*taḥbulâ*) means *direction, counsel* as being probably originally used "of *rope*-pulling, i.e. *steering, directing* a ship," and related to *ḥōbel*, a sailor (i.e., rope-puller).[63] Our word *taḥbulâ* occurs only in the plural (*taḥbulôt*), and only in the Wisdom literature.

This is a difficult word to render, as attested by the breadth of translations that have been offered:

> "A man of understanding will attain to leadership" (MLB)
> "let the discerning get guidance" (NIV)[64]
> "a perceptive man learns the ropes"[65]
> "[Let] the man of understanding take to himself rules of conduct"[66]

So what does it mean? It probably builds off the literal idea of a rope in a sailing vessel, steering the course by directing the sail or the rudder.

---

[61] BDB, article חָבַל. HALOT says the derivation of the noun is uncertain (article תַחְבֻּלוֹת).

[62] As an area measured off by a measuring cord.

[63] BDB, article חֹבֵל. Evidently "rope-puller" because sailors pulled ropes to move sails (cf. Delitzsch, 1:57), and thus move and steer the vessel.

[64] "Guidance" is also reflected in the CSB, NET, NLT, TNIV, ESV; and in the translations in commentaries by Waltke, Fox, and Longman.

[65] McKane, 211; cf. Kidner, 37.

[66] Delitzsch, 1:54.

McKane helpfully explains that

> it is...a term for a kind of nautical expertise, the ability to steer
> a course through the trackless sea; and it lends itself readily to
> becoming a metaphor for the negotiating skills which discern the
> beginning and the end of a problem and perform each operation in
> the right place at the right time.[67]

For that reason, Fox suggests "navigational skills,"[68] and Waltke says that it
"connotes that [Proverbs'] guidance enables the insightful to lead himself and
others through life like a well-steered ship."[69]

So the man with discernment will gain from Proverbs the ability to chart his
life's course and direct himself aright. Proverbs is perfectly suited as a textbook
to provide just such a benefit. Remember, a proverb is often compressed wisdom
gained from experience. By virtue of his God-given wisdom, his restlessly
observant mind, his international contacts, and his broadly-accomplished life,
Solomon was a fount of just such experientially-refined wisdom.

God used Solomon's unique personality and experiences. The Holy Spirit's
inspiration worked through the temperament and individuality of the men whom
He employed for the writing of Scripture. It is as Warfield said: "the colors of the
stained glass window have been designed by the architect for the express purpose
of giving to the light that floods the cathedral precisely the tone and quality it
receives from them."[70] Solomon was the perfect vessel to convey "knowledge of
the ropes." Proverbs distills just such an accomplished grasp of the details of life.

---

[67] McKane, 266.

[68] Fox, *Proverbs*, 1:37. Fox himself prefers the notion of design or plan, which (as Waltke observes, 1:96) is not all that far-removed from the idea of guidance.

[69] Waltke, *Proverbs*, 1:96. HALOT suggests "the art of leadership" (article תַּחְבֻּלוֹת). Cf. A. Cohen, *Proverbs* (Soncino Books of the Bible; Brooklyn: Soncino, 1946), 2.

[70] B. B. Warfield, "Inspiration," in Geoffrey W. Bromiley, vol. 2, *The International Standard Bible Encyclopedia, Revised*, 846 (Grand Rapids: Wm. B. Eerdmans, 1988; 2002).

Seventh Benefit (1:6)

> For discerning a proverb and a satire,
> The words of wise men and their enigmas.

Solomon promises that his book will grant insight into *four bundles of knowledge.*

First Bundle: a *Proverb*

We have already discussed a *māšāl* under 1:1, where it was defined as a compressed statement of wisdom, artfully crafted to be striking, thought-provoking, memorable, and practical.

Second Bundle: a *Satire*

The word is the Hebrew מְלִיצָה, *mᵉlîṣâ*. This is rather a startling word, in that it is derived from לִיץ (*lîṣ*), to *scoff, mock, scorn,*[71] which is characteristically a negative term. In fact, the לֵץ (*lēṣ*), the scorner or scoffer, makes regular appearances as a "bad guy" in the OT.[72] The scoffer is someone who "makes fun," who mocks and scorns—usually mocking and scorning God and His ways, people who walk with Him, His truths. The scoffer is the worst kind of incorrigible fool.

So how is *mᵉlîṣâ* used here? The "satire," the *mᵉlîṣâ*, is a mocking poem.[73] Tim Powell says that it is "a saying laden with satire, sarcasm and innuendo."[74] I take it that it is the sort of saying that "pokes fun" at and satirizes folly. It is what we might call a humorous exposé.

Proverbs is bejeweled with quite a few satires: see Proverbs 6:6–11; 7:6–27; 19:24; 23:29–35, and others. They serve most effectively to unveil the true nature of "the Emperor's new clothes." Proverbs such as these expose and lampoon our foolishness, pricking our attention.

Wait! Sarcasm? In the Bible?

Many today take a milquetoast attitude, asserting that nothing merits cutting remarks. When I taught at a seminary, a professor (now a well-known author)

---

[71] Cf. BDB, by ranging the article for מְלִיצָה under the heading לִיץ.
[72] Cf. Psalm 1:1; Proverbs 1:22; 9:7, 8; 13:1; 14:6, etc.
[73] See it used this way again in Habakkuk 2:6, the only other use.
[74] לִיץ, in NIDOTTE, 2:799.

astonished me with the remark that "sarcasm has no place in Christianity." What shocked me 25 years ago is a common attitude today. Above all, we must be sure never to offend others, or make anyone look foolish. Popular writers often seem to dedicate themselves to preserving the honor and dignity of unbelief.

The perhaps-uncomfortable truth is that the Bible is brimming with sarcasm. As we just saw, Solomon used it frequently. So did Yahweh,[75] so did the Lord Jesus,[76] so did the apostle Paul,[77] and so did James[78]—among a great many others.

The fact is that God moves His servants to communicate His truth, and to warn people away from deception, by all sorts of means. He moves them to employ instruction, explanation, reasoning, pleading, warning, and yes, even acerbic, sarcastic satire. Indeed, the most common forms of humor in the Bible are satire, sarcasm, and irony.

And so, we must prepare ourselves for the *satires* of wise men. If the shoe does not fit at the moment, we may breathe a sigh of relief, square our shoulders, and prepare ourselves for the next volley. However if it does fit, if it is ourselves we find being lampooned, we had better be ready to slip that shoe on, rather than taking refuge in whiny excuses and evasions (cf. 28:13).

Third Bundle: *the Words of Wise Men*

Solomon could appreciate wisdom mediated through any source. He explicitly includes such words in this collection (cf. 22:17–24:34), including possibly the two guest appendices (30–31).

Fourth Bundle: *Their Enigmas*

The word here is a form of the noun חִידָה (*ḥîḏâ*). Occurring seventeen times,[79] the term's meanings range from "riddle" (Judg. 14:12–19, where Samson does a turn as "the riddler") to enigmas and hard questions (1 Kings 10:1; Psa. 78:2). It signifies "difficult speech requiring interpretation."[80]

Here the idea is probably *enigma*, meaning a hard word that must be pondered because it defies instant and easy unraveling. Kidner says that the term is used "of

---

[75] Cf. Isaiah 1:3; and the most brutal chapter in the Bible, Ezekiel 16.
[76] Matthew 23:4, 5, 15.
[77] Galatians 3:1; 4:21; 5:12.
[78] James 4:4.
[79] Edwin Yamauchi, TWOT, 1:267.
[80] Gerald Wilson in NIDOTTE, 2:107.

anything enigmatic, which needs interpreting,"[81] and notes that

> the secondary purpose of Proverbs is to introduce the reader to a
> style of teaching that provokes his thought, getting under his skin
> by thrusts of wit, paradox, common sense and teasing symbolism,
> in preference to the preacher's tactic of frontal assault.[82]

Solomon knows that there is not only one way of communicating. This
approach—communicating by riddles and obscure sayings—is expressly designed
to demand and provoke thought and reflection.

This need for such writing is great. Communication is being "dumbed down"
by increasing degrees. Simpler and simpler versions of the Bible (8th-grade reading
level, 6th-grade reading level, 4th-grade reading level—for adults!) are coming out.
People are impatient of anything requiring thought, concentration, focus, effort.
Folks rush to churches featuring interpretive dance, snazzy musical entertainment,
dancing bears and skits—and stay away in droves from the rational, systematic,
demanding exposition of the Word of God.

At the same time, attention spans lessen. People become accustomed to the
flip-flip-flip of movie camera angles. Anything taking longer than five minutes of
concentrated thought wears us out and quickly loses our attention.

Against all this, Solomon says, "Here is something knotty. Here is something
you cannot have without hard thought. Here is something you will have to
ponder, consider—even untangle. Slow down, stop. Fix your attention on this!"

And so we should. Only so will we reap the promised sevenfold reward.

And Then...

Solomon has introduced himself (1:1) and identified both his aims and his
audience (1:2–6). Now comes the most important part, the pivot, the critical turn
that sets the stage for the entire book. In the verse that follows—Proverbs 1:7—
Solomon isolates what will be the foundational axiom for his entire book. It is the
all-controlling element that forever removes Proverbs from being a mere book full
of axioms, advice and quaint sayings.

The fear of the Lord is the beginning of Knowledge.

---

[81] Kidner, *Proverbs*, 58.
[82] Ibid., 59.

Fools despise wisdom & instruction.

Questions for Thought or Discussion

1. How is the Hebrew/Biblical concept of wisdom different from ours, in our culture, today?

2. Why is it important to stress that wisdom must be listened to, received, and acted on?

3. When have you had to exercise discernment? When have you failed to do so and regretted it?

4. Have you known Christians who isolate theory from practice? To what result?

5. What is the relationship of wisdom to morality and godliness in the Bible? Cite at least one text as proof.

6. What are the virtues and dangers of open-mindedness? How can you tell when the virtue has become a vice?

7. What signs do you see in your contemporaries that they have no plan?

8. What does it mean to "listen" for the wisdom of God?

9. What would a wise man do during a sermon? Be specific.

CHAPTER THREE

The Foundation of Wisdom

What Is This Book's Axis?

> The fear of Yahweh is the beginning of knowledge;
> Wisdom and discipline, dense people belittle. (Prov. 1:7 DJP)

Here we encounter the foundational truth of the book of Proverbs: the utter, indispensable centrality of the fear of Yahweh. This thought opens (1:7) and closes (31:30) the book, occurring fourteen times in all.[1]

Today, the concept of the fear of God is more often mouthed than understood. Yet if we are to gain the education Solomon offers in this book, we must not only grasp the notion, but must ourselves be grasped by it.

So, let us look at the fear of Yahweh closely and at length together.

Though he makes the fear of Yahweh the centerpiece of his book, Solomon did not invent the concept. Here is yet another point at which an understanding of Solomon's point in history, and a respect for canonical indications of authorship, pay rich dividends. We will approach the concept of the fear of Yahweh first by examining the conceptual world that Solomon inherited, as found in the Scriptures that he had been taught from infancy. When we understand what preceding Scripture means by the fear of Yahweh, we will have a good and solid angle on what Solomon means by it.

---

[1] Clifford, 35.

What the Fear of Yahweh Involves

When we study the fear of Yahweh in the Scriptures which preceded Solomon, we soon find that fearing Yahweh involves a subject and an Object. That is, there must be someone to do the fearing, and Someone to be feared.

The Fear of Yahweh Involves a *Subject*

The fear of Yahweh is not a concept without a context, hanging on nothing. It is not a vibration, not a virus. We don't catch it, and it doesn't happen either outside of us, or to us. It is an attitude, it is a mindset. More, it is a worldview: it is the grid through which we perceive, arrange, understand, interpret and interact with the world.

And what is a worldview without a viewer?

Prepare yourself to be involved.

The Bible depicts people fearing or not fearing God. Abraham feared for his safety among Abimelech's people, because he assumed there was no fear of God in that place (Gen. 20:11). Though Egypt has already been hammered by God's miraculous plagues, Moses says "But as for you and your servants, I know that you do not yet fear the LORD God" (Exod. 9:30). After the crossing of the Red Sea and the judgment of the pursuing Egyptians, "the people feared the LORD" (14:31). Israel was repeatedly commanded to fear Yahweh (Lev. 19:14, 32; 25:17; Deut. 6:13, etc.). None can fear God for or in the stead of another; each person must himself fear God. He himself must be involved.

So it is that Solomon states without qualification that the fear of Yahweh is the beginning of knowledge (Prov. 1:7). He does not suggest that priests can fear God for their people, or parents for their children. Nor does he hint that only certain classes, sexes, races, tribes or occupations are being called to fear Yahweh. We have seen that Solomon addresses himself generally to the young, the gullible, and the learned. In the course of Proverbs, Solomon further reaches out to boys, men, women, parents, children, slave-owners, and kings—in short, all sorts of people. *All* are challenged to build their lives and their worldviews on the fear of Yahweh.

Stop and think.

This in itself is worth a moment's reflection. Even in the age when there was an actual priestly class, God did not address Himself to them alone. God did not

Help me Lord, to be a ~~god fea~~ God fearing Woman.

provide that only a special subset could learn of Him and live God-centered lives, to the exclusion of the people at large.

If that was the case under the Law of Moses, how much more will it be necessary for every church-age believer to invest himself personally in the fear of Yahweh? Every participant in the New Covenant by definition knows God (Jer. 31:34). We are all called to learn, grow, and be of service to Christ (Eph. 4:11ff.). So we must avail ourselves of what we will learn in Proverbs.

Further, each of us must make personal application of what we learn here. True, we may well learn something of help to a friend or relative. Still, we should think primarily in terms of how we can learn and personally apply the fear of Yahweh in our own lives.

It is I who must learn to fear Yahweh, myself. And so must you. No one can or will do it for us, as our substitute—not even the Holy Spirit.

The Fear of Yahweh Involves an *Object*

This "fear" is not a free-floating attitude fixing now on this object, now on that object. It is not a sort of generalized anxiety, a sort of *pantophobia* (fear of everything). No, this fear is directed toward a person, a specific person, a divine person whose name is Yahweh.

As I mentioned earlier, Yahweh is God's personal name in the Hebrew Old Testament. Traditional translations such as the KJV, ESV, NAS, and RSV, whatever their other differences, unfortunately agree in obscuring God's name behind "Lord," all in capital letters.[2] Only three somewhat well-known translations that I can think of have broken with the bad tradition: the American Standard Version (using "Jehovah"), Rotherham's Emphasized Bible, and the Jerusalem Bible.

Hide and Seek with God's Name?

In spite of its "mainstream" support and whatever its origins, this use of "Lord" has become a strictly superstitious device. Every time you see "Lord" or "GOD" printed all in caps, it means that the Hebrew text has God's personal name, יהוה (YHWH, probably pronounced "Yahweh"), which is used some 6,823 times.

---

[2] I have often wondered how many Bible readers this unfortunate practice has utterly baffled. "Now what does *that* mean?" I envision them thinking. "Am I supposed to say 'Lord' twice as loud as I say 'Lord'?" It was a bad idea all around. And then, to make matters worse, when the actual Hebrew word for "Lord" occurs with Yahweh, these and other translations (except NIV) say "Lord GOD." What possible sense can that make to new Bible readers? It might be simpler just to learn Hebrew. Which isn't simple.

Although God clearly meant His name to be used, verses such as Leviticus 24:16 have been misunderstood by some to mean a blanket prohibition against using His name. So, after the close of the Old Testament, Jewish readers in the synagogue avoided saying God's name altogether.[3] Every time readers came to *Yahweh* in their oral readings, they vocally substituted either the Hebrew word for God (*ᵉlōhîm*), or the Hebrew word for "Lord" (*ᵃdōnay*).

The Hebrew alphabet is all consonants. For that reason, the original text had no vowels. Only in later copies of the Hebrew text were markings inserted that signify what the vowel-sounds are. And so, after centuries of a tradition of reading the words for "Lord" or "God" instead of "Yahweh," the vowel-markings for "God" or "Lord" got stuck into the text at these points. So do you see now how Y-H-W-H got to be written as Yehōwah? It is the consonants from YHWH hooked in with the vowels of *ᵃdōnay* ("Lord").[4] From there, by way of Latin, we got the impossible hybrid form "Jehovah" found in the ASV and some great hymns.

It has become a sad matter of unthinking traditionalism, in my opinion, that English versions perpetuate this device of "Lᴏʀᴅ" or "Lord GOD." We really should rid ourselves of it. It was nurtured by misinterpretation, perpetuated by superstition, and now is encased in tradition. Knowing better, are we not obliged to do better? *Yes*

Further, returning to the text would serve our generation well, in view of the prevalence of cults and religions and philosophies which deny the personal nature of God. We need the reminder that God has a personal name. He is not a principle, a force, an impersonal spirit. He is an infinite person, and He has named Himself Yahweh.

Besides, there are two perfectly good words for "Lord" in Hebrew, and "Yahweh" is neither.[5]

---

[3] Hamilton says that the practice goes back as far as the Septuagint and the Dead Sea Scrolls, and apparently was not related to fear of violating the third commandment, though he does not explain the origin of the practice (Hamilton, 54.)

[4] Cf. Terence Fretheim, "Yahweh," in NIDOTTE, 4:1082; and Gerard Van Groningen, "Yahweh," in Elwell, W. A., & Beitzel, B. J., *Baker Encyclopedia of the Bible* (Grand Rapids: Baker Book House, 1988).

[5] I've had a scholarly type or two respond that we don't know for certain how "YHWH" was pronounced. True; however (1) we do have evidence indicating that "Yahweh" was the pronunciation; (2) we do know that it was not pronounced *ᵃdōnay*, (3) we do know that it does not mean "Lord," and (4) we do know that it is a personal name, and not a title like "Lord" or "God."

Because God is a person, and people have names

The name Yahweh almost certainly derives from the verbal root הוה (*hwh*), meaning *to be* or *become*.[6] Of the many explanations of its significance, I take "Yahweh" to signify God as the one who is *present faithfully to keep His covenant*, the promise-keeping God who is personally present. It is God's covenant-name; if you will, it is the name by which He signs His covenants. The closest to an explanation comes in Exodus 3:14, "I am who I am," in the context of expressing God's presence to keep his covenant with Abraham and his sons.[7]

And now, a brief word from the liberal wing

It is instructive to note what more liberal commentators have done with this phrase. For instance, Crawford H. Toy was exactly wrong when he said

> The use of the name *Yahweh* instead of the more general *Elohim* [sic] is not significant as to date or as to ethical feeling. Yahweh, though in name nothing but the national deity of the Jews, is here regarded as the supreme and only God.[8]

Or gawk with me at this bewildering statement by J. Alberto Soggin, which reads almost like a parody:

> However, the attentive reader who is versed in the history of religion will not miss the fact that the mention of the God of Israel is made more in the form of a concession to the dominant faith than as a personal confession: we could easily substitute the more general phrase 'fear of God' or even 'of the deity' for the expression 'fear of Yahweh', without facing the problem of the identity of the deity to which reference was made. The expression could very well be considered as equivalent to the popular modern saying that a bit of religion never does anyone any harm.[9]

These gentlemen could hardly have been more mistaken.

---

[6] Cf. BDB, article יהוה.

[7] Cf. J. Barton Payne, *The Theology of the Older Testament* (Grand Rapids: Zondervan, 1962; used by permission), 148; also Merrill F. Unger and William White, Jr., *Nelson's Expository Dictionary of the Old Testament* (Nashville: Nelson, 1980), 229.

[8] Toy, 10.

[9] Soggin, 379–380. One wonders whether Soggin had as liberal an attitude about his own name. Would Soggin have accepted it if his book were published with no author's name at all, or with

The point of this point

"What's in a name?"[10] A great deal, fair Juliet, in this case.

There is a big difference, say, between saying, "I would like you to get to know *women*," and saying, "I would like you to get to know my wife, *Valerie*." A personal name brings the focus down tight and specific. If I say "book," you have no idea of my specific point of reference. If I say, "J. I. Packer's *Knowing God*," then I mean one book, and not another. I have named it. It is particular.

In the same way, when Solomon writes "the fear of *Yahweh*," he is not talking about some generic "God," the Force, the "Higher Power, however you conceive of her/him/it" of many 12-step programs. Solomon had a particular God in mind, a God with a particular name. This God's name is Yahweh, the creator of heaven and earth, the self-revealing, covenant-keeping God of Abraham, Isaac, and Jacob; the God of Moses and the exodus and Mt. Sinai. He is also the God and Father of our Lord Jesus Christ. Yahweh is the God who committed Himself to covenants, and revealed Himself by word and deed throughout the Bible.

Solomon is saying in effect, "The true God has revealed Himself. If you want true wisdom, you must start with Him, on His revealed terms. You must have a living, vital relationship with that one true God." Solomon's short-hand phrase for that relationship is—"the fear of Yahweh."

Now let us move on in our understanding of the meaning of this most-important concept. We need to gain a great deal more depth and specificity, if this reality is to steer our lives as Solomon says it must.

The Content of the Fear of Yahweh

Solomon writes that "The fear of Yahweh is the beginning of knowledge; Wisdom and discipline, dense people belittle" (1:7 DJP).

The fear of Yahweh, as I hinted at the outset, is a major pan-Biblical concept. It reels out a long thread, running all through both Testaments. But what does it mean? How do I *do* it? It is too easy to mouth this familiar phrase without any true understanding of it.

What does the fear of Yahweh involve? We shall see that the fear of Yahweh

---

some other scholar's name on it? As to Soggin's notion that a little religion never did any harm: many of us would say that "religion," understood Soggin's way as being a man-made philosophy involving some concept of divinity, has caused immeasurable harm in world history. Such a mish-mash certainly was no part of Solomon's view.

[10]   *Romeo and Juliet* (II, ii, 1–2).

involves at least three elements: it involves *revelation*, it involves *direction*, and it involves a *relationship.*

The Fear of Yahweh Involves Revelation: There Is Much to Learn

When we think of *fear*, our first thought is probably of the emotion—that paralyzing, mouth-drying, stomach-clenching dread that seizes hold of us in the face of an imminent threat. This connotation is not altogether absent. Anyone who can think of God and shrug is not thinking of the God of Scripture.

However, a primary and basic element in the fear of Yahweh is *revelation*. Read Deuteronomy 4:1–15, a passage with which Solomon would have been intimately familiar. The chapter opens with a call to Israel to hold tight to the words of God (vv. 1–3), which is equivalent to clinging to God Himself (v. 4–5). Moses stresses that it is the possession of this verbal revelation which is both their national wisdom and their point of distinction on the international scene (vv. 6–8). So they must hold fast the words and the memory of their encounter with God (vv. 9–10).

Of particular interest to us is Deuteronomy 4:10, where Moses recalls

> "...the day that you stood before the LORD your God at Horeb, the LORD said to me, 'Gather the people to me, that I may let them hear my words, so that they may learn to fear me all the days that they live on the earth, and that they may teach their children so.'"

From this verse and the larger context I isolate two observations:

1. "Fear" here clearly is not merely an *emotion*—or else I think that the fire and all (v. 11) would have done the trick.

2. "Fear" here is something that must be *learned*, and that *requires revelation* from God. God commanded that the people hear His words "so that they may learn to fear" Him, and that they might teach the fear of Yahweh their children.

And then we see in verses 12–14 where Yahweh Himself directs the spotlight in that entire encounter. So many today pine and yearn for anything remotely supernatural—and here it is, on bold display. Darkness, clouds, fire, the very voice of God. Is that where Yahweh fixes their attention?

No. In fact, Yahweh expressly says, "You heard the sound of words, but saw no form; there was only a voice" (v. 12b). He goes on to relate at length the fact that He revealed and inscribed the Ten Commandments (v. 13) and commanded Moses to teach them "statutes and rules" that they might do them (v. 14). There was no form, only the word of God (v. 15). God emphasizes His word, and specifically stresses that He spoke to them, that He rendered Himself *quotable*.

Therefore, if anyone wishes to learn to fear God today, he will not chase off after reports of supernatural outbreaks here and there. Instead, he will open his Bible, and he will pray that God open his heart to hear His voice speaking through it, and will teach him to fear God thereby (cf. Psa. 119:18; Heb. 3:7ff.).

The point comes up again in Deuteronomy 31:9–13, where Moses commanded the Levites to read the Word of God to the people at their national assembly "*in order that* they may *hear* and *learn* and *fear* the LORD your God, and be careful to observe *all the words* of this law" (v. 12 NAS, emphases added), and that their children may also hear, and learn to fear Yahweh (v. 13).

The soul of national worship, then, was not music or dances or entertainment or emotions. If those elements were present, they were not what Yahweh stressed. What He stresses is the reading of His Word as essential to Israelites coming to fear Him.

Deuteronomy 31:13 is worth further emphasis, in that God expressly declares that this is how the children "who have not known" would learn to fear Him. "Have not known" what? In context, they have not known His miraculous deeds (cf. 11:2). By saying this, God is indicating that the truth and power of His Word are sufficient. Unlike some late-arrivers who have attempted to make the case that supernatural "special effects" are necessary for vital Christian faith, God says that His Word is not only sufficient, but superior.

In his extended masterpiece on the wonders of God's Word, the writer of Psalm 119 prays, "Establish Thy word to Thy servant, As that which produces reverence for Thee" (Psa. 119:38 NAS). This once again puts the focus where it should be. All of us should desire to cultivate this fear of Yahweh. All church leaders should hold this goal for themselves and the souls in their care. But how to pursue it?

The answers commonly proposed to that question—assuming that the goal is even accepted—fill Christian book lists today. The Bible's answer is simple: fear for God is produced by the Word of God. Many modern trends boil down to self-expression. Self-expression, however wonderful it may feel, tells us nothing of God.

God's Word produces the right attitude toward Him, because His Word reveals Him, His mind and His ways to us. His Word alone gives content to our faith.

- Without content, there would be no *reason* to fear
- Without content, there would be no *object* for our fear
- Without content, there would be no *form* to give to our fear

This finds a strong echo in the words of Jesus, recorded in John 8:31–32—

> Therefore, He was saying to the Jews who had believed Him, "If you remain in My word, truly you are My students; [32]and you will know the truth, and the truth will free you." (DJP)

Our Lord here provides both the promise and the definition of discipleship. His progression of thought is very definite:

1. To be set free, we must know the truth

2. To know the truth, we must be students (disciples) of Jesus

3. To be disciples of Jesus, we must continue in His Word.

So we see another way in which being a God-fearer and a disciple of Jesus are parallel: both rooted fundamentally in submission to God's Lordship and commitment to His verbal self-revelation. Neither fear of Yahweh nor belief in Christ can be melted down to "a numinous sense of awe," or any other mystical bibble-babble. Biblical faith has distinct content, form, and edges.

The Fear of Yahweh Involves Direction: There Is Much to Do

Though it dates after Solomon's time, a fascinating narrative in 2 Kings 17 teaches us that the fear of Yahweh can and must be *taught*, with a specific content.

We read in verses 24–28 that the king of Assyria had transplanted people from various pagan cities, and settled them in the cities of Samaria alongside the chosen people. Of course, those immigrants were pagan idolaters, not worshipers of Yahweh. After they were settled, God exercised His property-rights by sending lions to kill a number of the intruders.

So the besieged populace discerned that "the god of the land" was angry because they didn't know his ways, his customs. The king of Assyria found this reasonable and directed that a Jewish priest be sent back to Israel to teach the pagans the law of Yahweh.

And so we read in verse 28 that "one of the priests whom they had carried away from Samaria came and lived in Bethel and *taught* them *how* they should *fear the LORD*" (emphases added).

Once again, it fairly leaps out of the text that "fear" is not primarily an emotional response, nor is it primarily a matter of being afraid. The inhabitants were already afraid! That is why they had called for the priests. They needed no tutelage in how to feel fear. (Besides, what would such tutelage look like? "Okay, everyone bug your eyes out, wave your hands in the air, scream, and run!"?)

Here, then, we have a group of people who were *frightened of* Yahweh, but did not yet *fear* Yahweh. For that, they needed teaching in areas both of faith and practice. (Unfortunately, they never got the fundamentals of fearing Yahweh, and mix-n-match Samaritan syncretism was born.)

Deuteronomy 17:18–19 is a passage that would be close to Solomon's own heart and much on his mind. This was Yahweh's famous direction that Israel's king manually copy out the Law of Yahweh, under the watchful eye of the Levitical priests. The king would copy the law, retain it, and "read in it all the days of his life, that he may learn to fear the LORD his God by keeping all the words of this law and these statutes, and doing them" (v. 19).

Note the words closely. Even though he was arguably the most powerful and the busiest man in Israel, the king was expected daily to study the Bible. Why? That he might learn to fear Yahweh, which is the beginning of wisdom. What form would this fear take; how would it show itself? By carefully observing everything he finds in the law.

Even though he lived in the day of ongoing revelation, with prophets hearing words straight from God's mouth, the king was not directed to focus on them. He was not told to have daily coffee with a prophet, asking for the latest scoop from Heaven. No, he was directed to the written word that he (and all Israel) already possessed.

How ironic that today, when each of us has in his hands the completed Canon of Scripture, so many folks restlessly find God's written revelation insufficient. What a judgment against our Eve-like spirit, that we pine after something other than the treasure God has entrusted to us, something to which even the king was not directed.

This vital connection between fear of Yahweh and righteous, godly living is a frequent theme all over Scripture. Reaching back (as I take it) to pre-Mosaic times, we find Job speaking thus: "And he said to man, 'Behold, the fear of the Lord, that is wisdom, and to turn away from evil is understanding'" (Job 28:28). Noting the parallelism, we find Job taking "the fear of the Lord" in Line A, and expanding it in Line B with "to turn away from evil." That is, to fear the Lord is to turn away from evil. One cannot do either without doing both equally at the same time.

Similarly in Psalm 128:1, we find that "everyone who fears Yahweh" is made more definite by "who walks in His ways." Or Solomon himself will put into the mouth of Lady Wisdom the words

> The fear of Yahweh is to hate evil;
>> Pride and arrogance and the wicked way,
>> And the mouth of crooked things, I hate! (8:13 DJP)

The wording is even stronger here. To fear Yahweh is not only to turn away from evil, but positively to hate it.

The anonymous Psalm 111:10 adds:

> The beginning of wisdom *is* the fear of Yahweh;
>> Good intelligence *belongs* to all who do them;[11]
>> His praise stands to eternity. (DJP)

Starting at the verse's middle, perhaps my question is also yours: Good intelligence belongs to all who do what? What is "them"? For the answer, we need but run our eyes back to verse 7–9, where we read of Yahweh's precepts and His covenant. So here, the idea of fearing Yahweh is interpretively paired with the doing of His precepts.

We observe similar thoughts in many other Scriptures, where fearing Yahweh is coupled with obedience to His Word. In Deuteronomy 5:29, Yahweh sighs, "If only they had such a heart to fear Me and keep all My commands, so that they and their children will prosper forever" (CSB). Again, Deuteronomy 6:1–2 speaks of "the commandment, the statutes and the rules that the LORD your God commanded me to teach you… that you may fear the LORD your God, you and your son and your son's son, by keeping all his statutes and his commandments, which I command you, all the days of your life…"

---

[11] NAS "who do *His commandments*."

Or, turning back to the Psalms, we find the anonymous writer of Psalm 112 singing "Praise the LORD! Blessed is the man who fears the LORD, who greatly delights in his commandments!" (v. 1). Fearing Yahweh and delighting in His commandments are paired. They are best of friends here as they are in the conclusion of the book of Ecclesiastes: "When all has been heard, the conclusion of the matter is: fear God and keep His commands, because this *is for* all humanity" (12:13 CSB).

All these verses underscore the truth that the fear of Yahweh lives, breathes and thrives in the atmosphere of the verbal, written revelation of Yahweh. Old Testament scholar and theologian J. Barton Payne well said, "'Fear' is faith, as it submits to His will"[12]—His *revealed and inscripturated* will, I would add.

The Fear of Yahweh Involves a Relationship: There Is a Person to Fear

No one should infer from the preceding that "the fear of Yahweh" is a barren, bloodless, solely-propositional state of being. At its core is not a catalog of assertions, but the infinite-personal God of Scripture, who grants Himself to be described by revealed assertions. We fear Him that we may know Him, and we cannot know Him without fearing Him. This fear is the necessary tenor of our *relationship* with Yahweh.

This relationship requires that we be forgiven.

Let us first turn to Psalm 130:3–4, where we learn that this is a relationship requiring forgiveness and fear. Hear the psalmist

> If You were to keep iniquities, Yah,[13]
>   oh Lord—who could stand?
> [4] But with You is forgiveness,
>   in order that You might be feared. (DJP)

According to the title, Psalm 130 is an anonymous "Song of Ascents," presumably sung by pilgrims on their way up to Jerusalem for one of the annual feasts, such as Passover or Tabernacles. Although some have called it a "lament," it is actually a very hopeful song. Four thoughts are expressed in four pairs of verses:

---

[12] J. Barton Payne, *The Theology of the Older Testament* (Grand Rapids, Zondervan, 1962; used by permission), 307.

[13] *Yah* is the shorter form of *Yahweh*, found in poetic texts.

1. The psalmist calls on God to hear him calling from the depths (vv. 1–2).

2. God's forgiveness is affirmed (vv. 3–4).

3. The singer declares his utter dependence upon God and His Word (vv. 5–6).

4. Israel is exhorted similarly to trust in Yahweh and His loving-kindness and His redemption (vv. 7–8).

Quite strikingly, verses 3–4 combine *forgiveness* and *fear* in a relationship with God. Verse 3 affirms the Biblical doctrine of man's sinful guilt before God, a guilt he is powerless to assuage by his own efforts. Then, arrestingly, verse 4 assures believers that there is forgiveness with Yahweh *in order that* He might be feared.

Forgiveness… and fear? Odder still, forgiveness *in order to* fear? How can these concepts possibly be wed?

First, we must understand the Bible's premise concerning the place of man: we do not approach God as peers. We are not "valued collaborators." We are not His equals. The Bible is candid and univocal in asserting how we approach God: as criminals, guilty rebels who deserve His wrath and need His forgiveness.

This is why the psalmist bluntly affirms that, apart from divine forgiveness, we would all be utterly doomed before this holy God (v. 3). There would be no relationship, except that between judge and condemned, between convict and noose.

Thus the writer sings boldly of God's forgiveness, which alone makes a relationship possible. What kind of "fear" is this, then? We tend to think of "fear" as servile and cringing. To us, fear is an emotion that repels, rather than attracts. Clearly, this is not God's meaning here. Kidner notes that this verse "confirms the true sense of the 'fear of the Lord' in the Old Testament, dispelling any doubt that it means reverence and implies relationship."[14]

What forgiveness makes possible is reverential, worshipful fear. Fear, then, is our proper attitude toward God. It is how we cling to Him as our Redeemer and our Lord, looking to His redemption (vv. 7–8). It is how we recognize our subordinate and vastly inferior position. And the only reason we may thus worshipfully revere Him rather than fleeing in terror of His judgment, is because of His forgiveness. Spurgeon brings us right to the bottom-line:

---

[14] Kidner, *Proverbs*, 482.

If the Lord were to execute justice upon all, there would be none left to fear him; if all were under apprehension of his deserved wrath, despair would harden them against fearing him: it is grace which leads the way to a holy regard of God, and a fear of grieving him.[15]

It is as David sang: "The friendship of the LORD is for those who fear him, and he makes known to them his covenant" (Psa. 25:14). Had Solomon heard his father sing that song? In that same psalm, David also pled with God not to remember his youthful sins (v. 7), and asked that He forgive all his sins (v. 18). The covenant David knew of provided for forgiveness through blood atonement by an innocent victim (Lev. 17:11), which in turn pointed forward to the perfect atonement to be made by the Lamb of God, the Lord Jesus (John 1:29). All this would have fed Solomon's concept of the fear of Yahweh.

With this in mind, we can see that the coming of Christ, so far from eliminating the fear of God, makes it possible. Our knowledge of the redemption of God in Christ (1 Peter 1:18) motivates us to live our lives in the fear of God our Father (v. 17).

This relationship requires humility.

We gain some important light from Proverbs 22:4. Here is a painfully literal rendering:

> Result-of humility fear-of Yahweh
> Wealth and-honor and-life.

The wording is characteristically terse. In fact, the entire verse is verbless. The syntax is very non-English. We need to supply some verb—but which verb, and where? What is Solomon saying, exactly?

Translations are divided. Most give something like the ESV:

> The reward for humility and fear of the LORD
> is riches and honor and life.

In this reading, "humility" and "fear of the LORD" are paired as virtues, and they bring the reward of "riches and honor and life." Of course, this is a possible translation and interpretation.

---

[15] C. H. Spurgeon, *The Treasury of David, Volume 6: Psalms 120–150*, 119 (Bellingham, WA: Logos Research Systems, Inc., 2009).

Another possibility is seen in the God's Word translation, which leaves off its usual "dynamic" approach to give a fairly literal version:

> On the heels of humility (the fear of the LORD)
>   are riches and honor and life.

The old Modern Language Bible is similar:

> The results of humility—reverence for the LORD—
>   are riches, honor and life.

In this case, humility and fear for Yahweh are made equivalent. Both are interchangeable: one cannot be truly humble without fearing Yahweh; and one cannot fear Yahweh without being truly humble.

In meaning, the first two translations are fairly similar, in that Line B is the result of Line A, whether A is taken as naming two distinct virtues, or one interchangeable virtue.

The Christian Standard Bible gives a third possibility:

> The result of humility is fear of the LORD,
>   along with wealth, honor, and life.

In this case, humility results in fearing Yahweh, along with the three blessings of Line B. So humility is the single cause for all four following items.

How to choose?

Grammatically, all are possible. What tilts me is the very consideration Longman dismisses as irrelevant:[16] factoring in *who wrote the proverb*. This is an illustration of the value of seeing Solomon as author, and plugging in his biography for interpretation.

How did Solomon come to the wisdom that qualified him to write Proverbs? Remember the narrative in 1 Kings 3. Here, Yahweh appears to Solomon with the staggering offer, "Ask what I shall give you" (v. 5). Solomon's reply is the soul of humility: he acknowledges that both his father and he have been utter debtors to Yahweh's faithfulness (vv. 6–7a), and he confesses that he has neither the maturity, intelligence nor wisdom to govern Israel (vv. 7b-9). In other words, Solomon lies low before Yahweh, humbles himself, confesses Yahweh's Godhood and Lordship,

---

[16] Longman, *How to Read Proverbs* (Downers Grove: InterVarsity Press, 2002)—"…if we are quite honest, the authorship and date of the book have little or no impact on our interpretation of [Proverbs]" (159).

confesses himself (in so many words) to be Yahweh's servant, and confesses that what he needs most of all is Yahweh's own wisdom.

This is humility, *and* this is the fear of Yahweh.

But it gets even more exegetically significant. Notice what Yahweh, in His delight, pledges to give Solomon in response to this petition. In brief, He promises Solomon wealth, and honor, and life (vv. 13–14)—the *same three blessings* that Proverbs 22:4 promises to the humble Yahweh-fearer. First Kings is a real-life embodiment of the message of Proverbs 22:4, providing us with a beautiful example of how a short proverb *compresses* a longer narrative.

Therefore, I take "humility" and "fear of Yahweh" as appositional. [17] The two terms explain and condition each other. A humility that is not centered on fear of Yahweh—and thus submission to His person and revealed will—is a false humility. A professed fear of Yahweh that is not characterized by real humility before Him is a false religion.

We learn here the important lesson that humility does not arise from thinking less of myself than I ought, but from thinking as much of God as I ought. It is not a case of a six-foot-tall man trying to convince himself that he's only two feet tall. It is a case of a six-foot-tall man standing next to an enormous, towering redwood, and seeing himself dwarfed by it; or gazing at the vast array of the stars twinkling in the desert sky and gasping at the unimaginable immensity of it all.

What, then, is the key to humility? It does not lie in fantasy, or in finite comparisons: Nor is it a matter of trying to convince myself that I am worse than I am in various ways—though, Lord knows, I am certainly bad enough. It is not comparing myself to other people, for this is always a shifting, subjective, uncertain standard.

Rather, genuine humility rests in comparing myself to the infinite God. It is standing before the true and living God, in all of His holiness, vastness and glory. That is what puts us in our place.

Everett F. Harrison made an excellent observation, commenting on John the Baptist, who said of Christ, "He must increase, but I must decrease" (John 3:30). Harrison wrote:

---

[17] So also W. J. Dumbrell, עֲנָה, NIDOTTE 3:463; Waltke, *Proverbs*, 2:193 (Waltke translates it "humility—the fear-of-the-LORD sort," calling it a "sortal appositional construction"); Murphy, 163–165; Henri Blocher, "The Fear Of The Lord As The 'Principle' Of Wisdom," 28, *Tyndale Bulletin* (1977): 1, 9.

One becomes humble, not by opposing to the swellings of pride lowly or mean thoughts of himself, but one becomes humble by thinking upon Christ and exalting Him to others. While the multitudes were musing in their hearts about John, he was thinking of Another. John was a voice to proclaim His coming. The larger Christ loomed before him, the smaller did John become in his own estimation.[18]

This humility is a vital component in fearing Yahweh. My favorite brief definition of the fear of Yahweh comes from Derek Kidner, who wrote that the fear of Yahweh is "that filial relationship which, in the most positive of senses, puts us securely in our place, and God in His (a theme thankfully developed in, e.g., Ps. 34:7ff.)."[19] From Kidner's sublime wording, one could turn to the grittier (yet apposite) Two Pillars of Wisdom:

1. There is a God.

2. You ain't Him.

So the fear of Yahweh could be said to have a two-pillared impact on us, as it first confronts us. *First,* I see God as who He really is: vast, infinite, thrice-holy, beautiful in absolute perfection, limitless in power and glory. *Then,* I see myself as who I really am: puny, limited, dependent in every way for my very existence, morally defiled by nature and by choice, in need of every atom of grace, forgiveness, and wisdom that God can give, capable of salvation by no measure less extreme than the death of Christ on the cursed Cross.

The attitude both causing and born of the clash of these two visions is fear of Yahweh.

This relationship requires fear.

Our final point might seem like what the kids call a "duh"—so obvious that it needn't even be said. However, it clearly does need to be said. Evangelicalism has swung far in the opposite direction from any former day's *over*-emphasis on God's transcendent, fearsome might and majesty. There is no danger, in our day, of worrying that the average, casual, laidback, chuckling, chatting, coffee-sipping, entertainment-addicted churchgoer will err on the side of trembling in the presence of God.

---

[18] *Jesus and His Contemporaries* (Grand Rapids: Baker, 1970 [reprint]), 23.
[19] On Nehemiah 9:32, in *Ezra & Nehemiah* (Downers Grove: InterVarsity Press, 1979), 113.

To such, we must say that "fear" does involve *fear*. While the idea is not that of shrinking away in terror, neither is it well-expressed as a mere nod of the head or doff of the cap. Curtis and Brugaletta are right in cautioning that "fearing God does not entirely exclude components of fright and terror."[20] "Let us offer to God acceptable worship, with reverence and awe, for our God is a consuming fire" is not an Old Covenant sentiment, but a New (Heb. 12:28b-29). More on this, later.

Aside: a Trans-Covenantal Translation

We will show below that the concept of the fear of Yahweh is as fully a New Testament imperative as it is an Old. Here we pause briefly just to make one observation.

To fear Yahweh in practical terms, as we have seen, involves turning around in humbled conviction of our sins, taking the Word of God to heart, and submitting ourselves to Him as Lord and Savior. We could say fairly that the Word of God is its focus, and that it has elements of *recognizing, realizing,* and *resting.* That is, the fear of Yahweh requires that we *hear and understand* the word of Yahweh, that we *see the relevance and truth* of its revelation of Him and His will, and that we *rest our weight* upon it in such a way that a changed life is a result.

But in so describing it, what have we just done other than describe what it means to believe in the Lord Jesus Christ?[21] You see, either word (fear/faith) equally describes what a lost, rebellious sinner needs to repent and embrace; *and* what the heartbeat of the converted sinner's life is to remain. As surely as we say, "Faith comes from hearing, and hearing through the word of Christ" (Rom. 10:17), we could have said, "The fear of Yahweh comes from hearing, and hearing comes through the word of Yahweh." The only difference is explicit, revealed content. But everything that Solomon says about "fear of Yahweh" in Proverbs can be taken to heart and legitimately applied to "faith in Jesus" by the Christian believer.

Note also that, in the fourteenth chapter of Revelation we have a vision of an angel flying, who we are told has "an eternal gospel to proclaim to those who dwell on earth, to every nation and tribe and language and people" (v. 6). What

---

[20] Edward M. Curtis and John J. Brugaletta, *Discovering the Way of Wisdom* (Grand Rapids: Kregel, 2004), 128. They cite Exodus 20:18–21 in evidence.

[21] I develop the meaning of saving faith at great length in *The World-Tilting Gospel* (Kregel: 2011), chapter 7.

is that "eternal gospel"? The next verse tells us: "Fear God and give him glory, because the hour of his judgment has come, and worship him who made heaven and earth, the sea and the springs of water" (v. 7). Here in the last book of the Bible "fear God" is portrayed as an angelic proclamation of the Gospel.

Fear of Yahweh is Solomon's OT-context way of saying "faith in the Lord Jesus," though with a connotation of reverent, awestruck fear. It is a faithful fear, it is a fearful faith. It is the beginning and the ongoing backbone of a relationship with God.[22]

What Good the Fear of Yahweh Does

The fear of Yahweh is the beginning of knowledge;
  Wisdom and discipline, dense people belittle. (Prov. 1:7 DJP)

The preceding study should give us all a better, more Biblically-informed grasp of what the fear of Yahweh means. But what are its benefits? Is it worth the trouble? What good does the fear of God do me?

Solomon packs a number of benefits into this terse verse. Let's unpack them together.

The Fear of Yahweh Serves as the Beginning of Wisdom

The word "beginning"

The Hebrew word translated "beginning" is *rēšît*. It is the feminine singular construct of a Hebrew noun which means "beginning, chief." [23] It alternately can mean what comes first; beginning; starting point; the first and best; or first-fruit, choicest portion.[24] It is used of absolute beginning in Genesis 1:1 ("In the beginning [*b*ᵉ*rēšît*] God created the heavens and the earth"). It also denotes beginning an activity (Prov. 17:14). Sometimes it means the most important, or the chief (possibly Prov. 4:7; also Amos 6:1).

There is disagreement among Hebrew scholars as to what the exact sense of "beginning" (*rēšît*) is as used in Proverbs 1:7. Waltke well sums up the leading possibilities: it "might mean, temporally, 'first thing,' qualitatively, 'chief thing'

---

[22] We will revisit the NT continuance of this theme once again in the Postscript at the chapter's end.

[23] BDB, article רֵאשִׁית.

[24] HALOT, article רֵאשִׁית.

(i.e. the choice part), or, philosophically, 'principle thing.'"[25] In the abstract, all are possible, and each makes some kind of sense. The second sense Waltke lists is the least likely, as it suggests that the fear of Yahweh is but part of wisdom, meaning that wisdom could be had on other terms as well.

Fox makes a convincing argument[26] for taking "beginning" here in the sense of "starting-point." He points out that the parallel 9:10 ("The fear of Yahweh is the beginning of wisdom") uses a synonym (*t^ehilla<u>t</u>*), which unambiguously means "first in time." Also, 15:33 reads

> The fear of Yahweh is wise discipline
> And before glory *is* humility. (DJP)

Line B clearly means that glory must be preceded by humility; and so Line A means that wise discipline must be preceded by the fear of Yahweh, which leads the way to it.

Solomon is saying, then, that the fear of Yahweh is where we must begin, if we are to have any hope of gaining wisdom. It comes first. All else must and can only come afterwards.

We must not miss the shot across the bows of the ungodly and the scoffer. Solomon is laying it down categorically that "fear of Yahweh" is where we must *start*, if we are ever to hope to gain wisdom and understanding. Where does that leave the man who is still at mankind's default-setting of "no-fear" (Psa. 36:1; Rom. 3:18)?

It leaves him a fool. It means he has not even arrived at the starting-line. He does not even know the ABCs of wisdom.[27]

The Big Idea

The idea of "beginning" here, then, is not that of a rudimentary lesson that one learns and then leaves for greater and deeper things. The idea is more that of a foundation, of the first element that must be set firmly in place before anything else can come. We could say in philosophical terms that it functions "as a presupposition or preunderstanding," and "is the first thought that makes all other thoughts fall into place."[28]

---

25 Waltke, *Proverbs*, 1:181.
26 Fox, *Proverbs*, 1:67–68; cf. Waltke, *Proverbs*, 1:181.
27 Cf. Blocher, "The Fear of the Lord as the 'Principle' of Wisdom," 15.
28 Longman, Commentary, 102.

The example that leaps to my mind is the relationship of learning the alphabet to reading. The ABCs are the beginning of reading. But they are hardly learned and then left behind. One uses and re-uses that knowledge all the way through, indeed every second he spends reading and writing. Without that knowledge, all subsequent effort is haphazard at best.

The Hebrew alphabet is, to English eyes, a bizarre and alien sight. When I taught Hebrew, I always told my students at the very outset that they needed to master the alphabet and vowel-signs. They needed to do that before they did anything else.

Further, I warned them that they would never progress, and would soon leave Hebrew behind, if they didn't learn the alphabet and vowel-signs cold. Learning the alphabet was *fundamental* to learning to understand and use Hebrew.

The alphabet was, if you will, the *beginning* of Hebrew.

Some students believed me, and some evidently didn't. Those who believed me started down the path of learning to read and use Hebrew by mastering the alphabet. They advanced. The ones who didn't heed the warning worked at Hebrew as if those marks were all secret code, and as if the grammar books and lexicons were their codebooks. For them, Hebrew was a brief, painful, and unrewarding experience.

The Hebrew alphabet is the beginning of knowing Hebrew. In much the same way, the fear of Yahweh is the beginning of knowledge. It is fundamental. Without it, one cannot acquire true knowledge or wisdom.

And so the fear of Yahweh is foundational to the wisdom and knowledge the book of Proverbs promises. We must start with that fear. It will control, shape and inform all that follows. A genuinely God-fearing worldview is a markedly different conceptual grid than any other. A man or woman who fears God simply will and must see things differently from how others see them.

Such an all-encompassing attitude bears a wide variety of fruit in the lives of its possessors. Let's trace out *eleven* of those fruits.

The Fear of Yahweh Brings...

From the book of Proverbs alone, we can identify at least *eleven benefits* resulting from the fear of Yahweh.

First: knowledge (1:7)

> The fear of Yahweh is the beginning of knowledge;
>> Wisdom and discipline, dense people belittle. (DJP)

The form of this verse is contrast, or antithetical (A, but B), even though the word "but" is not used. This verse impresses upon us that you and I absolutely must start out by learning where we stand before God. If the proper estimation of God, and our place before Him, is not our premise, then all that follows is an increasingly wild miscalculation.

If we are gripped by the fear of Yahweh, we are ready to learn and apply God's wisdom-principles for life. We will accept both instruction and rebuke from the Word, equally. We will approach Scripture to hear God speak to us.

If we aren't straight on the fear of Yahweh, our approach (if any) will be utterly different. We will pick-and-choose after our fancies and prejudices. We might like this or that proverb, but we will remain our own lords, our own gods, and true knowledge will elude us (cf. Prov. 14:6).

Second: wisdom (9:10)

> The beginning of wisdom is the fear of Yahweh,
>> And the knowledge of the Holy Ones is discernment. (DJP)

The form is synonymous (B rewords A). "Wisdom" in Line A is focused into "discernment" in Line B, and "the fear" of Yahweh" in A is opened by "the knowledge of the Holy Ones" in B.

The idea obviously is a close parallel to 1:7. One difference is the word translated "beginning," תְּחִלַּת (*tᵉhillat*), which unambiguously means a starting point, a first thing. So if one wants this wisdom, which is skill for living in the fear of Yahweh, he must start by gaining a firm grasp of what it means to fear Yahweh.

The parallels ("fear of Yahweh," "knowledge of the Holy Ones") teach us that fear of Yahweh and knowledge of Him are related ideas. Hence, this is a fear that clings, rather than recoils. It is a fear that grounds a relationship on submissive reverence. Such fear/knowledge bring wisdom (skill for living in the fear of Yahweh) and discernment (the ability to tell right from wrong, worthwhile from worthless).

Third: long life (10:27)

> The fear of Yahweh adds days,
>> But the years of the wicked will be shortened. (DJP)

The form combines antithetical (A, but B), and consequence (B is what happens when you A) for both lines.

To understand this verse, we should remember two things: *first,* we must keep in mind the general-principle nature of Proverbs. A proverb is "an adage without paddage." There is no long list of lawyer's warnings. By nature and design, a proverb is not meant to say all that can be said on a given subject. Often one is helped by mentally prefixing the words, "Other things being equal..." Some God-fearing men such as David Brainerd will die young, while some godless fools will love long lives.

Second, we must remember Proverbs' setting within the Mosaic Covenant. This covenant included these promises of health and prosperity for believing obedience (Exod. 15:26; Deut. 7:12–15). Beyond that, there was quite a list of capital-offense crimes under Moses, none of which would befall the man walking in the fear of Yahweh. So to promise longer life to those walking with God and shorter life to the wicked is simply to reword one provision of the Mosaic Covenant under which Solomon and his readers lived.

What of New Covenant readers? Has this any application? In principle, absolutely. On the most literal level, the fear of God will likely remove us from liability to various forms of death, such as:

- Death at hands of jealous spouse, mobster loan shark, angry drug contact, vengeful rival gang, mistress' jealous husband, police officer.
- Venereal diseases (of which AIDS is only one well-known example).
- Liver disintegration due to chronic drunkenness.
- Execution for capital offenses.

Beyond this, Waltke argues that "life" in Proverbs means more than what he calls "clinical" life, which is to say the mere circulation of blood and maintenance of greater than room temperature for the body. "Life" is God's life, the life God gives—full, blessed, meaningful, God-centered life.[29] This is a life that God would see as purposeful, fruitful, and worthwhile.

---

[29] Waltke, *Proverbs*, 1:104–107.

Fourth: strong confidence and a refuge (14:26)

> In the fear of Yahweh is strong confidence,
>> And his sons will have a refuge. (DJP)

The form of this proverb is consequence (B is what happens when you A). When you are walking in the fear of God, you can be strongly confident:

- That God loves and accepts you personally
- That God is in control of all of the details of your life
- That what comes into your life has been "okayed" by His sovereign will first, or it would not have happened
- That your conscience can relax, and you can live without constantly looking over your shoulder in guilty fear (cf. Prov. 28:1).

Not only do you gain personally, but you set an example for your children, in both word and deed. Your legacy to them is a legacy of real-life faith in God, reverent submission to Yahweh. In this, you have something greater than gold to bequeath to the next generation (Line B: "his sons will have refuge").[30]

Fifth: a fountain of life (14:27)

> The fear of the LORD is a fountain of life,
>> that one may turn away from the snares of death.

The form is consequence (B is what happens when you A). The meaning of this verse is related to 10:27 (see above). Beyond that, it has a valid application on the eternal level. We are all born rebels, enemies of God and under His death sentence. When we come to know and fear God as He truly is, we receive eternal life, and turn away from the snares of everlasting death under His judgment in Hell.

This is one of many proverbs that suggest to me that "fear Yahweh" is the Old Covenant equivalent of "believe in the Lord Jesus" (Acts 16:31). It is a distillation of the Gospel, in Old Covenant terms. It could be "translated" for Christians with no changes other than greater New Covenant specificity:

---

[30] It is possible that "his sons" in Line B refers to *Yahweh's* sons. However, since that idea appears relatively infrequently in the Old Testament, and since Proverbs is often concerned with the legacy of the faithful, I incline toward seeing it as referring to the sons of the one who fears Yahweh.

> Faith in Christ as Lord is a fountain of life,
> For turning away from the snares of death.[31]

Sixth: peace and satisfaction (15:16)

> Better is a little with the fear of the LORD
> than great treasure and trouble with it.

This is an "evaluation proverb" (A is better than B). When we contrast the two lines and the two lives envisioned, we glean that fear of Yahweh brings the opposite of turmoil. Walking with God, applying His wisdom-principles to life, can alleviate problems with people and with powers-that-be (cf. 16:7).

Loving Yahweh with all our beings makes Him our highest value and goal, and puts everything else in perspective under His value and sovereign care. Therefore, the fear of Yahweh brings contentment, satisfaction, peace—even when it is not accompanied by material wealth. [32]

Seventh: the discipline for wisdom (15:33)

> The fear of Yahweh is wise discipline,[33]
> And before glory *is* humility. (DJP)

The form is perhaps synonymous (B rewords A). Again, fear of Yahweh brings with it discipline (which, remember, is training; it is education with *pow*). The fear of Yahweh instructs us, "Here is God's high and lofty place, and here is yours as you stand before Him: resist Him at your peril, embrace Him for your delight and blessing."

It is chastening to realize that God is God, that He is my A and Z, and that His Word is my law. As a son of Adam, I would much rather be God—and the fear of Yahweh tells me that I am not.

Notice that, as in 22:4, fear of Yahweh parallels humility; the second term explains the first.

---

[31] Cf. John 4:10–14; 5:24; and 7:37–38 (NET).

[32] Note too that this is one of several proverbs which disprove the notion that Proverbs guarantees that the godly man will always be materially wealthy.

[33] Or "discipline *that brings* wisdom."

Eighth: preservation from evil (16:6)

> By steadfast love and faithfulness iniquity is atoned for,
>   and by the fear of the Lord one turns away from evil.

I take this as a consequence proverb (B is what happens when you A). Having said that, it is a challenging verse, bristling with questions. A detailed exposition would have to deal at length with a series of queries:

- Are "steadfast love and faithfulness" qualities of God,[34] or of man?[35]

- Is "iniquity" sin before God, or sin against man?

- Does "atoned for" refer to divine forgiveness of sin, or pacifying human relationships?

- What kind of "evil" is in view: moral (sin) or circumstantial (calamity)?

- Does one turn away from evil's grip, or avoid it in the first place?

- Does the verse assert that horizontal morality atones for vertical guilt—in other words, that if Brenda is nice to Joyce, does God forgive all her sins without requiring blood sacrifice?

Kitchen correctly notes, "The first line seems to teach salvation by works."[36] However, we can take it in that sense only if we rip the verse out of the Bible,[37] which is both poor scholarship and poor thinking. Calvin correctly denies that Solomon is saying that, by these virtues, "compensation is made to the Lord, so that he being thus satisfied remits the punishment which he would otherwise have exacted."[38]

It's a very difficult interpretive call, with good reasons pointing in both directions. On balance it seems to me that the other two proverbial pairings of the words translated "steadfast love and faithfulness" in 3:3 and 20:28 are

---

[34] So Raymond Van Leeuwen, "Proverbs," *The New Interpreter's Bible* (Nashville: Abingdon, 1997), 159; and Fox, *Proverbs*, 2:612.

[35] So Kitchen, *Proverbs*, (353), and Waltke (2:13). How one answers this question fairly determines his answers to the following two questions.

[36] Kitchen, *Proverbs*, 353. Kitchen then refutes that impression.

[37] Michael L. Brown responds to suggestions that this verse renders blood sacrifice unnecessary in *Answering Jewish Objections to Jesus, Volume 2: Theological Objections* (Grand Rapids: Baker Books 2000), 123ff.

[38] John Calvin, *Institutes of the Christian Religion* (Bellingham, WA: Logos Research Systems, Inc., 1997).

ambiguous, but probably refer to human qualities. This is strengthened by Line B, and by the following verse's application to human relations.

Taken that way, "The first intimates how sin is to be expiated, the second how it is to be avoided."[39] In human relations, we are to treat each other with loyal kindness and faithfulness, making right our offenses against each other by fruitful repentance and restitution. That will correct many wrongs, appease many quarrels.

But better still, if we walk in the fear of Yahweh, we will avoid calamities in relationships in the first place. We will heed His warnings against gossip, slander, harping on petty wrongs, stirring up strife, bringing up the past, breaking our promises, and other relational sins and follies. We will follow His counsel to show love, patience, kindness.

Thus godliness is a proactive grace on the horizontal plane. The virtues Yahweh teaches us help us deal with current wrongs; the fear of Yahweh steers us away from getting involved in them to begin with.

Ninth: life, peace of mind, and preservation (19:23)

> The fear of the LORD leads to life,
>   and whoever has it rests satisfied; he will not be visited by harm.

The form is consequence (B is what happens when you A). This proverb sounds notes similar to the third, fourth, and eighth benefits above. It is a general principle in this life, open to exceptions. However, on the eternal plane, it is literally true. Since the fear of Yahweh equates to saving faith, an eternity of fullness of life and peace await the worshiping servant.

Fear of Yahweh brings life at its best and highest.

Tenth: riches, honor, and life (22:4)

> The result of humility—the fear of Yahweh—
>   *Is* riches, glory and life. (DJP)

The form is transparently a consequence proverb (B is what happens when you A). To understand Line B, again, we must place it in the context of Mosaic

---

[39] *The Pulpit Commentary: Proverbs*, W. J. Deane, and S. T. Taylor-Taswell, ed. H. D. M. Spence-Jones, 311 (Bellingham, WA: Logos Research Systems, Inc., 2004).

Law, which promised material blessing to the faithful. We must also remember the general-principle nature of Proverbs.

However, once we raise the proverb to its eternal reference, we are able to see that the proverb will be fulfilled beyond our richest visions in the presence of Christ. Conversion is humility that revolves around Christ. In conversion, the sinner sees God's holy majesty, and is brought low. In his humiliation, he calls on Christ to do for him all that he is powerless to do for himself—in short, to save him from his sins (Matt. 1:21).

As a result, he has unspeakable wealth in Christ (Eph. 1:3ff.; Col. 2:3), the promise of eternal glory (Rom. 8:29–30), and life everlasting (1 John 5:11, 13, 20).

Eleventh: praise (31:30)

> Charm is deceitful and beauty is nothing;[40]
> A woman who fears Yahweh, it is she who shall be praised. (DJP)

In form this is an evaluation proverb (B is better than A). As mentioned earlier, this verse forms an *inclusio* with 1:7, thus framing the book as being about the fear of Yahweh. Specifically, Lemuel's mother contrasts the internal quality of fearing Yahweh with mere external beauty.

The apostle Peter will say something similar in the NT 1 Peter 3:1–6, where he praises women who respect their husbands, regard them as their "lord" in their hearts, and cultivate a gentle and quietly faithful spirit which God finds precious.

In that God the Holy Spirit ultimately moved Lemuel's mother to compose these words, as He later guided the apostle Peter, they combine to testify as to what God prizes in a woman. God is unmoved by how fads, societies and cultures estimate feminine pulchritude. The quality He finds worthy of praise, and valuable, is the quality of a gentle, God-fearing heart.

This, then, is the highest of the eleven benefits. It signals the approbation of God. To a genuinely God-fearing heart, it just does not get better than that. On the other hand, anyone who does not see this as much of a prize thus marks himself as a stranger to the fear of God. It calls to mind Paul's words in Romans 2:29—"But a Jew is one inwardly, and circumcision is a matter of the heart, by the Spirit, not by the letter. His praise is not from man but from God."

---

[40] Or "vain"; the term *hebel* means a vapor, a breath.

The Opposites of the Fear of Yahweh

We gain understanding not only by grasping what a thing *is*, but also what it *is not*. Having identified a number of positive traits of the fear of Yahweh, we now turn to contrasting vices. In this way, we will form a dark background against which the luminous quality of the fear of Yahweh will stand out more distinctly.

We will single out three dark obstacles: *evil*, *conceit*, and the *envy of man*.

Evil

In Proverbs 3:7, we read:

> Do not be *someone who is* wise in your *own* eyes,
> Fear Yahweh, and turn away from evil. (DJP)

The grammar of the Hebrew sentence stresses not being the type of person who is wise in his own eyes,[41] rather than merely not making the mistake. That arrogant type of person would not hesitate at evil, if he thought that it served his own ends. The antidote to the one is also the antidote to the other: the fear of Yahweh.

This leads naturally to Proverbs 8:13—

> The fear of the LORD is hatred of evil.
> Pride and arrogance and the way of evil and perverted speech I hate.

The speaker here is Lady Wisdom. Syntactically, the first line expresses the idea that it is of the essence of fearing Yahweh to hate evil. Some think that the truly godly person is relaxed and unconcerned about immorality, crime, bad doctrine, heresy, hypocrisy. To care (they imagine) is to be harsh, judgmental, unloving.

However, to the person passionate for the glory and truth of God, moral numbness is not an option. Indifference to perversions of God's truth is not an option. The God-fearer's model is not the apathetic, aloof postmodern Christianoid, but the Lord Jesus Christ. Of Him it was said that He "loved righteousness and hated wickedness" (Heb. 1:9), that zeal for the holiness of God's house consumed Him (John 2:17), and that He came "to destroy"—not *start a conversation with*—"the works of the devil" (1 John 3:8).

Lady Wisdom says that she herself hates evil, and then she specifies what she means by evil. It is interesting to note that the terms in Line B—pride, arrogance,

---

41 The Hebrew text is literally "Do not be a wise-in-your-own-eyes *person*."

the way of evil, perverted speech—denote the self-reliant, self-centered, self-deluded walk. She does not merely hate evils such as rape, murder, and child abuse. Her hatred lights upon pride and arrogance (attitudes opposed to the fear of Yahweh), the evil way (behavior patterns and choices violating the Word of God), and the perverted mouth.[42]

To the degree that we are indifferent to those things, to that degree we are deficient in fear of Yahweh.

In Proverbs 14:2, we read that

> He who walks in his uprightness fears the LORD,
>> But he who is crooked in his ways despises Him. (NAS)

This is another consequence proverb, specifically arguing from the *effect* to the *cause*. We can visualize it in this way:

Line A	
Effect	*Cause*
Walking in personal uprightness; moral/spiritual straightness	Fear of Yahweh

Line B	
Effect	*Cause*
Deviousness in behavior and choices	Thinking little of God

Some evangelicals might bristle at this stress on behavior and dismiss it as "works-righteousness." However, this is no more "works-righteousness" than the book of James, nor than our Lord's statement that one knows a tree by its fruits (Matt. 7:16–19). Solomon does not say, "If you behave yourself, then you will come to fear Yahweh." Rather, the argument is that one's behavior *reveals* one's heart. Our core attitude comes out in our walk.

The word translated "despises" means "to accord little worth to something."[43] If someone strays from God and His Word, in heart and choices and deeds, it reveals his true thoughts of God. He may be formally orthodox, or he may not.

---

[42] The Hebrew text is literally "the mouth of crooked, twisted, perverted things"; this would include lies, slander, and *bad doctrine.*

[43] Waltke, TWOT I:98.

He may make lofty claims about his reverence of God. However, the life reveals the reality.

When a person elects to deviate from God's Word, he is saying in effect, "God? No big deal"—which is the opposite of the fear of Yahweh.

Conceit

We have focused on Line A of Proverbs 1:7. Now let us look a bit more closely at Line B.

> The fear of Yahweh is the beginning of knowledge;
>> Wisdom and discipline, dense people belittle. (DJP)

It is axiomatic that one does not desire that which he does not value. When I pray, for instance, I do not seek the intercession of departed saints, whether Mary or any other. I meet the fullness of God in Jesus (Col. 2:9), who is the sole Mediator (1 Tim. 2:5) and my great High Priest (Heb. 4:14–16; 10:19–22). While I might follow the Biblical example of soliciting prayer from living believers (1 Thess. 5:25), I see no value in violating God's law by seeking after the dead (Isa. 8:19–20).

I don't value it, so I don't want it. Or, equally, you could say that I don't want it because I don't value it. I belittle it.

So why do dense people belittle wisdom and discipline? It is because they do not see value in them. And since wisdom and discipline are based on the fear of Yahweh, that means they think that they do not need that fear either. They are gripped with that form of Godless self-sufficiency which is the very height of arrogance.

The point is deftly made in Proverbs 3:7 (DJP):

> Do not be *someone who is* wise in your *own* eyes,
>> Fear Yahweh, and turn away from evil.

Line A warns against being the sort of person who is self-impressed, a legend in his own mind. Line B prescribes the antidote: fear Yahweh.

What, then, is the opposite of the right view of God, and my place before Him? It is that arrogant conceit which is immune to all instruction and correction (12:15; 26:12), no matter how painful (27:22).

Arrogance is the opposite of fear of Yahweh.

Envy of Man

> Let not your heart envy sinners,
>> but continue in the fear of the LORD all the day.
> [18] Surely there is a future,
>> and your hope will not be cut off. (Prov. 23:17–18)

It is, of course, tempting to look at the outward prosperity or even the immoral fun of sinners, and think, "Gee, that looks exciting. Why do I work so hard at this godliness thing?" In fact, a whole psalm was devoted to this very thought (Psa. 73).

If I am upset by the good fortunes of those without a relationship with God, I betray a lack of perspective. God does not have His rightful place in my hierarchy of the universe.

Put more simply, the fear of Yahweh is the antidote to envy of the lifestyles of the rich and infamous. Solomon, accordingly, sets things back in focus for us (as he is at great pains to do in the book of Ecclesiastes as well).

Our Lord does the same even more brilliantly in the Parable of the Rich Fool (Luke 12:16–20), to which the punch-line is, "So is the man who lays up treasure for himself, and is not rich toward God" (v. 21).

Wrong Side of the Equation: the Dense Man

> The fear of Yahweh is the beginning of knowledge;
>> Wisdom and discipline, dense people belittle. (Prov. 1:7 DJP)

We'll not do justice to the motto if we do not consider the sort of person who rejects God's counsel. After all, one of Solomon's brilliant thematic refrains is "Consider the end"—that is, before you take a step down a path, think about where it terminates.

What sort of person shrugs off the centrality of fearing Yahweh? We shall examine who he is, what he does, why he does it, and what befalls him as a consequence.

Who the Dense Man Is

The Hebrew word here is אֱוִילִים, *ʾwîlîm*, plural of the noun אֱוִיל, *ʾwîl* [eh-WEEL]). This is one of about four synonyms translated "fool" in Proverbs.[44] It may be related to an Arabic word meaning "to grow thick (of fluids)."[45] This would then mean "thick-headed"; in fact, Louis Goldberg suggests "thick-brained,"[46] and the old Koehler-Baumgartner lexicon gave *Dummkopf.*[47] I use the translation "dense."[48] British readers might prefer "thick."

The issue is not the man's IQ nor his sanity, per se. He is morally and spiritually obtuse (cf. 14:9).[49] He can look straight at the wealth of God's wisdom and see no value in it (1:7). Nor is he quick to learn and rethink. You can beat him like a bongo drum and grind him like pepper, but he will stay just as morally and spiritually dense, barring a miracle (27:22; cf. 20:12). In his helpful chart of a fool's declension, Kitchen puts the "dense" man at midpoint between the gullible (*pᵉtî*) and the stupid man (*kᵉsîl*), on the one (and more hopeful) hand, and the fool (*nābāl*) and the scoffer (*lēṣ*), on the other (and less hopeful).[50]

What the Dense Man Does: "Belittle"

In this verse, we see that he belittles wisdom and discipline (1:7). What does it mean to "belittle"? The Hebrew verb בּוּז (*bûz*)[51] means to "hold as insignificant."[52] This means "to look down on with contempt and scorn," and "regard with dislike and repugnance." The special nuance of this English word is its indication of an emotional response—which is not the main idea of the Hebrew verb.

To my mind, "despise" would describe the way I feel about eating the emetic vegetable called "squash," or slimy asparagus. I recoil; the thought makes me

---

[44] Not counting related words *not* translated by some variation of "fool"—such as those I would render "short on brains," and "gullible/naïve," as well as the other descriptives of specific kinds of fool such as the "sluggard" and the "scoffer."

[45] Cf. BDB, article אֱוִיל, listed under אול; Louis Goldberg in TWOT, 1:19; Longman, *Commentary*, 102.

[46] TWOT, 1:19.

[47] Ludwig Koehler and Walter Baumgartner, *Lexicon in Veteris Testamenti Libros* (Brill: 1958), 19.

[48] Waltke's suggestion is "idiot" (Commentary, 1:112).

[49] Cf. Fox, *Proverbs*, 1:40.

[50] Kitchen, *Proverbs*, 733.

[51] The term *bûz* "is probably a by-form of *bāzâ*" (Elmer A. Martens, בּוּז, TWOT).

[52] Elmer A. Martens, בּוּז, *bûz*, in TWOT, 1:95.

unhappy and queasy. It is a physical, emotional response. Again, that is not the core of this word.

Though most English versions stick with "despise," I think "belittle" would be a better translation; or "undervalue," "depreciate," or even "hold in contempt." We observe in this verse that it is the opposite of fear or reverence, which connotes a very high estimation—thus it means to impute very low value. This idea is reinforced by 12:8, where it is the opposite of being *praised*.

We glean further light from seeing *bûz* in action in three proverbs (emphases added):

> People do not *despise* a thief if he steals
> to satisfy his appetite when he is hungry. (Prov. 6:30)

In the case of theft born of hunger, Solomon says that people will understand. They may prosecute the thief, but they will not belittle him for stealing for survival. They disapprove of his actions, but they understand them, they can see a sort of sense in them.

> Whoever *belittles* his neighbor lacks sense,
> but a man of understanding remains silent. (Prov. 11:12)

Solomon says that it shows a lack of brains to belittle your neighbor, to fail to love him as yourself. In fact, such contempt may backfire in any of a number of ways. Since it is contrasted with keeping silent, it suggests a verbal display of contempt, not merely a feeling or thought. The thought is similar to our, "If you don't have anything nice to say, don't say anything at all."

> Do not speak in the hearing of a fool,
> for he will *despise* the good sense of your words. (Prov. 23:9)

The fool will not recognize the value of your wise words; he will undervalue them, belittle them. Very likely, he will mock and twist them. For that reason, Solomon says, it is sometimes wise just not to bother, not to toss your pearls to the pigs.

The point of 1:7, then, is that the fool does not fear Yahweh, and by this fact he shows that he does not think much of wisdom or discipline. Wisdom or knowledge are not worth the indispensable "price" of fearing Yahweh. He may feel strongly negative feelings toward wisdom, or he may have no feelings at all.

It just isn't his priority. When Lady Wisdom says that God-centered knowledge and wisdom are better than silver and gold (Prov. 8:10), the dense man shrugs.

An illustration may underscore the point. The Lord saved me when I was seventeen, and a senior in high school. Immediately, I set about trying to talk with my non-Christian friends about Christ.

One fellow to whom I spoke about Christ had a passion for writing. He said that he just couldn't see himself becoming a Christian at this point. His problem was not that he had any objections to or problems with the Gospel per se. It was that he couldn't see the *use* in becoming a Christian. He said that he had tried to convince himself that "getting born again" would make him a better writer, but he just couldn't see it.

So I had to try to persuade him that one becomes a Christian because Christ is true—not because Christ will do some trick to serve our ends. My plea fell on deaf ears. He was a nice guy with a pretty nice life, and he saw little value in the knowledge and wisdom that could only come as a consequence of fearing the Lord through repentant faith in Jesus Christ. He was *dense*. I pray he has awakened by now.

Why the Dense Man Belittles

Everyone does what he does for some reason, for some benefit—imagined or real. In this case, I see three reasons suggested in Proverbs for the dense man's destructive course.

We note, *first*, the dense man *does not know what is good for him*. Proverbs 1:7 says "Wisdom and discipline, dense people belittle." Knowledge, wisdom and understanding are precisely what he needs, and precisely what he lacks. However, to have them, he must have fear of Yahweh—and this is what he refuses, to his own ruin.

Again, Proverbs 10:21 tells us

> The lips of the righteous man nourish many,
> but dense men, by lack of brains, die. (DJP)

Righteous people, since they by definition fear Yahweh, have what they need and much more. By what they say, they are an influence for life and blessing to many others (cf. 10:11; 12:18; 15:4, 7; 31:26). The dense, however, haven't the brains to see the value of God-centered wisdom. As a result, they forfeit their own lives.

Second, the dense man *has a mouth problem*—which always means a heart problem. Note the following uses of this word *ᵉwîl,* dense (uses are *italicized*):

> The wise of heart will receive commandments,
>> but a babbling *fool* will come to ruin. (10:8)
>
> The wise lay up knowledge,
>> but the mouth of a *fool* brings ruin near. (10:14)
>
> The vexation of a *fool* is known at once,
>> but the prudent ignores an insult. (12:16)
>
> Even a *fool* who keeps silent is considered wise;
>> when he closes his lips, he is deemed intelligent. (17:28)

I paraphrase a common saying: "Don't let your mouth write a check that you can't cash." But that is precisely the dense man's problem: his mouth is forever writing checks he can't cash. But the mouth speaks what fills the heart, and the heart is dim, dank and dense—and so this man is forever on the wrong side of the equation.

Third, he is *stubborn.*

> The way of a *fool* is right in his own eyes,
>> but a wise man listens to advice. (12:15)
>
> A *fool* despises his father's instruction,
>> but whoever heeds reproof is prudent. (15:5)
>
> Crush a *fool* in a mortar with a pestle along with crushed grain,
>> yet his folly will not depart from him. (27:22)

Not knowing something is not necessarily disgraceful in itself. Refusal to learn is. This is the dense man's shame: he is not merely ignorant, which would be bad enough. He is willfully ignorant, and refuses to learn what he most needs to grasp.

What Befalls the Dense Man

In this universe scrutinized (Prov. 15:3) and controlled (16:33) by Yahweh, such a resistant attitude to His truth necessarily reaps a harvest. But what a grim harvest it is:

> He who belittles the word[53] will be in debt to it;
>> but he who fears the commandment, he will be rewarded (13:13 DJP)

This proverb is another pair of stories, compressed into eight little Hebrew words. The first envisions the man of the world, talking big and walking proud. He is despising the Word of God and getting away with it—or so he imagines.

What he does not realize is that he's simply running up his bill. He is like Ebenezer Scrooge, unaware that he was already bearing chains far longer and heavier than Jacob Marley's. Higher and higher above his head towers the dense belittler's debt, and one day it will come crashing down on him. Then he will realize his great miscalculation, in mistaking God's patience for His acquiescence or approbation (cf. Psa. 50:21; Rom. 2:4). His will be the endless misery of the two saddest words in the English language: *too late*.

This dense man's experience will be a little like an incident from my distant youth (single digits, as I recall). A friend and I went bowling together one day. We happily bowled and bowled, set after set. Finally, a manager came up and asked if we knew what the bill was, and were prepared to pay it. I remember my shock. I had no idea that as I played and played, my debt kept rising and rising. I was that young and ignorant.

And so this man's years of blithely ignoring God's Word are running up a bill which may well begin to come partly due in this life, and which will certainly come fully due before the Throne. It is as Lady Wisdom warned the stupid, the naïve, and the scoffers in Proverbs 1:20–33—ignore the day of grace and opportunity, and she will laugh when disaster falls, as it surely will.

The Lord Jesus sounds the same warning in Matthew 7:24–27. The man who agrees with Jesus builds his life on His words. The man who does not build his life on Jesus' words shows that he disagrees with Jesus, that he belittles Jesus' words. The man who hears His words, and goes on unchanged, is headed for calamitous disaster.

Again, recall what Jesus said in John 12:48—"He who rejects[54] Me, and does not receive My words, has one who judges him: the word[55] which I spoke—that

---

53 "The word" in Line A is made specific by "the commandment" in B, removing ground for doubt that Solomon had the authoritative word in mind, which in the final analysis is the Word of God.

54 Or "sets aside," "disregards."

55 Or "message," "doctrine."

will judge him in the last day" (DJP). We note here that the rejecter does not necessarily do anything vile or violent. He does not necessarily curse Christ, defile a cross, or wear a T-shirt that says "I hate God!" What he does is more a passive sin, a sin of omission: he sets Christ aside, and he does not receive Christ's words.

We also note that Christ leaves no more room than Solomon does for the modern invention of the God-loving Scripture-ignorer. Jesus parallels disregarding His person with not accepting His words. To do one is to do the other. Or, to take the flip-side, to honor Jesus requires accepting His words.

The case is identical with the dense man of Proverbs 13:13. By his very attitude of passive disinterest in God's Word, he marks himself as one who "belittles wisdom and understanding" (Prov. 1:7). He could have had both, yet he let them go, and lived according to his own counsels.

So we note in closing:

- The opposite of fearing God is not only hating God or mocking God.
- The opposite of fearing God is ignoring God, of which the chiefest manifestation is indifference toward His Word.

This is the dense person.

Summary of Old Testament Teaching

The fear of Yahweh is the beginning of knowledge;
    wisdom and discipline, dense people belittle. (Prov. 1:7 DJP)

1. The fear of Yahweh is *personal*; it is a specific person fearing a specific person.
2. The fear of Yahweh *must be learned*, so that we might learn of His *person* and His *will*.
3. The fear of Yahweh grows directly out of and depends upon His *Word*.
4. The fear of Yahweh *motivates obedience*.
5. A brief way of explaining it, then, would be *repentant, reverent, obedient faith*. In fact, I have argued that the case could be made that "the fear of Yahweh" is the Old Testament equivalent of Acts 16:31—"Believe in the Lord Jesus, and you will be saved, and your household."

Step Back for the Big Picture

Two critical truths we have now won bear special stress.

First, we have seen that Solomon frames the entire book as being about living life in the fear of Yahweh. We see that in how he brackets the book as a whole (1:7; 31:30), and by his frequent repetitions within the book (1:29; 2:5; 3:7; 8:13; 9:10; 10:27; 14:2, 26–27; 15:16, 33; 16:6; 19:23; 22:4; 23:17; 24:21; 28:14; 29:25).

The practical impact of that observation is that *every verse* should be read against that backdrop. Whether Solomon is writing about kinds of kids or marriage or work or the courtroom or palace-life, we must throw each individual proverb against the conceptual frame of the fear of Yahweh—or we will miss Solomon's point.

Second, we have seen that this concept itself ushers us right back into the Pentateuch and beyond. Solomon did not invent either the phrase or the idea. He assumes that we know as much. So what the king is doing in Proverbs is "communicating the great truths of… the Pentateuch, and chiefly Deuteronomy… in new, surprising, and memorable ways."[56] Therefore we must constantly anchor our understanding of each saying in the Scripture that Solomon had in hand. Only thus can we hear what Solomon says as Solomon meant it to be heard, which is also as God intends it to be heard.

Postscript: Is the Fear of God Solely an OT Concept?

There is a notion, most popular among those whose knowledge of the Bible is secondhand, that the Testaments are polar opposites. The Old Testament (we are told) is all about fear, wrath, judgment and fire, whereas the New brims with love, peace, joy and puppies. According to this impression, "fear" would be a perfectly appropriate element in the religion of Moses and the Jews, but it could have no part in the preaching of Christ and the apostles.

However, so far from being a notion confined to the Old Testament, the fear of God is a *pan*-Biblical theme, literally found from Genesis (20:11, etc.) to Revelation (11:18; 14:17, etc.). Rather than a dividing concept, it is a uniting reality joining the faith of both Testaments into a single, unfolding unity.

---

[56] Hamilton, 291.

Did Jesus balk at the language of fear and wrath? Hardly. Baptized under the ministry of John, fiery preacher of God's wrath against sin (Matt. 3:1–16), Jesus' first recorded sermon in Matthew was as sharp as it was brief: "Repent, for the kingdom of heaven is at hand" (Matt. 4:17).

Our Lord Jesus was quite emphatic about the necessity and centrality of fearing God. Hear Him from Luke 12:4–5—

> I tell you, my friends, do not fear those who kill the body, and after that have nothing more that they can do. ⁵ But I will warn you whom to fear: fear him who, after he has killed, has authority to cast into hell. Yes, I tell you, fear him!"

From this we glean a number of truths. Let's count out three:

1. Far from replacing the image of God as worthy of fear, Jesus vastly intensified it.[57]

2. Jesus specifically impressed "fear" as an appropriate attitude among His loyal disciples ("my friends," v. 4).

3. Exactly as in the OT, "fear" has the effect of exalting God above all else, and positioning us as vulnerable to Him and subordinate to His will.

Does the theme extend beyond Calvary and Pentecost? Some have carved such sharp dispensational lines in redemptive history that one scarcely expected to see concepts transcend from epoch to epoch. "Fear" might have been supposed to be appropriate to the dispensation of law prior to Calvary, but not the dispensation of grace afterwards.

However, surely we must bow to the authority of the apostle Paul in the matter of God's plan of redemption. The apostle specifically bids his Christian readers: "Since we have these promises, beloved, let us cleanse ourselves from every defilement of body and spirit, bringing holiness to completion in the fear of God" (2 Cor. 7:1). The fear of God is not here a pre-Christian, Law-imposed state of oppression. It is the very motivation for gracious, holy, Spirit-led Christian living.

---

57 While the OT passages warning of God's judgments tended to stress temporal judgments, Jesus here holds out the prospect of eternal suffering of the wrath of God. If anything, He *heightens* the factor of fear in our relationship with God.

Paul would motivate slaves to exemplary Christian practice in the same manner: "Slaves, keep submitting in all respects to *those who are* your[58] lords according to the flesh, not with superficial service[59] as man-pleasers, but *rather* in singleness of heart, because you fear[60] the Lord" (Col. 3:22 DJP). Again and famously, Paul urges the Philippians, "just as you have always obeyed, not as in my presence only, but now much more in my absence, work out your salvation with fear and trembling; [13]for it is God who is at work in you, both to will and to work for *His* good pleasure" (Phil. 2:12–13 NAS). This passage has no whiff of the Old Covenant nor of the Law of Moses, yet "fear and trembling" motivate the blood-bought Christian believer.

Nor does the apostle Peter hold out any different impetus in 1 Peter 1:17–19—

> And if you call on him as Father who judges impartially according to each one's deeds, conduct yourselves with fear throughout the time of your exile, [18] knowing that you were ransomed from the futile ways inherited from your forefathers, not with perishable things such as silver or gold, [19] but with the precious blood of Christ, like that of a lamb without blemish or spot.

We see specifically that Peter identifies God as our Father in Christ, and our state as having been ransomed by the priceless blood of Christ. Yet in our case—no less than in Moses', nor Solomon's, nor Daniel's—the fear of God motivates us to lives of faith and obedience.

Finally, we saw previously that the last book in the New Testament (and in the Bible), the book of the Revelation, the "eternal gospel" is expressed in the words "Fear God" (Revelation 14:6–7). The fear of God is truly and literally a pan-Biblical, trans-covenantal concept.

Conclusion

At the very least, this study should reform our vocabulary. For decades it was an American fixture to call any moderately moral and religious (unconverted) person a "God-fearing" man or woman. There is no Scriptural warrant for such creamy twaddle.

---

[58] Literally "the," the definite article standing for the pronoun.
[59] Literally "eye-slavery."
[60] Literally "fearing"; grammatically termed a "causal participle."

It is the characteristic of the lost that "There is no fear of God before their eyes" (Rom. 3:18). Wholehearted, open submission to the sovereignty of God in every area of life is neither congenital nor congenial to us. We must *become* God-fearers; indeed, we must *be made* God-fearers by a sovereign work of God's grace (cf. Jer. 31:33; 32:40; Ezek. 36:26).

A God-fearer today is the man who has repented of his good works as well as his bad, trusted Christ alone as his Savior, relied on Christ's righteousness alone, by the grace of God alone, and taken God's Word alone as his marching orders, with God's glory alone as his uniting motivation.

That is the man who fears God.

Questions for Thought or Discussion

1. Why not just study "the fear of Yahweh" in Proverbs alone?

2. Compare and contrast "the fear of Yahweh" with "belief in 'God,' whoever you conceive 'God' to be."

3. What is the relationship between the Bible and fearing God?

4. Is being frightened of God the same as fearing God? Explain.

5. What is the connection between fearing Yahweh and godly living?

6. What does fearing Yahweh have to do with having a relationship with Him?

7. What does forgiveness have to do with fearing Yahweh?

8. How does humility factor in to fearing Yahweh?

9. What are some of the benefits of fearing Yahweh? How have you experienced those benefits?

10. Is there a right way to preach the benefits of fearing Yahweh? A wrong way? Explain.

11. How does fear of Yahweh factor into one's worldview?

12. How many of the eleven listed benefits of fearing Yahweh can you name from memory?

13. What are some characteristics of the dense man?

14. What is the opposite of fearing God?

15. Is the fear of Yahweh strictly an Old Testament concept? Explain.

CHAPTER FOUR

WISDOM:
Seeking and Finding

How to Wise Up

Opening Thoughts

The godly man or woman knows the value of God's thoughts and wants to gain God's wisdom. We want to possess and practice skill in godly living.

So, how is this done? How do we gain wisdom?

Thankfully, Solomon tells us, in just so many words. But before we study what the sagacious sovereign says, we must consider a very important truth. Let us approach it by way of analogy and two simple questions.

How to Get Bread

First simple question: *How do you get **bread**?*

Some pious Bible students might immediately come up with the answer. "Why, you *pray* for it, just as Jesus modeled in Matthew 6:11—'Give us this day our daily bread.'"

And so, taking off on that one verse, one might build a whole Theology of Bread Procurement. He might teach that God's glory shines out at its greatest brilliance when we do absolutely nothing for our bread, aside from prayer. We sit in public, praying for bread. We "trust God" for bread. We are careful to add no fleshly human works of our own. Then, when bread falls into our mouth from Heaven in the sight of all the watching crowds, God alone is glorified.

But then another Bible student might remember another verse, and cry out, "Wait, wait. Don't just pray. If you did that, you would dishonor God by your laziness." But then, just as the rest of us are letting out a sigh of relief, this person might go on:

> "In fact, don't pray at all. Just *work* for your bread, as Paul says in 2 Thessalonians 3:10—'For even when we were with you, we were ordering you this: that if one is not willing to work, neither let him eat.' There it is, and it is an apostolic command: if you want to eat, you must work…not pray."

There, is that all better?

Of course, we all recognize immediately that it isn't "all better." In fact, it is just as bad as the first answer. If the first errs in the direction of slothful presumption on God, the second errs in the direction of arrogant independence of God. Both are grave errors.

So what is the answer? In this area at least, most of us recognize that the answer is that we must do *both*. We must pray for our bread, then we must use the strength and opportunities that God provides and go work for our bread. We have no problem recognizing, in this area, that *God works through means*. He does not simply materialize bread, deposit it on our tongue, start us chewing, then tamp it down into our tummies. He gives us abilities, opportunities for gainful work, and commands us to get out and do our part to acquire what He provides.

How to Get Wisdom

All right, we've dealt with bread. Let's ask the second, more directly "spiritual" question: *How do you get wisdom?*

Again, an observant Bible student named Bud might pop up and proclaim,

> "Why, that's easy. God tells us that we just need to pray for it, and He will give it to us. We read in James 1:5–7 that those who lack

wisdom should ask it from God in faith, and they will receive it from him. So there it is, straight from God. The way to wisdom is prayer. Just close your eyes, bow your head, and ask God for wisdom. He will graciously pour it right into your head, or maybe He will even speak to you by His 'still, small voice'."

But while brother Bud is talking, sister Ofelia nearby is becoming visibly agitated. She can barely contain herself. No sooner does Bud pause than she springs up and bursts out,

"No, no, no! That lazy mysticism only brings shame to God. Don't pray for wisdom—you've got to listen, learn, and do. You left off too soon in James. Keep reading, and when you get to James 1:22–25 you'll read that we need to be doers of God's Word who act on it, and not self-deluded hearers only. So get off of your rear end, Bud, crack open that Bible, and start studying and learning. And forget all of this 'prayer' nonsense."

So, how about this one? Some of you may have been more uneasy with the example about wisdom than the one about bread. The answer to the question about bread was obvious, but the answer about wisdom mightn't be as clear to some Christians.

Through the years, you have been exposed to a lot of people who talk, preach and write just like Bud. They seem very assured, and very spiritual. They insist that the most important way to learn is by praying. When we pray, God speaks to us directly in some quiet, mystical way (we are told), and opens His wisdom to us.

Yet you saw from James that the same principle obtains in both areas, whether we're after wisdom or whole wheat. The principle? Simply put, *God works through means*. He does not make bread appear in our mouth—and He does not make wisdom appear in our head. In both areas, we must pray, *and* we must work.

What, then, are the *means*—the instrumentality, mode, mechanism, method, approach—that God has provided for us in our search for wisdom?

Solomon will tell us, if we will listen.

STUDY OF PROVERBS 2:1-6

Translation

My son, if you receive my sayings,
> and my commandments you treasure up with you;

[2] by making your ear attentive to wisdom,
> turning[1] your heart to insight;

[3] For if for discernment you call,
> for insight you give your voice;

[4] If you seek for her as silver,
> and as hidden treasures you search for her;

[5] Then you will discern the fear of Yahweh,
> and knowledge of God you will find.

[6] For Yahweh gives wisdom;
> from His mouth, knowledge and insight. (DJP)

Overview

Solomon provides us with…

1. Three conditions (introduced by *if*);

    a. Verses 1–2

    b. Verse 3

    c. Verse 4

Then we meet…

2. The prize (vv. 5–6; introduced by *then*).

---

[1] Hebrew students will notice that "by making …attentive" translates a Qal infinitive, but "turning" translates a Hiphʿil imperfect. Most translations (ESV, CSB, NIV, TNIV) and commentators (Longmann, Fox, Clifford, Murphy) simply make the two coordinate. Waltke sets the whole off by dashes to set it off, thus: "—by making your ear attentive to wisdom, you will apply your heart to understanding—" (*Proverbs*, 1:213). He calls it an "aside," and says its two lines respectively nuance the charge of v. 1 by specifying an attentive ear, and promise a changed heart (*Proverbs*, 2:220–221). While this is certainly possible, I'm more persuaded by Fox's suggestion that such infinitive/finite verb parallelism is "a stylistic fillip to avoid monotony" (*Proverbs*, 1:191).

THE THREE CONDITIONS

First Condition: Build a Foundation (vv. 1–2)

Relationship of the Two Verses

Verses 1 and 2 form one condition. The first verse features a favorite Hebrew poetic touch called "chiasm." What is a chiasm? Glad you asked.

Aside: "Chiasm"? Huh?

A *chiasm* refers to a poetic structure shaped like the Greek capital letter *chi* (X), with two pairs of terms, crossing in the middle. They are very common in the book of Proverbs, though sometimes the English translation obscures it for the sake of smoothness.

Chiasm can be explained painlessly. Let me illustrate from Proverbs 2:1. We will use A and B, in this case, to label the elements of a single line; and A¹ and B¹ to label the elements that mirror the same. So, we may think of "if you receive" as "A," and "my sayings" as "B." Then "my commandments" thought-rhymes with "B," so we will call it "B¹"; and "you treasure up with you" thought-rhymes with "A," so it is labeled "A¹." The order within this verse, then, is A-B-B¹-A¹, which pointy-headed academics diagram thus:

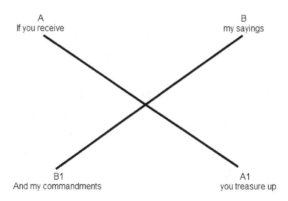

If we draw a line from element to mirror-element, the result looks like a Greek *chi* (X). Hence the name: *chiasm*.

Then the second verse is grammatically framed in a way that indicates that it makes verse one more specific. It shows the way verse one must be done.

"Receive"

In verse one, then, Solomon begins

> My son, if you receive my sayings,
>> and my commandments you treasure up with you…

His son must *receive* his sayings.[2] The verb is related to *leqah* in 1:5a, where it suggests a repository, a storehouse of received instruction.

The verb here is not meant to convey a transitory reception. We are not to receive God's wisdom like a radio receives radio waves and immediately loses them. Rather, the idea is that we "receive" them "for keeps," like a digital recorder receives sounds and hangs on to them, or like a computer's hard drive receives and stores data.

Implications

God wants us to see ourselves as students who advance, but who never graduate. Little-known fact: "student" is the meaning of the NT term usually translated "disciple." Most churchgoers I ask think "disciple" means "follower," or even "apostle"; but in fact the underlying Greek word *mathētēs* simply means "pupil," "student."

All Christians should see themselves as students of Biblical instruction, scholars who never graduate. However, very few seem to have embraced that self-image.

When I have passed out sermon or lesson outlines in various churches, I have received varying reactions—and the reactions tell me a lot about my audience. One church was thrilled and couldn't stop commenting on how nice it was to receive outlines and be able to take notes. They loved being able to follow the flow of the sermon, and being able to preserve what they were learning.

Others, by contrast, have been stiffly offended. The criticism comes: it's like being back in school. What seems to be escaping notice is that the Christian is always in school. He is to learn throughout his entire life. Church is to function as his center of instruction.

"My sayings"

The noun here (*ᵃmārāy*) was already used in 1:2 ("Sayings of discernment"). In Job 23:12, this noun refers to the words of God.[3] By using this word, Solomon

---

[2]   The Hebrew verb is *lāqah,* which was already encountered and discussed in 1:3.

[3]   As it does many times, including Numbers 24:4, 16; Psalm 107:11; 138:4. The related feminine

prepares us for the idea that not only the thoughts, but the very words and sayings of God are important.

"And My Commandments" (v. 1b)

This term escalates both the specificity and the authority of Line A. What basis does Solomon have for speaking so authoritatively? Was he just an authoritarian, demanding teacher?

Ultimately we find our explanation in Hebrews 12:5–7, where Proverbs 3 is quoted and applied as being God the Father's words to His children. We recall as well that Solomon's wisdom was a direct gift from Yahweh. Though Solomon did not speak a "Thus says Yahweh," as the prophets did, he did speak with authority, and expected his words to be accepted as such.

"You treasure up"

This is the Hebrew *tiṣpōn*, from *ṣāpan*, to hide, keep, save up, store, treasure up.[4] The verb was used of hiding baby Moses in Exodus 2:2. Clearly, "hide" here does not mean that the baby's mother put him where she could not find him. Rather, she put him where she could keep him and would not lose him.

The application to us is that we are to put God's words where they will remain intact, where they will not be lost. Where would that be? The answer is found in the use of the same verb in Psalm 119:11.

> In my heart have I *treasured up* Your saying,
>> in order that I might not sin against You.
> (DJP, italics added for emphasis)

This wonderful verse plainly does not suggest that we should put God's Word out of sight. Rather, the words direct us to make God's words so much our own possession that they cannot be taken from us.

Without using this verb, Solomon will show in 3:1 that he intends his teachings to be memorized.

> My son, my law[5] do not forget,
>> and my commandments let your heart guard. (DJP)

---

noun *'imrâ* is also used frequently of the word or words of God, as in Psalm 12:7; 18:30; 119:11, 38, 41, 50, 58, 67, 82, and so on; also Proverbs 30:5.

4   See BDB, article צָפַן, HALOT, article צפן.

5   As I shall explain in Appendix Two, *tôrâ* means "law" in the comprehensive sense of authoritative

What is it to "not forget" something, but to remember it? My heart guards God's written revelation, so as to keep it safe.

How many Christians even have the ghost of such an attitude toward the Word of God? If we treated our money as indifferently and neglectfully as we deal with Bible doctrine, there is no question but that every one of us would be penniless. Familiarity with the Word of God is a treasure-trove to be preserved and continually increased. This should rule our personal lives, and should set the agenda in how we seek a church. The learning, treasuring, and doing of the Word of God must be central in everything.

"With You" (v. 1b)

BDB explains this word as meaning (among other things) to have in the knowledge or memory, citing numerous examples.[6] We *literally* keep our ID, our driving license, or our wedding ring *with* us. We *figuratively* treasure our mental image of the faces of loved ones, or the savor of our relationships and commitments.

The sad reality is that God's goal for the believer is higher than many believers' goals for themselves. Many are content to let their pastor know Biblical truths (or, God help them, men relegate that duty to their wives), while they bumble on in thundering ignorance. God's intention is that you and I make His wisdom our own. We are to learn it from the Bible. Nobody is to know it in our stead. Pastors are charged by God with helping us to grow, but we must make His Word *ours*, so as to keep it "with" us.

"By Making Your Ear Attentive" (*lᵉhaqšîḇ*) to Wisdom (v. 2a)

To make one's ears "attentive" here means to be rapt, absorbed, captivated. It summons to mind the picture of leaning forward, so as to listen closely. An important usage of the same verb is in 1 Samuel 15:22 (NAS).

> And Samuel said, "Has the LORD as great delight in burnt offerings and sacrifices, as in obeying the voice of the LORD? Behold, to obey is better than sacrifice, and to listen [*lᵉhaqšîḇ*] than the fat of rams.

---

instruction. It is used of the Mosaic Law, but it is also used of all the Old Testament. Proverbs uses it both of canonical law and of parents' authoritative instruction in line with that law.

6   BDB, article אָת.

Could Samuel (or Solomon) even conceivably mean that believers should *listen* to a supposed mumbly inner voice of God, to some subjective urging? In context, absolutely not. Both Samuel and Solomon mean to listen to the objective Word of God. God wants us to lean forward and give our rapt attention to His objectively revealed Word.

Note too that this is something *we* are directed to do. It isn't up to a riveting, charismatic speaker (or father) to compel his hearer to attend. The Holy Spirit will not do this in our stead. If you and I want wisdom, this is a choice and commitment we must make.

"Turning Your Heart to Insight" (v. 2b)

The *heart* in Hebrew is *lēḇ*, or *lēḇāḇ*. BDB defines the Hebrew word for "heart" as "inner man, mind, will, heart."[7]

Contrary to years of Christian traditional definition, the heart is not primarily the seat of the emotions, but rather of intellect, volition, and evaluation. It is used specifically of *memory* in various places, including Deuteronomy 4:39 and Proverbs 4:21.[8]

Wouldn't "brain" be the better modern term for this idea? Why is the heart used for the mind, rather than "brain"? As a matter of fact, the word "brain," as a part of the body, is never mentioned in the OT.[9] The word simply was not in use in the Hebrew working vocabulary as it is in modern English. The question is not, "Why didn't the Hebrews use our word," but rather, "What Hebrew word (if any) has a meaning equivalent to 'brain'?"—and usage shows that the answer is, "Heart."[10]

When he speaks of "turning" the heart, Solomon uses the Hebrew verb *taṭṭeh*, from *nāṭâ*. The form here is a verbal stem called the Hiphʿil imperfect, which usually means that the verb causes something to happen or exist.[11] That form is

---

7   BDB, article לֵב; HALOT adds a range of meanings which include: one's inner self, seat of feeling and emotions, inclination, disposition, will, intention, attention, consideration, reason, mind in general and as a whole, and conscience (article לֵב).

8   Cf. BDB, article לֵב, where they cite also Deuteronomy 4:9, 39; 6:6; 30:1; 2 Chronicles 6:37; Job 22:22; 1 Samuel 21:13; Jeremiah 51:50; and Ezekiel 38:10.

9   Cf. Toy, 33.

10   BDB says that the use with reference to the *mind* is "characteristic" of this word, citing such passages as Deuteronomy 8:5; 32:46; Joshua 23:14; 1 Kings 2:44; 1 Chronicles 29:18; Job 9:4; 12:3; 34:10, 34; Psalm 77:6 [Hebrew 7]; 90:12; Ecclesiastes 9:3; Isaiah 6:10; 10:7; 32:4; Haggai 1:5, 7; 2:15, 18; Zechariah 10:7; 8:17, among many others.

11   The Hiphʿil stem (to generalize) makes a verb causative. In other words, if the base verb means "turn," the Hiphʿil will mean "cause to turn."

Playing music "by heart"

built from the verbal root which means to *stretch out, spread out,* but only rarely so in the Hiph'il, where it more commonly means *incline, turn.*[12]

The word is used literally of a donkey turning aside (in the Qal verbal stem) into a given road, and then of Balaam turning it back (in the Hiph'il stem; both in Num. 22:23).

> When the donkey saw the angel of Yahweh standing in the way with his drawn sword in his hand, the donkey *turned off* [simple Qal stem] from the way and went into the field; but Balaam struck the donkey *to turn* her *back* [Hiph'il stem, as in Proverbs] into the way. (NAS, emphases added)

The first turning requires decision—albeit on the part of a donkey. The second turning requires decision and effort. Perhaps the reader has tried to turn a donkey from the direction in which it wanted to go? I never have, but I understand it isn't for the easily discouraged.

This verb is used in a parallel prayer in Psalm 119:36, "Incline my heart to your testimonies, and not to selfish gain!" We see here that the psalmist realized that his own effort was not enough. On his own, he could not direct his heart. So he calls on God for help.

The psalmist prays that God will incline his heart; Solomon says we must incline our hearts. How can those two ideas be wed?

We must be sure to remember the lessons of Matthew 6:11 and James 1:5:

1. We pray for bread and wisdom;

2. *Then* we work and study.

It is we who must do this. God does not grant to anyone else the power to study or to memorize for us. It requires conscious effort and concentration on our part to direct our mind to something. It is not enough merely to pray that God will do this, and then hope for the best. After all, remember that Solomon's command is not addressed to God.

We must also mark well that it would be sinfully tempting God for us to "wait on the Holy Spirit" to cause us to do this. It is the Holy Spirit who inspired this text, and it is He who addressed it to believers. If we want to grow in our understanding of God's wisdom, you and I must direct our minds to it.

---

[12] See BDB, article נָטָה.

Yet at the same time, we must not imagine that we can do this by ourselves. If all holiness required was the issuance of a perfect law or command, the Mosaic Law would have done the job. But it did not. Hence we must take this command as ours, yet we must come to God for help. We must pray. And when God hears our prayer and grants it, our case will be like Paul's apostolic paradox:

> But by the grace of God I am what I am, and his grace toward me was not in vain. On the contrary, I worked harder than any of them, though it was not I, but the grace of God that is with me. (1 Cor. 15:10)

Second Condition: Pray (v. 3)

For if for discernment you call,
  for insight you give your voice;

Introduction

Does the principle that God works through means eliminate the need for prayer? Not at all. Indeed, when we realize that our lives, our footsteps, and even the very breaths that we draw are under the sovereign control of God (Jer. 10:23; Dan. 5:23b), we see all the more the need for prayer.[13]

Note the *fervency* of this prayer. What does Solomon tell us to do? Solomon does not simply urge us to "pray" or "ask" for discernment and insight. Rather, Solomon urges us to "cry," and to "give [our] voice."

What tone does this strike? Does this sound like a cultured lady politely requesting another napkin in a fine restaurant? Does it bring to mind the man in the old commercial politely asking for a little "Gray Poupon" mustard?

Or does it not more sound like a baby screaming loudly and insistently for a bottle?

---

[13] Some would reason the opposite: if God controls all, why pray? This objection suggests an underlying misconception about prayer. Prayer is not the way we get God to do our will. As the book of Psalms alone should teach us, prayer is how we communicate with God. It may be by thanks, confession, praise, exclamation, musing aloud, cries of anguish, cries for help, or petition. (W. Bingham Hunter develops these themes in his little study, *The God Who Hears* [Downers Grove: InterVarsity, 1986].) Prayer at its "best" is an expression of our dependence upon God, and our desire to be fully-engaged in doing His good pleasure. Understood that way, the truth of God's sovereignty underlines the importance both of prayer and of responsible use of the means He provides us.

I pick the latter!

When we realized the importance of our possessing (and being possessed by) God's own viewpoint, we will not think of it as a nice extra, a sprig of parsley on our dinner plate. Rather, we will cry out for it, we will give our voice for it, as if our very lives depend on it...which they do.

Placement and Contents of This Prayer

We should note *first* that Solomon's overall counsel is *two-thirds study*. Thrice the bell tolls for intensive study, research, memorization: verses 1–2 and 4 (i.e., *receive, treasure up, make your ear attentive, turn your heart, seek, search*). Then one sustained note calls for prayer, verse 3.

Is it shocking, then, to suggest that our priorities should reflect this same structure? By my observation, too many substitute prayer for the hard work of study. They pray and pray and pray for God's wisdom, yet they seldom if ever crack open the Bible for intensive personal study, let alone give the effort to find and participate in an emphatically Bible-teaching church.

By contrast, I have run into far fewer who study without prayer. Solomon's priority directs us to study, study, pray, and study.

Our *second* observation is that, this prayer follows the building of a foundation. The first two verses counsel us to build that repository of wisdom; *then* we are to pray. So, when we pray, we are not simply firing off some well-intended thoughts into the infinite, unknown void. Rather, Solomon is counseling an informed, contentful, Biblically-directed[14] prayer.

Third, to understand the role of prayer, we must keep in mind what Solomon had written in 1:2–6. Would Solomon say, in effect, "My book will give you wisdom; so when you want wisdom, throw the book away and pray"? Though this is logically absurd, many mystically-inclined Christians think and live just so. The Bible is a pleasant extra, to them; but the real marrow of their lives consists of emotions gained in mystical encounters—such as are neither urged nor even described in Scripture.

What this command does show is that mere personal study, while crucial, is not enough. We must not merely read and think; we must pray for insight as well.

---

[14] Some may see "Bible study" as anachronism, as the whole Bible did not exist when Solomon wrote. This fact underscores my point, however. If study was to precede and direct prayer when only a handful of books had been revealed, how much more would this be the case now, when the whole counsel of God has been inscripturated?

I think it helpful if we take a moment to consider a parallel scripture: Psalm 119. In this psalm, famously, we repeatedly see expressions of praise and adoration for God's revealed Word. At the same time, these celebrations are *coupled* with prayerful cries for greater insight into that Word.

For instance, consider specific examples such as Psalm 119:12 and 18.

> You are blessed, Yahweh;
> > teach me Your statutes. (Psa. 119:12 DJP)
>
> Open my eyes that I may behold
> > wonderful things from Your law.(Psa. 119:18 DJP)

Both of these verses take God's revealed Word as the basis for all knowledge. Equally, both of these are cries for greater understanding of and insight into the Word of God. Prayer couples with Scripture study in seamless harmony.

Perhaps you have had experiences in prayer such as I have had. While praying, my mind has been directed to specific Scripture. Sometimes this actually interrupts my prayer time. At first, I thought of the interruptions as symptoms of how unspiritual I was, and resisted them. I have come to see, however, that this is how God the Holy Spirit speaks to God's children: through the living and abiding Word of God. And what better time to speak than during a time of prayer?

The process of thinking through Scriptures while praying often was itself the answer to my prayers.

Third Condition: Study (v. 4)

> If you look for her as silver,
> > And as hidden treasures you search for her.

This verse suggests two prominent thoughts:

1. Wisdom *requires* effort.

2. Wisdom *repays* effort.

The image Solomon suggests is that of a *miner*. The miner sweats and strains and exhausts himself to gain something very valuable. He expends every effort in locating it, and making it his own.

Think about this on a personal level. What would your attitude be if you knew that there was a great treasure—such as a huge and rich ore of purest gold—buried a few feet under your backyard lawn? Would you yawn and go back to your Play Station? Would you sit around watching folks on TV talking about their mines?

Or would you not rather obtain the necessary tools, get out there, and start digging?

Yet God has assured us that great treasures lie open to us in His Word, if we would but search, seek, and dig. God wants us to be miners for His truth.

Now let your imagination enter the doors of a Christian church. If this verse gripped everyone in attendance, what would we see? In a manner of speaking we should all show up at church with our mining helmets on, pickaxes and blasting caps ready. That is, we should all come with the attitude of being prepared to go to work, digging and shoveling in our search for God's truth.

Far too often, the reality is very different. At best, to flog the metaphor a bit more, too many church meetings are cheap imitations of variety shows, with perhaps passing reference to "miners" here and there—or reassurances that they're all "miners," though no actual mining ever takes place. Or they may feature a lot of music and chit-chat, plus an occasional story about miners. Or perhaps there are slide shows about silver. Or, again, they may be reminiscences about how wonderful it was back in the days of John Calvin and John Owen, when there was still silver and gold to be mined, and men and women dug with the conviction that rich ore still remained to be found.

At worst, Christian assemblies are merely convocations of pew-potatoes, who have shown up to be entertained and to have their feelings manipulated. These would find the very mention of mining offensive and "legalistic."

So, we build a foundation, pray, and study. What do we get for it? What kind of ore does this mine produce?

The Prize (vv. 5-6)[15]

> Then you will discern the fear of Yahweh,
> and knowledge of God you will find.
>
> 6 For Yahweh gives wisdom;
> from His mouth, knowledge and insight. (DJP)

---

[15] Actually, the rewards of wisdom are expanded throughout the remainder of Proverbs 2. We will examine only the first two verses here, but the reader would do well to review the entire chapter.

In digging into the prize, we will single out three aspects: the What, the Why, and the Why Bother?

The What (v. 5)

In characteristically parallel fashion, verse 5 presents the prize in two lines. The form is *chiastic*, which (as we saw above) is to say it can be diagrammed as A B B¹ A¹, like so:

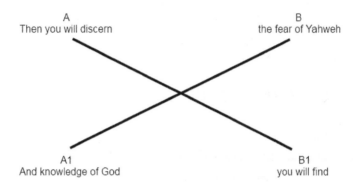

You see? "Then you will discern" in Line A is furthered in "you will find" in Line B; and Line A's "the fear of Yahweh" is developed in B's "knowledge of God." Let's delve in a bit more deeply.

"Then you will discern the fear of Yahweh"

Once one has studied, thought, reflected, memorized, prayed, he will gain *discernment*. He will have a specific insight, will pick out this central truth from among all the alternatives.

What truth will he pick out? None other than the fear of Yahweh. "Say, wait just a minute," one will say. "How can 'the fear of Yahweh' be the crowning achievement of a search for wisdom? Didn't 1:7 say that it was the *beginning* of wisdom, that you can't even start your search for wisdom without it? How can it be the start *and* the finish?"

True enough, as far as it goes. But remember, the fear of Yahweh is not something that we simply learn and then outgrow. We could think of it this way: we start out in "First Year Fear of Yahweh"—but it is intended that we go on to "Second Year" and "Third Year Fear of Yahweh," and so on, without end.

The truth of it is: the more we grow in our fear of God, the more we see our need for fear of God. Having been a Christian by God's grace for more than thirty-eight years, I can say with conviction that there is no problem in Christian living that isn't related to the fear of God. Every last defect in my character would be addressed by deeper fear of God, Biblically defined. Every failing or weakness I've met in fellow humans can be traced to defective fear of God. Every bit of growth in Christ-centered graces relates to growth in the fear of God.

So yes, the critic would have it right... partly: one *begins* the Wisdom curriculum by fear of Yahweh (1:7); one *continues* the curriculum in fear of Yahweh (14:26; 16:6; 19:23; 23:17). The more one grows in wisdom, the more one discerns the fear of Yahweh (2:5).

"Knowledge of God you will find"

The Hebrew concept of "knowledge" discussed above, under Proverbs 1:2, steers us away from two extremes.

On the one hand, "knowledge of God" cannot refer to a mystical encounter with God that excludes facts, statements and propositions. Bluntly put, neither the Old Testament nor the New know anything of such a relationship. Both Testaments are jam-packed with propositional statements about God's past and future acts (Gen. 1:1; Rev. 22:20), as well as categorical assertions about His character (Exod. 34:14; 1 John 1:5) and about how to be right in His eyes (Gen. 15:6; Rom. 5:1).

If we were to stay with the curriculum model, perhaps we could think of it this way. If we are unbelievers, we are strangers to the fear of Yahweh. We are not even enrolled in the "school." If we are believers, we are enrolled—and every last one of us has "The Fear of Yahweh" as our major. We may take a wide variety of courses, but they all relate to and are controlled by our major.

On the other hand, there simply is no such thing as a relationship without knowledge. If you don't know anything about a person, you don't know the person. The moment you say anything about anyone, you are dealing with propositional statements. Likewise, say one thing about God, and you are talking theology. The fact is unavoidable. The only issue is whether it will be good theology or bad theology.

Thus as far as Proverbs 2:4 reflects on theology—which it does—it is the promise that the search for wisdom will lead one to *good* theology, to the ability to make *true* assertions about God.

Also, given the parallelistic relationship of verses, we will be warranted in saying that this knowledge of God is a God-fearing knowledge of God. It is a knowledge, for instance, unshared by would-be theologians who do not submit themselves to the full authority of the entire Bible. True theology is done from a position at God's feet, out of a reverent heart. It births the earnest, prayerful search depicted in 2:1–3, and it reaps the rewards of 2:4.

At the same time, this knowledge *is* an encounter with God. It can never be a mere arid affirmation of truth-statements, a cold-hearted, distant recitation of even the best of creeds. These propositions are meant to describe the person of God, and lead us to a personal, direct encounter with Him.

Solomon knew of this from his father David. The great king treasured the word *and* person of God. One simply cannot read the Psalms without confronting those inseparable realities in David. Let us take Psalm 18 as one example. What are the first words of the psalm, following the title? "I love you, O LORD, my strength." Ardent personal devotion to God bubbles from the very opening words.

Yet the very next words are "The LORD is my rock and my fortress and my deliverer, my God, my rock, in whom I take refuge, my shield, and the horn of my salvation, my stronghold" (v. 2). These are categorical statements, assertions about a God who can be described in truth-statements. God is these things, and He is these things *to David*. It is because of these attributes, and because of His deeds, that God is "worthy to be praised" (v. 3). David knows these things because the word of Yahweh is tried, pure, and true (v. 31).

In this expectation, Solomon says what the whole Bible says. Recall the words of the beloved apostle:

> That which was from the beginning, which we have heard, which we have seen with our eyes, which we looked upon and have touched with our hands, concerning the word of life—[2] the life was made manifest, and we have seen it, and testify to it and proclaim to you the eternal life, which was with the Father and was made manifest to us—[3] that which we have seen and heard we proclaim also to you, so that you too may have fellowship with us; and indeed our fellowship is with the Father and with his Son Jesus Christ. (1 John 1:1–3)

John shared with the other apostles an encounter with Christ that was personal and unforgettable. But the distilled, transmittable essence could be proclaimed (v. 3)—and it was *that proclamation* which would lead his readers to "fellowship" with the Father and His Son, the Lord Jesus. The words of God ground, shape, and lead to our personal encounter with Him (cf. also Rom. 10:17).

This is precisely the vision the Lord Jesus had taught John. Jesus taught that His words were spirit and life (John 6:63). He said that the only way truly to be free is to be His disciple, His student; and the only way to do that is to continue in His words (John 8:31–32). The true believer is the person who hangs on to Jesus' words—and that is the person who comes to know God (John 14:21, 23–24).

We must not miss this point. It is a clarion call to our spineless, gelatinous, and ultimately Godless generation. Knowledge of God is the result of diligent, prayerful, systematic, earnest, demanding, pedal-to-the-metal study of His words. We may say it categorically, on the basis of Scripture: anyone who will not study God's words will not know God—except as Judge (cf. Luke 16:29–31).

This accounts for the lamentable condition of the church today. A fragment of professing Christians are like friendless sociologists, who have studied about people but never actually connected with any. The remaining majority resemble virtual-game addicts, relating to objects that do not exist. Both are fatal flaws. Neither leads to God.

Solomon unites with all of Scripture to point to the only way to gain that wisdom which centers in a truth-based relationship with God.

The Why (v. 6)

> For Yahweh gives wisdom;
>> from His mouth, knowledge and insight. (DJP)

"For" introduces the reason that a prayerful, earnest search for wisdom will invariably lead us to fear and knowledge of Yahweh. It is a little bit like saying, "If you want to catch some nice rainbow trout, you're going to find yourself by some cool, clear water." Why? Because that's where trout can be found.

And so similarly, if we want to find wisdom, we are going to find ourselves fearing and knowing God. Why? Because that is where wisdom, knowledge and insight have their source. How does Yahweh give wisdom, knowledge and insight? He does it as we diligently and prayerfully study His words (vv. 1–4).

We get further light on "from His mouth" by considering 1 Samuel 15:24, where Saul confesses to Samuel, "I have sinned, for I have transgressed the commandment of the LORD and your words, because I feared the people and obeyed their voice." Here, "the commandment of the LORD" is more literally "the mouth of Yahweh." So His mouth is His revealed command; it is actually verbal revelation, which had come from God's mouth.[16]

This, too, is how such knowledge comes to us: from the word of His mouth, the Scriptures.

The emphasis of Proverbs 2:6 is not the method for gaining wisdom (which had been opened up in vv. 1–4), but the source of wisdom. God does not give wisdom immediately and directly, bypassing His inscripturated revelation. Solomon here emphasizes the truth that it is Yahweh who is the source of the wisdom found in His Word. There is no other source.

This thought already formed part of Solomon's "mental furniture," as we can see from Deuteronomy 4:5–8, where Moses charged the nation Israel to keep and do the statutes and rules he had taught them, because the law and their adherence to it is what would create an international testimony to the wisdom of Yahweh.

The wisdom was revealed by Yahweh in His Word. By studying that word, we gain the wisdom that He gives, and which comes from His mouth through His servants the prophets.

Why Bother? (vv. 7–22)

Many commentators observe that Proverbs 2 is actually one very long sentence.[17] Though we are focusing only on vv. 1–7, I would be remiss in not pointing out that Solomon immediately goes on to open up some of the many benefits issuing from the wisdom and knowledge we gain through this prayerful, targeted search.

Earlier, we had already seen that wisdom averts great harm (cf. Prov. 1:20–33, particularly vv. 28–32). This section in chapter 2 adds more items to the list, specifying God's protection and deliverance from bad men and from the wrong woman.

Looking to the larger Canon, we could expand the list greatly. We just noted Deuteronomy 4, in which the surrounding nations would have their attention directed to Yahweh by Israel's believing embrace of His Word. The New Testament

---

[16] This is not an uncommon idiom; see also the Hebrew text of Numbers 4:27; 9:18, 23; 10:13.

[17] Cf. Waltke, *Proverbs*, 1:216.

echoes just the same thought. The Lord Jesus urges us, "Let your light shine before others, so that they may see your good works and give glory to your Father who is in heaven" (Matt. 5:16). When we embrace God's Word and His wisdom for our lives, we bring glory to God.

Paul sounds that very same note in Ephesians 5:15–17—

> Look carefully then how you walk, not as unwise but as wise, [16] making the best use of the time, because the days are evil. [17] Therefore do not be foolish, but understand what the will of the Lord is.

Solomon anticipates both the Lord Jesus and His apostles, in holding this wisdom out as obtainable and necessary. He tells us how to lay hold of it and make it ours. The only changes for those living under the New Covenant are (1) we have a yet richer treasure-trove of revelation available, and (2) we have a richer and fuller ministry of the Holy Spirit to aid us in our pursuit.

Follow this path and nothing but blessing will reward our believing efforts; ignore it, and the shame of folly is ours.

Questions for Thought or Discussion

1. What does obtaining bread have to do with obtaining wisdom?

2. What does "God works through means" mean, and what does it have to do with gaining wisdom?

3. What does "disciple" mean? What are the implications?

4. How does one gain wisdom?

5. What do many Christians do in order to gain wisdom, and how does this differ from what Solomon says to do?

6. How is the growing disciple like a miner?

7. How is the growing disciple like a baby?

8. What is the relationship between theology and knowing God personally?

9. What does it mean to say that wisdom and knowledge come *from the mouth* of Yahweh?

10 . What is the result of gaining wisdom as depicted in Proverbs 2?

CHAPTER FIVE

Relating to God by Trust and Worship

Opening Thoughts

The key element in relating to God is *the fear of Yahweh*, which has already been discussed in our exposition of Proverbs 1:7.[1] We cannot experience a genuine walk with God unless we have both clearly grasped and fully embraced the truths of who He is and who we are by contrast. We must see His greatness, His Godhood—and our creatureliness, guilt, dependence, and need for both redemption and subsequent obedience to Him.

The fear of Yahweh is an attitude of which we are in daily need. As Peter says, we are to live out all of the days of our pilgrimage here on earth in the fear of God (1 Peter 1:17). Now let us focus on one other essential and much-misunderstood component in a genuine walk with God: the element of *trust*.

Trust is a vital, crucial component in a real, vigorous relationship with God. We shall see that far too many Christians do not have a Biblical grasp of this key mindset. Mystical mythology is a gloppy river flowing overabundantly from American pulpits and bookstores today.

---

[1] See Chapter 3, "The Foundation of Wisdom."

Trust In Yahweh: the Basis

We begin with a closer look at Proverbs 16:20.

> Whoever gives thought to the word will discover good,
>   and blessed is he who trusts in the LORD.

"Whoever Gives Thought"

The term translated "he who gives thought" is מַשְׂכִּיל (*maśkîl*).[2] It means to give attention to, consider, ponder,[3] understand, comprehend,[4] with an emphasis "on the act of attentive observation, of perception and scrutiny, through which one becomes 'insightful.'"[5]

Obviously, this is nothing that can be accomplished while one is passively "yielded," or in any sort of mystical trance. This verb calls for diligent mental and intellectual activity and intelligence.

The verb already had wide use before Solomon's time. In the following passages, the ESV's translation is italicized. The verb is used in Deuteronomy 32:28–29 of Israel needing to *discern* their latter end, and in Nehemiah 8:13 of the remnants' leaders gathering to *study* the written law of God. In Job 34:27, it refers to the wicked who have no *regard* for any of God's ways (34:27). In Psalm 41:1 blessing is pronounced on one who *considers* the poor, and in Psalm 64:9 men are to *ponder* God's works (cf. 106:7). In Proverbs 21:12, Yahweh *observes* the house of the wicked, to bring them to ruin.

Then after Solomon, Isaiah says that restored Israel will *consider* the miraculous work of Yahweh in gathering and blessing them (41:20). Then Daniel confesses Israel's sinful failure to *gain insight* by Yahweh's revealed truth.

"To the Word"

Solomon is referring to the Word *par excellence*, the Word of God. Notice the parallel with Proverbs 13:13. There, Solomon had written, "He who belittles the word will be in debt to it; but he who fears the commandment, he will be rewarded" (DJP). Since "the word" in Line A parallels "the commandment" in Line B, Solomon plainly means the Word of God.

---

[2] Hiphʻil participle from *śākal*; the verb is always in the Hiphʻil, excepting only 1 Samuel 18:30.
[3] See BDB, article שָׂכַל.
[4] HALOT, שׂכל.
[5] TLOT, 1270.

What Solomon is urging is the same endeavor that would later be pursued under Ezra's leadership (cf. Neh. 8:13), the study of God's Word.

Note the parallel within the verse: "He who trusts in Yahweh." Solomon lays side by side the activities of intelligent attention to God's Word, and trusting in Yahweh. The two are natural corollaries. Trusting in Yahweh and attending to Yahweh's revealed words are related ideas in Solomon's thinking (cf. Prov. 22:19;[6] 1 Kings 2:3).

It will also be helpful to consider the *form* of 16:20. Remember the genius of Hebrew parallelism: one line develops, explains, and/or intensifies and specifies the thought of the other. In this case, we must analyze the parallel in this text:

> Whoever gives thought to the word will discover good,
> and blessed is he who trusts in the Lord.[7]

This is yet another instance of chiasm:

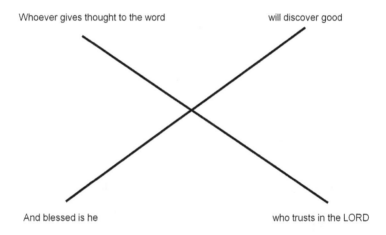

What we will call the "A" and "A¹" elements in lines 1 and 2 are—

- "Whoever gives thought to the word" (A)
- "he who trusts in the Lord" (A¹)

What we will call the "B" and "B¹" elements in lines 1 and 2 are

- "will discover good" (B)
- "blessed" (B¹)

---

6   See discussion, below.

7   The relationship of the two lines is *synonymous* parallelism (cf. Kitchen, *Proverbs*, 362).

Therefore, "shall find good" expands on the idea of what it means to be "blessed"; and…

"He who trusts in Yahweh" expands on the idea behind the words "He who gives attention to the word."[8]

To trust in Yahweh, then, is to give thought to the Word; and to give thought to the Word is to trust in Yahweh. There is no doing the one without doing the other. Any attempt to do so is bereft of God's blessing, and thus doomed from the outset.

It is not too difficult to make practical application of this verse. Armed with Solomon's sage perspective, we see too many signs of ill health in today's church. One of the crippling maladies among professed believers shows up in statements like the following:

- "I'm not into doctrine, I just love the Lord."
- "I'm no theologian."
- "Give me a sermon that isn't loaded down with a lot of doctrine!"
- "Doctrine divides; love unites."
- "A man with a theory is never at the mercy of a man with an experience."
- "I want to worship, not listen to a lecture."
- "'Sermon'?! Where's my sofa and caffè latte?"

The underlying notion behind such ideas is that love for God, worship, and Christian living may (and should) be divorced from doctrine, from teaching, from learning, from considering, analyzing, and systematizing the facts and truths revealed in the Bible.

In fact, one might imagine a modern church leader coining an opposing proverb:

He who gives thought to the word is a legalistic hater,
  but blessed are they who trust whatever makes them feel good. *really*

---

[8] In my judgment, Waltke's commentary here provides an example of how excessive eagerness to create a contextual flow can ill serve the interpretation of individual proverbs. Waltke sees vv. 16–30 as dealing with "wise and foolish speech" (2:22), and thus finds in 16:20 a play on words in which Solomon sort of gives revealed wisdom a nod, but really is talking about listening and speaking wisely (2:28–29). In this, I think Waltke does not do justice to the parallelism within the verse. Garrett makes a similar mistake (157).

What does the Bible do with the modern "faith [or love or Christian experience] versus doctrine" division? This text is one of many which reveals that trust in God and intelligent analysis of His Word are inseparable. Faith and doctrine are wed in the Bible. They are divorced only in sick and straying quarters of modern Christendom.

The point cannot be stressed too emphatically. Not only are faith/trust and doctrine *not opposed* to each other in Scripture, but there simply *is* no Biblically-defined "trust" *without* doctrine. Consider: it is only by Bible doctrine that we learn—

- Who God is
- Who we are
- What God's will is
- What our deepest needs are
- What God's provisions are

The list could be multiplied almost without end. Without Biblical doctrine, we don't know whom to trust, or what to trust Him for. Absolutely everything we need to know as believers, in order to know and serve God, is revealed in Scripture (2 Tim. 3:15–17). Anyone imagining a relationship of trust that is not grounded on the certainties of God's Word is envisioning something other than Biblically-defined faith.

Next we turn our attention to Proverbs 22:19.

> So that your trust may be in Yahweh,
>   I have made *them* known to you today—yes, you! (DJP)

In Solomon's aside here, we see that the goal of biblical teaching is not mere intellectualism. God's objective is not to create a mass of pointy-headed intellectuals, people who know great oceans of facts and details, and bear themselves with barren, fruitless, useless, and insufferable arrogance.

This is likely the sort of thing Paul had in mind when he said, "Knowledge puffs up, but love builds up" (1 Cor. 8:1a DJP). Obviously, the apostle is not opposed to knowledge per se. How could he be? If he were, wouldn't knowing that knowledge puffs up, itself, puff up? Why would Paul write any letters to help any Christians *know* anything, if he were opposed to knowledge per se?

Rather, the point is the sort of possession of knowledge that is used chiefly to tear down others, and to magnify oneself inappropriately. This knowledge does not produce a God-honoring, neighbor-loving, fruitful lifestyle (cf. James 3:14–18).

The goal of teaching wisdom, of communicating God's Word, is cultivating a vital relationship with God. This, Solomon says, is why he taught what he taught: that his son would come to trust in the Lord, nourished by the faith-producing words of Solomon.

We noted this same phenomenon earlier in 1 John 1:1–3. The apostles communicated what they knew of Christ, and that knowledge led their readers into fellowship with God. Therefore, the Christian has "fellowship" with God by what he *knows* from the apostles' writings.

It is essential that a Christian study Scriptures most carefully. At the same time we must never forget: our goal is not mere knowledge of facts and details. Our goal is knowledge of facts and details that enable us to know and serve God better.

Trust in Yahweh: the Opposites

It isn't easy to pick out a white rabbit against a snowfield. Placed against some dark granite, however, it stands out bright and bold.

As we continue to work toward grasping what it means to trust Yahweh, it may be useful to note two contrasting attitudes. What is the opposite of trusting Yahweh?

Arrogance

Keeping in mind the close relationship we have established between trusting Yahweh and attending closely to His Word, let us closely consider two verses from Psalm 119. First, note verse 21:

> You rebuke the insolent, accursed ones,
> who wander from your commandments

The cursed "insolent" ("arrogant," NAS) ones are named in Line A, then depicted in Line B's explanatory phrase, "who wander from your commandments." Accordingly, the essence of arrogance is not (as the postmodern would have it) the claim to know anything with certainty. Rather, arrogance is exposed as the refusal to bow the knee to God's Word.

Next we turn to Psalm 119:85—

> The insolent have dug pitfalls for me;
>> they do not live according to your law.

"The insolent" (again, "arrogant" in NAS) in Line A are once more explained in Line B. The ESV is less terse than the Hebrew, which bluntly has "who are not according to Your law." They do not line up with God's revelation.

What is arrogance, then? In God's eyes, there simply is no greater arrogance than rejecting Yahweh's viewpoint in favor of my own. It is grimly fascinating that some Christians abhor the believer who dares to think that he or she knows something from the Word. To such folks, claiming certainty on any given issue is the height of arrogance. They are certain that certainty is certainly bad.

By contrast, it is the height of arrogance to have a word from God and refuse to trust it by incorporating it into our way of thinking and living. To do that is to commit two fundamental sins:

1. It is to ape the primal Serpent, by confronting a word from God with that "Has God really said…?", which always evolves into rejection and denial. It is nothing other than arrogance posing as humility.

2. It is to exalt my judgment over God's judgment. This may not be my direct claim, but how else can it be analyzed? I have God's ruling on a matter, but I prefer another view. What can that possibly be, but finding another's thoughts and conclusions (my own) more compelling than God's? It is arrogance posing as open-mindedness.

Fear of Man (Prov. 29:25)

> The fear of man lays a snare,
>> but whoever trusts in the LORD is safe.

The noun translated "fear" is *ḥerdâ*. It is a feminine noun meaning trembling, fear,[9] anxiety. The noun is built from the verb meaning to tremble, be terrified. We find it used literally of mountains trembling in an earthquake, of islands, and of people.[10] The verb is used in Exodus 19:18 of smoke-swaddled Mount Sinai shaking violently under the weight of Yahweh's descent.

---

[9] HALOT, article חֲרָדָה.
[10] See BDB, article חֲרָדָה.

For this reason, BDB translates this phrase *ḥerdaṯ 'āḏām* here as "trembling before man," which well brings out the meaning. This is a person who trembles with anxiety about men and their opinions of him. He is absorbed with concern over such questions as—

- What do *They* think of me?
- Am I well-liked and respected?
- Am I seen as reasonable, deep, nuanced, balanced?
- What can I do to widen the circle of my admirers, and avoid giving offense?

In other words, it is being exactly the sort of persons who are endlessly drawn to "church growth" fads and methodologies, ever chasing the latest movement in the hopes of being better-liked by the world. To be addicted to the latest crowd-pleasing craze is to be motivated by fear of man.

Solomon is warning us against running our lives by the opinions of people who are not walking with God. He would have us trust God, rather than shrink back from saying and doing what pleases God for fear of catching heat for it. Solomon wants us to see that trusting Yahweh and fearing man are mutually exclusive.

David's greater Son would later say just the same thing, even more intensely. The Lord Jesus revealed that this attitude not only is *damaging*, but can be *damning* as well:

> "How are you able to believe, while *you are* accepting glory from one another, and *yet* you do not seek the glory which is from the only God?" (John 5:44 DJP; cf. Matt. 10:28)

The Pharisees were obsessed with remaining in good standing with their little religious community, which they were assured was correct and straight. In this community, Jesus was an outcast, and those who believed in and followed Him were coming under increasingly open and intense hostility. None of the VIPs believed in Jesus (John 7:48–49)—and that was sufficient reason to shun Him.

Therefore, Jesus says that it is not possible for a man to believe savingly while he is in hot pursuit of popularity. This fear of man would snare them to eternal doom. Spurgeon aptly quotes Thomas Manton: "The soul that cannot entirely trust God, whether man be pleased or displeased, can never long be true to Him;

for while you are eyeing man you are losing God, and stabbing Christianity at the very heart."[11]

Trust in Yahweh: Putting it Together (Prov. 3:5–7)

Perhaps one of the best-known, yet most-misunderstood "trust" passages in all of the Bible is Proverbs 3:5–7. When we look closely at these beloved words, we shall see a number of Biblical themes uniting in a vitally important message.

The Larger Section

Proverbs 3:1–12 forms a unit with a distinctive pattern. Read it through, and you will note that the verses alternate in sense: first an exhortation, then a consequence. For instance, verse 1 bids the son to memorize his father's teaching; verse 2 then promises life and peace. Verse 3 urges the son not to let steadfast love and truth forsake him; verse 4 promises that this is the key to favor with God and man. And so it continues (with slight variation) through the section.[12]

As I will demonstrate, we must keep this flow in mind, lest we yank any part of verses 5–7 from their intended thought-flow and miss Solomon's point.

Exposition of Verse 5

> Trust unto Yahweh with all your heart,
> > and unto your own discernment do not keep leaning. (DJP)

The common view

The danger with being familiar with a verse is that one assumes an unwarranted level of understanding. These words are so familiar and well-loved that many feel no need to think them through carefully or Biblically. As a result, this verse is more often misused than used as intended by Solomon, or by the God who inspired him to write these words.

Many assume that the meaning of the verse runs like this: to "trust in Yahweh with all your heart" is to have the very deepest feelings of confidence in God, to feel sure that He will take care of me, to feel good about God and His fatherly

---

[11] C. H. Spurgeon, *My Sermon Notes, Volumes 1 & 2: Genesis to Malachi*, 199 (Bellingham, WA: Logos Research Systems, Inc., 2009).

[12] Waltke sees 3:1–12 as a lecture consisting of "six quatrains, each of which presents one (v. 9), two (vv. 1, 3, 7, 11), or three admonitions (vv. 5, 6a) in the odd verses and a motivating argument in the even verses, containing one (vv. 4, 6b) or two promises (vv. 2, 8, 10), or a reason (v. 12)" (Waltke, *Proverbs*, 1:238–239).

care. To "not lean on your own understanding" is piously to refuse to think or analyze with my own mind, but simply to wait in silence on God without understanding, to trust that He will bypass my mind and send me the leadings and feelings that I will need in order to handle any situation. Or He will simply control the situation without my needing to engage, mentally or volitionally, in any way.

The more biblical view

Let us apply some steps in Biblical interpretation, one by one, to understand these verses in the way intended by Solomon.

First, we must analyze the Hebrew parallelism. Two verbs are paired: "trust," in Line A, parallels "lean" in Line B. Therefore, the idea of "trust" is made more specific in the image of seeking and finding support. Kidner sees the idea of the verbs as related to each other, noting a suggestion from G. R. Driver "that the Heb. for *trust* had originally the idea of lying helplessly face downwards."[13]

Then we turn to the prepositional phrases. "Unto Yahweh" in the first line is opposed to "unto your own discernment" in the second.[14] These are two rival ways of thinking, two antagonists. The one leaves me locked into my own inborn foolishness and waywardness (Prov. 12:15; 22:15; cf. Psa. 51:5). The other puts me in the way of God.

Note, too, that "Yahweh" is laid in contrast with "your own discernment." Solomon has in mind a mental/volitional process, not an emotional vibration. Knowing God affects not merely our feelings, but our entire mental grid.

This truth is highlighted when we note the additional prepositional phrase in Line A, "with all your heart." We recall the Biblical meaning of "heart," discussed earlier. In the Bible, the heart is not "the seat of the emotions." Rather, the heart is the center of thinking, treasuring, and deciding. It is the mind. Thus our entire thinking is to bear the impress of the Lordship of God.

Finally we must apply the context of Proverbs, beginning with the broad context and ending with the decisive near context. Does Proverbs teach— *ever*—that we should wait mystically upon God, minds passive and all a-quiver?

---

[13] Derek Kidner, *Proverbs,* 61. Kidner cites Psalm 22:9b and Jeremiah 12:5b as examples of this sense.

[14] The repetition of the Hebrew preposition אֶל (*'el,* "unto") underscores Solomon's intent to put the two options in stark opposition: one may trust *unto* Yahweh, or lean *unto* his own discernment—but he may not do both. They are contradictories.

Or does Proverbs rather teach that we must learn, understand, memorize, and put into practice the words of God?

In response, we're tempted merely to gesture at the book itself, and rest our case. What possible purpose did God have in mind when He moved Solomon to write this book, if He wished His children to be passive, reactive, gelatinous mystics? Why load a book with practical warnings and calls to thought and action, only then to turn and bid His children to float along like God's little jellyfish?

More specifically, we could call to mind Proverbs 1:2–6. There, Solomon says in so many words that the whole point of the book is to serve as an education for skill in godly living. He would provide us *things* to learn and ponder. He absolutely intended intensive mental activity as a result, and as a natural component of fearing Yahweh. We gain God's perspective, embrace it, absorb it, and then act on it.

Solomon's assumption is that we do not natively possess that understanding ourselves. We are neither born with it, nor does it simply "come to us" as we watch and wait in pious immobility. If we had the knowledge of all of these truths either naturally or directly supernaturally, we would need no book of Proverbs.

This is reinforced in Proverbs 2:1–6, which we studied in-depth earlier. We must seek, memorize, analyze; and we must do it with earnest, sweaty diligence. Otherwise, we can expect no other word nor hint from God.

In fact, we could simply ask: Does any part of Proverbs teach that our minds per se are our enemies? Is there any hint that the truly godly man will not fully employ his mind?

In response, we could point to a battery of verses from Proverbs, with brief comments, remembering that "heart" always refers to *the center of thinking, treasuring, and deciding*.

For instance, in 2:2 the son is urged to incline his *heart* to understanding. It is something he must do, and it is a specifically intellectual undertaking. Again, in 4:23 we see that the way we live flows from our hearts, because our hearts are the nursery of our convictions and values. We must guard that nursery, which calls for intense spiritual and intellectual action. Proverbs 6:18 condemns "a heart that devises wicked plans"—and a planning heart is an intellectually-active heart. Here the activity is evil. God does not hate people who plan (see 16:1, 6; 19:21), but He does hate those who plan evil.

A better use of our heart is found in 6:21's call to bind God's words on our hearts always. This is figurative language calling for the intellectual activity of memorization. Further, the activity is urged on us, not the Holy Spirit. To attempt to shrug this God-given responsibility back onto God would be the rankest form of pious hypocrisy. Similarly, 7:3 bids us bind God's Word on our fingers, again promoting the rigorous discipline of memorization. After all, it is the "wise of heart" who "will receive commandments" and hold onto them (10:8). The heart moves one to learn, memorize, and obey commands. There is no praise here for him who is empty of heart, or "yielded to the Infinite" of heart.

As a result of this disciplined mental activity, "Wisdom rests in the heart of a man of understanding" (14:33), in his mind. Thus wisdom, and not a pious vacuum, fills the heart of the person whom God praises. This wise man must use his mind to plan his way (16:1, 9; 19:21). That's right: God intends that we use our hearts (=minds) to make plans. There is no comfort in these verses for the person who avoids analytical thought in the name of trusting Yahweh with all his heart. God means us to use our minds to focus on, acquire, understand and retain His wisdom (18:15; 22:17; 23:12). ❧

Aside: misuse of the heart

If Solomon is not warning against intellectual activity per se, then what is he cautioning us against doing? We are to invest all our intellectual, volitional, and treasuring powers in trusting Yahweh, and not lean on our own understanding.

We may understand Solomon better by means of a brief detour to Proverbs 28:26—

> He who trusts in his own heart—he is stupid!
> But he who walks in wisdom—he will be delivered! (DJP)

The contrast seen in the parallelism is instructive. The opposite of trusting in one's own heart is not having an empty heart that vacantly trusts God in a passive, intellectually-comatose way. Rather, the opposite of trusting in one's own heart is *walking in the light of God's revealed wisdom*. One cannot walk in wisdom without knowing wisdom, without the intellectual activities of learning, analyzing, memorizing, and applying. Therefore, trusting in one's own heart will have to mean the opposite of walking in God's revealed wisdom.

A parallel idea is found in Jeremiah 7:23–24, with Yahweh's lament that Israel did not heed His call to repent and obey, because they "walked in their own counsels and the stubbornness of their evil hearts, and went backward and not forward" (NAS). Israel's problem was not that they thought too much. Rather, their problem was that they thought too stupidly, too stubbornly, too rebelliously, too autonomously. Their problem was their refusal fully to employ their intellects in learning and obeying the Word of God.

Therefore, trusting in one's own heart means trusting one's own native, inborn, fallen wisdom, independently and in defiance of the revealed wisdom of Yahweh. We see this vividly in Jeremiah 17:5–8, where Yahweh curses the man whose heart turns from Yahweh to trust in man, and blesses the man who trusts in Him instead.

This passage is similar in intent to Proverbs 3:5ff. In fact, it is conceivable that Jeremiah had Solomon's words in mind. In Jeremiah's prophecy, Yahweh says that reliance upon mere human wisdom, in rebellion against Yahweh, brings God's curse. For this rebellion, the cure is not to empty the mind so as to achieve a passive, empty, vapidly pseudo-pious attitude of contentless "trust." Rather, the only cure is to fill the mind with God's Word and wisdom, and to understand and obey Him thereby.

The immediate context is to be found, of course, in the immediately-preceding verses: Proverbs 3:1–4—

> My son: my law, do not forget,
>   and my commandments, let your heart observe;
>
> 2 Because length of days, and years of life,
>   and peace will they add to you.
>
> 3 Loving-kindness[15] and faithfulness,[16] let them not leave you;
>   bind them upon your neck,
>   write them upon the tablet of your heart,
>
> 4 And you will find grace and good intelligence
>   in the sight[17] of God and of man. (DJP)

---

15 Or "loyalty," "covenant-kindness."
16 Or "truth."
17 Literally "eyes."

Mark well that these are the words that frame our verse. What does Solomon say, in them? How do they bear on verse 5?

Solomon has urged us to learn and retain understanding from the very words of God. Look at the king's terminology:

- "my law, do not forget" (v. 1)
- "My commandments, let your heart observe" (v. 1)
- "Loving-kindness and faithfulness, let them not leave you" (v. 3)
- "Bind them upon your neck" (v. 3)
- "Write them upon the tablet of your heart" (v. 3)

These are intellectual activities that Solomon has just urged upon us. We must keep all this in mind, if we wish to understand what Solomon meant by trusting in Yahweh, as opposed leaning on our own understanding.

Conclusion

Given all this, what particularly will Solomon be saying in Proverbs 3:5, when the nearer and further context are plugged in? We have two choices:

1. *Common* view: Solomon is saying, "Don't try to understand. Don't use your mind at all. Just feel trustful of God, lean blindly on Him, accept things as they come, and let Him worry about absolutely everything."

2. *Preferred* view: Solomon is saying, "Do not lean on mere human understanding, but trust God enough to study and learn and depend on His revealed understanding, which I am teaching you in this book."[18]

Illustration: my dear wife is an engineer, working in HVAC (designing heating and air conditioning for buildings). She is an expert, while I can barely even understand what she does. In fact, our running joke is that I say a room is cooled by blowing in cold air, she tries patiently to explain that it is really cooled by sucking out hot air... and hilarity ensues.

If I were to begin work with her as a lowly draftsman, and she were giving me direct guidance, she might conclude her instructions by saying, "Trust me"—particularly if I found her instructions difficult or challenging.

By saying "Trust me," what would Valerie be urging? Would she mean, "Have

---

[18] The first reference would be to the book of Proverbs, but by extension the point would apply to all of Scripture.

good feelings about me, just sit there motionless, and let me do everything"? Or could it be, "Have a positive attitude, and do what you feel like doing"?

Or would Valerie not rather mean, "From what you know about my character and qualifications and accomplishments, you can take my word that I know what I am doing. So trust me enough to follow my directions and do what I say"?

Clearly, the latter would be her meaning—as it is Solomon's meaning, in Proverbs 3:5.

Summary

At issue is whose understanding will rule my life: mine, or Yahweh's? If mine, then I can trust my own heart, be a fool, and invite ruin. If Yahweh's, then I trust His revelation wholeheartedly for my thinking and decision-making.

Exposition of Verse 6

> In all your ways know Him,
>> and He Himself will straighten your paths. (DJP)

"In All Your Ways"

The "ways" refer to life's pursuits, undertakings.[19] The phrase conveys the idea of all the details of life. No part or portion of life is "off limits" to God. The man or woman who says that he keeps his _____ separate from his "religion" is a stranger to this verse. The earth is the Lord's, and all those who fill it. Therefore, no segment of life is beyond God's purview. Christ's Lordship must mark the believer's behavior at home, at work, and at worship equally.

"Know Him"

This is a difficult word to translate and interpret. It is but one word in Hebrew, a verb with a pronoun-suffix: דָעֵהוּ (*dāʿēhû*), literally "know-Him." As we saw earlier, the Hebrew verb translated "know" means more than mere intellectual awareness.[20] To know is to be involved with, to relate to, even to experience. So, we could render this, "Be involved with Him, relate to Him."[21]

---

[19] Cf. 1:19, 31; 2:8, 12–13, 15; 3:31; 4:11; 10:9; 12:15; 14:2, 12, 14; 15:19; 16:2, 7.

[20] See the discussion in our opening study of 1:1–7.

[21] Discussing this verb in another verse, James Kugel makes this thought-provoking assertion: "In Near Eastern treaty language, 'know' was regularly used in the sense of 'acknowledge as sovereign'" (*The Idea of Biblical Poetry*, Baltimore: Johns Hopkins, 1981, 9). Though it would

Solomon's idea, I think, is to relate to God in all areas of life. Perhaps it is something like what I might say to a salesman at a convention, "You be sure to love your wife at that convention." He might reply, "But my wife won't be there." My response would be, "I know; so love your wife at that convention."

I trust that my meaning would be clear: he is to live out the implications of his love for his wife, even while away at a convention. Awareness of his marital vows and relationship will follow him wherever he goes, and affect what he says and does. Similarly, Solomon means that the knowledge of God is to affect every area of our lives—all of our ways.

It is more than possible that Solomon has in mind his father's final charge to him:

> "And you, Solomon my son, know the God of your father and serve him with a whole heart and with a willing mind, for the LORD searches all hearts and understands every plan and thought. If you seek him, he will be found by you, but if you forsake him, he will cast you off forever." (1 Chron. 28:9)

The command to know God is coupled here with the ideas of serving Him with a whole heart and a willing mind. It is a complete dedication of one's life to relating to God wholly, as individuals, citizens, friends, community-members, children, and spouses. It is an existential application of that wholehearted love that God commands (Deut. 6:5).

"He will make your paths straight"

The verb translated "He will make...straight" is the Hebrew יְיַשֵּׁר (*y'yaššēr*). The verb *yāšar* means to be straight, right, smooth, both literally and in a moral/spiritual sense. The root *y-š-r* is found in many forms in Proverbs, whether in referring to "the upright" (*y'šārîm*, 2:7, 21; 11:3, etc.), "equity" (*mêšārîm*, 1:3), or the like.

Here the specific form (*y'yaššēr*) is the Pi'el imperfect, in this case giving the verb a *causative* idea. Therefore, rather than "to be straight," it means "to make straight."[22] The imperfect (or "prefix," or *yqtl*, depending on what grammar you consult) aspect has nothing inherently to do with time, though the future

---

make good sense here, I could find no scholar who makes that connection with this verse.

[22] Cf. BDB, article יָשַׁר.

translation in English is appropriate here.[23] The verb *yāšar* used with the synonym *derek* can mean to make a path "free from obstacles, successful,"[24] or it can mean to make it morally/spiritually straight. Here it is used with the noun *'ōraḥ*, as in 9:15, where it means to be making one's way morally straight.

What exactly does this verse mean? Several views have been offered.

Wrong turn: promise of personal guidance. The worst misuse is also the most popular: Proverbs 3:6 is portrayed as guaranteeing individual semi-revelatory guidance in non-moral issues. This misunderstanding is so widespread that someone, somewhere is probably abusing the text this way as you read. Put on the mystic's torture-rack, this text is forced to say, "Pray, and God will show you what to do—whom to marry, what job to take, which car to buy, what words to use."

The problems with this view are several, and they are fatal.

1. The verb does not mean "direct" or "guide"; it means to make straight, or to make smooth.

2. The immediate context has everything to do with walking according to God's written revelation, and nothing to do with receiving fresh, direct semi-revelation.

3. The larger context of Proverbs contain no texts—zero—directing us to search for mystical, almost-prophetic sort-of revelation to make life's decisions. What we find instead is God's revealed Word, the responsibility of wise decision-making, and Yahweh's sovereign overruling. That is what Proverbs is all about.

Second-best view: promise of circumstantial success. A better view is one held by many commentators: basically, this is a promise of success in one's endeavors, as one walks with God. It is common for commentators to cite examples such as Isaiah 45:13, which uses the same verb and noun as in Proverbs 3:6.

---

[23] Not to give anyone a headache, but the Biblical Hebrew verb-system (unlike English) is not primarily concerned with time-frame, per se. Hebrew verbs are not past, present, future *tense*. While grammarians differ, the best view—grossly overgeneralized—thinks in terms of perfect or imperfect *aspect*. Thus, generally: the perfect views action as completed, the imperfect as not completed—whether that action is in the past, the present, or the future. Though naturally the past idea finds itself expressed in the perfect form, and the future in the imperfect.

[24] Cf. BDB, article יָשַׁר.

I have stirred him up in righteousness, and *I will make all his ways level*; he shall build my city and set my exiles free, not for price or reward," says the LORD of hosts (emphasis added)

It is possible that Solomon has this idea in mind, as a general principle. This was the interpretation I favored, until a fresh reading of the Hebrew text compelled me to another conclusion.

Best view: promise of moral/spiritual straightness. Appeals to word-use in Isaiah and other later writers should not carry as much weight as the usage in Proverbs itself. Let us take a closer look.

Proverbs is a book of *two ways*.[25] With the creative breadth of a master artist whose palette is filled with brilliant colors, Solomon sets up stark contrasts: wisdom vs. folly; righteous vs. wicked; and life vs. death, among others. For each of these, he has an array of synonyms at his disposal.

One neglected, paired cluster of words would be those used by Solomon to contrast what is *straight* with what is *crooked*, perhaps as a subcategory of the contrast of righteous versus wicked.[26] I have informally counted at least five different Hebrew terms Solomon uses to denote the "crooked" in Proverbs, describing the bad side of the contrast. To be crooked is to be out of line with God and His will, His wisdom. A small representation would be:

...men whose paths are crooked [*'iqqᵉšîm*],
  and who are devious [*nᵉlôzîm*] in their ways. (2:15)

The integrity of the upright [straight, *yᵉšārîm*] guides them,
  but the crookedness [*uᵉselep*] of the treacherous destroys them. (11:3)

Those of crooked heart [*'iqqᵉšê-lēb*] are an abomination to the LORD,
  but those of blameless ways are his delight. (11:20)

A man is commended according to his good sense,
  but one of twisted [*uᵉnaᵃwê*] mind is despised. (12:8)

---

[25] Daniel P. Bricker, "The Doctrine Of The 'Two Ways' In Proverbs," (*Journal of the Evangelical Theological Society* 38, no 4 (1995):501–517.

[26] Though if someone wanted to argue for it as a subdivision of wisdom versus folly, I could agree. To Solomon, being wicked is really stupid, and godliness is the wisest course a person could follow.

> Whoever walks in uprightness [straightness, *yošrô*] fears the LORD,
>> but he who is devious [*nᵉlôz*] in his ways despises him. (14:2)

> The way of the guilty is crooked [*hᵃpakpak*],
>> but the conduct of the pure is upright [*yāšār*]. (21:8)

Literally from start (1:3) to finish (29:27), Solomon contrasts the morally/spiritually "straight" and the morally/spiritually "crooked."

We can see an extended series of these contrasts in Proverbs 2:9–15. This follows the section we studied in Chapter 4, and lays out the second of the benefits of seeking wisdom diligently and prayerfully. See the constant clashing of the straight and the crooked ways:

> Then you will understand righteousness and justice
>> and equity [*ûmêšārîm*, straightness], every good path [*maʿgal*];

> ¹⁰ for wisdom will come into your heart,
>> and knowledge will be pleasant to your soul;

> ¹¹ discretion will watch over you,
>> understanding will guard you,

> ¹² delivering you from the way [*derek*] of evil,
>> from men of perverted speech [literally "speaking perverse things," *tahpukôt*],

> ¹³ who forsake the paths of [*ʾōrḥôt*] uprightness [*yōšer*, straightness]
>> to walk in the ways of [*darkê*] darkness,

> ¹⁴ who rejoice in doing evil
>> and delight in the perverseness [*tahpukôt*][27] of evil,

> ¹⁵ men whose paths [*ʾōrḥōtêhem*] are crooked [*ʿiqqᵉšîm*],
>> and who are devious [*nᵉlôzîm*] in their ways [*maʿgᵉlôtām*].

Again and again Solomon warns against the twisted, the crooked, the perverse, as the way on which God frowns—the way of folly. These refer not to circumstantial difficulties, but to deviations from God's revealed, moral will.

By contrast, Solomon repeatedly holds out the straight way, the straight character, the straight path, as the way of wisdom and blessing. This suggests a

---

[27] Eight of the nine occurrences of *tahpukôt* are in Proverbs.

mental image of God's way as a straight road; any variance is "off true" (cf. 4:25–27). The king employs several variations of the *y-š-r* ("straightness") root, such as:

> …to receive instruction in wise dealing,
>> in righteousness, justice, and equity [straightness, *mêšārîm*]. (1:3)

> who forsake the paths of [*'orḥôt*] uprightness [*yōšer*, straightness]
>> to walk in the ways of [*darkê*] darkness. (2:13)

> …for the devious person is an abomination to the LORD,
>> but the upright [*yešārîm*] are in his confidence. (3:32)

Again and again, the picture of the straight is not of good circumstances, but of godly character—as the crooked is not normally the disastrous situation, but the deviant character.[28]

For instance, note 15:21—"Folly is a joy to him who lacks sense, but a man of understanding walks straight ahead." The original wording of "walks straight ahead" is interesting. It is *yeyaššer-lāket* in Hebrew, using the same verb as in 3:6. The contrast isn't a circumstantially successful life versus a difficult one, but a foolish life versus a wise, godly life. To "make straight to walk" is not to enjoy smooth sailing, but to walk with wisdom and intelligence.

The noun translated "path" (*'ōraḥ*) is used both in the singular and plural in Proverbs. It regularly means lifestyle, behavior, course of life (1:19; 2:19; 22:25). It has to do with the moral/spiritual tenor of a man's life, whether godly (2:8, 13, 20; 4:18; 8:20; 10:17; 12:28) or godless (2:15; 4:14).

In sum

When Solomon urges us to "know" God in every department of our lives, then assures us that God Himself[29] will make our paths straight as a result, he is not saying that if we know God, things will go well for us. This may or may not follow.[30] Rather, the wise king is assuring us that if we have a close, vital relationship with God in all our lives, God Himself will cause us to have a godly, wise life that is morally and spiritually straight.

---

[28] It is true that, for Solomon's proverbic depictions, bad (ungodly) character generally leads to a bad (ruined) life, and vice-versa. But I would argue that this is secondary. The moral/spiritual is fundamental.

[29] The pronoun is added for emphasis in Hebrew.

[30] Cf. 16:19; 19:1, 22; 24:15–16; 28:6.

What Does it Mean? ⊙

Solomon's focus is characteristically practical. Solomon points to knowing God in all our ways. "Ways" refers to the details of life—our roles as worshiper, friend, spouse, parent, child, citizen, employer/employee, neighbor.

God has no interest in creating people who are "so heavenly-minded that they are no earthly good." God will not be compartmentalized, set in a safe corner and told to mind His business. Everything is His business.

God is too massive to agree to be confined to some small space. As Creator and Lord of all, God's sovereignty and His authority extend to everything. Therefore the man, woman, or child who truly knows God will reflect that knowledge of God in every compartment of his life. God is very interested in how you and I conduct ourselves, 24 hours a day, in every room of the house and down every street and byway of the city. A knowledge of God that leaves no imprint on all of life is a barren, fruitless, and useless theoretical faith that will neither save nor sanctify.

Tell Me How

Solomon would never have meant his readers to have fine little theories of knowledge and straightness and crookedness, and leave it all on paper. None was more eager to put truth into sandals and get it walking than Solomon was. So we must ask:

- *How* do I know God from within the details of my life?
- *How* do I enjoy His "straightening" of the paths of my life?

Scripture alone gives the answer.

Psalm One

One of the most delightful depictions of this kind of life may well have been penned by Solomon's father:

> Oh, the blessings of the man who does not walk in the advice
> of wicked ones,
> and in the way of sinners does not stand,
> and in the seat of scorners does not sit.
>
> 2 But instead in the law of Yahweh is his delight,
> and in His law he keeps musing—day and night.

³ And he shall be like a tree
>   transplanted by channels of water,
>   which keeps giving its fruit in its season,
>   and whose leaf does not wither,
>   and everything that he does prospers.[31]

⁴ Not so, the wicked!
>   But instead they are as chaff which the wind drives away.

⁵ For this reason the wicked will not stand in the judgment,
>   nor sinners in the community of the righteous.

⁶ Because Yahweh knows the way of the righteous ones,
>   but the way of wicked ones will perish. (DJP)

This is the picture of the godly man, in the pursuits of his life. He is *blessed*, which is to say that he enjoys the good hand of God bringing joy to his life (v. 1). His conduct distinguishes him, because his worldview is different. In the living of his life, he neither seeks the counsel, nor the status, nor the company of rebels against God (v. 1). Rather, he actively reflects on and engages the word of Yahweh throughout the day (v. 2).

As a consequence, his way is fruitful and successful (as God defines success; v. 3). Most of all, "Yahweh knows the path of the righteous ones," which is to say that God is personally and lovingly involved in his life as he goes about his various pursuits. This is how that "blessed" man knows God and is known by Him: he is mentally occupied with the Word of God in all the contexts of his life, in every part of the day.

Psalm 119:9

This anonymous song is an extended love-poem dedicated to the Word of God. In this verse, the author poses and answers a critical question:

> With what shall a lad keep his way pure?
>   By keeping watch over *it* according to Your Word. (DJP)

What is good for a "lad" is no less true for a "lass," or for biddies or codgers. The only way to keep our way—our lifestyle, behavior, pursuits—pure is by

---

[31] Or "in everything he does, he prospers."

keeping watch over it according to God's Word. This means that God's Word is the standard, and constant conscious reference-point for the godly person's life.

Bring It Home

The reader might just ask himself two questions right now:

1. What am I? (Man, woman, child; spouse, single; employer, employee; citizen, government official; etc.)

2. What does God's Word specifically say to me (as a man, woman, spouse, etc.)?

The idea Scripture is pressing on us is that we must

- Embrace God's viewpoint
- Absorb His Word
- Trust Him so much as to learn and choose His way over our own, and
- Live out the life of an obedient student of the Word of God.

Exposition of Verse 7

Do not be wise in your own eyes,
    Fear Yahweh, and turn away from evil. (DJP)

Exposition

This verse is free from the controversies that attended the previous verses. In fact, we find here strong confirmation of the interpretation given above concerning verse 5:

- The opposite of being wise in my own eyes is not searching for nor heeding some "inner voice" of God.
- The opposite of being wise in my own eyes is turning away from evil, which I can only do by heeding the written Word of God.

Solomon has in mind our embracing that wisdom which can be gained only through God's Word, and shunning the merely human wisdom which rises up in opposition.

Application

There is, as we have seen, no greater arrogance than the refusal to consider God's Word above every other factor. Every one of us is occasionally wise in our own eyes. But it is not when we try to conform to God's Word. Rather, every time we fail to consider God's Word in our ways, we are being wise in our own eyes. We do it every time we imagine we have a better way than God, or that His ways are insufficient.

The only remedy is careful and humble study of Scripture. For a person to seek to understand Scripture, and to do it, is the opposite of arrogance. True humility leads a person to humble himself to the point where he cares more about understanding and doing the wisdom of God than he cares about wisdom from any other source, including himself.

Summary of Proverbs 3:5–7

Solomon told us right up-front that everything in his book is to be related to the fear of Yahweh, without which there is no knowledge nor wisdom. When we make that connection, we see that Blocher was right to see this as a commentary on what the fear of Yahweh means: it is "the renouncing of autonomy, and trusting acknowledgement of the LORD at every step of one's practical or intellectual progress."[32]

The Worship of Yahweh

Now let us consider somewhat briefly what Proverbs teaches about the practice of religion.[33] It has been alleged that Proverbs knows nothing of the religion of Israel. As we have already seen, this is far from true. The first verse alone, coupled with the dozens of occurrences of the covenant-name of the God of Israel, are ample refutation.

To those we may add the following elements.

Sacrifice

Proverbs 15:8—

The sacrifice of wicked *people* is an abomination to Yahweh,
    but the prayer of upright *people* is His delight. (DJP)

---

[32] Blocher, "The Fear of the Lord as the 'Principle' of Wisdom," *Tyndale Bulletin* 28 (1977): 17–18.

[33] I use "religion" of a belief in God that expresses itself in action. Obviously, I do not here mean "religion" in the popular, specialized sub-sense of a man-made system of works invented to earn the favor of God.

The "sacrifice" was a bloody offering. As such, it was enjoined by God, and this verse does not frown on that Divinely-instituted worship. The problem is not the offering, but the offerer.

"Wicked" people are rebellious against Yahweh. They have no intention of walking with Him in faith and obedience. Rather, here they "check the 'religion'-box" with outward observance. Perhaps they make a religious gesture to cover up for the sin which they have no intention of forsaking. If so, they are trying to mask internal corruption and impenitence by means of an outward show of piety.

In their book about the penal, substitutionary death of Christ for His people, Jeffery, Ovey and Sach note how the later prophets raised warnings about the misuse of sacrifice. Some mistakenly see the prophets as objecting to sacrifice per se, as they might also see this verse. But the authors observe that the Israelite problem to which the prophets and Solomon objected was *presumption*:

> The people seemed to think that so long as they continued to offer the occasional sacrifice, the moral demands of God's law could safely be overlooked. Such an attitude is condemned in Isaiah 1:11–17 and Jeremiah 7:21–24 (cf. 1 Sam. 15:22–23).[34]

Or perhaps the wicked are trying to manipulate God, as if by magic. Maybe they imagine that God will be won over by their sacrifice, brought over to see things their way and give them what they want. If so, they are practicing idolatry, because such bribes could never work on the God who sees the depths of the heart and weighs the inner man (Prov. 16:2; 17:3; 20:27; 21:2; 24:12).

Either way, this verse issues a stiff warning against merely formal worship, worship that is a matter of external acts which do not express a hearty faith. In so doing, Solomon both echoes and anticipates many similar refrains. Perhaps the classic text, which Solomon would have known, comes from 1 Samuel 15:22–23. Here, Saul has disobeyed God by failing to wipe out Amalek (vv. 8–9). When the prophet Samuel confronted him, Saul responded with some pious nonsense which the prophet swept aside with this trumpet-blast:

> "Has the LORD as great delight in burnt offerings and sacrifices, as in obeying the voice of the LORD? Behold, to obey is better than sacrifice, and to listen than the fat of rams. [23] For rebellion is as

---

[34] Steve Jeffery, Michael Ovey, and Andrew Sach, *Pierced for Our Transgressions* (Wheaton: Crossway Books, 2007), 50–51.

the sin of divination, and presumption is as iniquity and idolatry. Because you have rejected the word of the LORD, he has also rejected you from being king."

It may even be that Proverbs 15:8 is a compression of that story, for Saul's sacrifice was the sacrifice of a rebel, a man who put his judgment over God's.

Decades after Solomon, the prophet Isaiah will thunder against Israel's religious hypocrisy. Through Isaiah, Yahweh will tell the Jews that their sacrifices and feasts have become nauseating and repulsive to Him, and that He can stand them no longer (Isa. 1:10–17). He will harshly denounce their human traditions as empty worship, not being brought by believing, submissive hearts (Isa. 29:13–14). These words will be echoed by the Lord Jesus Himself, in denouncing the empty religious shows of those who hated Him (cf. Matt. 15:1–11).

Then, later still, the writer to the Hebrews will add a testimony that points around all the way back to the dawning days of human history. He speaks of Abel by faith offering to God "a more acceptable sacrifice than Cain," receiving God's attestation of his believing worship—for faith is the indispensable element in drawing near to God (Heb. 11:4, 6).

God despises the more impressive, costly, outward sacrifice offered by the man whose heart is not right with Him.

This proverb should provoke the man or woman who has perhaps been a faithful churchgoer, a loyal tither, diligent in every sort of show of religion—but always had a nagging unease of heart. It is possible to be very religious, and very lost. The task of earning God's favor by ever so many religious observances is hopeless. Even were we to do all we are required—which none of us does—we would merely be meeting the minimum owed, and leaving our sins unforgiven (cf. Luke 17:10). The only way to peace with God is through Jesus Christ (Rom. 5:1), on the basis of *His* infinitely-valuable sacrifice (Rom. 3:20–28).

Proverbs 21:3—

> To do righteousness and justice
>   is chosen by Yahweh above sacrifice. (DJP)

This proverb may be another example of a narrative being condensed into two lines. Specifically, it could also be a compression of 1 Samuel 15:22–23 into six little Hebrew words.

Clearly, Yahweh is not saying that He utterly negates sacrifice. He is the one who created the sacrificial system of Israel. This verse is not a denigration of sacrifices offered in believing obedience.

The principle behind this proverb should be easy for parents to understand. We always teach our children that they should apologize when they break or spill something, or if they wrong someone. If we are responsible, we also teach our children that it is better still to be more careful and wise, so as not to have to apologize in the first place. In fact, you might say, "To be wise and careful is chosen by parents above apologies."

This verse, I think, says the same thing: God does not want people who heedlessly do wrong and blithely commit injustice, because they know they can just pop by the Temple later and slice a lamb. Rather, God wants people who so believe in and love Him that they obey Him, and "do righteousness and justice."

Therefore, a godly walk is one part of acceptable worship to God.

Proverbs 21:27—

> The sacrifice of wicked *people* is an abomination;
>> how much more when one brings it with a scheme! (DJP)

We studied the idea of Line A under 15:8. This is what is called an *a fortiori* argument. That form amounts to saying, "If A is bad, A + B is worse." Specifically, Solomon is saying, "If it is *bad* for an unrepentant sinner to offer a sacrifice, it is *worse* for him to do it with an ulterior motive!"

The "scheme" (*zimmâ*) is the wicked man's scheme to get something out of God. It is saying, "I give You an offering, You bless my plans." Or, alternatively, it may be intended to impress others with a show of pious religiousness, as if to say, "Sure, you can trust me, folks, because I'm very religious. Look, here I am making my offering/waving my big black Bible."

But, as Solomon's father had heard, God sees the heart (2 Sam. 16:7). He cannot be "bought off" by us in this way, or in any other way. So outward shows of religion are not merely unhelpful, they are positively harmful.

Offerings (Prov. 3:9)

> Glorify Yahweh from your wealth,
>> and from the tops of all your income. (DJP)

Here we can see that Line B intensifies the thought of Line A. The verb is not repeated, so the thought of "glorifying" or "honoring" Yahweh dominates both lines. But the strong "your wealth" of Line A is made even more intense by "the tops of all your income" in B, using a Hebrew word built off the word for "head," and meaning "first and best"—or, as we say, "tops."

The principle is clear: keep God first. Give Him, not the leftovers, but the very best. He is a great King, and our gifts should reflect His honor. When people offer lame "seconds" and "remnants," it reflects poorly on their real thoughts of God (cf. Mal. 1:6–14).

The application to finances is plain enough, but we should not stop there. How does it reflect on the place of God in our lives, if we pray only when we've nothing better to do? If we start our day off with TV, the internet, or the papers, and then maybe cobble together a scant few sleepy and distracted moments hearing Him speak in His Word at the end of the day, as we drop off to sleep?

Prayer

Proverbs 15:8—

> The sacrifice of wicked *people* is an abomination to Yahweh,
> but the prayer of upright *people* is His delight. (DJP)

Of the two (sacrifice and prayer), sacrifice is of course the more outward and visually impressive. But God here says that it means a lot more to Him when a spiritually "straight"[35] person simply prays, with no outward show.

This is someone who is right in God's eyes through faith (cf. Gen. 15:6), who approaches out of love. The relatively quiet, relatively small, relatively un-"flashy" prayer of such a man or woman delights God more than the expensive, impressive offering of the unbelieving rebel.[36]

Prayer from a heart that is right with God, then, is one element of worship that pleases God.

This is greatly encouraging. It is easy to look at the Jonathan Edwardses and Charles Spurgeons of history, or to the leading lights of our day or of our church, and conclude that we haven't much to offer. We don't do big flashy works, we don't have massive ministries. We just aren't much.

---

[35] This is the literal meaning of the word translated "upright" (*yāšār*).

[36] Proverbs 28:9 will warn against using even prayer as this wicked man tries to use sacrifice.

But if what matters to us is what pleases God instead of what looks impressive, Solomon points the way. The proverb is particularly striking, coming as it does from the man who "offered as peace offerings to the LORD 22,000 oxen and 120,000 sheep" at the dedication of the Temple (1 Kings 8:63). Solomon tells us that it is the prayer of faith from the repentant, redeemed, loving heart that is Yahweh's pleasure.

Proverbs 15:29—

> Far is Yahweh from wicked *persons*,
> > but the prayer of righteous *persons* He hears. (DJP)

The form is interesting, a sort of chiasm. At each end of the verse we have "Far" and "He hears," and in the middle we have "wicked persons"—as such, period, no matter what they do—and "righteous persons."

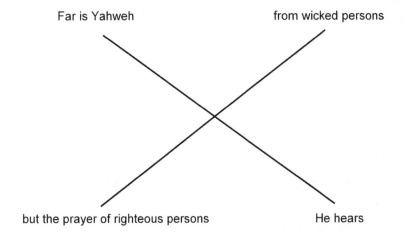

Toy brings in an element not in the proverb:[37]

> It is involved that the wicked may pray (that is, ask for some favor), but their prayer will not be favorably received. The case of a bad man's repenting is not considered; such a man, in the view of the OT. [sic], would, by his repentance, be transferred from the category of the wicked to that of the righteous.

---

[37] Toy, 316.

But the wicked man is not depicted as praying. It doesn't matter what he does, whether he prays or doesn't, whether he gives offerings or steals, whether he kisses his wife or rapes a stranger, he is wicked, and Yahweh is far from him.

By contrast, it is implied that Yahweh is close to the righteous, and that is why He hears their prayers. A father will hear his child's requests, if that child is sitting in his lap; and so we are assured that those who are right in God's eyes have His ear, because they are close to him (cf. Psa. 73:28; Prov. 3:32 [NAS]).

The next verse is a shocker. I am convinced that most Christians have never even seen it.

Proverbs 28:9—

> He who turns his ear away from listening to the Law,[38]
>> even his prayer is an abomination. (DJP)

It is popular in Christian circles today to exalt the importance of prayer to the most dizzying heights. Many would say that prayer is the most important element in the Christian life. Prayer is held to be the sovereign key to holiness, power, effectiveness, revival, and personal spiritual growth. It is not uncommon for those newly professing faith in Christ to be told that the single most crucial activity that they can pursue is prayer.

I daresay that this verse calls some of these lofty claims and notions into serious question. We must remember at the outset three important Biblical truths about prayer:

1. Prayer is you talking to God—it is not God talking to you.[39]

2. Prayer is anything you say to God—it has nothing to do with God saying something to you.

3. Prayer is not a dialogue.

In Proverbs 28:9, then, God says that if you and I are not listening to His Word,[40] prayer is worse than a waste of time. Solomon says it is so bad, that it is an *abomination* (tô'ēḇâ) to Yahweh.

---

38 The Hebrew text has no capital letters. I capitalize "Law" for *tôrâ* here to reflect my understanding that Solomon has particular reference to the written Word, such portion of Scripture as was possessed in his day.

39 When a man talks to God, it is *prayer*; when God talks to a man, it is *revelation*.

40 John A. Kitchen is correct: while "the 'law' normally refers to the wisdom instruction of a father or teacher...here, given its intimate connection with God it probably has reference to God's

We must not miss the force of this condemnation. "Prayer" is meant to be a drawing near to God with adoration, confession, supplication. Solomon says that when the person praying is one who turns a deaf ear to God's law, "even" his prayer—even that act meant to win God's heart—is unspeakably repulsive to God.[41]

In the books that would have informed Solomon's use of the word, an "abomination" is a disgusting, repelling moral offense against God, such as—

- homosexuality (Lev. 18:22)
- idolatry (Deut. 7:25–26)
- apostasy (Deut. 13:14)
- transvestitism (Deut. 22:5)
- burning one's child alive to a false god (2 Kings 16:3)

Application

This is a truth that needs to be both laid to heart and broadcast. While Biblically defined prayer is a wonderful and vital thing, it is easily abused. It is, itself, a no-commitment endeavor. A person can pray heartily and often, while walking in stubborn defiance of God and His Word. No one can observe externally whether or not his prayer is passing the ceiling, nor offered to any deity but himself. There are no clashes of thunder that distance God-pleasing prayer from its opposite.

Worse, the deluded individual can comfort himself that he is a great and godly man… because, after all, he *prays*, and prayer (we are endlessly told) is a powerful thing.

The Biblical counter needs to be sounded out loud and clear. Not only is prayer in and of itself utterly devoid of power and benefit, but the prayer of a man who ignores God's Word is positively harmful. If we do not hearken to God speaking in His Word, not only does He not hear our prayers, but they are offensive and disgusting to Him.[42]

Law given through Moses (cf. v. 7 also)" (*Proverbs*, 632). The point merits stress: "listening to God's Word" always and only refers to heeding His revealed Word as now recorded in Scripture.

[41] "So much for religious exercises as a sop to conscience," Kidner tersely observes (162).

[42] I phrase myself carefully. Anyone who reads this book has access to the Word of God in printed form. People who have been or are literally unable to access printed copies of the Word are not under consideration at this point.

The first and greatest need of Christendom is not prayer. The first and greatest need of Christendom is the preaching, teaching, studying, embrace, and faithful practice of the Word of God. That will give birth to prayers that please God.

Prayers from a defiant heart repel God and damage the rebellious hypocrite who offers them.

Yahweh and Other Relationships: Proverbs 16:7

The Principle Stated:

> When a man's ways please [Yahweh],
> > he makes even his enemies to be at peace with him.

Approaching a Correct Understanding

At first glance: this verse seems to be saying that if we just concentrate on pleasing God, He will see to it that everyone gets along with us. However, we must recall that proverbs are general principles, not iron-clad, unconditional guarantees.

This verse is a classic example of this principal. Think of Abel, Noah, Moses; Elijah, Jeremiah, Ezekiel; Stephen, James, Paul; Luther, Calvin, Spurgeon—and above all, the Lord Jesus. What great and godly man hasn't been a contradiction to this verse, if it is read as a legal contract binding God always to make everything nice for the holy?

Additionally, we could point to a number of Scriptures which seem to indicate precisely the opposite principle, such as Matthew 5:10–11, Luke 6:26; John 15:18–21; and 2 Timothy 3:12.

Clearly this verse is not a guarantee of happy relationships for all godly people. What is it, then?

The Point

On what we might call the "lowest" level, God's Word contains wisdom principles to help us win and retain worthwhile friends, and to pacify strife (i.e. Prov. 15:1; 17:14). This is—other things being equal—a promised benefit of wisdom. Recall Proverbs 3:1–4, with its commendation of "loving-kindness and faithfulness" that will enable us to "find grace and good intelligence in the sight of God and of man" (vv. 3–4 DJP).

It would, however, be more to the point of Proverbs 16:7 to say this: my primary relationship must be with God. If I am right with Him, he can put all horizontal relationships in order.[43]

Here we have numerous illustrations in Scripture itself. For instance, Joseph had seen what Yahweh could do, in reconciling his brothers to him (Gen. 39:1–4). Solomon's father David had experienced respite from hostilities under God's hand, at God's will (1 Sam. 24:15–22). Solomon himself saw how God could pacify his enemies (1 Kings 5:3, 4).

The fullest play is seen in the life of our Lord Jesus. Remember that countless people hated Him, and still hate Him today, precisely because none has ever pleased God as He did and does. They hate God. He loves and mirrors God, so they hate Him (cf. John 7:7; 15:18, 23). His own nation rejected Him *en masse* (John 1:11).

However in our day, the Spirit of God is working in people's hearts to transform them from hating Him to hearing and loving Him (Acts 2:37ff.; 16:14). And one day, we read, He will bring the nation of Israel to repent *en masse*, and embrace Jesus as their Messiah (Zech. 12:10–13:2). Ultimately, every knee will bow and every tongue will confess Christ's Lordship, precisely because His ways fully pleased His father (Phil. 2:5–11).

At present, then, we must follow Him who bade us put God and His kingdom above all things (Matt. 6:33) and relationships (Matt. 10:34–38), knowing that we must suffer with Him if we are to reign with Him (Rom. 8:17; 2 Tim. 2:11–13).

We examined Proverbs 16:7 as touching our relationship with Yahweh, and as identifying that as necessarily the central relationship of our lives. Let us now turn to the horizontal and see what wisdom Solomon has for us concerning human relationships.

Questions for Thought or Discussion

1. How is arrogance the opposite of trusting Yahweh?

2. What is the practical essence of arrogance?

3. How is the fear of man the opposite of trusting Yahweh?

---

[43] The reverse is also true: if God needs to discipline me, He can bring great pressure in horizontal relationships (see 1 Kings 11 for a distasteful lesson Solomon himself had to learn).

4. What is the common view of trusting Yahweh with all one's heart? What's wrong with that view?

5. What does it mean, concretely, to trust Yahweh with all your heart?

6. What does "in all your ways" mean?

7. What does it mean to "know Him" in all your ways?

8. What is the popular view of "He will direct your paths / make your paths straight"?

9. What do those words actually mean?

10 . How can sacrifice, which Yahweh commanded, be an abomination to Him?

11 . What relevance does the sacrifice issue have for the Christian?

12 . What is prayer? What is it not?

13 . Is it always appropriate to pray?

14 . When is it not only inappropriate, but positively offensive to God, to pray?

15 . What does it mean to put the vertical above the horizontal in relationships? In practical terms?

CHAPTER SIX

Skill in Godly Relationships

Beyond a doubt, our friendships are woven into the most intimate fabric of our lives. We mold our friends, and are molded by them. Our friends can help lift us to a godly walk, or lead us to disaster, like the cars of a train plunging over a cliff.

Thankfully, our Lord has given us wisdom to guide us through this determinative aspect of our lives.

PRELIMINARY WORDS OF CAUTION

Caution Against Isolation (Prov. 18:1)

Whoever isolates himself seeks his own desire;
he breaks out against all sound judgment.

This is the picture of the man who deliberately disassociates himself from society and from relationships: he is a social hermit. Solomon provides us with God's X-ray of such an attitude, a view which (as so often) does not reflect the man's view of himself.

This "loner" obviously feels that he has good reasons for his isolationism. The man himself may plead how bad others are. He may tell heart-breaking tales of how he has been burnt and stung in public situations. Or perhaps he feels himself to be absorbed with pursuits so lofty and noble that none can attain to his level.

All of these things may be at least partly true, as far as they go. We might grant some of what the recluse is saying.

God's vision, however, is most penetrating. God does not see this man as a noble pioneer, a lone beacon of light standing alone against the corruption and ugliness of the world.

Rather, God sees this man as a selfish fool.

Individualism?

There is such a thing as Biblical individualism, of course (cf. famously Ezek. 18). God saves and judges us on an individual basis. Each of us will stand before His judgment and answer for himself (Rom. 14:12). Further, each must receive Christ by faith individually, and become a child of God individually. God has no grandchildren (John 1:12; 3:16).

Each of us must take full responsibility for himself and bear his own load (Gal. 6:5). We must not have as our goal in life to be sponges, vacuums of bottomless need, forever sucking life and time and resources from others while never loving anyone enough to take measures to give and serve and spend ourselves.

Context Under the Law of Moses

Still, no man is saved as an island. Think of Solomon's own day. Each Israelite was born into the community of faith, at least formally. Each Israelite was involved in communal, group-spirituality from his very birth. Each Israelite was commanded to love his neighbor (Lev. 19:18). Each Israelite was commanded to take part in group worship, and obliged by the very nature of God's covenant with Israel publicly and corporately to worship God in contrition and in thanksgiving.[1]

There simply was no provision for the man who wanted to have his own private relationship with God, worshiping at his own little home-altar, continuing in insular isolation from the rest of the community. Utterly to refuse to participate would be to sin, and (to say the least) "to quarrel against all sound wisdom."

---

[1]   Think of the three annual feasts, where every man had to journey to Jerusalem to worship in company with his fellow Israelites.

If a man was a proselyte, then he still needed to become part of the community of faith, and still would participate in the life of the believing community. There would be no sitting at home, worshiping via the internet, television, or iPhone.

As it was in Solomon's day, so it is even more intensely under the New Covenant, as we shall see...

Context Under the New Covenant

Misanthropes might hope that the situation would be "better" in the NT, now that God's plan is not under ethnic stewardship. We are not part of a national spiritual entity during this economy. Therefore, one might hope that our walk is more individual. Perhaps one can now just watch DVDs of sermons, listen to MP3s, blog, Tweet, email, Facebook, or take an iPod packed with sermons to a mountain glade each week.

The layout of the book of Ephesians provides a dramatic counter to this illusion. The letter is six chapters long. The first three chapters are heavily and richly doctrinal in emphasis, opening up the wonders of God's eternal redemptive plan, in His sovereign selection of individuals, and His powerful life-giving work in bringing them from being sons of wrath to being His own sons through Christ. Three glorious chapters, filled with these truths.

Then, in the fourth chapter, we perceive a pivot. In what direction, exactly? Study the words of the apostle, in Ephesians 4:1–6. The apostle takes us right to church. Paul wants his readers to put those wonderful truths into practice in a "walk" that is marked by love and shown in the context of Christian community. His mind immediately turns to how we relate to "one another"[2] in the eyeball to eyeball context of the local church. He continues on in this vein until the last words of the letter. Paul envisions the Ephesians living out these truths in relationship, exercising love and patience to their fellow-believers.

We see a similar cluster of exhortations in Romans 12:9, 10, 13, 16, where Paul calls for genuine, affectionate love for one another that shows itself in showing honor, meeting needs, showing hospitality, and forging relationships characterized by humility and service.

God clearly moves Paul to give us all sorts of instructions about relating to one another as Christians. *None* of them includes hiding from other people

---

2   Paul's thought is frequently concerned with how Christians relate, in person, to "one another": Rom. 12:10, 16; 14:13; 15:5, 7, 14; 16:16; 1 Cor. 6:7; 11:33; 12:25; 16:20; 2 Cor. 13:11-12; Gal. 5:13; Eph. 4:2, 32; 5:19, 21; Col. 3:9, 13, 16; 1 Thess. 3:12; 4:9, 18; 5:11, 15; and 2 Thess. 1.

or floating above their heads in smug, superior self-satisfaction (see especially Romans 12:16).

To take one last Pauline sample, in Philippians 2:2–4 the apostle calls for loving, other-oriented humble service. The language is so exalted, that we might miss Paul's point: he is saying in effect, "If you want to make me happy, treat each other with Christ's kind of love." After this, in fact, Paul lifts up the incarnation and death of Christ as the model for the love he has in mind.

We could easily add passages from other NT writers. The author of the letter to the Hebrews calls his readers to a worship of Jesus that must feature regular assembly with other believers and regular service rendered to one another (Heb. 10:19–25). The apostle Peter says that the necessary result of purification through faith is a fervent, sincere love for other Christians (1 Peter 1:22). Finally, "the beloved disciple" John makes love for the brothers an indispensable mark of genuine saving faith (cf. 1 John 2:10; 3:10–18; 4:7–8, etc.).

Summary

Through both Testaments, God calls His children lovingly to involve themselves in others' lives, in His name. To do otherwise is utter folly in His eyes.

Now we move from one end of the pole to the other.

Caution Against Excess (Prov. 18:24)

> A man of many companions may come to ruin,
> but there is a friend who sticks closer than a brother.

Translation

When I evaluate a commentary on Proverbs, this is one of the verses I invariably turn to. The Hebrew is very difficult. If a commentator doesn't at least note the fact, I come away thinking he hasn't tussled with the original text very seriously.

One needn't know Hebrew to see that. Consider the following assortment of versions of line A, with their original footnotes, grouped by rough similarity:

> A man that hath friends must shew himself friendly (KJV)
> There are friends who spend time with you (Clifford)
> There are friends who want to associate (Longman)
> There are companions for socializing with (Fox)

A man has many friends[3] for companionship[4] (MLB)

There are friends who only seek society (Toy)

A man of many friends comes off a loser (Delitzsch)

He that maketh many friends[5] doeth it to his own destruction; (ASV)

A man of *many* friends comes to ruin[6] (NAS)

A man of many companions may come to ruin (NIV)

One who has unreliable friends soon comes to ruin (TNIV)

A man with many friends may be harmed[7] (CSB)

There are "friends" who destroy each other (NLT)

Friends can destroy one another[8] (GW)

A person who has unreliable companions is about to be broken (Waltke)

Some[9] friends play at friendship[10] (NRSV)

There are[11] friends who pretend to be friends[12] (RSV)

There is a companion who does nothing but chatter (McKane)

It is hard not to feel dizzy, looking at such an array. Clearly, the Hebrew text of this verse is difficult. Not to get bogged down in details, here are my renderings of the unaltered Hebrew text. First, extremely literally:[13]

A man of friends to break himself;

but there is one loving *such as* sticks more than a brother.

Now, smoothed out a bit:

A man of many friends tends to get himself[14] broken;

but there is a loving friend who sticks *closer* than a brother. (DJP)

---

3   Literally "a man of friends."
4   Literally "to act as companions."
5   Heb. *A man of friends.*
6   Lit., *be broken in pieces.*
7   Some LXX mss, Syr, Tg, Vg read *friends must be friendly.*
8   Or "A person has friends as companions."
9   Syr Tg: Heb *A man of.*
10   Cn Compare Syr Vg Tg: Meaning of Heb uncertain.
11   Syr Tg: Heb *A man of.*
12   Cn (correction) Compare Syr Vg Tg: Heb *to be broken.*
13   There is a textual issue with the first word, forcing a translator to choose between almost identical words meaning "man" or "there are."
14   Or "ends up getting himself."

Interpretation

"A man of many friends" refers to a man who values popularity above all, and whose highest aim is that he has a lot of friends. He is empty within. Unless he has the approbation of a broad circle of friends, he is restless and unfulfilled.

"Tends to get himself broken" may refer, *first*, to the dissolution of his character of a man who will do anything to have friends: "Like a muddied spring or a polluted fountain is a righteous man who gives way before the wicked" (Prov. 25:26). Not everybody wants to be a friend of a godly man. Something has to give: either the ungodly man will repent and choose to walk God's way with the godly man, or the godly man will compromise or mutate himself sufficiently to retain his "friend's" acquiescence and approval.

A man who is not discriminating in who he calls "friend" will suffer for it. He will pick up the bad behavior of his "friend" (Prov. 22:24–25). As Paul says, "Bad company ruins good morals" (1 Cor. 15:33).

A *second* reference may suggest the calamity that a faithless friend is in rough times. Proverbs 25:19 puts it in picturesque terms: "*Like* a bad tooth and an unsteady foot Is confidence in a faithless man in time of trouble" (NAS). Loyalty and strength of character are character traits of the godly. When godliness is not a filter in our selection of friends, some will be fair-weather folks who buckle and flee (or worse) when needed.

A *third* way in which too many friends can be ruinous is when one incurs judgment by association. In 1:10, 18 and 19, Solomon had warned that joining a gang means sharing in their violent end. More pointed, in 13:20 he observes that "Whoever walks with the wise becomes wise, but the companion of fools will suffer harm." Climb into a boat with someone, and where the boat goes, you go.

It's rough to end up as "collateral damage." Ask King Jehoshaphat (2 Chron. 19:1–3; 20:35–37).

Application

The practical upshot can be phrased succinctly:

- One good friend (cf. Prov. 17:17) is worth fifty bad friends (cf. Prov. 25:19).

- Therefore, choose your friends very carefully.

Extension

We can also see a legitimate New Testament extension. The counsel of God has not changed since Solomon wrote these words. God does not urge us to be everyone's friend. In fact, in some cases, He warns us against being "friends." For instance, God positively urges us to avoid associating with:

1. People who cause divisions because of their doctrinal deviation (Rom. 16:17).
2. Professing believers under church discipline (Matt. 18:17).
3. The "so-called brother" who is immoral, covetous, idolatrous, a reviler, a drunkard, or a swindler; we are "not even to eat with such a one" (1 Cor. 5:11).
4. Unbelievers who are plunging into immoral behavior (1 Peter 4:4).
5. The world, since friendship with the world is hostility against God (James 4:4).

All of this flows from the single relationship we as believers prize more than any: our bond with the Lord Jesus Christ. He is our hope of glory (Col. 1:27), our life (Col. 3:4), our all (1 Cor. 1:30). Only He literally sticks closer than a brother, since He is the vine and we are branches who draw our spiritual vitality from Him (John 15:1–8), and since all the spiritual good we have, we have in Him (Eph. 1:3ff.).

Therefore, it is of paramount importance to us to abide in His love (John 15:10). Nothing that would bring shame on Him, or break our fellowship with Him, or hamper our service of Him, can be tolerated. To walk in a worthy manner requires wisdom (Col. 1:9–10). This necessitates our applying a wise filter in choosing those with whom we will share the intimacy of friendship.

What to Seek and Cherish in Friends

God provides us with guidelines both in the form of "green lights" and "red lights." Proverbs praises some characteristics, and condemns others. By these signposts, we know the sorts of friends we should embrace, and those whom we must avoid. Let us study the qualities which God says make for desirable friends.

Wisdom (Prov. 13:20)

> Whoever walks with the wise becomes wise,
> but the companion of fools will suffer harm

Introductory: types of relationships

I find it helpful—if not very imaginative—to think in terms of three categories of relationships:

1. *Give* relationships
2. *Take* relationships
3. *Give and take* relationships

We should have *give*-relationships. That is a case in which perhaps you may have more to offer your friend than he has to offer you. Perhaps you are more mature, better-off financially, or more knowledgeable in some particular field of shared interest. It is simply Christian giving to have such friends, to give in love (Matt. 20:26; Rom. 12:10, 16; Phil. 2:3). If we build all of our relationships on what we will get out of them, then our primary drive is self-concern, and Christ's love has little to do with it.

When *taking* or *getting* is top priority, love is definitely not our prime motivator. Perhaps, though, great-hearted folks will take us under their wings and do us great good. So we seek to show them what love and service we can... but we know ourselves to be in their debt.

But then we all need friends who will be our confidants, our trusted partners. In this level of friendship we must exercise great discernment. These are *give and take* relationships. Here there is greater intimacy, openness, and trust. In a give and take relationship, we are peers, sharing back and forth—now giving, now receiving; now teaching, now learning. This is what the NT calls *fellowship*, a sharing of commonality and kinship. We are more likely to take on the characteristics of such friends.

For that reason, only Christians are candidates for such an intimate level of friendship (cf. the principle of 2 Cor. 6:14ff.). More specifically, only Christians who are learning and applying the Word of God are candidates for this level of friendship.

Why so? Let us think it through.

The principle

We might say very simply, "We *become like* those whom *we like*." It is natural to take on the characteristics of those whom we trust and admire. Thus, we must be very careful in whom we choose to embrace in close friendship.

If we join with those who are applying the wisdom of God in their lives, we will benefit from their example. However, the opposite is also true: if we embrace as close friends those walking contrary to God, their characters will have a negative impact on our own walk.

Other scriptures certainly reinforce this principle. Remember the portrait of the godly man in Psalm 1:1, who "does not walk in the advice of wicked ones, and in the way of sinners does not stand, and in the seat of scorners does not sit" (DJP). We see this man first depicted in terms of what he does not do. He does not choose wicked associations. Specifically, he does not take the advice of godless men as his life-map. He does not adopt the lifestyle of those violating God's standards. He does not identify himself with God's enemies.

Failure at this point has been the downfall of more than one king. Remember that Solomon himself was tragically and hideously corrupted by the pagan, idolatrous wives he "clung to …in love"(1 Kings 11:1–8).

Remember that Israel was split in two when Solomon's son Rehoboam, perhaps the primary student addressed in Proverbs, took the advice of the "young punks" with whom he had evidently associated himself from his tender youth (1 Kings 12:5–14).

Remember that even godly King Jehoshaphat suffered by his association with evil King Ahab (2 Chron. 18:1–3; 19:1–3). Recall the stinging rebuke from Hanani the seer: "Should you help the wicked and love those who hate the LORD? Because of this, wrath has gone out against you from the LORD" (19:2).

Remember that King Joash did well while godly priest Jehoiada advised him (2 Chron. 24:1–3), but then he went astray when new court officials took over after Jehoiada's death (vv. 17ff.).

And so our Lord Jesus warns us against seeking to be accepted by the wrong people for the wrong reasons (Luke 6:26).

The proof

The test of any given intimate friend can be expressed in a question: "If I become more like my friend, will I love the Lord more deeply, or less so? Will I know Him better, or more feebly? Will I be more useful to the Lord, or less useful?" If the answer is, "More love, deeper knowledge, greater usefulness," this is a tremendous friend to have—indeed, a tremendous friend to emulate.

However, if the answer is in the deficit column, we are seeing at least a yellow light, if not a full red light.

Loyalty

The problem (Prov. 20:6)—

> Many a man proclaims his own steadfast love,
>> but a faithful man who can find?

Time underscores this point. Thirty years ago, I would have said a sincere "Amen" to this principle. Now I can write it in capital letters, italicized, underscored, and in my own (metaphorical) blood.

There are few areas where it is truer that talk is both easy and cheap. Many could affirm that the quality of devoted loyalty does not seem to be particularly prized in many Christian circles.

Nor is the virtue easy or cheap. A man I knew was offered the choice of "selling out" a dear friend, at the threat of losing his reputation and future ministry. This man's friend was innocent of the charges, but he was offered an easy out: disown his friend and keep his reputation in this circle. But that simply was not an option to him. He could not conceive of doing what they were demanding, particularly under threats.

What happened? The persecutors did their best to deliver on their threat, but last I heard this man never regretted his demurral. He felt it his duty before God to be the kind of friend he himself wanted to have: faithful, even when it costs.

Which segues nicely to the next verse.

The quality

Proverbs 17:17 says:

> A friend loves at all times,
>> and a brother is born for adversity.

This verse implies good news and bad news. The good news is that a friend worthy of the name is born for bad weather. This is a blessed truth, as the path from this world to Christ's presence always leads through bad weather.

The bad news is that we often do not know for sure whether a friend is of this caliber until the bad weather comes—at which point it might be too late.

Solomon observes that "a brother is born for adversity." He is holding up as a wonderful example of the true friend and brother, who virtually welcomes the rough times. This solid-gold friend is contrasted by implication with the flitty, spineless majority who can be put to flight by a few blustery clouds on the horizon.

With the perspective of years, I must say that I would not trade my real friends for anything but Jesus.

Candor

Solomon highly values the quality of honesty, of frank (but gracious) truthfulness. Let me single out *two* reasons such a friend is so important.

First, you and I want a truthful friend. Note Proverbs 14:5—

> A faithful witness does not lie,
> but a false witness breathes out lies.

A friend is not necessarily someone who will tell us what we want to hear. But a friend certainly is someone who will tell us what is true—and what we need to hear.

Second, you and I *need* a truthful friend (Prov. 27:5–6):

> Better is open rebuke
> than hidden love.
>
> ⁶ Faithful are the wounds of a friend;
> profuse are the kisses of an enemy.

Actually, when you consider all the grief that one can catch for administering needed rebuke, we realize that someone who is willing to take the risk is likely to be a true friend. Remember: the only person who does not need a friend who is willing to rebuke him is the man who has no sin or error to rebuke—which, at present, is a phonebook with no names in it.

As a postscript, we must not neglect our part in this. If we want friends who feel free to correct us or reprove us, we should make it easy for them. Remember, Solomon wrote "Give instruction to a wise man, and he will be still wiser; teach a righteous man, and he will increase in learning" (Prov. 9:9). Where did Solomon learn this attitude? Perhaps from his father, who sang "Let a righteous man strike me—it is a kindness; let him rebuke me—it is oil for my head; let my head not refuse it" (Psa. 141:5).

Ask yourself: Do my friends find rebuking me to be a low-stress experience, or even a rewarding experience? Or would they rather wrestle a wild boar?

What to Beware and Avoid

Now we single out four qualities, in rapid succession, which Solomon identifies as "ROAD OUT" signs for a close and trusting friendship.

First: Foolishness

The precept

> Whoever walks with the wise becomes wise,
>> but the companion of fools [*k*sîlîm, stupid men] will suffer
>> harm. (Prov. 13:20)
>
> Leave the presence of a fool [*k*sîl, stupid man],
>> for there you do not meet words of knowledge. (Prov. 14:7)

The problem: How do you tell a fool?

The answer, in principle, can be seen in Proverbs 1—

> The fear of the LORD is the beginning of knowledge;
>> fools despise wisdom and instruction. (1:7)
>
> "How long, O simple ones, will you love being simple?
>> How long will scoffers delight in their scoffing
>>> and fools hate knowledge?" (1:22)
>
> For the simple are killed by their turning away,
>> and the complacency of fools destroys them. (1:32)

A fool can be identified first of all by his lack of the fear of God, as described in Proverbs 3:5–7. His worldview is not being reconstructed with the infinite/personal God of Scripture at the center, and himself at His feet. Not only is he in that state, but he is comfortable in it. He is complacent, smug, and settled. He is a fool, and he is no fit friend.

We find a New Covenant echo of the same idea in Paul. Let us single out just two passages. First, in 2 Thessalonians 3:14–15 Paul urges us to note the person who does not submit to apostolic teaching, mark him, and avoid fellowship with him in the hopes of producing shame that leads to repentance.

Similarly, in 1 Timothy 6:3–5 Paul notes the person who not only does not submit to Christ speaking in the apostles, but goes so far as to advocate contrary doctrine. Paul stigmatizes such a person, brands him, condemns him, and points Timothy and all his readers away from him (cf. Rom. 16:17).

Since Calvary, the mark of a man who does not fear Yahweh is that he does not bow the knee to Jesus as Lord and take on himself the yoke of discipleship. The words of God are not "law" to him. Whether he positively rejects and perverts central apostolic doctrine, or whether he passively displays no interest in learning and growing in them (cf. John 8:31–32), he marks himself as a fool. As such, we may evangelize him, we may reach out to him to point him to Christ, but we aren't walking in the same direction.

Second: Hot Temper

Solomon issues this warning more than once:

> A man of violence entices his neighbor
> > and leads him in a way that is not good. (16:29)
> A man of great wrath will pay the penalty,
> > for if you deliver him, you will only have to do it again. (19:19)
> Make no friendship with a man given to anger,
> > nor go with a wrathful man,
> ²⁵ lest you learn his ways
> > and entangle yourself in a snare. (22:24–25)

It has been a fad in America, in recent years, to admire the person who just "lets it all hang out," who gives instant expression to his emotions, passions, urges and thoughts. The more unfiltered, the more fun we think he is. We go to movies to watch men respond in violent anger, taking vicarious satisfaction in their unbridled rage.

Solomon's God-given wisdom provides a different perspective.

A perpetually (or easily) angry man has not learned to trust Yahweh to settle scores for him (20:22). Perhaps he has not taken to heart God's charge about dealing with people who hate us (Exod. 23:4–5). Regardless, one who cannot or does not control his temper marks himself as a foolish man, not an admirable example (Prov. 14:29; 15:18; 16:32; 19:11; 25:28; cf. James 1:19).

To be patient and self-controlled is to be like God (Exod. 34:6; Psa. 103:8; Joel 2:13; Jonah 4:2; Nah. 1:3). To allow oneself to blow up at slight offenses is to act as if we *think* we're God.

To nurse wrath and grudges is to set up a nice little cozy room for the Devil (Eph. 4:26–27).

Third: Mouth Problems

A *first* category of mouth problems is *gossip and slander*. We find these among the six… no, *seven* things Yahweh says that He hates (Proverbs 6:16–19). Note that three out of four are mouth sins, including telling lies (v. 17; slander is a subcategory of this sin), and spreading discord (v. 19). We may initially be drawn to such a person when he—in violation of the Word of God (Exod. 23:1; Lev. 19:16; Psa. 15:3; Eph. 4:31; Col. 3:8)—dishes up some gossipy "scoop" to us. But then we (A) find that we begin to emulate his bad example… or (B) find ourselves the subjects of his next whisper campaign.

Well says James that

> …the tongue is a small member, yet it boasts of great things. How great a forest is set ablaze by such a small fire! [6] And the tongue is a fire, a world of unrighteousness. The tongue is set among our members, staining the whole body, setting on fire the entire course of life, and set on fire by hell. (James 3:5–6)

The slanderer is one who says untrue, harmful things about someone. Because of the pervasiveness of tongue sins and slander, a slanderer can even break up close friendships if he is let in, entertained, and listened to. Solomon says to have nothing to do with such a person:

> The one who reveals secrets is a constant gossip;
>   avoid someone with a big mouth. (Prov. 20:19 CSB)

Kidner pungently observes that "The point of the first line is that it may be *your* secrets next."[15] Or, to consider the flip side, "The definition of a best friend is someone who knows enough to ruin you—and doesn't."[16]

---

[15] Kidner, 139.

[16] Chuck Swindoll, from a broadcast sermon.

It is simply wise not to disclose too much to a new acquaintance, until we see how he handles confidences. The best way to "let someone in" is bit by bit; see how he handles some confidence, then some more, then some more. Also note carefully how he handles the confidences of others. Bear Solomon's warning in mind.

A *second* category of mouth problems is *flattery*. Solomon warns against this in a couple of ways:

> Faithful are the wounds of a friend;
>> profuse are the kisses of an enemy. (27:6)

> A man who flatters his neighbor
>> spreads a net for his feet. (29:5)

Ultra-simple example: someone tells his friend, untruthfully, that he has a "wonderful singing voice"—so the man embarrasses himself by croaking aloud in public. But the applications are far broader than that. You and I already harbor deadly flatterers in our own bosoms (Jer. 17:9). It is best to counter our internal Jacob with some honesty among our friends.

Fourth: Disloyalty

> The *problem* is framed by Solomon in Proverbs 20:6—
>> Many a man proclaims his own steadfast love,
>>> but a faithful man who can find?

> The *price* for trusting such a "friend" is described in 25:19—
>> *Like* a bad tooth and an unsteady foot
>>> Is confidence in a faithless man in time of trouble. (NAS)

Allow Solomon's picture to linger a moment longer. What is the problem with a "bad tooth" and "an unsteady foot"? What do a bad tooth and an unsteady foot have in common?

The answer to both comes when we pose a third question: When do both show their natures? Is it when we are sitting about, watching TV? No. In both cases, their weakness is exposed only when pressure is applied—when we bite down on something hard, or put our weight on our foot. Then the faulty part gives way.

It is an awful experience to trust to something, only to have it buckle from under you. Have you ever been hiking or climbing and entrusted your full weight confidently to a stable-looking rock—only to have it shift or roll or give way? (I have!)

It is even more disastrous and distressing to go to lean on a trusted, sworn ally, in time of great need, only to find that he really is a cowardly, knock-kneed invertebrate.

How do you recognize this person? Loyalty requires holding to a commitment, particularly when it becomes inconvenient, when there's pressure to "bail out."

Signs of a disloyal person, then, would include one who will not honor commitments, or is not committed to being a man of his word. How does this person behave under pressure? Does he go with the crowd? Is he willing to take principled stands, even if they are unpopular?

The *poignancy*: any leader, such as was King Solomon and his father, knows the bitterness of treachery and disloyalty. Some of the most moving words ever written on the stinging experience of betrayal were penned by Solomon's father David in the Psalms; perhaps this was the matrix for Solomon's own vehemence on the subject.[17]

Perhaps it was David's experiences with his conceited, treacherous son Absalom, and with Shimei, that burned this lesson into Solomon.

Pitfalls to Relationships

Friendship takes work. The wise person knows how to identify potholes and black ice. Solomon gives us guidance as to what to avoid, which we will distill under three categories.

First: Mismatched Intimacy (Prov. 25:17)

> Let your foot be seldom in your neighbor's house,
>   lest he have his fill of you and hate you.

The terms

The verb translated "seldom" is a form of *yāqar*, meaning to be precious, scarce, prized. It gives birth to the adjective *yāqār*, which means precious, rare, splendid. The particular verb form used (*hōqar*, the Hiph'il imperative) means to *make*

---

17 Cf. Psalms 3, 11, 12, 55, etc.

rare.[18] The primary idea is, "Make your foot rare" or "scarce." There could be the additional thought that by making your foot rare, you are making it valuable.

The idea then would be to be a good marketer. Scarcity drives up prices. Drive up the value of your visits by avoiding excess. Be sure your friend wants to see more of you, rather than less.

"Lest he have his fill of you" translates the Hebrew *pen-yiśbāʿkā.* The verb *śābaʿ* means to *be sated, satisfied, surfeited;*[19] to *have enough* or *get enough.*[20] This particular use signifies to have in excess, be glutted or stuffed with to the point of nausea (cf. Isa. 1:11; Prov. 25:16).[21]

The idea

Solomon is counseling us to avoid constantly barging into someone's life and overwhelming him with our needy, demanding presence. Commentator Franz Delitzsch catches the thought well, citing a German proverb, "Let him who seeks to be of esteem come seldom."[22] Delitzsch later warns against "a restless impetuosity, which seeks at once to gain by force that which one should allow gradually to ripen."[23]

Our presence should be valuable and valued, not excessive. Solomon's point certainly is not *never* to spend a lot of time with a friend. Rather, he is counseling us to spend the time appropriate to the friendship, to nurture and cultivate it without saturating and drowning it. This calls for consideration and sensitivity.

Second: Flattery

> A lying tongue hates its victims,
>> and a flattering mouth works ruin. (26:28)
> A man who flatters his neighbor
>> spreads a net for his feet. (29:5)

The problem

A relationship characterized by flattery is one in which hard truths are held back and untruthful praise is lavished. It may look like love, but it isn't. Solomon

---

[18] BDB, article יָקַר.
[19] BDB, שָׂבַע.
[20] HALOT, article שׂבע.
[21] Cf. BDB, ibid.
[22] Delitzsch, 2:163.
[23] Delitzsch, ibid.

rips the mask off the flatterer: he is not being kind, he is not being loving, and he is not doing good. Rather, he is setting his "friend" up for disaster.

Is that not immediately apparent? If a doctor discovered cancer but, from a desire not to upset, told his patient he was the very picture of health—would that be a kindly doctor? If an ordination committee found a candidate to be Scripturally ignorant and spiritually deficient, would ordaining him regardless be a loving act? If a young man knew his friend had no chance with a girl who caught his eye but egged him on anyway, would he be a good friend?

The principle

Beware mutual admiration societies. Failing to administer needed correction can involve treating serious faults with adoring blindness. Or it can signify a relationship so fragile that it cannot bear the weight of reality. Or again, it may indicate a "need" for a friend that is so unhealthy and unwise that it will chain us to someone who cannot bear the truth.

Regardless, a relationship characterized by flattery is a very sickly and unbalanced relationship, overall.

If you have no friends who criticize you, ask yourself:

- "Is it because I am above criticism?" Anyone who thinks this should check for coins on his eyelids. Seriously.

- "Is it because I flee criticism, and those who deal it out?" If so, then one has become like the scoffer in Proverbs 15:12, who "does not love one who reproves him," and thus "will not go to the wise" (NAS).

If our friends never reprove us, we must ask God to help us cultivate the attitude of the wise man, who desires to grow, and welcomes truthful criticism (Prov. 9:8–9).

Third: Offense Given

Overview

We "set the table" for this topic by noting both the danger and the solution from Proverbs 10:12—

> Hatred stirs up strife,
>> but love covers all offenses.

A hostile inclination will transform any offense into a major offense, as in our expression "to make a mountain out of a molehill." Love, however, covers over such wrongs. "Love hides transgressions, not by condoning wrong, but by making allowance and forgiving; it leads a man to cover up not his own faults (this is condemned in 28[13]) but those of others..."[24]

We see a similar factor at work in 17:9—"Whoever covers an offense seeks love, but he who repeats a matter separates close friends." Paul reveals the dynamic for this in 1 Corinthians 13:5, where he says that love "does not insist on its own way" and "is not irritable or resentful."

Having scanned the hazard and its preventer, let us approach it a bit more closely.

Dilemma

Solomon analyzes in 17:14 why strife in a relationship is such a disaster—

> The beginning of strife is like letting out water,
>> so quit before the quarrel breaks out.

Here he envisions a situation such as a breach in a dam. First, a little water gets out. But then this flow causes further erosion of the dam, and the flow increases. If nothing is done, the dam eventually breaks down entirely and a flood results.

Let us transfer the simile back to human relations. Let us say that we have been wronged in some relatively minor way (i.e., a cross word in a marriage, as opposed to adultery). We know that it is best to "love it over." However, we find ourselves obsessing on the offense, with all our feelings of injured pride clamoring at us.

So what do we do? Do we keep bringing it up until a fight starts? Solomon counsels wisdom and self-control. He observes that a quarrel is easier to start than it is to resolve, and less difficult to prevent than to stop. "Opening such a sluice lets loose more than one can predict, control or retrieve."[25]

Accordingly, Solomon's advice is to forsake, abandon, leave the quarrel before it even starts. Perhaps second thoughts will drive one back to the first solution: love it over.

---

[24] Toy, 206.
[25] Kidner, 125.

Disaster

Solomon also reveals the unhappy results of not simply dropping a relatively trivial wrong,[26] in 17:9.

> Whoever covers an offense seeks love,
>> but he who repeats a matter separates close friends.

This is the portrait of somebody who neither simply loves a matter over, nor successfully resolves it. Whether his attempt at a direct confrontation met with failure, or whether he is refusing to forgive an offense that has been repented of, he keeps pecking at it. He "repeats a matter"; the ASV quaintly renders it "harpeth on a matter."

When we are offended, there are three possibilities:

1. We can love it over and drop the matter.

2. We can confront and maybe enjoy a satisfactory outcome, whereupon we drop the matter.

3. We can confront and not be satisfied with the outcome, whereupon we either:

   a. "Play a little traveling music" (i.e., distance ourselves from the friendship); or—

   b. Resolve to drop the matter; or—

   c. Keep bringing the matter up until the relationship self-destructs.

Demolition

We see the ruin that a mismanaged offense can cause revealed in 18:19—

> A brother offended is more unyielding than a strong city,
>> and quarreling is like the bars of a castle.

Here Solomon addresses himself to the person committing the offense, urging him to avoid it. He has in mind an offense of more major proportions, something that is unlikely to yield to the counsel that it simply be overlooked.

I think Solomon envisions a case in which the culpable one will not accept responsibility, repent, seek forgiveness, and give himself to appropriate restitution.

---

[26] The word translated "offense" (*peša'*) can mean a serious crime against God, or a relatively minor

Perhaps the case is that the offense is so serious that the relationship simply cannot continue as before—a serious slander, betrayal, failure of loyalty.

Underlying this thought, I believe, is God's understanding that an intimate friendship creates vulnerability. It allows one's intimate friend an opportunity to do the kind of damage as none other can. When that vulnerability has been exploited so as to cause real damage, the injury is not easily undone.

Peaks

Having seen warning signs and hazards of friendship, we turn to the positive in Proverbs. Let us study *four* of the blessings and boons of close, healthy, wise, godly friendships.

First: Analysis and Criticism (Prov. 27:5–6)

> Better is open rebuke
>> than hidden love.
>
> ⁶ Faithful are the wounds of a friend;
>> profuse are the kisses of an enemy

Note at the outset of this evaluation proverb *what is better*, according to Solomon: open rebuke. We find the word translated "rebuke" (*tôkaḥaṯ*) paralleled by "counsel" (*'ēṣâ*) in 1:25 and 30; and by "discipline" (*mûsār*) some eight times, including 3:11; 10:17; 12:1; 13:18; and 15:32.

Here the modifier is "open" (*meʹgullâ*), which signifies the opposite of "hidden" in line B. It is uncovered or manifested, and means "frank, direct, from friend or foe."[27] We need friends who will candidly do that difficult office of a true friend, by telling us what we need (but may not want) to hear, out of love.

Second, we find that *what is worse* is love that conceals itself. This means that "The *love* is hidden, invisible, manifesting itself by no rebuking word, and therefore morally useless."[28] There should never be deception, repression of necessary truth, in a genuine friendship.

We note, third, that *what are faithful* are the wounds of a friend. They are said to be "faithful" wounds. The Hebrew term *neʹmānîm* is from the verb *'āman*,

---

wrong against an individual. In Proverbs, it often seems to have the latter sense (cf. 10:12; 12:13; 18:19; 19:11; 29:22).

[27] Toy, 483.

[28] Toy, 483.

which means to confirm or support. This form[29] signifies a thing that is made firm, and is therefore reliable, trustworthy. The wounds of a friend, then, are something that you can rely upon as sincere, reliable, and faithful.

Still, they are *wounds!* The idea of the word *piṣ'ê* is of a hurt, a bruise—a wound. At times a friend must say or even do things that hurt us. But what sets them apart from other bruises is that they are the wounds of a friend, administered faithfully and out of love. Indeed, the word translated "friend" here is *'ôhēḇ*, which is literally "one who loves." This is not, however, the idea of a romantic lover. Rather, it signifies a friend as someone who sincerely loves us.

This, then, is what makes an essential difference. What an enemy does is intended to hurt and destroy us. And, note well, he may do this by destructive, demoralizing criticism. Or equally he may do this by insincere, lulling flattery and false affection ("but deceitful are the kisses of an enemy"[30]). Either way, his intent is to do us harm.

By contrast, what a loving friend does is intended to help us, to improve us in our walk with God. He may help us by giving us heartening encouragement and demonstrating genuine affection. Equally, as we see here, he may help us by taking up and applying the scalpel, as needed. His cuts, however, are intended to bring long-term healing, even though they may bring short-term pain.

This loving ministry is not always immediately appreciated. Henry Alford, New Testament scholar from the nineteenth century, well calls the giving of Christian rebuke "the best and most difficult office of Christian friendship."[31]

The faithful friend should take heart from the words of Proverbs 28:23—"Whoever rebukes a man will afterward find more favor than he who flatters with his tongue." It may well be that the friend who issues a needed, loving rebuke is not immediately thanked for his services. However, afterward—when tempers have cooled and there has been time for calm reflection—he will be appreciated by his friend for the service done.

---

[29] Niph'al participle.

[30] Hebrew *śōnē*; literally, "hater," v. 6b.

[31] Henry Alford, *Alford's Greek Testament: An Exegetical and Critical Commentary*, Mt 7:5 (Bellingham, WA: Logos Research Systems, Inc., 2010).

Second: Helpful Counsel (Prov. 27:9)

> Oil and perfume make the heart glad,
>> and the sweetness of a friend comes from his earnest counsel.[32]

The terms "oil and perfume" are associated with celebration, feasting, joy, and joyous grooming. They make life sweet on the physical plane; so does a friend's earnest counsel, on the non-physical plane of life. "Earnest counsel" is more literally "counsel of soul," meaning heartfelt, sincere advice, counsel.

The thought is that a friend's heartfelt, sincere counsel is precious and gladdening for two major reasons:

1. Because a friend's counsel has our best interests in mind.

2. Because a friend's counsel arises out of familiarity with us, our motivation, our aims, our character.

Perhaps I can offer a personal illustration. I once was in an immensely complicated situation, needing to make some sharp decisions in a limited time frame. While I was trying hard to think Biblically, clearly, and objectively, some malicious folks were whispering untruths about me. I seriously considered even what they said, but primarily turned to my friends.

Why? Their counsel was based on intimate knowledge of where I was, and who I was. I did not need to start from Ground Zero to establish my character, convictions, and identity with them. I did not need to clear away the weeds, defend myself against slander. They knew who I was, they knew what truly motivated me, and we could start from there. They could ask hard questions, but not needless questions. We could get right down to the decisions that needed to be made and talk about what was real, instead of debating what was unreal.

Third: Loyalty

Recall Proverbs 20:6—

> Many a man proclaims his own steadfast love,
>> but a faithful man who can find?

This proverb underscores the importance of this quality in others. It follows as well that we must cultivate it in ourselves.

---

[32] The Hebrew text of Line B is difficult to translate, as a comparison of ESV, CSB, and NAS quickly shows. This discussion rests on the ESV's rendering.

This is a sort of lynch-pin trait. By definition, a person with no character is swayed and influenced by whoever he happens to be with at any given moment. Loyalty requires the ability to stick with a value (or a person) against pressure to the contrary. Accordingly, loyalty will simply not be an option for a man of poor character. A person who fears God must learn to be loyal to Him against contrary pressure. That sort of person is ready to show principled loyalty to a friend.

The importance of this truth is underscored in Proverbs 21:21.

> Whoever pursues righteousness and kindness
> will find life, righteousness, and honor.

It may not be too much of a stretch to see "righteousness" as summing up our relationship with God, and "kindness" (or "loyalty," NAS) as summing up our relationship with men.

These qualities, then, are seen as the key to finding good in our lives. Again, to have this quality of character one should build a Godward commitment and walk.

Finally, Proverbs 27:10 counsels

> Do not forsake your friend and your father's friend,
> and do not go to your brother's house in the day of your calamity.
> Better is a neighbor who is near
> than a brother who is far away.

Bridges says, with proverbial sagacity, "If other things are better when new, a friend is better that is old and tried. ...For how can you trust an untried friend?"[33]

Fourth: Mutual Refinement (Prov. 27:17)

> Iron sharpens iron,
> and one man sharpens another.

This sage saying underscores our need for real interaction. It is striking that God's first "not good" in all of creation was the spectacle of Adam's solitude (Gen. 2:18). This is all the more striking when one factors in that this estimation was voiced before sin entered the race. It reflected nothing broken in Adam, nothing wrong or sinful. God simply proceeded as He did to underscore the importance of society in general, and marriage in particular.

---

[33] Bridges, 511.

Whence comes this refinement of which Solomon speaks? Obviously, it cannot come through animals or inanimate objects, as Adam learned. So for our part, we must realize that books or tapes or CDs or videos or MP3s will not and cannot do what God intends to be done by face-to-face personal relationships.

However, not just any interaction will do. Literal iron is not sharpened by cheese or wood. So we are refined by no less than concourse with our peers—with *sharp* peers, with peers of strong enough conviction and character to serve as a sharpening influence for us. We must experience godly, personal interaction with those who are growing in Christ.

As Christians, our greatest goal in life must be seeking God and His glory (cf. Pss. 27:4; 73:28; Matt. 6:33). This goal of godliness will not be achieved by associating with those who are not seeking that same goal fervently. Such folks cannot sharpen us, but will rather dull and harm us (cf. Prov. 13:20; 1 Cor. 15:33).

We need to befriend folks who will complement and challenge our weak and flat areas, who will thus help us grow to be what God intends. The NT is accordingly all the more emphatic about being personally involved in a group of growing believers, submitting personally to an in-person pastor and experiencing the give-and-take of fellowship with other believers, serving side-by-side.[34]

Review: the Full Circle, and the Best Friend

We started out in this study of relationships by seeing God's command against willful, personal isolation (Prov. 18:1). We saw as well the dangers of being a social butterfly, a *philiolater*[35] (Prov. 18:24). We weighed God's guidelines for selecting friends, and for the care and nurturing of a friendship. Finally, we saw emphasized the need for the mutual sharpening of godly friendships.

This is one place where even the world sees the truth, albeit dimly and out-of-perspective: A man who has friends is indeed rich, it is often said. What is less often said is that the best friend a person can have is Jesus Christ.

It would be worthwhile to review the qualifications of Jesus Christ under each of the headings in our study. No mortal can perfectly fulfill the demands of friendship—but Jesus can and does.

It is Jesus who so loves at all times that He died to redeem us when we were enemies of God, utterly unable to lift one finger for our own spiritual good (Rom.

---

[34] Anyone wishing to can easily verify this by consulting Hebrews 10:24, 25; 13:17.

[35] A word of my coinage, meaning a *worshiper of friendship*, who lives for horizontal relationships over the vertical.

5:6–9). It is Jesus who so sticks with us with such indestructible loyalty that absolutely nothing in all time nor space nor all of creation can ever part us from His love (Rom. 8:35–39). This Jesus is the faithful and true witness (Rev. 1:5), whose words to us are spirit and life (John 6:63), and who reproves and disciplines us out of love (Rev. 3:19).

None is more committed to our good than He, none more loyal, none more truthful, none more present in difficult times. Even if we sin, He is our advocate before God (1 John 2:1), even as He calls and moves us to repent (2 Cor. 7:9–10; Rev. 3:19).

Wisdom tells us that the friendship we should cultivate above all others is friendship with Jesus Christ.

With that greatest of friendships in its proper place, we are ready to weather the inevitable failures among our fellow-mortals, as well as to deal with our own frequent failures.

Questions for Thought or Discussion

1. What was wrong with isolationism in an Old Testament context? In the New Testament?

2. What is the danger of having too many friends?

3. Is it right or wrong to pick who will and won't be our friends? Explain.

4. What qualities should one seek in friends?

5. What qualities should one shun in prospective friends?

6. What are some examples of "mouth problems"?

7. What are pitfalls to relationships?

8. What are the high points to wise, godly friendships?

9. Who is the best friend, and why?

CHAPTER SEVEN

Skill in Godly Marriage

There is no shortage of Christian material on the subject of marriage. I am not aware of any detailed, deeply exegetical, specific exposition of the material in Proverbs, however. Beyond that, it long has seemed to me that a number of Biblical truths about marriage, and specifically Proverbial truths, have not seen the light they merit.

There is enough material on marriage in Proverbs to provide the basis for a lengthy book. This will not be that book, but I hope it makes a contribution in that direction. First, however, we must ground this material in a larger Biblical context. Then we will be prepared to begin to study the wealth of material provided by Solomon.

The Foundations of Marriage and Family

If we are to frame marriage in its Biblical context, we must go back to the original design, fresh out of the box, previous to any tampering or corruption. This necessarily drives us to the opening chapters of Genesis, where we see the foundations of marriage in man's need, and in God's design.

Some might object that Genesis has little to say to us. After all, the conditions were (literally) Edenic. We are broken people in broken cultures, and need something more adjusted to our times. For that reason, popular writers are fond of citing this or that survey or study, finding statistics about what women and men want, what women and men think will make them happy, what their complaints about their spouses are, and so forth. Modern Christian thought often drinks long and deep at the trough of sociology and psychology, adds a sprinkling of Christianoid pixie-dust, and then merely closes in prayer.

It is important to note, however, how the Lord Jesus responded to a question about divorce in Matthew 19:3ff. Divorce—if anything is a symptom of our brokenness, surely it is the collapse of a marriage. This should make a perfect test-case.

How does our Lord answer? He goes directly back to the original creation of mankind and of marriage. He finds it relevant. Jesus quotes from the narratives of Genesis 1 and 2, affirms what we find there as God's perfect design, then responds to the question from within that framework (vv. 4–9).

We should follow our Lord's example. Beyond the fact that this is how a student of Christ should think, it makes perfect sense. If I want to fix a broken house, I don't measure a dozen other broken houses and make adjustments. No, I would go to the blueprint, see how the house is *supposed* to be made, and work with that design in mind.

So we will follow our Lord in looking back at the very beginning.

The Foundations of Marriage and Family in Man's Need

Phase one

We find phase one of the creation of man in Genesis 2:7–9, 15–18.

> Then Yahweh God formed the man, dust from the ground; then He blew in his nostrils the spirit of life; and the man became a living soul. [8]Then Yahweh God planted a garden in Eden to the east, and there He placed the man whom He had formed. [9]Then Yahweh God caused to sprout from the ground every tree *that is* desirable as to appearance and good for food; and the tree of life in the midst of the garden, and the tree of the knowledge of good and evil.
> …[15]Then Yahweh God took the man, and He set him down in the garden of Eden, to work it and to keep it. [16]Then Yahweh God

commanded the man,[1] saying, "From every tree of the garden you may eat freely, [17]but from the tree of the knowledge of good and of evil you shall not eat—for in the day of your eating from it you shall surely die!"[2]

[18]Then Yahweh God said, "The man being by himself is not good. I shall make for him a helper, corresponding to him." (DJP)

The creation narratives, in contrast to Proverbs, are not written as poetry but as historical narrative. All the Bible treats this section as having occurred in the same space-time world as the rest of history.

The first chapter of Genesis is a more general overview of creation, structured along the six days of creation. It might correspond to a "pan shot" on television, where the entire span of an area is taken in. Chapter 2 corresponds to a "tight close-up" shot, focusing on the creation of *man*. Here the order of events is not strictly chronological (sequence having already been established in chapter one), but thematic.

The picture Moses paints is clearly of man having absolutely everything that he could possibly need...or so it would seem, initially.

The problem of man is seen in the parenthesis of Genesis 2:18–20. In Genesis 1, we saw God saying "good, good, good" at each stage of creation (except Monday, 1:6–8). The first "not good" in all of creation is man's aloneness; it means that man's situation was not yet complete, he still had a need (v. 18).

Remember four things:

1. Man already was the image of God.

2. Man already had all the rudimentary spiritual and intellectual equipment he was going to need.

3. Man already had his task from God, his work to do, his responsibility of being in charge of creation.

4. Man already had company per se, in his fellowship with God.

In that light, think again of the "not good" of verse 18: "Then Yahweh God said, 'The man being by himself is not good. I shall make for him a helper, corresponding to him'" (DJP).

---

[1] Very literally, "commanded upon the man."

[2] Literally, "dying you shall die," which is to say "dying is what you will certainly do!"

From our perspective, we would likely have said that it was all really quite good. What was it that was not good? What does this teach us?

The least we must say, *first*, is that what Adam lacked was not a sense of God's love for him. Marriage was not created as the answer to lack of assurance of God's love. Anyone who does not have a God-centered worldview that assures him of God's love for him before marriage will not gain it from marriage. In fact, anyone who marries to fill a psychic hole will probably eat his/her mate alive, trying to fill that hole by the love of his mate.[3]

Second, what was lacking was not a sense of purpose, or a plan for life. Adam already had a life-calling: he was to subdue the earth for God. He already had a job: he was to take care of the garden. He did not get married so as to gain a purpose in life. Anyone who does not have purpose in life before marriage, will either not gain a purpose... or he will end up with the wrong purpose.

So, what was lacking in Adam or in his situation, so that all was "not good" in God's eyes? The text tells us that was lacking, specifically, was what God calls a "helper, corresponding to him," an *'ēzer kᵉnegdô*.

We must understand the meaning of the phrase. An *'ēzer* is a helper, an assistant. In itself, the word may denote an equal or subordinate, as in Isaiah 30:5.[4] Equally, it could denote a superior, as in Exodus 18:4, and often. The point, however, is that this is someone who will help Adam in realizing his created task, his life-calling.

The term *kᵉnegdô* hyper-woodenly means "as-in-front-of-him," or "like-opposite-him." The idea of the word is more than just "like him,"[5] but means "corresponding to him." The idea of complementarity is thus included. In other words, the idea that the helper God sees Adam needing is not just to be a living tool. Rather, this helper will be a complement to him, will fill him out, and will both assist him and be a companion to him.

We understand what an *'ēzer kᵉnegdô* is a little better by studying what an *'ēzer kᵉnegdô* isn't, in the narrative. For instance, an *'ēzer kᵉnegdô* could not be found among the animals (Gen. 2:19–20). True, the animals could "help" him as living tools; however, they could never be partners, and they could never correspond to him. They could never be soul-mates. Nor could they reproduce the species, as God desired.

---

3   Does Proverbs 30:23a reflect this reality?
4   The verb is also used this way in Joshua 10:4, 6; 2 Samuel 21:17; 1 Kings 1:7, and so forth.
5   As Wenham observes (citing Delitzsch), the word *kāmôhû* would express that idea better (Gordon J. Wenham, *Genesis 1–15,* Word Biblical Commentary [Waco: Word, 1987], 68).

Everything else had been created with its answering complement. The sky had birds and stars. The waters had fish. The dry land had animals. Each animal had its mate. Only man was created without his counterpart. As one rabbinical writing has it, the animals pass by Adam in pairs, and Adam laments, "Everything has its partner but I have no partner."[6]

It was this lack of a "soul-mate" that God had in mind in saying the first "not good." Adam needed a helper, and particularly a helper corresponding to him, for assistance and companionship. Adam would be in charge, as Scripture makes clear.[7] But that would not mean that Adam's wife was of inferior worth, since she would be "corresponding to him." She alone, of all creation, would share humanity with Adam, would bear the image of God with him.

The stubborn refusal to recognize the possibility of an equality of worth coexisting with inequality of function is simply a perversity of our culture.

Never forget, then, God's design: God created Adam—as He created all things—for His service. As such, God's design would never have been to create someone to make it harder or more miserable for Adam to serve Him. Rather, God would create someone to better facilitate Adam's service of Him.

Since this was the specific reason for which God created the first wife—to be a helper corresponding to him—this means that the woman would really find her greatest happiness in embracing what God created her to be. Unwise women might not think so (Prov. 14:1), but it remains true, nonetheless.

Apply this truth to the two kinds of wives we will see in Proverbs. Solomon will paint warning portraits of bickering, nagging, argumentative, shaming wives. We could sum it all up by saying that these are women who are not heartily embracing the role for which God created them. These women are not helping their husbands, they are hurting them. Ironically, by trying to get what they want rather than doing what they need, these women are always depicted as miserably unhappy individuals.

By contrast, Proverbs will also paint an encouraging portrait of the woman of excellence, such as that we find in chapter 31. We could sum up this model wife as a woman who heartily embraces, and finds her fulfillment in, the role for which God created her. She is always seen helping her husband, not hurting him.

---

[6] *Ber.Rab.* 17:5, quoted in Wenham, 68.
[7] Cf. Genesis 3:9, 16b; 1 Corinthians 11:3, 8, 9, etc.

As a result, while the foolish woman is always miserable and discontented in her self-directed course in pursuit of what she imagines as fulfillment, the woman of excellence is a beamingly happy, upliftingly positive, truly fulfilled lady.

When a marriage is unhappy, this is one area that is important to check. Although the wife's specific complaints may be many, it may boil down to this one matter: she has not embraced the role for which God created her.

Unfortunately, this besetting sin is not addressed much. Many marriage help books are written by men who seem to be embarrassed by and apologetic about what the Bible says. Many men are deathly afraid of being seen as benighted sexist Neanderthals.

Accordingly, I have found that many tend to skip lightly over this area, or to hedge it about with so many apologies and hyper-qualifications that it ends up buried well out of sight. However, we cannot understand Solomon's mindset (let alone share it) unless we grasp and embrace what older Scripture had taught him.

Pastors should be very straight on their commitments and convictions. First, they must calculate that they would be doing nobody any favors by watering down what God says, or by pretending that He hasn't said it, just so that nobody gets mad at them. Remember, "The fear of man lays a snare" (Prov. 29:25a). A faithful pastor needs to make peace with the likelihood being rejected by the "itching ears" crowd.

Second, and more fundamentally, a pastor will hardly fulfill his appointed task and please his Lord if he shrinks from declaring what is profitable, even the whole counsel of God—even the unpopular, out-of-style parts (Acts 20:26–27). No pastor should want to stand before God's final judgment and hear, "You refused to tell them what I said because you were afraid of *what?*"

Phase two

We next encounter phase two of the creation of man in Genesis 2:21–25. This is the completion of man's creation.[8] Adam recognizes that, in Eve, he finally has the soul-mate for whom he'd searched in vain, and he cries out in delight, "This one, this time, is bone from my bones, and flesh from my flesh! She shall be called Woman, because from Man was she taken" (2:23 DJP).[9] In naming her, Adam claimed her as his own. Along with this creation was the institution of marriage,

---

8   Cf. remarks on 1:26, below.
9   We might say that this was Adam's last act of the initial naming of creation (cf. Gen. 2:19, 20).

which was how God met man's need: "For this reason a man forsakes his father and his mother, and sticks to his wife, and the two shall become one flesh" (2:24 DJP).

Now they are wed, and they can enjoy mutual vulnerability as they work together to serve God ("And the two of them were naked, the man and his wife—but they were not ashamed of themselves" [2:25 DJP]).

The Foundations of Marriage and Family in God's Design

Now that we have reviewed the events of man's creation, we shall inquire anew as to His design. He did not create mankind, nor institute marriage, on a whim. Everything God does, He does in accord with His eternal plan (Eph. 1:11; 3:11). What part of that plan did man's creation occupy?

We shall study both the end and the means of God's design.

The end

We learn that the *end* was the exercise of *dominion.*

> Then God said, "Let Us make man in Our image, according to Our likeness, that they may rule the fish of the sea, and the birds of the heavens, and the cattle, and all the earth, and every crawling thing that crawls on the earth." (Gen. 1:26 DJP)

With appropriate apologies (if any) to the "animal rights" folks; man was created distinct from animal creation, and immeasurably superior to it. The image of God has its meaning in this charge that God gives man, to exercise dominion. The man and the woman, then, share in the same task: subdue creation for God, rule together for Him.

Marriage, then, must be neither an interruption or nor an obstacle to this God-given task. Marriage will be a means to God's end.

The means

Next, we learn that part of the *means* toward this end would be *creating a "staff."*

> Then God blessed them, and God said to them, "Be fruitful, and become many, and fill the earth, and subdue it; and exercise dominion over the fish of the sea, and over the birds of the heavens, and over every animal which crawls upon the earth." (Gen. 1:28 DJP)

Children were not designed by God because they were cute and warm, and thus darling and cuddlesome. Children definitely were not designated as an end in themselves, so that the mere having of children achieves an ultimate goal. Why did God create the mechanism for producing children? Children were brought in to be a staff, to work with their parents in subduing creation for the glory of God. The duties of "filling" and "subduing" were complementary.

The Duration of the Union

We find God's *intention* revealed in Genesis 2:24 and Matthew 19:6.

> For this reason a man forsakes his father and his mother, and sticks to his wife, and the two shall become one flesh. (Gen. 2:24 DJP)

> [After quoting Gen. 2:24] "Wherefore they are no longer two, but *rather* one flesh. Therefore, what God has yoked together, let man not separate." (Matt. 19:6 DJP)

We see here that God's intention is permanency, within this life (cf. Matt. 22:29–30). God created one man and one woman, for each other. The entire race was to be populated from that one union. God did not create Adam and Eve, and then a couple of spares for each of them in case their marriage didn't work out.

In affirming this, however, we must avoid here two errors:

First error

Some would argue that, because God intends permanency, a marriage may never and can never be dissolved.

This position, popular among some reactionaries today, is a bit like saying, "Because God intends that murder should never happen, there is no need for a police force and a justice system." Police and courts exist because sin exists. So does divorce.

None of the terms Moses uses means absolute, indissoluble permanence. The intent, clearly, is permanence. But also the intent is that there be no sin. Sin, unfortunately, changes the equation. In the Bible, some marriages are in fact terminated. To say that God "does not recognize" their termination is hardly complimentary to God. If man knows that something exists, so does God.

The Bible explicitly gives a number of possible grounds, under both the Old and the New Covenant, for divinely-permitted dissolution of a marriage (Deut. 24:1–4; Matt. 5:31–32; 19:9; 1 Cor. 7:13–15). The Biblical position is that, while God intends that marriage be lifelong, the Bible recognizes that certain categories of sin can terminate a marriage.

Second error

Others contend that, because a marriage can be dissolved at all, it may be dissolved at will, simply whenever the going gets tough or the joy is gone.

Everyone should take to heart that God's preference is the continuation of the union. No one should enter into the dissolution of a marriage lightly. While God allows some grounds for termination of the marriage covenant, those grounds are specific and restricted. At its very best, divorce is always only a "least-worst" option. God does not hate divorced people, but He does hate divorce, because divorce always means sin and treachery on some level (cf. Mal. 2:16 NAS).

If one approaches marriage with the thought, "…and if this doesn't work out, there's always divorce"—he is not seeing marriage as God sees it. Divorce is a miserable remedy allowed in a narrow range of circumstances to alleviate a *more* miserable situation. It is not a breath-mint to liven up mild unpleasantness.

The Foundational Pledge (Gen. 2:24)

> For this reason a man forsakes his father and his mother, and sticks
> to his wife, and the two shall become one flesh. (DJP)

How does one enter into marriage? One enters in *by covenant*.

Covenant

"Covenant" is not a word in common, modern use. We search around for modern equivalents, picking up "contract" or "deal" or "treaty"; but ultimately we have to put them back down. None of them really captures the idea of the Biblical covenant.

The best way to explain "covenant" is to define it as a *regulated relationship*. It is not merely a commitment to provide goods and services. A covenant relates two entities—whether nation and nation, God and His people, or (as here) a man and his wife. A covenant binds the two together, defines the relationship, outlines the edges, and fills in the participants' responsibilities to each other.

Bilateral covenants

Some covenants are bilateral (= two-sided) and therefore conditional. The two parties in effect say to each other, "If you do A, I will do B." We clearly see such a covenant at Sinai (Exod. 19:5–6; cf. Lev. 26 and Deut. 28).[10]

Unilateral covenants

Other covenants are unilateral and therefore unconditional, in that one party voluntarily pledges himself to do something for the other. There is no "if" to it. A clear example of a unilateral covenant may be found by comparing Genesis 12:1–3 with 15:9–21.

Marital covenant

Marriage is essentially a *bilateral, conditional covenant.* Husband and wife unite in obliging themselves to each other, thus creating and regulating the relationship, which is intended to be life-long, but which under certain specific circumstances may be abrogated (Deut. 24:1–4; Matt. 5:31–32; 19:9; 1 Cor. 7:13–15, etc.).

The covenantal nature of marriage is suggested at its institution in the words "leave...and cleave"; or, as I render them "forsake... and stick" (Gen. 2:24). One forsakes the relationship he had with his parents to establish a new family, founded on his covenanted commitment to "stick" to his wife. "This is the language of covenant commitment," Waltke rightly observes.[11]

The Bible expressly uses covenantal language of marriage. In Proverbs 2:17, the adulteress who in Line A "forsakes the companion of her youth" is said in Line B to be one who also "forgets the covenant of her God." Again in Malachi 2:14, God says of "the wife of your youth" that she is "your companion and your wife by covenant."

In this covenant, then, the man and woman commit themselves to be each other's companion on an exclusive level. In ancient times a covenant was celebrated by a feast. In marriage, the covenant is sealed and celebrated by the "feast" of sexual union ("the two shall become one flesh").

As an aside, we note that folks today reverse the order; or they omit the covenant part altogether—and they ruin a great many things in the process. Sex

---

[10] Though this might seem at first to be perfectly well-expressed by "contract," it still is a regulated relationship, rather than a simple agreement to perform certain services.

[11] Bruce K. Waltke and Cathi J. Fredricks, *Genesis: A Commentary* (Grand Rapids: Zondervan,

without marriage is a little like notarizing a blank piece of paper, or breaking open a bottle of champagne to celebrate a promotion one didn't receive.

People today engage in sex freely and frequently with many partners, and then dully wonder why they end up hollow and scarred. The answer is not hard to find. It is because they think themselves wiser than God, and reap the bitter consequences.

Now we pause for two asides.

First Aside: Does the Nature of Marriage as "Covenant" Have any Practical Impact?

It is absolutely imperative that we understand the nature of marriage as a conditional, bilateral covenant. Go wrong here, and we will not be able to make sense of anything the Bible says about divorce and remarriage. Worse, go wrong here, and we will not grasp the nature of the relationship of Christ and the church (cf. 2 Cor. 11:2; Eph. 5:22–32; Rev. 19:7ff.).

Beyond that, a grasp of this teaching would be revolutionary, both in pastoral, marital counseling and in Christian marriage per se. It brings us face to face with what I think is the single most neglected marital truth from the Bible.

What is that truth? I'll give you a few hints:

- A man who vows may not break his word, must keep his whole vow or oath (Num. 30:2)

- God expects one who makes a vow to fulfill it promptly or he incurs sin. Better not to vow, than to vow and not deliver (Deut. 23:21–23; cf. Eccl. 5:5)

- The mark of the man who is in fellowship with Yahweh is that he keeps his vows even when fulfilling them costs him and causes him pain (Psa. 15:1–2, 4b) [12]

- *After* the making of a vow is not the time to reflect on the vow's wisdom (Prov. 20:25)

To that large (but not exhaustive) list, we could add our Lord's words that our "yes" should mean "yes" (Matt. 5:33–37), as well as his half-brother's echoing of that same thought (James 5:12)—plus all the verses warning against and forbidding the telling of lies. For what is it to swear and not fulfill, but to lie?

2001; used by permission), 90; cf. also Victor P. Hamilton, *The Book of Genesis Chapters 1–18* (Grand Rapids: Eerdmans, 1990), 181.

[12] Cf. also Psalms 56:12; 61:4, 8; 76:11.

What does all this have to do with marriage? As we have just seen, marriage is by its very nature a vow, an oath, a covenant (Gen. 2:24; Prov. 2:17; Mal. 2:14). But in addition to that, at least in our culture, we usually take on ourselves oaths, vows, as part of the marriage ceremony.

Perhaps you recall the traditional vows, with their quaint old wording and abbreviations. In them, the man says something like, "I, John, take you, Jane, to be my wedded wife, to have and to hold from this day forward, for better for worse, for richer for poorer, in sickness and in health, to love and to cherish, till death us do part, according to God's holy ordinance." The woman responds along the lines of, "I, Jane, take you, John, to be my wedded husband, to have and to hold from this day forward, for better for worse, for richer for poorer, in sickness and in health, to love, cherish, and to obey, till death us do part, according to God's holy ordinance."

Note this about all such vows: not one of them is premised on the other's keeping his vows. In other words, we do not read, "*If* you keep your promise, *then* I promise that I will..." The promises are (in this sense) unconditional, and therefore binding as long as the marriage lasts. To be a husband or a wife is to be obliged to keep my vows. Period.

Here is the bottom line: Married folks: *keep your vows*, the vows you made before God and everyone, on the day you got married. If you are not doing so, you are sinning, and must repent, find God's forgiveness—and start keeping those same vows.

Let me add this. Many are "counseling-happy" today. Counseling with a pastor can be a great idea (cf. Heb. 13:17). I'd suggest that anyone wanting marital counseling first take out his/her wedding vows, and ask himself before God, with brutal honesty, whether he (or she) has provided any legitimate basis for charging that he (or she) is failing to keep those vows. If the honest answer is "No," then pastoral counseling may be an option.

If the answer is "Yes," then the only counseling he/she should seek from his/her pastor is to how to address and mortify this sin-pattern in his or her life.

To pastors and Christian counselors, I offer this suggestion: What if you started with this issue? Begin counseling by meeting with each spouse, individually. Tell each to bring the wedding vows, for review. Go over them closely and Biblically. Deal with sin honestly and brutally. Is each keeping his vows, her vows? The actions of the other are immaterial, at this point.

If they are not keeping the vows by which they defined their covenant, the vows they assured that trusting person to "bet" the rest of his or her life on—then you may well have isolated both the problem (sin), and the solution (repentance).

After that is all taken care of, then see if there is still really any need for further counseling.

Second Aside: Will this Study Offer Anything of Value for the Unmarried?

Valerie and I heard a sad story once from a local church. Its women's group was considering what book to use next for a Bible study. Someone proposed a very good book on being a Christian wife. It was summarily rejected. Why? "We don't want the unmarried women to feel left out."

My dear wife and I were aghast. What poor reasoning! Those were the very people who might profit most from such a study.

All Christians are concerned about the high divorce rates. Some, moved by this concern, think that marriages will last longer if we make it harder to get out of marriage, and work harder to shame and shun and sideline those who do. Others, concerned for individuals in damaging marriages, want to find ways to make it easier to get out and start again, free from shame or stigma.

Both attitudes miss the heart of the matter. There is no virtue (or wisdom) in trying to be stricter or more lax than God—on this or any subject. Since God's intention is permanency, would it not be far wiser to concentrate on making a wise marriage choice in the first place, and then helping married folks have the godliest marriage possible?

So how do we make that choice? How do we decide whether, and whom, to marry? And what shall we do once married?

To the first question, probably the majority "Christianoid" answer is that there is only one right man or woman, chosen by God for us individually. God wants us to find that one person; anyone else will be less than His perfect will. Since that person doesn't have his/her ideal match tattooed on his/her forehead, Christians have to get that information some other way.

One very popular view has it that God must tell me directly who that person is. He has to impart semi-revelation, subjective and fallible, discernable as if by divination. I am to lay my own mind and judgment aside, and concern myself with being "open to the Holy Spirit"—rather than with making a good decision.

If I am not "in tune" enough with God's vibrations, I miss out on God's "perfect will" for the rest of my life.

I actually knew a girl whose friend's mother felt she had missed God's best. She "felt called" to be a missionary, but married a man who did not feel that "call." And so she carried with her the knowledge that she was out of God's perfect will for good.[13]

A more Biblical answer would be to realize at the outset that the Bible simply does not teach that there is only one divinely-chosen prospective mate within God's will, whom each single Christian is obliged to divine—at the risk of being out of God's will and married to a "B-lister" forever. For decades I have challenged proponents to find me one single verse that even hints at such a notion. The challenge stands unmet.

The Bible teaches that we should choose a mate within revealed guidelines, and by application of revealed wisdom principles. A very important text in this connection is 1 Corinthians 7:39—"A woman has been bound as long a time as her husband lives; but if the husband dies, she is free to be married to whom she wishes—only in the Lord" (DJP). Did you see that? "Free to be married *to whom she wishes*." Not a hint of her needing to go into a trance or read tea leaves or portents. Paul gives one restriction: "only in the Lord." She must marry a fellow-Christian. That is the moral guideline. Beyond that, the choice is hers. She is "free."

We are about to study the traits of a godly husband or wife, and the opposing vices. How would people from the two groups I just delineated sit through this section?

Folks with the "majority," "bull's-eye" viewpoint might tune out. Though they might not be married, they believe that when The Time comes, God will simply tell them that they have found "The Right One." The Bible will be of no great help. It is insufficient for this crucial decision. As they themselves often observe, it does not name that special one for them. Rather than drawing the obvious conclusion from that fact (i.e., they are free), they choose instead to feel compelled to get the answer some other way—obviously without any direct Biblical guidance.

---

[13] Do not rush past the appalling effects of this popular view too quickly. Think: *I* knew this because my lady friend told me. *She* knew it because her friend told her. And *her friend* knew it because *her mother* had told this to her—about *her father!* By implication, then, this girl knew her father was "second-best," *and* she knew that she should never have been born! Poor man, poor daughter. Horrible teaching bears horrible fruit.

What of folks holding the other position, which I think to be the more Biblical stance? They will remember that all Scripture is God-breathed and profitable (2 Tim. 3:16)… and *sufficient* (v. 17). They will realize that God does not promise to bypass our thinking and whisper directly into our hearts when we meet The Right One—in part, because Scripture does not teach that there *is* only one "Right One" to be located and married. Convinced of the sufficiency of Scripture, they will reason something like this:

1. Proverbs tells what a wise wife is like, and what a foolish wife is like (and what a wise man is like, and what a foolish man is like).

2. I want to marry a wise woman (or a wise man).

3. Therefore, I will learn *everything I can* about marriage from God's Word, and

   a. Focus on seeking God's grace to become a wise man (or woman); and

   b. Apply Proverbs' standards of wisdom in my search for a mate.

The Husband

We will reverse the usual order of the apostles, who addressed the wife and then the husband (cf. Eph. 5:22f.; Col. 3:18f.; 1 Peter 3:1ff.). Instead, we will follow the order of Yahweh in the Garden. He had left Adam in charge. Something went terribly wrong. Whom did God seek and call to account? The man, the husband, the putative leader (Gen. 3:9f.).

That is where we shall start as well.

Characteristics of a Godly Husband

Of course, there is no such thing as an all-godly or an all-foolish man or woman. But there is Biblical warrant for characterizing someone by the dominant trait of his life and character. Otherwise, the book of Proverbs could never speak of the fool, the wise man, or the sluggard.

These are, if you will, green lights and red lights indicating the nature of a man's character. I will single out three:

1. A godly husband displays all the qualities of a wise man.

2. A godly husband displays intimate enjoyment of his wife.

3. A godly husband displays appreciation of his good wife.

Qualities of a wise man

First, then, a godly husband displays all the qualities of a wise man. That is, all the things that make for a wise man also make for a good husband.

Some may bristle at the outset that Proverbs does not as vividly portray a bad husband as it does a bad wife. We find no extended poem such as Proverbs 31:10–31, setting up an impossibly high bar for men also. Is it sexist that Proverbs seems to go easy on the men, and hard on the women?

I would offer a few thoughts in response.

At the outset, we should note that the challenge misses the point. In our study, are we seeking truth, or are we seeking affirmation? Do we expect Scripture to mirror our culture? Do we have some politically-correct standard, or some personal notion of "fairness," that we wish to try to impose on Scripture?

If that is the case, then we have already pre-decided what we will and will not accept. In that case, Bible study is a sham and a waste of time. After all, if I already have all the answers, I don't need God. I will pick and choose what I will accept from the Bible according to my own prejudices. In that case, I don't need a god—I think I am one.

After that, I would propose three sets of questions and answers:

> First set.
>> *Question*: Who are the most-frequently-encountered negative models in Proverbs?
>> *Answer*: the fool (under several different synonyms), the sluggard, the thief, the liar, the mocker, the unjust, the drunkard, the brawler, and others.

> Second set:
>> *Question*: In what sex are these horrible people usually depicted?
>> *Answer*: they are virtually always cast as *men*.

> Third set:
>> *Question*: How is the embodiment of wisdom depicted at length in chapters 1, 8 and 9?
>> *Answer*: as a *woman*.

We should accept the deep truth that men and women are different. They are not different as to humanity and worth, but they are different as to created makeup. Therefore, it should not shock us into a coma if we see some uniquely masculine flaws exposed, along with some uniquely feminine flaws.

Reflect on God's rationale. The man is to lead, and his wife is to help him. The same things that make the man a failure in life—ungodliness, lying, foolishness, laziness, naïveté, hot temper, short-sightedness, etc.—will make him a failure in marriage. By the same token, the same things that make him a wise and godly man—fear of Yahweh, wisdom, honesty, hard work, self-control, a gentle tongue, kindness—will make him a wise and godly husband.

It follows, then, that all of the qualities of wisdom and folly can be applied to a man's life in general, or equally to a man's life as a husband. Therefore, as we study all these truths from Proverbs, we will be studying qualities that make for a good husband. So we will try to single out the things about men that are particularly relevant to men as married men.

Intimate enjoyment of his wife

Second, a godly husband displays intimate enjoyment of his wife. This truth is grounded on Genesis 2:24.

> For this reason a man forsakes his father and his mother, and sticks
> to his wife, and the two shall become one flesh. (Gen. 2:24 DJP)

We note once again that the sequence is: marriage covenant, *then* sex.

- In that order
- Both, or neither

Morally, there is no difference between "one-night-stands" and un-married cohabitation. If people are "shacking up"—living together in a sexual relationship—they are simply fornicating with each other on a regular basis. Sharing an address in itself does not affect the moral crime against God.

As we shall see, the Bible portrays married sex as a blessing. Sexual intimacy is moral; it is a gift from God—within marriage. Solomon urges his son to enjoy "water" from his own "cistern," to delight himself with his wife's breasts, his wife's love (Prov. 5:15–19). In fact, verse 19 says "be intoxicated," which translates the verb šāgâ (v. 19). The verb normally means to err or go astray.[14] Here it means "to be wholly captivated by her, so that one is no longer in his own power, can

---

[14] See Delitzsch, 1:131.

no longer restrain himself—the usual word for the intoxication of love and of wine, xx. 1."[15] The same verb *šāgâ* is also used in 5:23, "in the greatness of his folly he will go astray" (NAS).

I once heard a conference speaker somberly warn married men against lusting… for their own wives! Like the speaker, I was unmarried at the time, and I thought that was one of the most preposterous things I'd ever heard. Several decades later, I've heard a lot of silliness—but that one still ranks up near the top.

Solomon knows nothing of such asceticism within marriage, nor does the rest of the Bible. This text encourages a man to let himself go a little crazy in sharing sexual joy with his wife. Remember, God invented sex. The intense pleasure that healthy sexuality brings within marriage was created intentionally and did not take God by surprise.

Think about it, at least a little. Had He so chosen, God could easily have made reproduction as unmoving and deliberate as shaking hands, or as involuntary as spreading germs. However, God deliberately designed sex within marriage a thrilling, releasing, exhilarating event.

According to this text, it is the one normal time when God says we can get drunk, though not with liquor.

Now again, some might protest that this revolves around the husband's needs. It is true that this text focuses on the husband's enjoyment. That is because Solomon is talking to the husband, warning him against adultery. If we want to read everything through a tinted microscope, then men could equally complain that only they are singled out as adultery risks.

Paul adds further revelation on married sexuality in 1 Corinthians 7:4b—"the husband does not have authority over his own body, but the wife does." The wife actually has authority over her husband's body, to assure that her needs to are met as well.

Since sexual enjoyment within marriage is a shared right and responsibility, this text could readily be aimed both ways. As Solomon counsels the husband directly to go to his wife for the fulfillment of his sexual needs, so it would be the wife's responsibility to communicate her needs to her husband in an honest and straightforward way as well.

---

[15] Delitzsch, 1:132. Proverbs 20:1 reads, "Wine is a mocker, strong drink a brawler, And whoever is intoxicated [*šōgeh*] by it is not wise" (NAS).

Appreciation

Third, a godly husband displays appreciation of his good wife. We see that at the very start of the Ode to the Excellent Wife, in Proverbs 31:29–30—

> "Many daughters have done excellently,[16]
> But you—you have surpassed them all!"
>
> [30] Charm is deceitful and beauty is nothing;[17]
> A woman who fears Yahweh, it is she who shall be praised (DJP)

What is it that she has done to elicit such praise? So special a person is this woman, that she crowns the book, she closes the *inclusio* between Proverbs 1:7 and 31:30. How does she so distinguish herself?

I have long thought that the center, heart and key lie in verses 11–12. This is fundamentally why she is such a show-stopping Godsend to her husband:

> The heart of her husband trusts in her,
> And he will not come short of profit.
>
> [12] She does him good, and not evil,
> All the days of her life (DJP)

This woman gives her husband every reason to see that she has wholeheartedly embraced God's revealed plan for her. She is not numbered among the bitter women who profess religion yet ceaselessly seek "loopholes" in God's Word to them. This woman is his helper and soul-mate in God's service, and she exults in that role.

So, he gives her what she so richly deserves: trust (v. 11), and praise (vv. 29–30)—including public acclaim (v. 31).

As a result, you see that the godly husband displays great confidence in his good wife, in terms of her delegated responsibilities. She has freedom to exercise her sharp, sage, decisive mind. She presides over the supplies and services of the household (vv. 13–15).

> She searches for wool and linen,
> And her hands keep working with pleasure.
>
> [14] She is like a ship of a trader,
> She brings her bread from afar.

---

[16] Hebrew *'āsû ḥāyil*, "have done excellence."

[17] Or "vain"; the term means a vapor, a breath.

[15] Then she arises while it is still night,
>   And she gives food to her house,
>   And a prescribed portion to her young ladies.

She even purchases property (v. 16).

>   She considers a field and gets it,
>   From the fruit of her hands she plants a vineyard. (DJP)

She engages in charitable endeavors (v. 20).

>   She spreads out her palm to the afflicted,
>   And she stretches out her hands to the poor. (DJP)

She owns and operates her own business (v. 24).

>   She makes a linen wrapper and sells *it*,
>   And she gives a girdle to the merchant. (DJP)

She enjoys some public prominence of her own, due to her achievements (v. 31).

>   Give her of the fruit of her hands,
>   And let her works praise her in the gates![18] (DJP)

From all this, we see that godly male leadership is not…

- …a matter of having a wife who is chained to a post in her home; or
- …a matter of having a wife who has no interests or pursuits of her own; or
- … a matter of having a wife whose whole world is her husband and her children within their four walls; or
- … a matter of having a wife who is afraid of venturing an inch beyond her little rut.

Rather, godly leadership is a matter of…

- …working with one's life-partner; and
- …leading her to become all that God has made her to be; and of…
- …showing confidence and trust in her.

Any lout with a few abilities can just do everything and give his subordinates the impression that they are incompetents who cannot do anything right, and

---

[18] Remember that the "gate" was basically the City Hall of the ancient city. Legal and public matters were settled at the gate.

who dare not try anything. It takes real leadership to inspire others to try new things and branch out, while still remaining centered on the shared family goals.[19]

So, once again, we see the godly husband leading his children, setting the example, in giving her full and out-loud credit for her remarkable character and her accomplishments (Prov. 31:28–31).

Women tell me that the husband's opinion is what means the most to the wife. Therefore, it will mean a lot for the husband to praise his wife, to give her full credit for who she is and what she does. Accordingly, this blessed husband sings his wife a "hallelu" (v. 28),[20] which is fitting, and is based on the quality of her character as shown in her lifestyle.

This is in keeping with Peter's word to the husband in 1 Peter 3:7—"Likewise, husbands, live with your wives in an understanding way, showing honor to the woman as the weaker vessel, since they are heirs with you of the grace of life, so that your prayers may not be hindered."

Proverbs 31 teaches men that they should be quick to praise. For one thing, as a general rule, praise is the surest way to encourage healthy, good behavior in anybody. Neglecting to offer genuine praise can crush a wife's spirit. Nothing can be more crushing to women (and men) than to labor away and feel that it is for nothing, that everything is taken for granted.

It is dispiriting to feel that it is simply assumed that we will function, as you and I assume that the light-switch will work, and never praise it when it does. This is a real weakness for many men. The wisest thing that a man can do is make sure that he gives his wife a lot of praise.

How much praise is "a lot" of praise? For most men, probably about 150% of our current output should be just about right.

Verse 31 directs that the excellent wife be allowed to appreciate the fruits of her own labors.

> Give her of the fruit of her hands,
> And let her works praise her in the gates!

---

[19] Of course, as long as we have a Bible that so bluntly describes the foolish behavior of the Twelve during Jesus' life, we cannot assume that every failure is the leader's fault. It is the same in a family. A father can lead well, and still have a failed family. Equally, a family can excel in spite of being subjected to a wretch at the helm.

[20] The verb in the Hebrew "he praises her" is that from which "Hallelu-yah," "Praise ye Yah[weh]," comes.

The verb translated "give" is plural. That means, more than one person is being ordered to give credit to the excellent wife. This includes at least whole family... and maybe everybody else as well—but at least her husband.

One way in which she appreciates the fruits of her labor is her knowledge that the nest she is living in is partly of her own construction.

Sidebar: Dynamic Wives

I think that some men feel threatened by the thought of wise, powerful, accomplished wives. Of course, a superior woman can hold her giftedness over her husband, and can treat him in a belittling, demeaning way. But this is by no means necessarily the case. In fact, the most powerful man ever was a man who had His power under control[21] and willingly submitted to the authorities in His life (Luke 2:51; John 4:34).

Men who are blessed with such Proverbs 31 wives should remember: your wife is "one flesh" with you. She is your partner and helper. You and she form a team.

In 1988, an injured Kirk Gibson drove an amazing home run, helping win the World Series for the Los Angeles Dodgers. I can still see it in my mind's eye. What greeted him at the plate, as he hobbled in? Did we see all the other players sulking and moping around, worried that Gibson had made them look like a bunch of nothings? Were they yelping out their fear that Gibson would earn more next year than they would, that people would forget about their contributions and make a big deal about him instead of them?

Far from it. What we saw were men going crazy with delight, with high-fives and bear-hugs all around. Why? Simple: because *their team had* won.

So, when a man's wife "hits home-runs," he should take the lead in making a big commotion about it. Nothing more eloquently teaches sons to love their future wives, nor daughters to look for wise husbands, than learning from the example of a father who celebrates his wife's excellence.

Any husband who is slow, reluctant, or half-hearted in giving such recognition only succeeds in coming off as a large, threatened baby. The man who is secure in his manhood has nothing to lose by publicly and loudly praising his wife.

---

[21] This is the meaning of *praus*, translated "gentle" in Matthew 11:29—*power under control.*

Characteristics of an Ungodly Husband

Seven major traits can be isolated within Proverbs that identify the unwise, ungodly husband.

Qualities of a fool

First, an ungodly husband is one who displays the qualities of a fool.

Let us focus on *four* specifically germane aspects of the foolish husband, *beginning* with the fact that he will be a *zero in listening* (12:15)—

> The way of a dense man is straight in his own eyes;
> But he who listens to counsel is wise. (DJP)

The assumption of the verse is that the counsel that is being listened to is good counsel. We are always subject to the caution expressed in 14:15—

> The gullible man has faith as to every word,
> But the shrewd man has discernment as to his steps. (DJP)

Nobody ever receives praise in Proverbs for heeding poor counsel (cf. Prov. 1:10ff.; 17:4).

Let us consider the man who never listens to his wife: on the one hand, a man is not obliged to agree with his wife's advice. Sometimes the best, wisest, and most loving thing a husband can do is to choose a course other than what his wife would choose. Ask Adam (Gen. 3:6b), ask Abram (Gen. 16:2f.), ask Job (Job 2:9).

However, nothing excuses a husband who, as a matter of policy, simply never seriously considers and follows his wife's input and advice. I have always wanted to ask such men, "Why did you marry this poor woman, if you didn't think that she had anything going on between her ears?"

God's intention is that a man's wife be his helper. A wife does not help her husband only by cooking, sewing, having sex, and making and rearing little Rufuses and Hephzibahs. A wife helps her husband by giving him the benefit of her viewpoint, her counsel. She shares the image of God (Gen. 5:1–2), she is a fellow-heir of the grace of life (1 Peter 3:7).

A man who does not listen to his wife, out of sheer arrogance and stubbornness, is at the very least being a poor leader. He is failing to give his wife an opportunity to do, to stretch, to grow in a positive and encouraging environment. Also, he is being a poor servant of God. He is not allowing his God-given helper to help him where he needs it the most. He is being like a man who has a top-of-the-line computer, and uses it exclusively as a doorstop.

I appreciate the way my mother-in-law put it: the wife should be the putty that fills in the man's gaps and cracks. A godly, wise man will be able to consider the wife's counsel seriously, giving a sincere and fair hearing. He who will not do so is simply dense. Or so says God, through Solomon.

Quarrelsome

Second, an ungodly husband is quarrelsome (20:3)—

> It is an honor for a man to keep aloof from strife,
> but every fool[22] will be quarreling.

In the arena of marriage, this is the man who always welcomes a fight, who rises to and enjoys domestic strife.

Perhaps you have heard the conventional wisdom that fighting is healthy for a marriage, that a little "clearing the air" (by means of a fight) is actually constructive and helpful. I have come to be absolutely convinced that this is a lie, and harmful one at that. A married couple should *never* fight.

By "fight," of course, I do not mean "disagree," nor do I mean have lively discussions nor debates. It is probably not only impossible, but positively undesirable that disagreements never take place in a marriage of two redeemed pilgrims on their way to—but not yet arrived at—the Celestial City. (More on that, later.)

Probably any couple knows when a disagreement becomes a fight. When lines are drawn up, tempers flare, hurtful accusations are hurled, and verbal blows are exchanged, a disagreement has degenerated into a fight. One opponent seeks to defeat the other, at almost any cost. Victory becomes the only goal.

This should never happen between two Christians.

Why not? Glad you asked.

Sidebar: Why Christian couples should never fight each other

1. A *husband* should never participate in a fight (I choose my words deliberately here) because:

   a. A veritable pile of proverbs praise self-control and condemn giving in

---

[22] The Hebrew word is *ʾwîl*, meaning a dense man.

to temper, of which this is only a sample: 14:29; 16:32; 17:27; 20:3.

b. He is to care for his wife as Christ cares for the church—which excludes identifying her as a target or an opponent to be "taken down" (Eph. 5:23).

c. "She started it," *even if true*, simply means that the husband should respond as Christ calls all Christians to respond to attack, as the following small selection may serve to remind:

- "…if anyone slaps you on the right cheek, turn to him the other also" (Matt. 5:39b) Remember that this slap is an insult, as one's wife might become insulting during a fight. In Matthew 5:38–42 Jesus rules out responding in kind.
- Cf. also 1 Peter 2:21–23; 3:8–9.

2. A *wife* should never participate in a fight because:

a. See "a" above.

b. The wife is called by God to subordinate herself to her husband (Eph. 5:22, 24, 33; Col. 3:18; 1 Peter 3:1–6), and there simply is no room for fighting, as defined above, from such a position.

c. See "c" above.

d. A woman who sees herself free to resist, denigrate and fight her husband is not emulating Proverbs 31:12, and cannot expect the blessing of Proverbs 31:11.

Abusive

Third, an ungodly husband is *abusive* (29:11)—

> A fool gives full vent to his spirit,
> but a wise man quietly holds it back.

The first phrase is literally, "All his spirit a stupid man discharges [literally *causes to go out*]." This means that he gives full vent to his temper, exercising no self-control. A wise man will keep a check on his temper.

Some women are upset if their husbands do not become as upset and demonstrative as they are during a disagreement. The loving and respectful assumption would be that he is keeping a rein on his temper and exercising self-control. If she is wise, she will see this as a godly trait and will be grateful for it, never "egging him on."

Refuses to learn from mistakes

Fourth, an ungodly husband refuses to learn from his mistakes and grow. Proverbs paints a grim picture of such a person:

> The way of the wicked is like deep darkness;
>> they do not know over what they stumble. (Prov. 4:19)

> Like a dog that returns to his vomit
>> is a fool who repeats his folly. (Prov. 26:11)

> Crush a fool in a mortar with a pestle along with crushed grain,
>> yet his folly will not depart from him. (Prov. 27:22)

How many of us have known men who spend their families into a financial hole, barely bail out—and then do it again…and again …and again…. Or they lose job after job, or wreck car after car, amass ticket upon ticket.

One observes such a man, and thinks, "Surely *now* this boy is going to wake up and smell the coffee." Yet then he turns right around and does the same destructive thing, if not worse, all over again.

Every mere mortal makes mistakes. That is not this man's issue. That is not the question to us. The issue is:

- Do we learn from our mistakes?
- Do we accept correction and criticism?[23]
- Do we think carefully about our choices and paths, learning from past mistakes, and avoiding future ones?[24]
- Or do we just blunder on like dullards until we (and our poor family) are shattered?[25]

Destructive

Fifth, an ungodly husband is destructive to his own family. "Whoever troubles his own household will inherit the wind" (11:29a). How does one do this?

---

[23] Proverbs 12:1.
[24] Proverbs 14:15; 15:28.
[25] Proverbs 29:1.

A man can trouble his house by directly wronging them through his own undisciplined, rash idiocy. Remember Saul's rash curse on anyone who ate during a particular battle, in 1 Samuel 14:24. His son Jonathan had not heard the curse. When he saw some honey, he ate it and felt better—and was displeased when he heard of his father's foolish oath. He knew the soldiers would have warred better if they'd eaten.

Yet when Saul learned of what Jonathan had done, he did not have the wisdom to regret his folly. No, he was ready to execute his own son, to save face. Foolish man; unfortunate family.

Also, a man can indirectly trouble his house by his own godlessness. Think of Dathan and Abiram in the rebellion of Korah (Num. 16, especially vv. 3, 27). They rebelled against God's delegated authority, and their families died as a result. Then Achan comes to mind. He stole goods under the ban, and his family joined him in death (Josh. 7, especially verses 1, 24, and 25). Eli harmed his sons by his refusal to discipline them appropriately (1 Sam. 2, especially vv. 29–32; and 3:13). Perhaps most sadly, when David indulged his arrogance and lust with Bathsheba, and had her husband killed (2 Sam. 11), not only did their illegitimately-conceived child die, but the sword did not depart from his family after him (2 Sam. 12, especially vv. 10, 14).

Consider this a moment longer. One of the most sobering, arresting, convicting realizations I carry as a husband and father is this very truth: my own folly, my sin, can harm not only me but my family as well. The prospect of suffering discipline for my failings is weighty; the thought of my family suffering for them is unbearable. None should lose sight of this truth.

Does not discipline his children

Sixth, an ungodly husband does not diligently discipline his children (13:24):

> He who holds back his rod hates his son,
>   but he who loves him seeks him early with discipline.[26]

The man needs to set the pace by training consistently, deliberately disciplined children. His discipline should be proactive rather than reactive, crisis-aversion rather than crisis-management.

---

[26] We are going to look at this in great detail later.

Of course, our evaluation today is backwards: We in our society have come to see the lax, indulgent, permissive TV father as being the model. The media tend to ridicule or condemn a father who does attempt to discipline.

Yet the wisdom of God tells us that it is the lax, permissive father who does not love his son. He does not love him because he is not preparing him for life. He does not love him because he is not preparing him for a relationship with God, who *certainly will* discipline him (Heb. 12:5–11). He does not love him because he will not submit himself to the wisdom of God for fathers, and thus he is setting up a legacy of self-indulgent ungodliness.

Flip-side of wise man's positive qualities

Seventh and finally, an ungodly husband personifies the flip-side of the positive qualities found in a wise man.

Go back to the start of the list and reverse the good to the bad. If the positive quality is intimate enjoyment of the wife, then its flip-side is passive or active sexual sin—immorality, in one of its several forms; defrauding; and the like. If appropriate appreciation of the wife is the positive quality, then withholding of appreciation (a very common male sin, unfortunately) is the flip-side. We could continue down the list in this way.

In parting: some have complained that there is no masculine equivalent to Proverbs 31:10–31. While that is formally true, one could well say that the entire book of Proverbs is the man's equivalent, both in what Solomon praises and in what he lampoons.

Further, one actually can find an extended portrayal of the foolish, ungodly husband. It is a tale Solomon would have known well: the narrative of "The Man Called 'Fool.'" I speak of *Nabal*, whom we meet in 1 Samuel 25. The Bible is far from letting men off the hook.

The Wife

Characteristics of a Godly Wife

As I remarked earlier, there is no such thing as an all-godly or an all-foolish man or woman. However, as we did with the man, so we can notice specific red-light and green-light counsel by which women can be encouraged, warned and instructed.

We should note in starting that all of the general, non-sexual wisdom qualities apply equally to women (i.e. Prov. 1:7, the foundational verse; and countless others such as 13:20, and so forth). Even grammatically-masculine proverbs mostly or all contain wisdom for women.

In illustration of this, we will now study *seven* characteristics of a godly wife.

Wisdom

First, the godly wife displays wisdom. A number of verses highlight this truth. One which does so in a humorous way is Proverbs 11:22.

> A ring of gold in the snout of a pig,
>> a beautiful woman and yet turning away from *good* taste. (DJP)

The mental image is that of looking at a lovely, sparking gold ring, admiring it twinkling in the sun—then seeing that it is in a pig's snout. Wasted! Misplaced! Thus, Solomon says, is a lady with a beautiful outside and nothing going on inside.

The word I translate "good taste" means literally just that: "taste" (as in Exod. 16:31). Then it comes to mean a discerning palate, good taste; and then the ability to discern, to judge, to distinguish among "flavors" of good and evil, of wisdom and folly, as here.

The picture is not simply of a pretty woman without a lot in the area of native IQ, as if by accident of birth and heredity. She is not simply "lacking," but she "turns away." This woman chooses not to develop her God-given brains, turns aside from the things that would develop her judgment and taste—primary among such things, of course, is the learning of the Word of God.

The NT ties this all together for us and shows the way to having a discerning taste, in Hebrews 5:14—"but solid food is the diet of the mature, who on account of habit have their faculties drilled[27] for distinguishing good from evil" (DJP).

Wisdom matters infinitely more than looks. Think of all the time and money that women have wasted sheerly on external cosmetics, only to end up as they started: hollow and empty inside. Real beauty will come with time invested with the Book, not the mirror.

It is said, truthfully, that a lot of men are just after good-looking things, regardless of what is between their ears. They pursue such women as if they were

---

[27] Or "exercised," from the verb *gumnazō*.

little living bangles, cute as a button and half as smart. And if so? What of it? Would a woman of substance *want* such a man as a husband? Such a man never grew up. He does not value what God values (Luke 16:15).

Too many women carry their worst enemy within, and are driven by it to marry worthless men. The wise woman is able to resist such temptation to ruinous "decisions of the heart."

Imagine here a woman who may not be physically "attractive" to such men; who instead is developing her heart after God and cultivating a quiet, gentle, godly, feminine spirit. She should find genuine courage and comfort herself in these truths. She is pleasing God and is thus a fully-valuable, precious, feminine woman who doesn't need a man in order to be worthwhile as a woman. She is developing qualities which, unlike outward appearances, are literally eternal in their value.

A particularly critical verse is Proverbs 14:1.[28]

> Feminine wisdom[29] builds her house,
>   but feminine denseness tears it down with her own hands. (DJP)

What is being called her "house," from God's perspective? First, it will be her husband, without whom none of the rest could follow. Second, it will be her children.

This calls to mind the model wife of chapter 31:10–31 and her priorities. We see that she has an exceptionally well-built "house." She does her husband only good, and he can safely trust her. He has gained prominence in the land. Her children are well-clothed, well-taught, and well-cared-for. The physical dwelling place is being cared for and built up.

All of this contrasts with a relatively newlywed young lady with whom I spoke once, whose stated priorities were (1) God, (2) her baby, and (3) her husband. What to make of that hierarchy? Right, wrong, and wrong, respectively.

How do you build a house? Solomon gives us his answer in Proverbs 24:3–4.

> By wisdom a house is built,
>   and by understanding it is established;
> [4] by knowledge the rooms are filled
>   with all precious and pleasant riches.

---

[28] This verse will be discussed at much greater length, below.
[29] Literally "Wisdoms of women."

One fears that many well-meaning women tell themselves that they are "feathering their nest" while they bustle about arranging, cleaning, and decorating—while, however, they are not growing in the Word of God, and thus cannot fully be a helper to their husband. It is possible to have a really nifty building and still be tearing down one's *house*, in Solomon's sense. Every "finer" neighborhood features magnificent buildings which contain miserable people.

What counts, and what builds a house, is *wisdom* built on the fear of God and reverence for His ways and priorities. Only that equips a woman to be God's kind of first-rate house-builder. Wisdom from God's Word will show a woman how to be a godly, feminine, divinely-powerful woman. It will tell a woman how to treat her husband with a "building" spirit. It will teach a woman how to rear her children, and what does and does not matter in family life and child-rearing.

This all rests on the foundational truth that is not welcome today. A wise woman will know the transcendent value of building her house, of devoting herself to its overall welfare from the central point of loving God and her husband and on down. She will not search for fulfillment by shooting off frenetically in a dozen different directions.

A glance from this verse to our culture forces the conclusion that there are not many wise women today. When a public woman dares to speak up for marriage, family and home, she is hated, vilified, and targeted for public humiliation.

Many women are slowly learning that, as they pursue what they *want*, they do not obtain what they *need*. A woman who is married and stays at home with the children should not envy her businesswoman friend who has a great career and a miserable husband and family—or (worse still) a broken family. What the world calls "successful" seldom overlaps God's definition of success.[30]

More insight is gained from Proverbs 19:14.

> House and wealth are inherited from fathers,
> but a prudent wife[31] is from the LORD.

---

[30] My point here is to praise women whose priority is building their home. None should read into any of this a condemnation of all women who work outside the home. Circumstances differ, and individual strategies for meeting individual families' needs differ. The nice, tidy, safe, blanket generalizations of which so many are too fond should be avoided. My own test-questions would simply be: Is any given arrangement for the betterment of the *family*, for the building of the *home*, or for the advancement of a woman's individual career? Is her husband fully on-board?

[31] Hebrew *'iššâ maśkelet*.

Inheritance is, as it were, an accident of birth, though even that is controlled by God. However, a prudent wife is depicted here as so rare and wonderful that one can only thank God if he has such a woman. After all, even if a man applies the canons of wisdom to the fullest of his abilities, he is just a man. His knowledge is finite, as is his intended's. No man knows whether or how a woman will change after the exchange of vows.

And so Solomon here affirms that, whatever a man has done to choose wisely, when he finds that he has indeed married a prudent woman, he can and must thank Yahweh alone.

Note, too, what it is that is valued in a wife here. It is not merely that a woman is able to make a lot of babies, or that she is a hard worker or a good cook, nor that she is "pretty." What God values is her prudence, her intelligence, the way she uses her head. God prizes an intelligent, insightful, thoughtful woman.

A crowning grace is found in Proverbs 31:26.

> Her mouth she opens in wisdom,
>   and the law of loving-kindness is on her tongue. (DJP)

This, from the song of the strong wife, reveals the importance of the lady's grasp of Bible doctrine. As a woman, she will have a very powerful "mouth." It is axiomatic that the mouth speaks from what fills the heart (cf. Luke 6:45). Therefore, it is crucial that a woman's heart be filled with God's wisdom, with the law of loving-kindness.

With a heart thus filled with good treasure, what comes out of her mouth will be edifying and beneficial.

Intimate enjoyment of her husband

Second, the godly wife intimately enjoys her husband (Prov. 5:18–20). In 1 Corinthians 7 (especially vv. 3–5), Paul speaks of sexuality as a divinely-mandated, mutual obligation. In fact, in a daring (and unparalleled) turn of speech, the apostle speaks of the wife as exercising authority over her husband's body (v. 4). As protection against immorality, among other things, both husband and wife owe intimacy to each other. Each must be personally committed to the sexual satisfaction of the other.

According to both Solomon and Paul, the spouse who refuses to obey God in this is exposing his mate, and therefore his marriage, to Satan's attack without the protective provision that God has built into marriage. To deny one's spouse is a violation of God's law, it is a form of immorality. Clearly, the intent of this and other related passages is to make the marriage bed a place of pleasure and mutual giving and receiving.

Now, a spouse of either sex could lie there with arms folded, waiting for his or her needs to be met. This is a sure recipe for mutual frustration and strife. Or one could apply the Golden Rule in the bedroom, approaching one's spouse to give and serve and delight in love—rather than to nurture demands, conduct tests, set up for failure, and condemn. Approach marital intimacy as yet another way to show love and to give, and one will be well on the way to happiness.

Graciousness

Third, the godly wife displays graciousness (Prov. 11:16).

> A gracious woman[32] attains honor,
> But violent men attain *only* wealth. (DJP)

Here we meet the beautiful trait of *grace*. Graciousness is a loveliness and gentleness of spirit. Since this is a contrasting proverb, we can learn about Line A from Line B.

- Line A praises the positive quality of being a gracious woman.
- Line B contrasts this characteristic against bold, truculent aggression.

Graciousness, then, is the opposite of ruthless violence.

Note: Proverbs 31 paints a portrait of a very powerful woman, a woman of great personal strength.[33] What makes this woman so powerful? The secret of her power is not masculine aggressiveness, nor is it grabbing what she wants at any price. She is not angry that she is a woman. She is not trying to be a man.

The key to this woman's strong character is that she practices the fear of Yahweh, as v. 30 highlights:

> Charm is deceitful and beauty is nothing;[34]
> A woman who fears Yahweh, it is she who shall be praised. (DJP)

---

[32] Literally "woman of grace."

[33] The opening title, "excellent wife" (31:10) is more literally "a woman of strength" or "might" or "excellence."

[34] Or "vain"; the term means a vapor, a breath.

By this fear of Yahweh, *she knows who she is*: a person created in God's image, specifically designed to serve Him as a woman. By this fear of Yahweh, she is content with the role for which God has created her, and is submissive to His revealed plan. By this fear of Yahweh, she has convictions and principles that provide the bedrock for all she is, and the foundation of all she does.

We gain yet more insight into this characteristic by way of 1 Peter 3:1–6. Given our current cultural mood, we will be struck first by v. 1, where Peter urges women to take the path of functional subordination. To almost any modern without faith in Christ, verse 1 is what would be deemed a "non-starter."

But let's turn the matter about. Let us ask: How does a wife *win*, God's way? In verses 1 and 2, Peter provides the answer.

The God-fearing wife does not win by physically or verbally abusing and battering her husband. She does not win by bludgeoning him into submission, compelling compliance with her will. Nor does she win by wearing him down until he is submits out of emasculated exhaustion.

Rather, the godly wife wins by obeying her husband ("subordinating yourselves," v. 1),[35] by obeying God ("pure," v. 2), and by revering her husband ("respectfully," v. 2a).

What matters least about a woman? Verses 3 and 4a tell us: a woman cannot make up for internal deficiency by external splendor. In saying that, Peter's point is not that a woman must never wear jewelry,[36] but that it is not to be the focal point of her real beauty.

What matters most in a woman? Verse 4a reveals God's answer: her spirit is *gentle*. The Greek word is *praus*, which as we noted earlier signifies power under control. It is used in Greek literature of a soothing medicine, of a tamed horse or wild animal,[37] and by a child asking his doctor to be gentle with him.[38] Jesus uses the word to describe Himself (Matt. 11:29): now, there was a *powerful* man; and at the same time there was a man whose power was *always under control*.

Every woman is created with great verbal and emotional power. God says

---

[35] The limitation is the same with all human authority: no man or woman has the right to compel another either to do what God forbids, or not to do what God commands.

[36] In that case, the apostle also would be saying, in the same verse, that she is never to wear clothes—which I am confident was not his point.

[37] TDNT, article πραΰς.

[38] William Barclay, *Flesh and Spirit* (Grand Rapids: Baker, 1976), 112, citing this as from *The Laws* by Plato—though, as usual, aggravatingly providing no specific citation.

that she must control that power. By the virtue praised in Proverbs 11:16, God is saying in effect:

> "Daughter, it is true, you could blow your man away with a verbal torrent, and you could drown him in an emotional flood. But trust Me: I will be honored, you will be happier, and your husband will be happier and probably a better husband, if you control that power, apply what I tell you, concentrate on mortifying your own sin patterns and cultivating godly graces, and use the capability I gave you to serve me by helping him. When you do, you can have the assurance that I place a high value on you and your spirit."

We note also from Peter's words that this woman's spirit is quiet (*hēsuchios*). This is a matter of being trusting, patient and self-controlled. It is the opposite of being loud, nagging, obnoxious and what is commonly called "witchy."

How important is this quality of spirit? No doubt, this age would find such an attitude abhorrent, repulsive, despicable, and craven. But we must face the truth squarely: any woman (or man) who cares about the estimate of this age is a stranger to the fear of God.

To the delight of any lover of God, verse 4b reveals that this quiet and gentle spirit is "precious" in the sight of God. "Precious" translates *polutelēs*, which means very valuable, very expensive, very costly. This means that, regardless of the husband's response, the wife can know that God places a high value on such a spirit in a woman.

A godly woman should ask herself, "In a million years, whose opinion will matter most? My husband's, my culture's, or my God's?"

Do the math.

Strength of character

Fourth, the godly wife shows strength of character. See Proverbs 12:4—

> An excellent wife[39] is the crown of her husband,
>   but she who brings shame is like rottenness in his bones.

---

[39] Hebrew *'ēšet-ḥayil*, literally "woman of strength," as in Proverbs 31:10.

Kidner says that the Hebrew term *'ēšet-ḥayil* has the "root idea of strength and worth… The modern phrase, 'she has a lot in her', expresses something of the meaning."[40]

The ESV translates the word *ḥayil* in its various usages by the following words, among many others: strength, excellent, able, host, riches, force(s), mighty, valiant(ly), wealth, valor, and army. Cohen sees the *'ēšet-ḥayil* as denoting strength of character, morally and intellectually.[41] McKane translates as "a woman of quality."[42]

The phrase is used by Boaz of Ruth in Ruth 3:11—"And now, my daughter, do not fear. I will do for you all that you ask, for all my fellow townsmen know that you are a worthy woman."[43]

Moderns caricature the godly woman as a servile nonperson, by disparaging the very concept of submission. This taunt is not an option for a Christian. Consider: Who is the most submissive person, of either sex, who ever lived? Who is the strongest person who ever lived? One name answers both questions: the Lord Jesus. Jesus is both the strongest and the most submissive person who ever lived (cf. John 5:30; 1 Cor. 11:3; 15:28).

By the way, the husband of this strong, excellent woman had better be all the more an *'īš-ḥayil*, a man of excellent, strong character himself.

Another telling verse is Proverbs 31:10.

> A woman of strength, who can find?
> And far beyond corals is her value! (DJP)

This would prepare the searching, unmarried believer with the advance knowledge that his search will not be an easy one. Once a strong woman is found, the man can yell a joyous "Jackpot!" for the rest of his life. That is why, Christian husband, you should thank God daily, loudly, and publicly, if you have a wife who is anything like this ideal.

This verse also provides focus for the believing woman. A Christian woman's first emphasis should be on pleasing God, having what He assesses as an excellent character, and finding satisfaction in that standing before God. In this way, even if her husband is not the most appreciative man alive, she will have her sense of worth where she needs to have it: in her relationship with God (cf. Matt. 6:1).

---

40 Kidner, 90.
41 Cohen, 73.
42 McKane, 228.
43 Hebrew *'ēšet-ḥayil*.

For surely it is sufficient motivation to know that, when a woman develops a strong, godly, feminine character, no less than God Himself says that her value is far beyond corals.[44]

Devotion to her husband

Fifth, the godly wife exhibits devotion to her husband (Prov. 31:11–12, 23).

> The heart of her husband trusts in her,
>> and he will not come short of profit.
>
> [12] She does him good, and not evil,
>> all the days of her life.
>
> [23] Her husband is known in the gates,
>> when he sits with the elders of the land.

All of my single life, I saw verse 11 as the peak of the song's praise of this woman as a wife. There is surely no higher praise than to say that a husband can trust his wife, trust that she will never act to harm him. This praise will be hers, if she wholeheartedly embraces being what God created her to be: God's servant, and her husband's helper.

Verse 12 explains verse 11, showing that the husband's trust is won and sustained by her performance. Candidly, I am aware of no Biblical command to the effect of "Husbands, trust your wives." Presumably, a man trusts a woman when he marries her. This trust must be won and sustained by her actually being trustworthy in their relationship. If she snipes, picks, tears him down in shame (cf. 12:4), she can hardly expect his trust to be very deep. But if she is committed to doing him only good, as God means her to be, she should enjoy the freedom of trust.

Verse 23 shows the heart of this excellent woman. As a result, in part, of her intelligent, godly devotion, her husband is freed to attain prominence and influence. Remember the woman's created design: she is to be his helper in subduing creation for God. And so, when he shines and excels, she is delighted and has done her job.[45]

---

[44] The word *p'nînîm* is sometimes translated pearls and rubies, but it probably means corals. Corals were valued as precious.

[45] The reverse does not necessarily follow. A foolish loser is not necessarily so because of his wife. He probably is just a foolish loser! (Remember Nabal and Abigail: sharp wife, drooling-idiot

Fear of Yahweh

Sixth, the godly wife practices the fear of Yahweh (Prov. 31:30).

> Charm is deceitful and beauty is nothing;
>> A woman who fears Yahweh, it is she who shall be praised. (DJP)

Coming at the end of the poem, and of the book, this pinpoints the organizing factor in this brilliant woman's universe. It is her fear of Yahweh that enables her to see that real greatness will come to her, not through self-centered aggressiveness, and not through merely external beauty, but through godly devotion and the wholehearted commitment to God's creational intention for her.

Flip-side of negative qualities

Seventh, the godly wife practices the flip-side of negative qualities (which follow).

Characteristics of an Ungodly (or Foolish) Wife

Solomon will alert us to *six* ungodly, foolish feminine characteristics. A woman who fears Yahweh will steer clear of these as if they were bloated, rotting, pustulent, pestiferous corpses.

First, infidelity

An ungodly, foolish wife displays marital unfaithfulness (violating God's intention for marriage). We encounter this early on in the picture of the "strange" or "forbidden woman" in Proverbs 2:16–19. This woman is depicted as a stranger and a foreigner, because she is foreign to the man's proper sphere. Notice that she hits on what is men's weak point: *flattery* (v. 16; cf. 7:5, 21). Basically, all men want to hear, "You're doing a good job. I think you're amazing." If a man doesn't feel that his wife is saying that, he will be more vulnerable to the right words from the wrong lips.

Longer portraits can be found in Proverbs 5:3–14; 6:24–32; 7:10–27; and 9:13–18. What we find in those tableaus is a woman who knows how to prey on man's weakness for sweet talk (5:3; 6:24; 7:13–18, 21; 9:17). She may have a superficial smattering of religion (7:14), but inside she is spiritually rootless, clueless and unprincipled (5:6; 7:11–12; 9:13). She destroys both the man and

---

husband.)

herself.

Second, insincerity

We can see this defect in Proverbs 2:16.

> So you will be delivered from the forbidden woman,
>   from the adulteress with her smooth words

She knows that the way to a man's heart, if not through his empty stomach, is through his fat head. But the words are smooth and flattering. She does not say what she means. She says only what will get her the evil thing that she wants. Proverbs 5:3 adds that

> ...the lips of a forbidden woman drip honey,
>   and her speech is smoother than oil.

A wise man would spot this a mile away. He would be aware of the male's Achilles Heel for flattery. He would fight this tendency by seeking out, valuing, and marrying only a woman who will be kind and yet utterly candid with him.

But this woman is not looking for such a man. She knows just the bait, and it is damnably effective. The tragedy is that neither she nor her victim find what they need, for both are looking in the wrong place.

Third, disloyalty

This note is sounded poignantly in Proverbs 2:17, where the immoral woman is described as one "who forsakes the companion of her youth and forgets the covenant of her God."

There are a billion reasons to stay light-years away from adultery. One reason is that it is the very height of the very lowest crime: treachery. This verse highlights that fact by the use of the relatively uncommon word translated "companion."[46]

Here Solomon subtly brings out the truth: there are *two* acts of betrayal in the *one* act of adultery. Focusing on the woman here, he says she abandons the companion of her youth, the man to whom she pledged her singular loyalty and exclusive devotion. But she also "forgets"—deliberately—the covenant of her God. For when she pledged herself to her young husband, she called on God as

---

[46] Hebrew *'allûp.*

witness. He did witness. And now He witnesses her betrayal. She betrays God when she betrays her husband.

The note of disloyalty is sounded again in the scandalous, cautionary vignette in Proverbs 7, there particularly singling out verses 18–20. The husband's *trust* becomes the occasion of his covenant-companion's betrayal. He has gone on a long journey, and his wife uses that to betray him. Some of the clues are subtle. For instance, "my husband is not at home" more literally is "because the man is not *in his home*." It is *his* home, which *he* secured for himself and his wife; but she will make it the scene of her treachery.

She echoes herself in v. 20b, where she literally says "on the day of the full moon he will enter his house." It is still his house, and remains so. She has no designs to build a life with her new fool. She will continue to "live off the dime of" her now-betrayed husband.

So we could add a *third* betrayal, couldn't we? In addition to her God and her husband, she is betraying her paramour. She is simply using him. And why not? It has never, ever ceased to amaze me that a man will sexually use a married woman, and then imagine that she will be faithful to him. Why? When the relationship began with an act of treachery, how can it—indeed, why should it—continue in faithfulness?

Fourth, destructiveness

The most devastating little exposé of this disastrous attitude is found in Proverbs 14:1.

> Feminine wisdom[47] builds her house,
>> But *feminine* denseness tears it down with her own hands. (DJP)

Let us examine the woman in depth.

Who she is: the embodiment of feminine *denseness* (*'iwwelet*). This is the feminine abstract form of one of three main synonyms translated "fool" in Proverbs (*'wîl, kᵉsîl, and nābāl*). As I explained above, in Chapter 3, the term *'wîl* means "thick-headed." I render the masculine form as "dense."

We have all known men and women alike who were just *dense*, who were destroying themselves in ways obvious to us, but hidden to themselves. Proverbs

---

[47] Literally "Wisdoms of women."

abounds with pictures of dense men (1:7; 10:8, 14, 21, etc.). This is that same destructive quality in a woman.

God has revealed the importance of a healthy home to a woman. She has an inbuilt need to build that home in helping her husband, a need for her husband to lead her, and a need to serve God with him and complement him. The woman of Proverbs 14:1, however, is dense.

It is an axiom of human behavior that people do what they do because they believe it will make them happy. Therefore, this dense woman does what she does because she thinks that it will get her what she needs. Whether she is tearing her house down by out-of-kilter priorities, by emasculating her husband, or by neglecting her children, she is doing it in the dense pursuit of own happiness. In the process, by the unerring illogical irony of sin, she is actually tearing down what God says that she needs. It is a classic example, again, of mistaking a want for a need, and sacrificing the need to pursue the want.

What she does: she tears down her house with her own hands. Remember what the "house" is: her husband and her children, in that order. Like every man, every woman carries her own enemy within her. What is the woman's inner enemy? God reveals it to us in Genesis 3:16—

> Unto the woman, He said, "I shall greatly increase the pain of your pregnancy.[48] In pain will you bear sons; And unto your husband will be your aspiration[49]—But it is he who must rule[50] over you." (DJP)

In the temptation and fall, Eve believed a lie. She substituted a want (to become wise autonomously) for a need (to gain wisdom through believing submission to God). Then she led her erstwhile leader to follow her in sin.

God now says that this aspiration, this drive to dominate her husband, will be Eve's legacy. The woman will have a desire to control her husband, to usurp his position. God's solution is that the man must rule her, rather than returning to the Fall's inverted order.[51]

---

[48] Very literally, "your pain and your pregnancy"; a common way of expressing one idea by two words.
[49] This unusual word occurs again in the very similar Genesis 4:7, and in both places means "desire to overcome or master."
[50] Or "let him rule."
[51] God's intended authority-chain had been: God → mankind [husband over wife] → animal creation. In the rebellion, Satan had used an animal to lead the wife to lead her husband to rebel against God. The resultant topsy-turvy order was :

A dense wife destroys a situation by the very measures she takes to save it, denying her deepest needs by giving in to her destructive wants. Examples:

- A wife and mother needs a happily thriving home; but she may want a career at any cost.[52]

- A wife needs a husband who will be a man, who will lead—not just because she has to obey "another stupid Bible-thingie," but because she really needs it by created design; but she may want to control her husband, to force him to do things her way, no matter what it takes.

- A wife needs to be faithful to her marital covenant and work out her relationship with her husband; but she may want this other man, and thinks that he will meet her needs better than her husband is doing.

- A wife needs to use her tongue to help her husband, to convey God's Word, and not to destroy; but she may want to let her tongue loose cruelly, even though it may tear down her house.

In summary, then, how does she destroy her "house"?

She can destroy her husband (as we will see) by betraying him, by degrading and shaming him, by defying him, by withholding her best from him, by unnerving him, by unmanning him, by picking at him until he loses his will to try, until he wants to be anywhere else in the world but with her.

She can destroy her children by neglecting their care in favor of a career, or by indulging and spoiling them (Prov. 29:15—"The rod and reproof give wisdom, But a lad let loose[53] shames his mother" DJP), or by neglecting to teach them the Word by lesson and example.

In these active and passive ways, a dense woman can tear down her house with her own hands.

Fifth, nagging, argumentative, implacable contentiousness

A number of Scriptures single this out. First, note Proverbs 19:13—

---

       animal → mankind {wife → husband} → God.

[52] Remember: it is the "at any cost," not the "career" per se, that is the problem.

[53] The word means let free, left to himself (i.e. undisciplined).

> A stupid son is his father's destruction,
> and a wife's quarrels[54] are a repellent dripping.[55] (DJP)

This verse presents two ways to make life grim and joyless for a man: a stupid son, or an argumentative wife.

"Contentions of" (*miḏyᵉnê*, from *dîn*, judge), refers to strife, contention, quarrels.[56] Even more interesting is *ṭōrēḏ*, the word translated "continual" in the ESV. The word is literally "pushing, driving," and it occurs only here and in 27:15.[57]

> A constant dripping[58] on a day of steady rain
> and a contentious woman[59] are alike. (NAS)

Delitzsch says that *ṭōrēḏ* is literally striking (i.e., hitting), cognate to an Arabic word meaning hostile assault.[60] Indeed, Fox suggests this could be rendered "a dripping that drives one out."[61]

Solomon uses the word to describe a foolish wife's relentless, repulsive argumentativeness. This woman finds a way to disagree with or fault *everything* the man does. You have heard the joke: "If a man speaks in the forest and there is no woman around to hear him, is he still wrong?" To her, it is a way of life and an unconscious conviction, not a joke.

This woman gives his every effort a failing (or inadequate) grade, loudly and verbally. She may be saying "You never spend enough time with us! You don't care about us! You go everywhere but home! You've got time for your work and your friends and your bowling, but you never have time for us! You don't ever talk to me! You don't ever spend time with me!" On and on it goes; his efforts are unnoticed, his flaws greatly magnified, his spirit crushed.

Ironically, though, by this abusive nagging—which she engages, ironically, to *force* the intimacy she craves—she actually drives her husband away. Her further frustration is thereby assured, giving birth to more faultfinding contentiousness, creating greater distance.

---

54 Hebrew *miḏyᵉnê 'iššâ*.
55 Hebrew *delep ṭōrēḏ*.
56 Cf. BDB, article מָדוֹן.
57 This verse will be discussed further below; cf. Toy, 373.
58 Hebrew *delep ṭōrēḏ*.
59 Hebrew *'ēšet miḏwānîm*.
60 Delitzsch, 2:27.
61 Commentary on Proverbs, 2:654.

From a pastor's experience, John A. Kitchen accurately paints the unhappy domestic picture:

> By "contentions" may be meant the nagging demands of an unhappy and discontent woman. There is always something wrong. The man feels he can never do anything right. Something is always not to her liking. Faced with constant failure, soon the man quits trying to please her at all. This only inflames her discontent and increases her complaints.[62]

Some of what this wife is saying may be technically correct, but *all her husband hears* is "Drip, drip, drip," and "Wham! Wham! Wham!"

- ...and all he's feeling is, "Push! Push! Push!" toward the door, and the relative peace and quiet and freedom to be found outside.

- ...because in time, all he's thinking is, "I have got to get away from this."

Such a wife needs to realize that she may well have a valid point, but she must learn how evaluate it, how to confront and mortify her sinful passions as such, and (if valid) how to put her thoughts across effectively rather than repulsively.

One might retort, "But if I have a complaint, don't I have a right to make it?" To this, I would offer two responses:

1. Focusing on your rights instead of what is right in the sight of God is not living in the fear of God, and is a sure ticket to disaster as a Christian.

2. Granting that you have a valid complaint (if you do), consider two questions:

   a. Is there only one way to express your complaint: a sharp, critical, discouraging, degrading way?

   b. Would it be worth it to you to drive your husband away and tear down your house, on the altar of your "right" to pour out graceless, God-dishonoring, destructive self-expression?

In the nineteenth century, Delitzsch referred to an Arab proverb he'd heard

---

[62] Kitchen, *Proverbs*, 420.

from Wetzstein, "that there are three things which make our house intolerable," and they are...

> ...*altakk* (dripping; the trickling through of rain),
>
> ...*alnakk* (nagging; the contentions of the wife),
>
> ...and *albakk* (bugs).[63]

Clearly God is saying that this is dense behavior. Through Solomon, He calls to such a woman to wake up, come to her senses. She needs to ask, Does it honor God and serve my husband to be right in my mind, and drive my husband far away in the process? A woman would be wiser to learn three priceless skills:

1. How to evaluate your own thoughts objectively, aware of our universal tendency toward self-justification.[64]

2. How to express your thoughts respectfully and effectively.[65]

3. How to accept your husband's God-given role, even when you do not agree with him perfectly.[66]

The matter is put plaintively in Proverbs 21:9—

> It is better to live in a corner of the housetop
>   than in a house shared with a quarrelsome wife. [67]

This is obviously an evaluation proverb (A is better than B). Solomon is saying, in effect,

> "So you're considering marrying this young lady who is beautiful and fun, but who has just one problem: she's argumentative. Given the choice between letting something go or waging war to get her own way, she will battle you until either she wins, or both sides are in bloody ruins. You figure that's a problem, but 'it's better than being alone'? Wrong. It is not 'better than being alone.' In fact, 'It is better to live in the corner of a roof, Than in a house shared with a contentious woman.'"

---

[63] Delitzsch, 2:27.

[64] Proverbs 14:12; 16:2, 25; 21:2.

[65] Proverbs 15:1, 2, 28; 16:23; 25:15.

[66] First Peter 3:1–6 and, by extension of the principle, 2:18.

[67] Literally "a woman/wife of contentions, arguments, quarrels."

Think it through. If you are a single person, and a huge argument breaks out when you're with a friend, or on a date, at least you know that you can go home where it's quiet and peaceful. You can be through with it, go to sleep in peace.

But what if all the worst fights happen at home, with your one-flesh wife? And your bed contains an angry, hostile, bitter, relentless opponent? Where do you go then?

Specifically, I would ask my lady readers, What do you really want? The wise helper, the wise builder of her home, wants home to be the place where her man loves to be. She wants it to be the one place in the world he'd rather be than anywhere else, the place to which he would gladly go even if he didn't have to. And she wants to be the person her husband would choose to be with, above all other mere mortals.

That is the attitude of the wise home builder. The wise home-builder does not want home to be the place where her husband reluctantly has to go, only when he runs out of other, safer places to be. I am afraid that some women make home into Hell for their men, and then weep and feel sorry for themselves when their men in fact find a better place to be.[68]

Another vivid word-picture comes our way in Proverbs 21:19—

> It is better to live in a desert land
> than with a quarrelsome and fretful woman.[69]

In form, this is an evaluation proverb (A is better than B). It is interesting to note that God moved Solomon to pen the same central thought as in 21:9, which we just discussed. The pairing of the words pictures a woman who both argues and provokes anger in her husband. This is the woman who would rather lose her husband than lose an argument. As a result, she stands a good chance of losing both.

To be clear, Solomon isn't envisioning a pleasant winter or spring home in the desert. Israel *is* in the desert, more or less. He likely has in mind the barren, lifeless desert that would doom even "survivalist" experts like Bear Grylls. The wise king is saying that it would be better to be dying of thirst and starvation, far from friend or foe, than to be stuck in the same house with a woman who never seems to tire of provoking and prolonging arguments.

---

[68] Let me be crystal-clear: *there is no excuse for adultery*. Ever! However, each mate can *help* the other resist any temptation, and each mate can *expose* the other to fiercer temptation.

[69] Literally "than a woman/wife of contentions and vexation."

A similar thought is found in Proverbs 25:24—

> It is better to live in a corner of the housetop
> than in a house shared with a quarrelsome wife.

There are only two letters different from the Hebrew text of 21:9. Better to be on the *roof* of a house with nothing (except peace and quiet) than to be *in* the house with everything (except peace and quiet).

An aside: if anyone thinks that I am making too much of this theme, consider the fact that God moved Solomon to repeat himself, three times?

Did I say "three"? The truth is… four! Courtesy of Proverbs 27:15–16—

> A continual[70] dripping on a rainy day
> and a quarrelsome wife are alike;
>
> [16] to restrain her is to restrain the wind
> or to grasp oil in one's right hand.

How are "a continual dripping on a rainy day and a quarrelsome wife" alike?

Think of the literal picture of a constant drip on a rainy day. The dripping is only somewhat bothersome at first. You think the dripping may stop pretty soon, or that you will adjust to it and it won't bother you anymore. But then, as the dripping goes on, and on, and on, it is increasingly irritating, until you wince and cringe with every drip.

Finally, you're up and out of your chair, looking either to fix it or escape it.

And so it is with a woman who is contentious and argumentative. At first, early in the courtship or marriage, perhaps the arguments are only an annoyance. Surely they will pass, as we "work out the kinks," the man reasons.

But then, as the arguments continue, and continue, and perhaps worsen as the woman's "aim" improves (in the sense of becoming more damaging) over the years, those "drips" can well drive her husband out of the house—physically or emotionally.

Why does Solomon add in 27:16, "to restrain her is to restrain the wind or to grasp oil in one's right hand."? When you're talking to a six-year-old, and he says, "Is so," and you say, "Is not," and he says, "Is so"—when does it stop?

---

[70] As in 19:13, the Hebrew phrase "constant dripping" is a repellent, driving, pushing dripping, with the effect of driving one out of the house, to put as much distance between himself and the annoyance as he can achieve.

And so this contentious woman is driven by untamed, unmortified passions of the flesh, such as self-righteous pride and discontentment and fear and need to control. Rather than addressing her real problems as a Christian (Rom. 8:13b; 13:14), she has embraced them and projected them onto her husband.

Yet all he sees and knows is what his wife says. So he, reasonably enough (to him), answers what she says. When he does that, her bitter discontentment just twists about and keeps the argument going.

Is this a familiar pattern?

> SHE: You never said anything about my new dress.
> HE: I was just about to.
> SHE: You know it means a lot to me for you to compliment me.
> HE: Yes, I was going to do that very thing.
> SHE: You don't care if you hurt my feelings!
> HE: But… I didn't *do* anything to hurt your feelings.
> SHE: And you're not going to apologize, are you? Typical. Just like always. You're always right. You never apologize!
> HE: Well, if I had done something wrong, I'd apologize. I didn't do anything wrong. As I said, I was just about t—
> SHE: Oh, no; not you! You never do anything wrong!

(This goes on for a few more minutes…and a few more…and a few more, until…)

> HE: I think we've talked enough about this one. That's a really nice dress. I like it. Let's talk about something else.
> SHE   (in tears, loudly enough for the children to hear): Oh, sure; when you're through, that's it! His Majesty has spoken! Yes, sir! Yes, Your Highness! And you don't even care that you hurt me! [Door slams loudly. The children are quiet.]

And then if he does immediately say something nice about the next new dress, her acid response is, "I suppose you want 'points' for that?"

Here is a deep truth: it is possible to be 100% correct, and 100% wrong, at the same time.

Earlier, I said the man with a dripping roof gets up, determined either to fix it or escape it. Perhaps readers thought, "Why does he not 'fix' his wife, then?" My response would be to ask how readers propose that he "fixes" her? Where is the Scriptural formula for sovereignly changing the heart of a fellow human being with a death-grip on a sin-pattern? If it is there, whether for men or women, boys or girls, I have yet to find it.

This man reasons with his perennially-unhappy wife, he talks Scripture with her, he points her to Christ in a dozen different ways, and she simply becomes more and more furious, bitter, and hostile. She will acquiesce only if she gets exactly her own way... and even then, she is not happy.

What this woman needs to do is repent. She needs to regard these drives as what they are: passions of the flesh (Gal. 5:19–21) which need to be put to death (Rom. 8:13) for Christ's sake and without condition or provision or negotiation (Rom. 13:14). She needs to see them as her soul's enemies and her family's enemies. She needs to wage all-out war to the death—but with her fleshly passions, not with her husband. And she needs to seek God for the renewal of her mind (Rom. 12:1–2), that the fleshly passions will be replaced by the Spirit's graces (Gal. 5:22–25; 1 Peter 3:1ff.).

Now, leaving aside the sinful passions of the flesh, suppose a wife has a legitimate need or thought to offer to a husband who is not "hearing" her. What options are open to her?

I could offer the relationship I had with my late, much-loved, and bitterly-missed father as a distant analogy. My dad lived into his eighties, had heard the Gospel again and again, and had no good reason not to be a believer (that I ever heard; not that there is any good reason).

During his life, I could have gone down to Glendale, California, where he lived, could have caught him at the golf course, could have grabbed him by the collar right in front of all his slack-jawed golfing buddies in their plaid pants, and could have begun screaming at the top of my considerable lungs, "YOU MIGHT NOT LIVE MUCH LONGER, DAD! STOP WASTING YOUR TIME! BELIEVE IN CHRIST OR YOU'LL BURN IN HELL FOREVER! YOU HAVE NO GOOD REASON FOR NOT REPENTING AND BELIEVING RIGHT NOW! BELIEVE NOW, BELIEVE NOW, BELIEVE NOW!"

Is any one of those statements erroneous? No. Every word is 100% true. Might I have had good intentions? Yes; I might have had the very best intentions. I loved my father dearly.

Yet, if I had done that, I would have been 100% right...and 100% wrong at the same time. The likelihood that God would use such a tirade to lead to a genuine conversion in my dad would have been about zero, if not less.[71]

---

[71] As an afterword, I have reason to hope that my father came to the Lord shortly before his death. But that is another story.

The moral: you want to win and persuade, and not batter and repel—even if you're right.[72]

Among the many revealed ways to avoid this misery is Proverbs 17:14.

> The beginning of strife[73] is like letting out water,
> so quit before the quarrel breaks out (Prov. 17:14)

The best time to stop a destructive argument—a fight—is before it starts.

Once a woman tolerates nasty, destructive, argumentative contentiousness in herself, she will find the habit to be every bit as hard to break as habitual drunkenness. But it is not one whit less critical that she do so.

Sixth, a contemptuous attitude or behavior (Prov. 12:4)

> An excellent wife[74] is the crown of her husband,
> but she who brings shame is like rottenness in his bones

This foolish, ruinous behavior is the polar opposite of God's assigned role as helper. This foolish, ruinous woman is the opposite of the woman God praises in chapter 31, especially verses 10–12.

> A woman of strength, who can find?
> And far beyond corals is her value!
> [11] The heart of her husband trusts in her,
> and he will not come short of profit.
> [12] She does him good, and not evil,
> all the days of her life (DJP)

Delitzsch sagely comments,

> Like as the caries[75] slowly but continuously increases, till at last the part of the body which the bone bears and the whole life of the man falls to ruin; so an unhappy marriage gnaws at the marrow of life, it destroys the happiness of life, disturbs the pursuit, undermines the life of the husband.[76]

---

[72] *Especially* if you're right, I might add. A truly important point, something beyond petty preferences, is too momentous to risk its dismissal because of the childish, self-indulgent lack of restraint of the speaker!

[73] The Hebrew word is the same as is used repeatedly of the contentious woman.

[74] Hebrew *'ēšet-ḥayil*, as discussed above, and as found in 31:10.

[75] Decay of bones or teeth.

[76] Delitzsch, 1:252.

McKane translates the phrase as "a hussy," which he explains as

> a wife who gives a man a red face, who puts him to shame before the
> world. While an [excellent wife] raises him to the fulness [sic] of his
> powers, a [hussy, a wife who shames him] will be a drag on him all
> his days and an unfailing topic of gossip and ribald humour [sic].[77]

Zöckler says that *rāqāḇ* ("rottenness") is "literally a worm-eating," and so she
is "a ruin inwardly undermining and slowly destroying."[78]

The resultant idea is of a woman who deliberately shames her husband, not
caring whether friends, neighbors or (worse) the children hear her tearing her
husband down. Regardless of her complaints or her self-image, she is not a woman
of character. Ironically, she may imagine that her shameful behavior shows how
strong and fulfilled she is, when in truth it reveals the opposite.

The shaming wife will find that shaming does not get her either what she
wants or what she needs, which in turn will increase her frustration for at least
two reasons:

- First, she is doing what she's doing because she thinks it should
  work, and it never will, and that will frustrate her.
- Second, this shaming behavior will demoralize her husband ("as
  rottenness in his bones"), so that he is likely to be less effective in
  whatever he was or could have been otherwise.

Always remember God's created design. The reason the first woman was
created was to be a helper, an assistant or partner to her husband. She was to
help him fulfill his created role. Therefore, any woman who shames her husband
is rebelling against her very reason for being.

Further, any woman who shames her husband undermines his strength, which
she was intended to supplement. She topples his world, which she was supposed
to help him subdue—as he himself would topple if his bones were rotten. In the
case of a man with a shaming wife, it would not be "not good" for the man to be
alone. It would be far better for that man to be alone.

---

[77] Page 443.
[78] In Lange's commentary, 127. BDB, however, says that the word means "rot," and is used of
worm-ravages (article רָקָב).

Two Possible Objections

First: "But This All Makes Me Subordinate to Him"

That's right. It really does.

Our society has created many varied and often mutually-exclusive expectations and demands for marital happiness. Scripture, however, is relatively simple and straightforward; and the first thing Scripture says about woman is that she was created in the image of God to be a helper for her husband.

I see two "upshots" here.

First, the *theological* upshot:

- The conversion-belief and confession of every Christian is, "Jesus is Lord."

- This confession includes at least three truths:

  1. Jesus is utterly supreme in His wisdom, authority, and power.

  2. I accept His authority over me, and pledge myself to obey His wisdom.

  3. I am convinced that His way is the best way.

- Therefore, if any of us thinks that he knows better than God, he is giving the lie to his confession as a Christian.

- In plainer language, why should we bother to call ourselves Christians, if we do not intend to obey Christ in His Word?

Second, the *practical* upshot:

- If you didn't want to help your husband, you should not have married him, nor anyone else.

- Now that you have married him, this is the role to which God calls you. God Himself commands you to subordinate yourself to your husband, in just those words (cf. Eph. 5:22, 24; Col. 3;18). It is your obligation as surely as any other Christian duty. Further, as you seek to please God by being a godly wife, it is the only route to joy and blessing for you.

Second: "To Whom Are These Verses Directed?"

The verses about men are for the benefit of single women who are evaluating possible husbands, or men (regardless of marital status) who want to be godly.

Likewise, the verses about women are for the benefit of single men who are evaluating possible wives; and women (regardless of marital status) who want to be godly.

In Closing: Behavioral Marriage Skills for Husbands *and* Wives

Listening

> The way of a dense man is upright in his own eyes,
>> but one listening to counsel is wise. (12:15 DJP)

> The ear that listens to life-giving reproof[79]
>> will dwell among the wise. (15:31)
> Whoever ignores instruction despises himself,
>> but he who listens to reproof gains intelligence.[80] (15:32)

Gracious Words

1. There are at least two ways to say anything: pick the gentle way.

> A soft[81] answer turns away wrath,[82]
>> but a harsh word[83] stirs up anger. (15:1)

2. Here is a word of encouragement particularly for wives: Proverbs 25:15.

> By forbearance[84] a ruler may be persuaded,
>> And a soft[85] tongue breaks the bone.

When your husband does not see some point that you believe you see, what do you do? After making a good, respectful, friendly case, you know that the

---

[79] Literally *reproof of lives.*

[80] More literally: "The one neglecting discipline rejects his soul, but the one listening to reproof acquires a heart."

[81] Hebrew *rak*, gentle, soft, as in 25:15 below.

[82] Hebrew *ḥēmâ*, literally *heat*, and so hot wrath, temper, rage.

[83] Literally *word of hurt*, word of *'eṣeb*, meaning *hurt, pain*. This is the difference between a response such as, "I don't see it that way," and snapping off, "You mindless idiot!"

[84] Literally *by length of temper/anger*, being calm and slow to anger. See James 1:19.

[85] Hebrew *rakkâ*, feminine form of the word found in 15:1.

Bible enjoins submission, respect, and support. Sometimes it may be wisest just to say, "Okay, hon, that's what we'll do," give it your best support, and let the matter lie, with good grace.

But take a case where the point is important, though not moral.[86] You do not have only two options: instant silence on the one hand, or screaming destructive hurricane on the other. It is possible to discuss respectfully, and then to submit... and then to bring up the matter again gently and respectfully...and then again... and then again, without nagging and harping criticism.

Screaming and name-calling does not call for much creativity, does it? Nor does it build a house.

Let us take a relatively small but common matter. Suppose that one's husband won't put the toilet-seat down. What could a wife do?

- She could yell and scream, and call him a lazy, self-centered jerk—and, as she does so, listen to the nails popping out, the boards creaking, and the plaster cracking as the "house" that she is supposed to be building begins to fall apart.
- She could defy him, by Super-Gluing the seat to the ring.
- She could drop the issue and be glad to have the problem (i.e. "spinsters," to use the old term, do not have this difficulty).
- *Or* she could "negotiate" a trade: he puts down the seats for you, you scoot the car-seat back for him. Put a series of humorous "post-it" notices on the bottom of the seat, like "Hey! Put me back! I was sleeping!" Or, "If you promise to put me down when you're through, I'll promise not to fall down before you're through."

Strife Avoidance

> The beginning of strife is like letting out water,
>   so quit before the quarrel breaks out. (Prov. 17:14)

It is much easier to avoid a fight than it is to stop one. Fight-behavior should be regarded by both as a non-option, as surely as if it were violence. Agree in advance

---

[86] By this distinction, I mean that no mere human authority has the right either to command anyone to do something God forbids, nor to forbid something God commands. I have in mind more a situation where the wife may see with perfect clarity that the husband's action, while permissible, is unwise.

(maybe even in writing) as to what you will do in burgeoning fight situations:

- Cooling-off period at either's request, when either thinks that the water is getting too hot.
- Stop for a dance. (No skills? Perfect? Hilarity will ensue!)
- Praise the other for three things before each single criticism.

Questions for Thought or Discussion

1. How did the Lord Jesus approach issues relating to marriage? What should that teach us?

2. How was marriage founded in man's need?

3. What was God's specific reason for creating a wife for Adam?

4. What were the ends for which God created the family?

5. What would be the means for achieving that end?

6. What is marriage, fundamentally?

7. How permanent is marriage?

8. What establishes marriage?

9. What are the characteristics of a godly husband?

10 . What is the place of sex in marriage?

11 . How does a godly husband treat his wife?

12 . What are characteristics of an ungodly husband?

13 . What are characteristics of a godly wife?

14 . What are characteristics of an ungodly or foolish wife?

15 . How does a foolish woman drive away what she needs, by her folly?

16 . What wisdom is there for men and women in the power of a woman's tongue?

17 . Is a good fight occasionally healthy for a marriage? Why, or why not?

CHAPTER EIGHT

Skill in Godly Child-training

Introduction

If too many professing Christians *stumble* into marriage—and they do—then the same number *bumble* into children. This may be preceded by no more deliberate, targeted Bible study than what occurred before the marriage. It is as if folks expect that some gland will go off inside of their craniums upon the arrival of the little ones, giving new parents instant and intuitive knowledge of what to do.

Observably, this does not happen.

The children of Christians should be markedly different from the children of unbelievers. Too often, however, they are not. Why is this? Is it, perhaps, because God neglected to give us much specific counsel as to child-training, in His Word?

Of course, the lack is not on God's side. The Bible is brimming with wisdom and counsel for parents, in one form or another. The fact that the upbringing of believers' children is often indistinguishable from (or inferior to) those of unbelievers is not traceable to a defect in the Bible. Rather, it is a testimony to our stubborn, arrogant refusal to seek counsel and accept correction from God's Word.

Let us sample some of Solomon's wisdom on the subject, set in its broader Biblical framework.

God's Overall Intention for the Family

What Are Children?

What metaphor would you choose to describe children? Little bundles o' joy? Or big packages o' problems?

The Bible uses a striking and thought-provoking metaphor: "arrows of a warrior." Consider Psalm 127:3–5, with its positive depiction of children as "a heritage from the LORD," as "a reward," and as like "arrows in the hand of a warrior." This is a psalm written by Solomon, so it gives us good insight into how the author of Proverbs viewed children. The Spirit of God moved Solomon to employ the image of an *arrow*. Why?

Ask yourself, What does one do with an arrow?

- Does one just polish it, shine it, treat its feathers, and admire it?

- Does one aim at keeping it in one's quiver forever, just happy to know it's there?

- Does one set it on the ground, and say, "Go get 'em, boy. Hit the target, hit the target, that's a boy!"?

Those are all silly suggestions. We know the reality: arrows are shot at some target. That is what they are for. They are for hitting a target—whether that target is a bull's eye in a tournament, tonight's dinner, or the enemy coming to sack our city.

True, one wants the arrow to be straight, and one wants it to be sharp. One's prime concern is not to make something that makes him feel good, or makes him proud. Basically, one wants something that hits and penetrates the target.

Here, then, is our opening question: What is your target? What is your goal for your family, for your children? What would success be? Failure? How do you measure either, and what is your authority for that goal?

Importance of Having a Distinct Goal

If you have not done so already, you had better sit down and think this through. It is important for a family to have a specific goal, worked out before God on the basis of the directions in His Word. Without a goal, the sheer "dailiness" of life will force one down the path of pagan pragmatism, and anything else will lose by default.

Remember this undeniable truism: *he who aims at nothing tends to hit it, every time.*

What are your goals for your children? Here are some possible answers:

- That my child will earn a high school diploma.
- That my child will go to college.
- That my child will learn a trade.
- That my child will "stay out of trouble."
- That my child will not get pregnant (or cause a pregnancy), become addicted, join a gang, get killed, or contract venereal diseases.
- That my child will be a good citizen—and a _____ (Republican, Democrat, Libertarian, etc.—you choose).
- That my child will marry happily.
- (For the *really* spiritual—) That my child will become a Christian.

Each of these goals will give a different slant and group of emphases to the process of child-training. Go back and think of the differing impact on training that would be caused by each suggested goal.

When we do this, we are in a position to realize that none of these goals goes far enough. Many of the goals listed above are not even distinctively Christian or Biblical. It is not that they are bad goals; no item on the list is a bad goal. It is that they are not distinctively Biblical goals. Each goal (except the last) might be equally shared by our unbelieving friends, who aim everything toward academic excellence, professional excellence, material wealth, marriageability, politics, and the like. If the fear of Yahweh is to be the foundation of all our knowledge, that lack of clear distinction is a problem.

Someone might respond, "But what about the goal that the child should become a Christian? That is a 'distinctively Christian' goal." It is true enough in itself, yet even that goal can leave the family in the same place as many churches. Some pulpits feature salvation messages upon salvation messages. The pastors constantly tell folks how to become Christians. And then...nothing. Nothing except maybe... go out and make more Christians, presumably so they can go out and make more Christians, who then go out and make more Christians, and...

Thus the whole process aims at this one point, one climax: conversion, or at least a profession of faith. Then, presumably, we're done.

Similarly many Christians believe that their children become saved at very early ages, such as 3, 5, or 7. They repeated a prayer. In those cases, if that was our goal, what now? We are thus left with a gap of another decade-and-a-half with no great objective in mind.

This is particularly true of those parents who are certain that the "sinner's prayer" which the 3-year-old lisped guarantees his passage into Heaven, no matter what he does with the rest of his life.[1] We will see that Scripture has a goal that is far superior to any of those listed. It is a goal that is grand, it is comprehensive, and it reflects the heart of God.

First: God's Design *Stated* (Gen. 1:26–28)

> Then God said, "Let Us make man in Our image, according to Our likeness, that they may rule the fish of the sea, and the birds of the heavens, and the cattle, and all the earth, and every crawling thing that crawls on the earth." [27]Then God created man in His image; in the image of God He created him; male and female He created them. [28]Then God blessed them, and God said to them, "Be fruitful, and become many, and fill the earth, and subdue it; and exercise dominion over the fish of the sea, and over the birds of the heavens, and over every animal which crawls upon the earth." (DJP)

God creates man with a particular task in mind

First Adam, the leader, is created to "rule" and "subdue" the earth. Then Eve is created to help Adam "rule" and "subdue" the earth.[2] The family grows out of this union, and is a vital part of that original goal: for man to "rule" and "subdue" the earth. Therefore it follows…

The family is created to subdue the earth for God

Parents' role, then, is to train their children for this calling.[3] The propagation of the human race is for the end of subduing the earth and ruling it under

---

[1] This is a sad, wishful perversion of the Scriptural truth of eternal salvation. It has led many a parent to hope falsely in his child's salvation, and to lead his child to cherish a false hope.

[2] See further discussion in the chapter on marriage.

[3] I am not a "Reconstructionist." That is, I am not out to establish the Kingdom of Christ by either evangelism or socio-political reconstructionism, nor by bringing government or anything else under the Law of Moses. Although this study will contain no extended interaction with

God. Children must be brought up with that vision in mind, and taught the convictions and skills necessary to pursue it.

What does this training for the service of God in exercising dominion entail? To be sure, establishing a relationship with God is primary. This will mean evangelism of our children. The family, and not the church, should be the primary place of evangelism. We should not look to the ride-through hit-and-run evangelist to do our work for us. Of course, if a child who has been evangelized at home is converted under Gospel preaching in a church, to God be the glory. One plants, another waters—God gives life (1 Cor. 3:6–7). Regardless, as their father I shall labor to point my children to Christ as if no one else will ever tell them the Gospel.

Still, we must remember that there is more to evangelism than just telling the "four spiritual laws," or the "plan of salvation" (in whatever package one prefers). In all evangelism, we must give grounding in those fundamental truths without which the Gospel is meaningless. Accordingly, we must teach the nature and attributes of the triune God, the fall of man, man's spiritual ruin, and God's one plan and offer of redemption through Jesus Christ.

So, the teaching of theology is primary, even in evangelism. There is more to it than a five-minute presentation, followed by, "Jimmy, would you like to receive Christ right now?" "Sure, Mommy."

This comprehensive training also entails learning to serve God, which itself involves a number of areas of education. From their earliest days, our children must be taught about the whole Bible, which leads them to salvation through faith (2 Tim. 3:15). They must learn how to read and study the Bible. They must actually study the Bible. They must be shown the need for repentant faith, and a life which adorns that faith. They must learn to practice what they learn from Scripture. They must see and participate in the service of God in a local assembly, and must see the process of learning what their own gifts for service are.

This is what is involved today in the call to subdue the world for God.

Reconstructionism, it is important to note: one need not be a Reconstructionist to believe that the ultimate goal of God for mankind is dominion under His Lordship, in His name. Christian discipleship is the current, main stewardship of that dominion mandate. Matthew 28:18–20 is this age's specific expression of the extension of God's future kingdom by enlisting and training citizens now. The kingdom of Christ will be brought about only by the personal and bodily return of Christ at the end of the age to establish His kingdom. Believers shall rule in conjunction with Christ's personal, bodily exercise of kingship (cf. Dan. 7:14, 22, 27; 2 Tim. 2:12; Rev. 20:6).

Parenthetically, this is why I think it unfortunate that in some families church is viewed as an interruption or an interference. Church service and life should be incorporated as the way in which the whole family is being trained together to serve God together. In your family prayers, remember to pray for folks in your own local church. As a family, discuss strategies for the growth of your church. Encourage the kids to come up with ideas, and to implement them. Make sure that they are part of the family's ministry.

Subordinated to this overall goal will be such areas of training as

- ✓ Godly employment
- ✓ How to obtain his own vessel in purity (i.e. sexual self-control, marriage)
- ✓ Training for producing other servants of God.

But we must remember the point: successful child-training will result in how the child sees himself. He should not primarily see himself as a good "stateling," supporting and serving the political order above all. Nor should he even primarily see himself as a good representative of the family name. Primarily he must see himself as a servant of God, charged with the privilege-responsibility of learning to rule for the glory of God.[4]

Can you see how this brings everything together in a lifelong, comprehensive, uniting vision, as nothing else does? The child would view his education as self-equipment in understanding this world that he is to subdue for God. After all, one must first gain strategic understanding, if he is to rule.

This is the context of education; not merely social acceptability or employment, but equipping for God's service. The child is taught to ground all of his goals in, and relate all of his goals to, the honor and glory and service of God. He will not simply and solely look for material success, but for God-honoring employment. He will not just want a happy marriage, he wants a God-honoring marriage.[5]

---

[4] This first-things-first orientation will ensure that the child is more than a credit to the family name (cf. Exod. 20:12; Prov. 23:24–25; Eph. 6:1–3, etc.)

[5] And so the well-discipled son will not hunt merely for a *pretty* wife (Prov. 11:22), but for a wife who will be a good partner in serving and glorifying God (Prov. 31:10–12, 26, 30). The well-discipled daughter will not hunt merely for a "cute" or "exciting" man, but for one with those character-traits of godliness which Proverbs details, which qualify him as a competent servant of God, ready to lead her and their family in the work of God.

Second: God's Design Reinforced

We shall see how God reinforced His design for the family in three ways: by divine endorsement, by divine commands, and by divine sanctions.

God's design reinforced by His endorsement (Gen. 18:19)

> "Because I have known him, in order that he may command his sons and his house after him, and they will keep the way of Yahweh so as to do righteousness and judgment, in order that Yahweh will bring on Abraham what He spoke concerning him." (DJP)

This verse contributes to a Biblical understanding of foreknowledge and election. God says, "I have known Abram, *in order that* he may" disciple his children and experience God's promise. Abram's godly life and parenting were not *objects* or *grounds* of God's knowledge of him; rather, they were *results* of God's knowledge of him ("in order that"). God foreknew, foreloved Abram, and thus became involved in his life to produce genuine faith and godly living. Everything good in Abram's life was a result of the sovereign working of God.

Also, we learn that Abraham's child-training in particular was a result of his own relationship with God ("I have known him, in order that"). Abraham's effective child-training was in part a goal of Yahweh's sovereign election. God had a larger purpose than merely giving this older man some kids to bounce on his knee. God intended ultimately the raising up of a nation that would serve as the repository of divine revelation, and through whom would come the Messiah and Redeemer of mankind.

Then we see...

God's design reinforced by His command (Deut. 6:4–7)

> "Listen, Israel: Yahweh is our God; Yahweh is one! [5]And you shall love Yahweh your God with all your heart, and with all your soul, and with all your strength.[6] [6]And these words, which I am commanding you today, shall be upon your heart; [7]and you shall

---

[6]   Very literally, "your muchness."

teach them incisively[7] to your sons, and you shall speak in terms of them when you sit down in your house, and when you walk in the way, and when you lie down, and when you get up." (DJP)

Note the flow: identification of the one covenant God (v. 4) leads to love for that God (v. 5), which necessarily involves immersion in His words (v. 6), which in turn overflows to instruction of one's family in His words (v. 7). God desired the raising up of troops of trained servants of God, equipped from childhood with God's revealed mind.

Who was to do this equipping, primarily? Was it the Sunday Sch…er, rather, the Sabbath School teacher? No. By a circuit-riding evangelist, or priest, or prophet? Indeed, no.

By the parents? Emphatically so!

We see here, then, that God intends that we—we parents—concern ourselves with making our homes a Biblically-rich atmosphere. God intends that we immerse our kids in God's Word from their very earliest years.[8] God means our children to grow up with His viewpoint virtually incorporated at the instinctive level in how they think, reason, and behave.

God's design also reinforced by His sanctions (Deut. 21:18–21)

> "If a man has a stubborn and rebellious son who will not obey the voice of his father or the voice of his mother, and, though they discipline him, will not listen to them, [19] then his father and his mother shall take hold of him and bring him out to the elders of his city at the gate of the place where he lives, [20] and they shall say to the elders of his city, 'This our son is stubborn and rebellious; he will not obey our voice; he is a glutton and a drunkard.' [21] Then all the men of the city shall stone him to death with stones. So you shall purge the evil from your midst, and all Israel shall hear, and fear."

The purpose of the legislation was effectively to rule out career criminals. This law serves as an illustration of what we now call "tough love." We do not find

---

[7] Intensive form of a verb meaning "to sharpen"; alternately, from a similar verb and meaning "to repeat."

[8] As Timothy was taught the sacred writings *apo brephous*, since he was an infant (2 Tim. 3:15).

any coddling of the notion of "family-olatry" here, effectively putting the family above everything. This text reveals that even a child of the covenant community could ultimately forfeit even the privilege of life.[9]

The *picture* of this legislation is quite clearly of a child who has been faithfully warned and disciplined by his parents, who deliberately continues in a course of rebellion against God's laws. What is done with such a child? Are excuses and rationalizations offered for him and his "misguided" behavior? Are we told that his behavior results from his being the oldest...or the youngest? Are we made to sympathize with him for being "high-spirited," or for having inherited some family trait? Is society blamed, or his racial or cultural background, or some elusive syndrome? Is he and his lawlessness subsidized, either by society or by his parents?

No, indeed; "no" to all.

This little criminal is to be executed. His parents are to see to it that he is executed,[10] and everyone in the community is to know about it (v. 21). News of the execution would affect the entire nation for the better (v. 21).

There is little doubt that, if this law had been carried out with any consistency whatever, at least two results would have followed:

1. The law probably would not have had to be carried out very often.

2. Israel might well have been spared many of its troubles—or at least they might have been long delayed.

There is also little doubt that, if this were carried out in our society,[11] many parents of lawless children would never have parented their lawless children, because they would not have survived their own childhood.

Third: God's Original Design Confirmed and Transformed

Did the advent of the New Covenant mean an end to this view of children and family? On the contrary; we rather see...

---

[9] "Privilege" from God's perspective. Remember, Israel was an actual theocracy, not a "wannabe" theocracy. God declared the conditions under which life must be taken by human hands, as is His right (Deut. 32:39).

[10] Clearly this legislation would heighten not only the motivation of the child to learn and to behave, but would spur loving parents to train their children in a godly way.

[11] Which, by the way, I do not advocate.

God's original design confirmed and transformed by Jesus (Matt. 10:34–37)

> "Do not think that I have come to bring peace to the earth. I have
> not come to bring peace, but a sword. [35] For I have come to set a man
> against his father, and a daughter against her mother, and a daughter-
> in-law against her mother-in-law. [36] And a person's enemies will be
> those of his own household. [37] Whoever loves father or mother more
> than me is not worthy of me, and whoever loves son or daughter
> more than me is not worthy of me."

Jesus' motto was not, "The family *über alles*," the family over all. Jesus
recognized in advance that there would be situations in which loyalty to Him
just might sever that otherwise-closest of human relations.

In these situations, He does not say, "The family must be preserved at all costs.
Don't let your devotion to Me interfere with family relations." Rather, He quite
clearly says, "If the choice is between Me and your family—you must choose Me."
In this way, Jesus effectively puts Himself above the Fifth Commandment, which
is yet another subtle but powerful claim to deity, since only God took precedence
over father and mother.

Original design confirmed and transformed by Paul (Eph. 6:4)

> And fathers, do not provoke your children to wrath, but *instead*
> nourish them in the discipline and confrontation of the Lord. (DJP)

Paul clearly mandates the godly training of children, but he does not tell how,
in any detail. "Discipline" is *paideia*, which extends to and includes corporal
punishment. "Instruction" is *nouthesia*, which means confrontation, admonition,
warning. Literally, it means *putting-in-mind*.

This verse is virtually a New Covenant rewording of Proverbs 29:15, which
we will study at length below: "The rod and reproof give wisdom, but a youth
let loose[12] shames his mother" (DJP).

Why did the apostle not give more detail concerning child-rearing? Simple:
it would be "reinventing the wheel." Paul both affirmed and made use of the

---

[12] NAS "who gets his own way."

ongoing instructive power of the Old Testament (cf. Rom. 15:4; 1 Cor. 9:9; 10:11; 2 Tim. 3:15–17, etc.). Within that body of revealed literature, Proverbs already serves that very purpose, providing a great deal of detailed guidance, both explicitly and in principle, concerning child-training.

It is well to have such rich resources for, as we are about to see, the stakes are incredibly high.

The Stakes in Child-training

The Good News: There Are Grand Benefits to a Godly Child

Great and grand benefits can accrue both to parents and child, when a child *is given and receives* a godly upbringing.

For the *child* the *first* benefit is the fear of Yahweh (Prov. 2:1–5).[13] Solomon, standing as the model father, urges his son to commit his words to memory, and to seek wisdom diligently and prayerfully. When he does, what does the child discern? "The fear of Yahweh" and "knowledge of God."

Therefore, we see at the outset that the goal of the fatherly instruction was not merely safeguarding the family's reputation, nor making a good little citizen or wage-earner. It was not the bare impartation of a trade. Rather, we see clearly that the goal of fatherly instruction was the inculcation of the fear of Yahweh, which itself would be the key to all else.

If the parent taught as God would have him teach, and if the child would receive as God would have him take it to heart, the result would be a child with a real and growing relationship to God.

The *second* benefit would be *long life.* More than one section affirms this truth. Consider Proverbs 3:1–2—

> My son: my law, do not forget,
>> and my commandments, let your heart observe;
> ² Because length of days, and years of life,
>> and peace will they add to you. (DJP)

On the literal level, we see the model father speaking to his son, and encouraging him to memorize his teaching. Behind this we see our heavenly Father's voice to us.[14]

---

[13] Translated and studied closely in Chapter 4.
[14] See Hebrews 12:5ff.

Is there warrant in the text itself for seeing these verses in this light? Indeed there is—*if* we affirm Solomonic authorship.[15] We call to mind the pivotal moment when Yahweh offered Solomon *carte blanche* to ask what he would, and he asked for wisdom. Recall this part of Yahweh's reply:

> "And if you will walk in my ways, keeping my statutes and my commandments, as your father David walked, then I will lengthen your days" (1 Kings 3:14).

The two passages are tied together by the mention of "my commandments" (identical in both), and by the fact that "I will lengthen your days" is the equivalent of "length of days," expressed by a verb rather than a noun. What Yahweh says to Solomon in 1 Kings 3:14, the father echoes to the son in Proverbs 3:1–2.

That being the case, we can see in verse two that the benefits are not only length of life, but quality of life. It is not merely the extension of what Waltke calls "clinical life," but the impartation of what makes life *life*: a relationship with God, with the joy and peace and God's blessing that attends.[16]

Then we turn to Proverbs 4:10–11, 13, which very literally runs:

> Listen, my son, and receive my sayings,
> > that the years of life may be many for you.
>
> [11] In the way of wisdom have I directed you,
> > I have caused you to tread in the paths of uprightness.
>
> ...[13] Grasp hold of discipline, do not relax your grip,
> > Guard it, for it is your life. (DJP, very literal)

Why is this true? The basis is Exodus 20:12 (literal): "Honor your father and your mother, in order that your days may be long upon the land which Yahweh your God is giving to you."[17]

---

[15] At the risk of brutalizing a deceased equine, let me observe again how short-sighted was Longman's airy dismissal of introductory matters as having "little or no impact on our interpretation of [Proverbs]" (*How to Read Proverbs*, 159). Any information that the text of Scripture provides the interpreter *always must have* great and much impact on interpretation.

[16] See Waltke's treatment in his Commentary on Proverbs 1:104–107, 109. He says that Proverbs 3:2 "refers to abundant life in fellowship with the eternal and living God" (1:240).

[17] This truth is reaffirmed in a New Testament context, in Ephesians 6:1–3.

It is also true, as we have seen before, that godly child-training, taken to heart, would preserve from many potentially fatal situations, not limited to—

- Thievery;
- Venereal disease;
- Drug-dealing;
- Starving to death due to poverty;
- Being shot by a jealous spouse; and
- Violent friends, resulting in violent lifestyle, leading to violent death.

Godly child-training, taken to heart, would also preserve from capital offenses, which during Solomon's time would include murder, adultery, homosexuality, blasphemy. Godly child-training, taken to heart, would produce the sort of inner peace of mind and stability which would make for optimum health and longevity. Godly child-training, taken to heart, would eliminate any necessity for the parents' invoking Deuteronomy 21 (or, in their failure to do so, God's implementation of it).[18]

A *third* benefit for the child includes *security and guidance.* This is memorably held forth in Proverbs 6:20–22, which again runs literally:

> Guard, my son, the commandment of your father,
>   And do not forsake the law of your mother;
>
> [21] Bind them upon your heart continually,
>   Tie them upon your neck.
>
> [22] When you walk about, they will guide you;
>   When you lie down, they will watch over you;
>   And when you awake, they themselves will talk with you. (DJP)

Parental instruction provides comprehensive guidance for life. This was instruction that could accompany the child wherever he went, providing guidance for each twist and turn.

When we remember that Proverbs is Spirit-breathed, and that the voice of God the Father speaks to us through Solomon, this section is simply fascinating and instructive… though much of modern Christianity may not come off looking too pretty in the process. As an exercise, pluck out verse 22 thus:

---

[18] Remember Hophni and Phinehas.

When you walk about, _____ will guide you;

When you lie down, _____ will watch over you;

And when you awake, _____ will talk with you.

What would modern, trendy Christians be most likely to supply for in the blanks? Many Christians today would instantly supply "the Holy Spirit." This reflects the traditional belief of many Christians—gleaned from *no* direct teaching of Scripture—that the Holy Spirit guides us by hunches, whispers, intuitions, feelings, and some misty form of semi-revelation. This certainly appeals to the subjective, lazy modern mindset, to which "study" and "spirituality" are antonyms, not complementaries.

It is of great moment to note that the Bible never assigns any of these verbs to the Holy Spirit.[19] The activities which God directly applies to the role of His inerrant Scriptures are, sadly, seldom used by many Christians—and yet this is what the Bible holds out as normal Christian experience. We see it in church context, in Colossians 3:16—

Let the word of Christ dwell within you richly, in all wisdom teaching and confronting one another, singing gratefully to God with all your heart, with psalms, with hymns, with spiritual songs. (DJP)[20]

How have we strayed so far from the Biblical model? The only possible reasons that the Scriptural teaching does not grip us are (1) our love-affair with mysticism;[21] and (2) collaterally, our failure to remember that God works through means: and the regular means that the Holy Spirit uses is His Word.

The Holy Spirit does guide and speak to us. He does it by means of His Word. Before modern false teaching infects your child, teach him and show him that God talks to us through His Word. Instill in your child the Word of God, and you will be giving him guidance for life.

---

[19] The closest parallel being John 16:13, which speaks of the Spirit's inerrant guidance of apostles into that infallible truth which we now have in Scripture.

[20] Literally, "The word [or doctrine; Greek *logos*] of Christ, let *it* keep indwelling in you richly, in/ with all wisdom teaching and confronting yourselves; with psalms, with hymns, with spiritual songs, in/with grace, singing, in/with your hearts, to God."

[21] Put briefly, the idea that God communicates immediately, directly, with our "spirits" apart from our rational minds, and apart from the Bible. Christian mystics usually hasten to declaim that this communication would never be contrary to the Bible; yet it regularly supplants study of the Bible in the daily decision-making of adherents. As a movement, Charismaticism tends to exalt and encourage mysticism, although that error is not limited to this faction.

For the parents the chief benefit is joy and satisfaction

We see as much, pithily, in Proverbs 10:1—

> The proverbs of Solomon.
> A wise son gladdens *his* father,
>   but a stupid son is his mother's grief. (DJP)

I think it true that this proverb is reversible. That is, a wise son certainly also makes his mother glad,[22] and a foolish son also is a grief to his father.[23]

We could think of this verse as the Fifth Commandment (Exod. 20:12), brought down close and personal. Is that not the genius of Proverbs, to give personal specificity to the Law's generalities? God has more in mind than bare, grudging, occasional outward compliance to preferred parental commands.

This proverb, then, is a down-home picture of two children: one responds to the Fifth Commandment in the warmth and enthusiasm of a living faith. The other rebels.

We see here that the son has the capacity to bring joy to his father, and grief to his mother. Neither parent wants the child to be unwise, or stupid. Both parents want the child to love God and apply His Word to life. They can have no greater joy than to see that he now has made God *his* God, and walks in His wisdom.

Then we turn to Proverbs 15:20—

> A wise son gladdens *his* father,
>   but a stupid man disdains his mother. (DJP)

Parenting has to be one of the hardest jobs in the world. One loves, gives, sacrifices; one sows and sows—but only God knows what the harvest will be. The young child seems to be holding the same faith. But what will he do, where will she turn, once they're out of the house?

When that time comes, and parents see that the Word has gone home and taken root, theirs is a joy that can never be taken away. They know that they have seen the hand of God, right there in their house, in their family, doing what they haven't the power to do: give spiritual life and reality.

---

[22] Proverbs 23:24–25.
[23] Proverbs 17:21, 25; 19:13.

But both verses also somberly warn of the flip-side, the bitter heartbreak of a son who is taught in God's ways, yet grows into a "stupid" young man with contempt for God and his parents.

The happy thought is echoed and turned to an imperative in Proverbs 23:24–25.

> The father of the righteous will greatly rejoice;
>> he who fathers a wise son will be glad in him.
>
> ²⁵ Let your father and mother be glad;
>> let her who bore you rejoice.

As a generality, a successfully-trained child is a token of and credit to two parents, working together. The father certainly takes great joy, as he sees his name and the family's faith carried on in his son. If the son disgraces his name, however, the pain is beyond description.

Children: this is your God-given goal

We must not miss that Solomon turns it around and makes this an imperative to the son: *you* must give joy to your father and mother; *you* must give your mother reason to rejoice. This is nothing but an application of the imperative in Exodus 20:12, which morally and spiritually obliges children not merely *not* to dishonor their father and mother, but positively to seek ways to honor them. In that same way, a child is obliged, not only *not* to bring sorrow and grief to his parents, but positively to seek ways to bring joy and gladness to them.

In fact, parents should be able to expect that their children will do just that. As Proverbs 29:17 says,

> Discipline your son, that he may give you comfort,
>> and that he may give delights to your soul. (DJP)²⁴

Parents discipline their children because God commands it. It is right, and it brings God glory. Further, it is the loving thing to do for the children's welfare.

But, in addition to all that, it is to the parents' advantage to rear godly children. As Paul says in another connection, "the plowman should plow in hope and the thresher thresh in hope of sharing in the crop" (1 Cor. 9:10). Parents are

---

²⁴ The purposive rendering "that he may" is also seen in McKane ("Discipline your son that he may be a source of satisfaction, and may give pleasure to you"—257), and in Waltke (*Proverbs*, 2:401).

right to hope that, when the crop of his sowing God's Word and love comes to maturity, their sons and their daughters will bring them joy and gladness.

The call to "honor"

It is fitting to recall the first horizontal commandment of the Ten Words: "Honor your father and your mother, that your days may be long in the land that the LORD your God is giving you" (Exod. 20:12; cf. Eph. 6:1–3). To honor (*kabbēd*) means to give weight to, to regard and treat with respectful deference, to show honor to. In some texts, the words "despise" and "honor" are semantic opposites (cf. Psa. 15:4; Mal. 1:6).

Do not overlook the position of this command among the Ten. As the commands turn from the horizontal to the social, which would you have put first? The prohibition of murder, perhaps? Of theft? Surely these are fundamental issues.

Yet God positioned the command to honor father and mother at the crown of the social commands, the horizontal commands. Fundamental to all social structures both in chronology and God's moral hierarchy is how children regard their parents. When Jesus wanted to illustrate how fast and loose the Pharisees played with the Law, He went to their legalistic circumnavigation of this command (Mark 7:6–13).

How to honor?

How does the wise child show such honor? Proverbs itself gives us a great deal of guidance here. The wise child listens hard and closely to his father (Prov. 2:1), and memorizes what he teaches him (3:1; 6:21–23). The wise son does not merely remain outwardly silent but inwardly inattentive; rather, he gives his heart to his father (23:26). He internalizes his father's teaching, puts it to work in a wise and godly life, and knows God's blessing. In so doing, he gives both his parents rest and delight (29:17).

"Fear." Other texts grant still more light, though an exhaustive study is beyond our scope. Leviticus 19:3 adds an imperative to *revere* mother and father; the Hebrew *tîrā'û* ("fear"—the verb corresponding to the noun in Prov. 1:7). This introduces that element found frequently in Scripture, yet seldom in our society: that of a submissive respect that conditions a heart genuinely to shrink from giving offense. Indeed, Malachi 1:6 treats this honor that a son owes his father as a God-given duty, something inherent in the relationship, simply because one is his father's son.

By contrast, in Proverbs the foolish child is neglectful during his years of instruction and learning (10:5), disregards what he has been taught (19:27), is abusive and insulting to his parents (19:26), is stupid (17:25; 19:13), ignores correction (13:1), and hangs around with the sorts of people his father warned him against (1:10; 24:21; 28:7).

Take the Fifth. If the stupid man embodies the opposite of the Fifth Commandment, the wise son embraces and embodies its values. We read back in 10:1 that the wise son makes his father glad. The wise son embraces his father's God-centered values, and seeks to please him, to make him happy—not merely to avoid getting in trouble. His measuring line is not, "How much can I get away with?" It is "How can I honor God by pleasing my parents?"

"*Any* parents?" one might ask. The focus of the proverb is on the child, but I'd feel it amiss not to restate the obvious. As a proverb, it is brief and pointed, and makes certain assumptions. Would a believing child be expected to make a Baal-worshiping dad happy in every way? Of course not. The assumption is a wise and godly parent, operating within the bounds of his divinely delegated sphere of authority.

Questions for Application

Do you really honor your father and your mother? What part does their upbringing and their teaching play in your major decisions? Do you even consult them, let alone give weight to their input?

Do you think, not just of not angering them, or what you can get away with—but actually of gladdening your parents, making them happy by your choices, attitude, behavior?

Can your friends bear witness to the respect and honor in which you hold your mother and father? What would they glean from the way you speak of your parents? Do you bring them around to show your parents off to your friends, and to show your parents how you've taken their counsel to heart in who you associate with (Prov. 13:20)? Is it obvious to all your friends that you think God gave you a real blessing in your parents? Or do you clearly act as if you are embarrassed by them, or as if they are nothing to you? Is your behavior anything like Solomon's very public honor shown his mother (1 Kings 2:19)? Do you treat your parents as optional, dispensable "extras" in the drama of your life?

Let's just bring it home like this. Son, daughter: what if I were to look at your father, your mother, as they think about you? What would I see?

Glad Dad?

Or glum Mum?

God's Heart for Parents

Parenting is not for the fainthearted; it involves countless sacrifices, large and small. These verses hold out hope for the reward of joy in this life.

But even in the case of apostate, ungrateful, foolish children, these verses reveal God's heart. There are parents who have faithfully loved, and trained, and taught, and shown—only to have it cast in their teeth by a child who has gone the way that seemed right in his own eyes, turning a deaf ear to God's law. There are sons today whose only fame is in their father's name, and in the shame they spitefully cast on it.

In these verses, such parents see revealed God's regard of them. Though the child does not value their sacrifice, and did not receive God's Word, God values such parents. He says they should know joy. Though they do not know it from their child, they can look to know it in His presence (cf. Matt. 25:21, 23).

The Bad News: There Are Terrible Miseries for a Foolish Child

For the Child Himself

Proverbs 30:17

We see a harvest of terrible miseries for the foolish child. Solomon warns that foolish children reap disaster, in Proverbs 30:17—

> The eye that mocks a father
>   and scorns to obey a mother
> will be picked out by the ravens of the valley
>   and eaten by the vultures.

First, note that this child is not walking in the fear of Yahweh, which is the beginning of wisdom (1:7). We know this with certainty, because "Whoever walks in uprightness fears the LORD, but he who is devious in his ways despises him" (Prov. 14:2). God Himself has told the child to honor his father and mother

(Exod. 20:12), and warned the child fiercely against shaming and defying his parents (Exod. 21:15, 17; Lev. 19:3; Deut. 21:18–21).

This child is not walking in God's commands. He has found a way that looks better, in his own eyes. It seems logical, reasonable, promising. His friends affirm him in his choice.

But it is a path that leads to his own destruction (Prov. 14:12).

Solomon is providing us another unique, compressed picture. Think it through. Here is the child's "eye," his way of looking at life. In his attitude, he has "mocked" his father, and "scorned to obey" his mother. The first is an active sin, the second a passive sin. Not only did he (passively) dishonor God by failing to honor his father, but he (actively) mocked God by mocking his father. Additionally, he "scorns to obey" his mother, refusing her godly instruction.

This son is like the shocking fool of verse 11—"There are those who curse [sin of commission] their fathers and do not bless [sin of omission] their mothers." If this son hid behind a pious veneer, God Himself would scorn him. He has turned his ear away from listening to God's law, and even his prayer nauseates God (Prov. 28:9).

Where do we find this independent, "free" soul now, as a result of his choices? That *eye*, which rebelled against God, is being "picked out by the ravens of the valley and eaten by the vultures." What are ravens and vultures? They are birds of carrion. They eat dead things. Carrion-birds would not be attacking this young man and overpowering him if he were in good health, and certainly not if he were at home.

"Ah," you say, "he is dead." Not merely dead, though. Birds of carrion would not be feasting on this young man if he had died, and then had been buried or entombed, as was normal. His corpse must be lying out open and exposed in a field.

So how did this young man come to this end? These birds could only feast on a young man if he were both dead and unburied. He must be away from home, with none to care for him, else his parents would have seen to his burial.

Solomon's condensed picture, then, is of a young man who has estranged himself from his family by his sin. He has alienated himself, by his mockery and rebellion, from those who loved him most deeply and purely. He has met a violent end, unburied and unmourned and uncared-for.

What is the moral of the story? Every rebel against God thinks he has truly gotten away with a grand deed. He feels a flush of exhilaration. Yet "God is not mocked, for whatever one sows, that will he also reap" (Gal. 6:7). Initial joys will all be turned to the deepest stain of guilt and misery.

Foolish children reap the reverse of the benefits a wise child would enjoy

Every glad fruit of a godly childhood may be flipped on its head to predict the lot of the arrogant rebel. For instance, if a godly child reaps knowledge of the fear of Yahweh, the ungodly child learns no fear of Yahweh (Prov. 2:1–5). He cannot fear Yahweh if he does not bow at His feet. If the child disrespects his parents and refuses to learn their godly counsel, he is rejecting Yahweh (cf. Rom. 13:1–7). He lacks the irreducible starting point for wisdom, and dooms himself to folly.

If a godly child can expect a rich and long life (Prov. 3:1–2), an ungodly child can expect the opposite. As mentioned earlier, godly child-training, rejected, exposes one to many potentially fatal situations, such as thievery, venereal disease, starving to death due to poverty, the sort of combative behavior which could result in being murdered. Godly child-training, rejected, would expose one to capital offenses such as murder, adultery, homosexuality, blasphemy, idolatry. Godly child-training, rejected, would render impossible the sort of inner peace of mind and stability which would make for optimum health and longevity. Godly child-training, rejected, could ultimately necessitate the parents' invoking Deuteronomy 21 (or, in their failure to do so, God's implementation of it).

But beyond that, since "life" means more than a pulse and respiration, the child will lack the well-grounded peace of mind and security and joy that is a godly child's birthright. His sleep *will not* be sweet and free from dread of evil (1:33; 3:24–25), unless he is entirely delusional (Psa. 10:4, 11). *God is his enemy.* He will reap the fruit of his own ways, and find it a bitter and deadly meal indeed (Prov. 1:24–32).

If a godly child knows security and divine guidance (Prov. 6:20–22), the foolish and rebellious child will be bereft of both. If the reception of parental training brings these benefits, it follows that the rejection of that training prevents them. The child who is walking with God has God's revealed standards, as taught by his parents, to guide him, has the assurance of Genesis 50:20 and Romans 8:28. He can always call on God for aid.

The child who is not walking with God does not have God's revealed standards to guide him. As God is not pleased with the arrogant "cafeteria Christian" who picks and chooses what he likes from God's Word (cf. Luke 6:46; James 2:10–11), this lad is on his own. God is his opponent (Rom. 13:2, 5). He is not walking God's path out of love for God, so he lacks the assurance of Romans 8:28. He has turned a deaf ear to God's law, so he cannot call on God for wisdom nor aid without actually repelling God (Prov. 28:9).

As we noted above, this boy's lot is that laid out in Proverbs 1:24–32. Foolish children reap just exactly what we see them reaping today. Public officials do not understand why gangs, drug use, drunkenness, lawlessness, and immorality are skyrocketing. Teen suicide, pregnancy, violent crimes grow and grow—and the best answer our leaders can come up with is more money for public schools or government programs. God knows the answer. He has given the answer. He needs but to be heard and heeded.

The ungodly child is not the only one to suffer, however. There are as well…

Terrible Miseries for the Parents of the Foolish Child

Grief

First, the foolish child brings his parents grief. We just saw that in Proverbs 10:1, above. It takes a long time to produce a thoroughly foolish son; but when one is produced, he is there for a long, long time, as a constant pain and heartache.

Solomon's point here is to underline this point: folks, you don't want a foolish child. Therefore Father, you do your job. Mother, you help him.

Again, Proverbs 17:21 says

> He who sires a fool gets himself sorrow, [25]
> and the father of a fool has no joy.

Sad, but terribly true. The father as head of the house should set the tone for discipline. This means a lot of work, thought, sacrifice. But remember, a foolish son is a lifelong pain. A man must square his shoulders, pray for grace and wisdom, and do what it takes.

Again, Proverbs 17:25 says that "A foolish son is a grief to his father and bitterness to her who bore him." Both parents lose if they produce a foolish child. Therefore, both must cooperate in rearing, disciplining and training a wise child.

---

[25] Hebrew *l'tûgâ lô*, very literally *to suffering* (or *pain*) *for him*.

Humiliation

Second, the foolish child *brings his parents humiliation.*[26] This is at least hinted at in Proverbs 15:20 (discussed earlier), which says that "A wise son makes his father glad, but a man who is stupid disdains his mother" (DJP).

The thought is stated more frontally in Proverbs 28:7—

> The one who keeps the law is a son with understanding,
>   but a companion of gluttons shames his father.

Solomon here re-affirms God's design for the family. The goal of child-training is a law(-of-God)-abiding son. God wants dads and moms to rear servants for Him. The good son is characterized, not merely by his obedience to mom and dad, but by his orientation toward God and the law of God. Now, if he obeys God, he will obey his parents—but the reverse is not necessarily true (i.e. that he obeys his parents does not mean he will obey God).

The Hebrew word for "glutton" [27] indicates someone who lives lavishly, extravagantly—a materialist. By his idolatrous materialism and extravagance he shows that he has not taken to heart the need to love God first and above all. That life-orientation brings shame on his father, who (it is assumed) pursues a very different priority.

We will study Proverbs 29:15 at length later. At this point, we will simply note that the indulgent mother's idea of love is to let her child loose without sufficient discipline. In response, he turns around and shames her.

Ruin

Third, the foolish child *brings his parents ruin* (Prov. 19:13).

> A foolish son is ruin[28] to his father,
>   and a wife's quarreling is a continual dripping of rain.

These are two wretched, ongoing miseries: a man is made miserable by a foolish son, or by an argumentative wife. If a man's adult wife is in an argumentative

---

[26] In some cases this humiliation is due to the reflection on the child-training. We do well to recall the case of Eli, which we will look at later. In other cases it is simply due to the child's own chosen behavior.

[27] The participle *zôlelîm* is from *zālal*, to be light.

[28] Hebrew *hawwōt*, calamities, troubles.

pattern of behavior (Line B), it is difficult for a man to do anything about it. But, with a man's son (Line A), he can start in during infancy to head his son in a wise direction. Whether the son takes his father's instruction to heart, however, is a different matter.

Application of Godly Parental Wisdom: Three Focal Points

First: Embrace the Right Center and Goal

Now let us hone in on more specific teaching in Proverbs relating to child-training. As we do so, a few brief observations may help set the stage, as we contrast two entirely-different approaches.

Worldly wisdom regarding child-training

A great many parents—even professing Christian parents—would give as their goal producing children who are *happy*. This mutates what should be a by-product (happiness) into the actual goal. Everything becomes skewed around an inappropriate and inadequate axis.

This lame goal results in:

- Lack of an overarching Game Plan based on the fear of Yahweh.

- Crisis-management and ad-hoc, party-host duties.

- Absence of a long-term, God-centered perspective that gives shape and coherence to all else.

- Indulgence, materialism, permissiveness.

- Damage to the parents' relationship.

- A child who is self-centered, self-indulgent, unprincipled, undisciplined, aimless, and ungodly; and therefore

- A child who either knows nothing about God, or knows only untruths about God, imagining Him to be like his parents: shapeless, edgeless, unprincipled, and wholly devoted to no higher good than making the world revolve around the child's happiness.

All this spells ruin for the child, the parents, and society.

Biblical wisdom regarding child-training

God's revealed perspective is entirely different in every way. It features and is controlled by a fundamentally divergent view of the child, of the parents, of the family, of the world, and above all of God.

According to Biblical wisdom:

- Each of us exists for the glory of God. Therefore

- The center of the universe is not the child, the parents, or the family. The center of the universe is *God.*

- The purpose of the family is to produce and train servants of God.

- Happiness is not the chief goal, but is a by-product of discipline and godliness. I am not happy playing a violin, I have no freedom at all with it. I am not happy nor free because I can do nothing meaningful with a violin. I can do nothing with a violin because I have no discipline, no guidelines, no training.

- Happy children will be children who have been reared with God-centered, God-defined goals, values, and discipline, so that they can play life like a violin.

We shall now study the how. But first…

Second: Cherish Wise Expectations

Is this a guaranteed method?

Some people are drawn to the book of Proverbs because of what they mistakenly see in it. Misreading proverbial form as a series of ironclad guarantees, they virtually regard Proverbs as a magic book, such as one might find at Hogwarts. If a parent simply applies these principles faithfully, he will end up with a wise, godly child—guaranteed!

Some think so

Am I making this up? I wish I were. The mentality of Job's friends abounds among many who teach, either directly or in so many words, that parents actually can *cause* their children to be genuine, godly believers.

How does this show? When a prominent Christian politician's daughter became pregnant out of wedlock, a well-known Christian author immediately laid the responsibility at her father's feet, suggesting he had not loved her properly. The girl sins, but it is her father's responsibility. That must mean that, if he'd been a proper father, she would not have sinned.

The reasoning is identical to that of Job's friends. God blesses the righteous, and punishes the wicked. Job was suffering. Therefore he was being punished by God. Therefore Job must have sinned. QED.

Or sometimes the formula-approach is stated in so many words, as in *What the Bible Says About... Child Training*, by Richard Fugate.[29] The author writes:

> Training children is not a hit-or-miss proposition in which the parent has no control. It is not that some children just turn out okay while others may not.[30]

Note how the author presents his system:

> Is there a system for child training that you can know for sure is correct and can utilize to obtain the right results? This book sets forth the system for child training given in the Bible, a system you can use with confidence to become a successful parent.[31]

That quotation was from the 1980 edition. Has the author's estimate changed in over thirty years? As of this writing (March 2010), his website says this:

> Over the years, I have spoken to thousands of concerned parents and a particular question often arises: "Is it really a promise from God that our children will turn out okay if we properly train them?" Some Christian authors have denied this concept. Please note that it is not just Proverbs 22:6 *"Train up a child in the way he should go: and when he is old, he will not depart from it."* [sic] that indicates a guarantee. All of the other passages cited in this lesson warn us

---

[29] Aletheia Publishers: 1980.

[30] Fugate, 15. He does add, "Even though a child could conceivably reject all attempts to train him properly, he would have to choose clearly against what he knows to be right. Even the one who rebels against good child training is likely to return to a productive life after his period of rebellion" (ibid.). Which is it?

[31] Ibid., 9. The book does contain some good information and suggestions, though its value is lessened by such absolutist promises.

that young adults are the products of their upbringing. It seems very clear to me that parents who raise their child to be a fool (one who rejects God's Word in living his life) will reap the promise of cursing. Equally clear is the promise that training up a wise child, who honors his parents as well as God's Word, will result in blessings for both parents and child.

...I have never known of a child "going bad" who was raised by a Christian father and mother who both practiced: a right marriage (father in leadership, mother in support, both operating in love and justice), and; [sic] correct child training principles (with a proper balance between controlling and teaching). On the other hand, I have met a great number of young adults who have paid a terrible price because their Christian parents failed in properly training them.[32]

There it is. Use the system, and success is guaranteed. If the child turns out wrong, the parents failed in their marriage, in their parenting, or both.

I can see Job's friends standing by, nodding in agreement.

Biblical?

Biblical realism

Think of the first son, ever. Perfect Father, perfect environment, perfect upbringing—yet he rebelled against his Father, turned traitor, and followed his wife's lead to join with his Father's chief enemy in slandering His character and His judgment. Now, whose fault is that? Bad parenting? (I speak as a fool.)

I would say this absolutely categorically: the Bible *never* presents *any* formula by which one human being can control the soul and spirit of another human being, in *any* relationship. Not husbands, not pastors, not leaders, not friends, not neighbors, not evangelists, not church members—and not fathers.

If it were the case that parents had such power, then we would have to conclude that the wrong person is being executed in Deuteronomy 21:18–21. You will recall that this law directs the parents of a stubbornly rebellious son to bring him to the elders to be executed publicly. But if his sin is his parents' fault, shouldn't *the parents* be the ones brought out for execution, instead of the

---

[32] http://www.foundationforbiblicalresearch.org/CT%20excerpt%203.html/.

wretched son? If his rebellion is a sure sign of their failure as parents, shouldn't the punishment be theirs, as well?

Further, if good parenting had a sovereign, monergistic effect on the child, why is Solomon forever pleading with and urging his son to remember, hear, listen, keep, treasure, bind, lay up, and so forth? Why does he warn him against leaving, neglecting, and forgetting?[33] If all the responsibility is on the parents' shoulders, and all the necessary power in their actions and words, why bring the child in? Do parenting correctly, and success is assured … right?

Proverbs does warn of ill fruits following bad parenting. But when Solomon speaks to rebellious sons, shameful sons, foolish sons—the sin is roundly laid on *their* shoulders, not their parents'. It seems to be the case that apostate children hate their godly parents all the more for their attempts to point them to the Lordship of Christ.

Remember: the only perfect Father, ever, had a rebellious human son; the only perfect Son, ever, was reared by flawed human parents.

Further, it strikes me that the "guaranteed success" teachers hedge their bets just as cynically and transparently as the "faith healers" do. If they fail to heal, the sufferer had insufficient faith. If children turn out ungodly, the parents did marriage or parenting wrong. But this is a trick, it is a cheat. Can any faith, or any marriage or parenting style, stand up to absolutist examination? Imagine the spirit of parents who feel that their ideal children owe their spirituality to what flawless, model couple they are. "O God, we thank you that we are not as other parents…"

This was not Paul's attitude toward his own ministry.

> I planted, Apollos watered, but God gave the growth. [7] So neither
> he who plants nor he who waters is anything, but only God who
> gives the growth (1 Cor. 3:6–7).

"But," one might retort, "Paul planted *faithfully*, and Apollos watered *faithfully*." True enough. Yet in the case of (just to pick one) the Galatians, Paul was afraid that he might turn out to have run in vain (4:11). They were giving the heretics such a sympathetic hearing that Paul feared his efforts might be for nothing. Yet did Paul conclude that the blame could be laid at his feet, for doing ministry wrongly? Hardly (cf. 1:1–12; 4:15–16).

---

[33] For Scriptural documentation, see Appendix 2.

In sum

We must embrace a central truth, as parents: the way we train our children must be shaped by Proverbs 1:7, as indeed is true of all our lives. We must not rear our children in a certain way because it will work (pragmatism); we must rear them in such a way because it pleases and honors Yahweh (fear of Yahweh). As in all walks of life, whether marriage or pastoral ministry or evangelism or work, God's pleasure and glory must be our focus. Then we can trust the results to Him with a clean conscience (Prov. 16:1, 3, 9).

Third: Maintain the Right Focus

Discipline, involving civilization?

Proverbs is filled with practical, specific exhortations. In speaking to parents (as we shall see), Solomon is in line with the larger Canon in affirming parental authority. Parents are to teach, reprove, and not shy away from using the rod. They are to draw lines, enforce those lines, and expect (and receive) respect.

It is natural, perhaps, to be caught up in all those specifics as if they were the heart of the matter. Perhaps influenced by formulaic books and dynamic seminars, parents might set out with grim determination to enforce all these rules *as their primary emphasis*. They find themselves constantly cast as cops and judges, pulling their kids over, handing out citations, and enforcing sanctions.

All of this is legitimate, as far as it goes. Like it or not, the parent *is* governor, cop, judge and jury in the home. To refuse these roles because they are onerous is to refuse to be a parent.

However, it is critical that parents not lose focus of the real target, the real goal.

Let me sidle up to my point by posing a question. Suppose you succeed in corralling your child's behavior? He always treats you and your spouse with respect. He always says "Yes, sir" and "Yes, ma'am," and follows orders cheerfully and immediately. He puts away his dishes. He makes his bed. He studies hard, and gets straight A's. He reads his Bible every day. He is quiet and attentive in church. He is active in his youth group.

What have you achieved?

You've produced a fine little *moralist*, heading smugly off to Hell with all the other Pharisees.

...or discipleship, involving conversion?

As we have done so many times, we must turn back to the foundational statement of the entire book:

> The fear of Yahweh is the beginning of knowledge;
> Wisdom and discipline, dense people belittle. (Prov. 1:7 DJP)

What is the fear of Yahweh, once again? It is a *heart-attitude*. It is the repentant faith of a sinner who's been brought low by God's holiness, has bent the knee to His Lordship, and trusted Him alone for salvation, on the basis of His Word alone.

How does one receive the fear of Yahweh? Can we behave ourselves into it? Indeed, no. The fear of Yahweh works its way out from the heart in behavior; it does not work its way into the heart by behavior.

So we recall Solomon's other word:

> Above everything *you* watch, guard your heart,
> for from it flow the springs of life. (Prov. 4:23 DJP)[34]

Solomon would have been far from meaning his son should learn simply to compel outward compliance from his children. The wise king's view of the family would have been informed by Deuteronomy 6:4–9, where the father loves the one true God with all his heart. It is an overflow of that love which moves him to talk in terms of God's Word in every season of his family's life.

At the risk of seeming anachronistic, the father preaches the Gospel to his children. Fathers in Solomon's day would preach the Gospel of Yahweh who redeems by blood sacrifice, and declares His believing people righteous through faith; Yahweh who will one day come to accomplish perfect salvation. In our post-Cross day, it is the Gospel of Jesus Christ, God incarnate, who came into the world to save sinners by His penal, substitutionary atonement on the basis of grace alone, and by means of faith alone. It is fundamentally one Gospel, preached at different points in the unfolding of revelation (Heb. 1:1–2).

Solomon would have the parents affirm what he himself said, that there is no man who does not sin (1 Kings 8:46), and that God is a consuming fire who

---

[34] This verse has weighty ramifications for parenting, many of which are developed helpfully in Tedd Tripp's *Shepherding a Child's Heart* (Wapwallopen: Shepherd Press, 1995); see 19ff. in particular.

hates sin and cannot simply excuse it (Exod. 34:7; Deut. 4:24). But he would also have had them preach that God promised to send the Seed of the Woman to redeem mankind (Gen. 3:15), and would have had them preach that God credits righteousness to anyone who simply believes His Word, as He did with Abram (Gen. 15:3). He would have had them teach their children to believe Yahweh, trust His Word, look to Him for forgiveness and life.

This faith, Solomon knew, would arise from the heart and work its way outward (cf. Prov. 1:7; 4:23). It could not be achieved by works. But it would be the seedbed for works.

Having called their children to repentant heart-faith, Solomon would have the parents urge their children to live a faithful life. A child is known by his deeds (Prov. 20:11). If he fears Yahweh, he will walk a morally and spiritually straight path (Prov. 14:2). His life-course will express that saving, gracious faith through obedience and holiness (Pss. 1; 19:7–14; 119).

So Proverbs must never be viewed nor employed as a lawbook, a book of etiquette, meant to create smug, smirking little damned legalists who know all the answers.

Rather, it is a book for those who have already savingly embraced the fear of Yahweh (1:7), and want to live wise lives that adorn that faith.

Therefore the children's hearts must first be pointed to repose upon Yahweh by repentant faith alone; and then educated in that wise and righteous life that pleases Him.

With that paramount imperative firmly before our minds, let us study together specifically what Solomon urges wise parents to do, and to avoid.

THE TWOFOLD METHOD: THE ROD AND REPROOF (PROVERBS 29:15)

Though Proverbs says a great deal about child-training, Proverbs 29:15 offers a very nicely-compacted summary. It will repay our close attention.

> The rod and reproof give wisdom,
> But a youth let loose[35] shames his mother (DJP)

---

[35] NAS "who gets his own way"; ESV "left to himself."

The Rod (Hebrew *šēḇeṭ*)

What is the "Rod"?

As to the literal object,

> [The *šēḇeṭ*] was used for beating cumin (Isa 28:27), as a weapon
> (II Sam 23:21), and as a shepherd's implement either to muster or
> count sheep (Lev 27:32; Ezk 20:37), or to protect them (Ps 23:4;
> Mic 7:14).[36]

The noun *šēḇeṭ* was used in many settings. In Leviticus 27:32, it is the
herdsman's staff, counting out his animals (cf. Ezek. 20:37). In 2 Samuel 23:21,
it is the weapon of Benaiah, one of David's mighty men. In Isaiah 28:27, it is an
implement used to beat the seeds from cumin. In Micah 7:14, it is the shepherd's
staff with which Yahweh is urged to shepherd His people. Waltke notes that "The
rod was also used as an instrument for either remedial or penal punishment. As a
corrective instrument it was used for a slave (Ex 21:20), a fool (Prov 10:13; 26:3),
and a son (Prov 13:24; 22:15; 23:13–14; 29:15)."[37]

The term *šēḇeṭ* is used some 48 times in Proverbs.[38]

My Proposal

We should see "the rod" is emblematic. That is: the rod is a literal object
representing a metaphorical reality, larger than (but including) itself. It is similar
to "the sword" in Romans 13:4, which denotes government's legitimate punitive
power, not limited to but leading up to and including the death penalty. The *rod*
represents the parent's God-given authority to enforce house law, not limited to
corporal punishment, but including it and everything leading up to it. Standing
in a corner is a legitimate use of the rod; writing sentences or doing chores is a
legitimate use of the rod; a spanking is a legitimate use of the rod.

---

[36] Bruce K. Waltke, TWOT, II:897. It is also used in Genesis 49:10 of the "rod" of sovereignty.

[37] Waltke, ibid.

[38] Another word, *ḥōṭer*, is used in Proverbs 14:3a ("By the mouth of a fool comes a rod for his
back"), where it denotes "a supple green branch used as a whip" (L. G. Herr, "Rod," ISBE,
IV:206). That verse, however, is not immediately relevant to child-training.

Application of the Rod

Literalism

Some have argued insistently that a literal rod is very important. Christian parents should never use their hand to spank, it is said. They should use only an implement like a rod or a branch, or a wooden spoon.

Rationale

Punishment (they argue) should not be dealt out by the same hand that loves, caresses and comforts. If the same parent touches a child lovingly with his/her hand, then with that same hand swats or spanks, this will terribly confuse both the message and the child. A parent must not employ the same hand both ways.

Response

Why not? God does just exactly that with us, does He not? He controls every last dot of our circumstances by His hand (Prov. 16:33; 21:1), and sometimes designs those circumstances to humble and discipline us (Heb. 12:5–11; cf. Psa. 119:67, 71). The same God, out of the same love and by the same mighty hand, sends us providences we deem both smooth and rough, both light and dark. Is it confusing? Certainly, at times. Would we be wise to get used to the idea early on in life? Definitely.

The phobia of confusing a child in this way is not Biblically warranted. It is not the child who sees love and discipline as coming from the same source who is crippled for life. Rather, that child is crippled who sees love and discipline as being mutually exclusive. Such a child is unprepared for God's kind of love. The first time God brings painful discipline to bear, this person will conclude that God does not love him.

Besides, unless Mom carries a rod in her purse, and Dad keeps a telescoping model in his suit pocket, or unless Bobby promises never to misbehave away from home, a literal rod may not always be practical.

However, having said all that, there are genuine advantages to at least occasional uses of some sort of a "rod."[39] A wooden spoon or a belt or a smooth switch can deliver a stinging, attention-getting blow to a specific location with

---

[39] See the discussion in *Withhold Not Correction*, by Bruce Ray (Nutley: Presbyterian & Reformed, 1978).

less general impact, and thus without so much as risking any actual harm. God has thoughtfully provided parents with a "bull's-eye" that is a well-padded area which He kept free from sensitive internal organs.

An aside: am I pressing the language too much if I note that the parental "rod" is always spoken of in the singular, and always put in the hand of the father (when it is specified)? If it is legitimate to see any significance to this, I take it to mean that the father should be where the buck stops, as to discipline.[40] Mom and Dad should have a united philosophy and praxis. Woe betide the household in which the children perceive Mommy and Daddy as having differing "rods," divergent ideas about discipline.

What would be the signs of such division? One clue would be if little Bobby checks with Mommy every time Daddy says something. Another clue would be if little Susy keeps going behind or around Mommy or Daddy to circumnavigate unpopular orders or decisions from one or the other. (e. g., "Dad would say 'No,' so I'll ask Mom"; or, far worse, "Dad said 'no'; let's see what Mom says.") A third might be if the children keep going to one parent over the other with issues that might involve discipline.

Remember that husband and wife are the primary unit and are to function as a team. The husband is the indispensable leader, the wife the indispensable complement. Happy is the home where Daddy recognizes that he is better off with Mommy's input. Happy, too, is the home where Mommy realizes that she needs Daddy—that it is not merely "just one more stupid Bible rule" that the man leads, but that God has made the wisest and best decision in putting the man in charge.

Accordingly, please allow me these three *nevers*. If you neglect these nevers, you may meet your own ego-wants, but you will likely upset the balance that God intends for your family, and fall short of His goal. Ready? Here goes:

1. *Never* contradict each other in front of the children.

2. *Never* allow your children deliberately to play off one parent against the other. This offense should bring real, memorable discipline; it is wrong on so many levels. Nothing should be allowed to split Mom and Dad.

---

[40] My fundamental point is well-grounded, given that children are to submit to mother and father, and wife is to submit to husband (cf. Eph. 5:22–6:3). That it is best for children to see their parents as united follows from that truth. Whether the singularity of "the rod" supports that point, I admit, is debatable.

3. *Never* let your children perceive you as sympathizing with them against your spouse.

Sometimes an ego-starved person will find an unhealthy gratification in leading his/her children to see him/her as "softer," and therefore "more loving." If you do this, you are undermining your partner, and short-circuiting what should be your shared goal. You really need to get with the program.

What Do You Do with the Rod?

By way of this and related Scripture, I am going to suggest that a parent should *use* the rod rather than withhold it, he should use it *with conviction*, and he should use it *for his child's instruction*.

I know going in that what I am about to say is unpopular, it is untrendy, and it is politically-incorrect. The sole question that should occupy both author and reader, however, is: *Is it Scriptural?*[41]

First, use the rod, rather than withhold it (23:13–14).

> Do not withhold discipline from a child;
>> if you strike him with a rod, he will not die.
> [14] If you strike him with the rod,
>> you will save his soul from Sheol.

We must take a closer look at "withhold" (v. 13). The verb *timna'* is from *māna'* to withhold, to hold back.[42] It is frequently used of holding back something that is desired, or of something that has been requested. In Proverbs particularly, this verb is used of holding back—

1. What is *owed* (3:27)

2. What is *needed* (11:26)

3. What is *needed, requested,* and *wanted* (30:7ff.)[43]

Obviously, all those senses should not be forced into one occurrence of the verb. But they do give light on the breadth of the word's range, which in turn

---

41 For some, even the most direct statement of Scripture is insufficient. Clifford's comment on 13:24 is absolutely baffling: "It goes without saying that this paradoxical language cannot be used as an argument for the corporal punishment of children" (140). If not, then one wonders what language *could* be so used?

42 BDB, article מָנַע.

43 Cf. uses in Gen. 30:1–2; 1 Kings 20:7; Psa. 21:2.

may illuminate Solomon's intent. For it is true that corporal punishment is *needed* by the child. The next verse makes this clear; literally it reads, "You, with the rod you will beat him, And his soul from Sheol will you deliver." Then 22:15 adds, "Folly is bound up in the heart of a child, but the rod of discipline drives it far from him."

Nor it is too much of a stretch to say that "the rod" is also *desired* by the child, albeit subconsciously. I was about to teach on this subject years ago and asked one of my children (then 6) what I should say. Here was the answer: "Tell them, when their children are bad, to spank them or send them to the corner—but because they love them, not because they don't love them; and if they won't do that, they don't love them very much, and they aren't obeying the Bible."

Kids on a cliff. It is generally recognized that, at a deeper level, children want discipline and real, firmly-enforced limits. The story is told of a village on a high precipice, with sheer drop-offs all around. The elders had erected sturdy fences all around the sheer edges. It worked well. The children played happily, chasing balls up to the fence, running back, playing all over the village.

Then one day some genius got the idea that the fences were inhibiting the children. They should be set free to soar, to set their own limits and make their own boundaries. So he led a successful campaign to rip up all the fences.

The result?

A mass of terrified children, huddled in the dead-center of the village, afraid to move.

Of course, that's just a story, but it does make a point. The Adam in our children wants to rebel, but the remnant of God's image knows the need of a larger authority who knows what it is doing, and who does what it is supposed to be doing. We know we are finite, answerable creatures. We need to know where the boundaries are. Parents provide these limits within the larger boundaries of God's Word.

Children need this, and deep down inside they want it. This helps explain why undisciplined children are often such miserably unhappy and maladjusted individuals.

Indulged, yes. But happy? A boy I knew as a child comes very vividly to mind. His name was Chris. He had me over to his house, and I was amazed. I don't recall any father; I think there was none. But Chris' mother gave him everything. I couldn't believe how set-up that kid was (to my mind).

Was Chris happy? Was he giddy with gratitude for his posh life, and was he brimming with gratitude to his adoring mother? Mercy, no! Chris was unhappy and angry, and treated his mother horridly, with absolute contempt. And she let him.

Chris *so* needed "the rod." At some level, he so *wanted* it, wanted enforced boundaries. But they were nowhere to be seen, and Chris was angry and miserable, and made his mother's life miserable.

"Save his soul from Sheol." Now we focus on the words to "save his soul from Sheol." The Hebrew word "Sheol" means "the grave." It is a one-word OT way of saying "where we go when we die," along with all the ambiguity that comes with that phrase.

On the simplest level, remember the many capital offenses from which a disciplinarian Israelite would have delivered his children. The situation is not so terribly different with us. Parent, you are your little cherub's first experience with a divinely-constituted and divinely-appointed authority. You have the opportunity of building the category of obedience, as opposed to self-indulgence or mere expedience. If you do not discipline, if your child can defy you and get away with it, you will engender in your child an impulse to resist other proper Biblical authority, and an expectation that he can get away with it.

A child who is a "career criminal" at home first, will then carry his behavior to society at large. He may be rudely surprised if he learns that the world does not coddle him and make endless excuses for him, as Mommy or Daddy did. Perhaps our little lawbreaker will escape human justice for a while, but he shall not escape Divine justice.

How many times have you seen some murderer or criminal on television, and there is his mother, making excuses and blaming the police, the government, the school, society—everyone except her son? In such instances, you have an X-ray into the formation of a criminal character.

If we give our children a home life of disobedience with impunity, we will share some blame for their wretched end.

As a Biblical illustration of this, recall the tragic story of Eli and his sons, Hophni and Phinehas (1 Sam. 2–3). We read that these young men were worthless and evil (2:12–17). What did Eli do? Well, Eli *talked* with them, pleading and reasoning and going on and on like a good modern parent (2:23–25a). Although *we* would probably allow that Eli had reproved them, it is crucial that we note: his words *do not even register with God* as having been reproof, in any meaningful way (3:13).

In consequence of Eli's failure, and of their own sin, the boys were judged by God with death (4:11). Their death was a judgment on his failure as a father to mirror the authority of God to his sons. They had a notion they could get away with it, because they always had.

But not this time.

Parents must *use* the rod.

Second, use the rod with conviction

This truth is particularly spelled out in Proverbs 13:24.

> He who spares[44] his rod hates his son,
>   but he who loves him seeks him early with discipline. (DJP)

This takes us straight to the relationship between love and discipline. It may help if we analyze this verse by tracing from effect to cause.

> **Effect**: refusal to use "the rod."
> **Cause**: *According to our society:* love, understanding, patience,
>   enlightened thought drawn from the latest
>   psychological fashions.
>   *According to the Bible:* hatred.

What's "love" got to do with it? Solomon's thought runs contrary to many modern fads and trends. Our society has developed highly idiomatic ideas about what love is. Love is thought to be letting others alone, leaving them to find the way that their "heart" dictates, without judgment or stigma of any kind. Love pulls up all the village fences.

Biblically-defined love is very different. Genuine love proceeds from a God-fearing base and is a commitment to pursuing what is best for the other. In the case of parenting, God says that "love" will invariably entail reproof and various forms of discipline.

What is passed off as love in permissive families grows from dismal ignorance of Bible teaching, at best. It reflects little or no respect for God's standards for parents and children, and entails nothing of the long view that this God-given task requires. It turns away from the demands of thinking-through, remembering, and commitment which are necessary for consistent, Biblical child-training.

---

[44] Or "restrains, stills."

How to hate your child. Solomon here shows how to *hate* your son: still your rod. Note that the text speaks of "his [i.e. the father's] rod." This calls to mind Romans 13:1–7—

> Let every soul subordinate itself to superior authorities, for there is not authority except *established* by God, and those which are stand appointed by God. [2]Wherefore, the one who opposes the authority has resisted the institution of God, and those who have resisted will receive judgment against themselves. [3]For the rulers are not a *cause of* fear for the good work, but rather for the bad. And do you wish not to fear the authority? Do what is good, and you will have praise from it. [4]For it is a servant of God for you resulting in good. But if you do what is bad, do fear! For it does not carry the sword arbitrarily! For it is a servant of God, an avenger resulting in wrath against the one practicing what is bad. [5]Therefore it is a necessity to subject oneself, not only on account of wrath, but rather also on account of conscience. [6]For on account of this also do you pay taxes: for they are public servants of God, persisting for this very purpose. [7]Render your debts to everyone, tax to whom tax *is owed*, custom to whom custom *is owed*, fear to whom fear *is owed*, honor to whom honor *is owed*. (DJP)

Here Paul teaches that God has established all authority, and intends that His authorities be obeyed. It is important that we understand that this entire section is not primarily about government. Rather, verses 1 and 2 deal with all authority per se, which includes government officials, parents, pastors, bosses, and so on. Verses 3 and 4 bring in government officials as a "for-instance," not as the entire focus of the section. Verse 5 then draws an all-inclusive conclusion on the subject of authority, and verses 6 and 7 provide specific applications.

"Sphere sovereignty." This is a concept has been called "sphere-sovereignty." God has instituted authorities within various spheres and has given them the right to rule in that sphere. The "king" is taken as the ruler in the realm of government; in other spheres, there are other rulers. These rulers have their symbols of authority.

> **Government:** verse 4 says that the king has the "*sword*," symbol
> of the God-given power of *capital* punishment.
>
> **Home:** Proverbs says that the father has the "*rod*," which
> represents the God-given power of *corporal*
> punishment.

Either authority may be abused, of course, as can every good thing in this
fallen world. Still, we must not become so obsessed with the abuses of discipline
that we forget what God has legitimately mandated. It is a sad, sickening reality
that children are genuinely abused. Abuse is wrong; it should never occur. But
one does not help the abused by demonizing God-ordained parental discipline.
Indeed, one trivializes actual abuse by grouping it with loving correction.

Biblical discipline is not child abuse. Indeed, the text starkly suggests that
refusal to discipline comes closer to that definition. Opponents of Biblical
discipline attempt to link it to abuse by capturing the semantics, using phrases
such as "hitting children" (as if fist-fight were in view) and "violence."

This opposition is religiously-motivated. It springs from a fundamental
rejection of authority, particularly of an authority that cannot be ignored or
avoided. It reflects the libertine's own flight from God, and his dream that he can
get away with it. As parental discipline is meant to remind one of the judgment
and authority of God, those attempting to flee Him are desperate to remove every
reminder—and "the rod" is one such potent reminder.

For this reason, every child who is disciplined is cast as an abused child in
the media today. Grown children who have rebelled against God malign their
parents for having lovingly applied the rod. Meanwhile, teenage crime, suicide,
unspeakable violence, and profligate or perverted sexuality spread like wildfire,
and many of the same elitists wring their hands in anxiety as to what could be
behind it all.

The home is the father's "sphere" of authority.[45] God, then, has given the father
the rod as an emblem of that authority. He is to use it wisely and in love. It was
given him by divine grant, and the gift is not to be in vain.

"Early." In Proverbs 13:24, "Seeks him early with discipline" translates the
Hebrew *šiḥªrô mûsār*. The verb *šāḥar* is formed from the noun *šaḥar*, which means

---

[45] We should remember that *šēḇeṭ* was used of the ruler's scepter in Genesis 49:10, an association
that would not have been lost on Solomon's audience.

"dawn." It means to look early or diligently for; BDB translates this passage as *seeks him early (with) discipline.*[46] For another use of the verb, see Psalm 63:1 (by David, written while on the run):

> O God, you are my God; earnestly I seek you [*ⁿšaḥᵉrekā*];
> > my soul thirsts for you; my flesh faints for you,
> > as in a dry and weary land where there is no water.

Solomon's watch word here is *proactivity.* One must start from early days, and do so with a mind to the future. Do not be a crisis-manager; do not dispense wisdom when it is too late, when the proverbial cows have already fled the metaphorical barn. Believe it: if you wait until your teaching becomes relevant, it will be too late. Solomon taught his son while he was young to "treasure up" his commands (2:1), knowing that the application might have been a while in coming.

Of course we must be wise and age-appropriate. We must not hold a child responsible for what is impossible for their stage of growth (i.e., a ten-month-old probably is not ready to make his bed or empty the trash). At the same time, many parents expect far too little of their children, and thus end up with immature youth.

Think of this particularly in terms of obedience. We should start expecting our child to respect and obey us from the earliest reasonable days. I have observed for many years that far too many parents simply do not expect to be obeyed. If a child can obey, then he should be required to obey.

If your child cannot understand and obey what you tell him to do, cancel the order, change it, help him with it, or (better still) don't give it in the first place. If your child can understand and obey what you tell him to do, you must see to it that he does it.

Telling a child firmly to do something, and then doing it yourself, is not teaching obedience—it is teaching disobedience. Asking a child something, and then answering the question yourself, is not teaching obedience—it is teaching disobedience. Endlessly reminding a child to say "please" or "thank you" is not teaching him obedience—it is teaching disobedience. Giving an order, then allowing it to be ignored with impunity, is not teaching him obedience—it is teaching disobedience.

---

[46] BDB, article שָׁחַר. Cf. also Kidner's comments at 1:28 and 13:24; and Fox, *Proverbs*, 2:571. Murphy gives a similar sense (94).

To teach obedience, a parents must do at least two things:

1. Determine in your own heart that your child is going to learn to do as he is told right away.

2. See to it that he does it, no matter how long or how much discipline it takes.

This can be personally costly and time-consuming. Hopefully, you knew that about parenting before you put in your order for children. Let's spell it out a bit.

It may mean: putting your child in a corner and telling him that he may come out as soon as he will give a straightforward answer to the straightforward (if inconvenient) question that you asked him.[47] It may mean telling your child that he may not have anything unless he says "Please" all by himself when asking for it, or that he will lose the thing if he does not say "Thank you" after receiving it. It may mean telling your child that a whining tone will buy him the writing of ten sentences such as, "I will break this terrible habit of whining, and will speak clearly and respectfully."

I think that some parents put off the building of that respect and obedience too long. Then they face a tougher fight because they have allowed patterns of rebellion to set in early. The goal of discipline is to teach the child to obey his parents right away, cheerfully, and without challenge or complaint.[48]

Remember, if you yourself fear Yahweh, then you are not doing this out of self-serving motives. You believe Yahweh. You believe that He is a great King who deserves our honor and respect and obedience. You believe that He knows what is best for you and for your children. And it is He Himself who says they must honor you, because of the role He has given you in their lives (Exod. 20:12f.; Rom. 13:1ff.). It is for their good and blessing that they learn to honor the parents God has given them.

In fact, it is worth noting that it is more important for your children to *respect* you than it is for them to *like* you. This is a fundamental social lesson they need to learn, for their own good. Never forget this.

It may be important to you that your children like you, but it is more important for them that they respect you.

---

[47] "I don't know" and "I don't remember" can be passive-aggressive dodges for getting around answering questions that the child does not want to answer.

[48] Two exceptions: it is wise to begin involving an older child, who has learned to obey, in the process of thinking through decisions and proposed courses of action; and "challenge or

Also, too many parents fall into the well-intentioned trap of *explaining* every order to their children. The parent's intention is often to secure the child's approval and agreement. The parent's motivation is often to avoid having his child angry or displeased with him, because he wants to be "best buddies" with his child. The harmful effects of this include:

- Casting the child as an equal, a peer, whose approval must be secured.
- Failing to teach the child the simple practice of obedience: of obeying an order, of doing what he is told by an authority.
- Guaranteeing an expanding process of negotiation and discussion over every order, as the child ages.

The parent must remind himself of three basic truths:

First, "Folly is bound up in the heart of a child, but the rod of discipline drives it far from him" (Prov. 22:15).

- Your child is a born fool, as you were.
- Your child is not—or had better not be!—your equal.
- It is your job to drive out folly, not to accommodate it.

Second, *you* are the one whom God has put in charge in the home.

- God expects you to give orders.
- God expects you to see to it that they are obeyed.

Third, *you* are the first person who has the crucial role of teaching your child the meaning of obedience. If you fail in this task...

- You are setting your child up for trouble in school (home or otherwise).
- You are setting your child up for trouble in church.
- You are setting your child up for trouble with the law.
- You are setting your child up for trouble at work.
- You are setting your child up for *big* trouble with God.

Too late? Suppose someone reading this exclaims, "I just woke up to what you're saying. I have been messing up—what do I do now?" The true but

---

complaint" does not include honest requests for clarification.

uninspired proverb, "Better late than never," comes into play here. *Start now.* If your child is an indulged ten-year-old, it will be much harder than if he were a relatively unspoiled 1-, 2-, 5-, or 9-year-old. But it will be much easier now than if he were eleven, twelve, or (Heaven help you) thirteen.

The time to start obeying God is always right now; it may be later than it should be, but it truly is better late than never.

We are to use the rod *with conviction.*

Third, use the rod for his instruction

See Proverbs 22:15—

> Denseness is bound up[49] in the heart of a youth;
> the rod of discipline will drive it far from him.

God tells us that denseness is "bound up." This is a well-nigh inseparable connection. Jacob's soul was intimately "bound up"[50] in Benjamin's life, to the extent that Benjamin's death would mean his own (Gen. 44:30–31). You recall the story: Judah is telling Joseph (in disguise) why he does not want to go back without Benjamin. He says that old Jacob's soul is so "tied up" with Benjamin that it would mean Jacob's death to hear of any harm to Benjamin.

In the same way, Jonathan's soul was "knit"[51] to the soul of David (1 Sam. 18:1; cf. vv 3–4). Jonathan saw David's godliness, and he was won over. The covenant they made, and gift of Jonathan's own goods, formalized their friendship, linked them to each other.

Likewise the Word of God should be "bound" around our neck, heart, and fingers (Prov. 3:3; 6:21; 7:3). We are to memorize it, and take it everywhere we go. It should influence our values, our thoughts, our decision-making.

In saying that denseness is bound up in a child's heart, Solomon is asserting what we call total depravity. Children are not innocent, divinely-wise little cherubs by nature. They are neither good nor neutral. Actual denseness toward the truths of God is bound up in their very heart.

Scripture does not show the effect of sin commencing at maturity. Sin's effects are congenital. Think of tiger cubs. Beautiful, cute little things. Yet tiger cubs are

---

[49] Hebrew *q̆šûrâ.*
[50] Hebrew *q̆šûrâ,* same word as in Proverbs 22:15.
[51] Hebrew *niqšᵉrâ,* from the same verb as in Proverbs 22:15.

still tigers. They simply are not yet big enough and strong enough to cause the damage they will do later.[52]

God's intent is that the rod of discipline would drive this inborn folly from the child. The child's heart will naturally incline toward folly—and worse. It is necessary to apply pressure from without, in the right direction, while preaching and praying for transformation from within.

While the child is under your roof, then, you are able to tell him the truth about God and himself. You are able to preach the Gospel to him. This is truth that would never arise from within his own dense, deceptive heart (Jer. 17:9). Also, you are to enforce and teach discipline, self-control, civilized behavior, values—in a word, obedience. God may well use your discipline (in conjunction with your evangelizing) to convict him of sin, and turn him to Himself in repentant faith.

By contrast, the indulgent parent who leaves the rod on the shelf does nothing to distance the child from his own natural moral and spiritual denseness. He simply starts the child out accustomed to indulging his own sin and corruption (cf. Prov. 22:6). He gives him no effective pointer toward denying himself and following Christ.

Back to Proverbs 29:15.

> The rod and reproof give wisdom,
> but a youth let loose shames his mother. (DJP)

This is an antithetical proverb (A, but B). The second line gives the flip-side of the first. Therefore, the opposite of applying the rod and reproof is giving a child his own way.

"**Let loose.**" The Hebrew *mᵉšullāḥ* comes from the verb *šālaḥ*, which means to send out. It means let loose, sent out on his own way, set free.[53] Since denseness is bound up in the child's heart (22:15), the way he will choose will surely be the wrong way, apart from an external influence. With its Biblical starting-point, this proverb assumes that we understand that a child let loose is likely to go the wrong way.

---

[52] Various writers quote from the Minnesota Crime Commission report of 1926, which assesses all babies as born self-centered savages, lacking only the means to carry out the worst of crimes (cf. Swindoll, *Growing Wise in Family Life* [Portland: Multnomah, 1988], 102; and John MacArthur, *The Fulfilled Family* [Chicago: Moody Press, 1997], np).

[53] This is borne out in the usage; cf. also the TWOT treatment of *šālaḥ* in the Pi'el verbal stem.

Some parents commonly rationalize or defend disobedience or destructive behavior. They may say, "He's just being a kid." This excuse, however, misses the point. It may be true that he or she is "just being a kid," *if* by "just being a kid" you mean "just shaking his fist in God's face and heading for doom." But is that what any God-fearing parent wants for his child?

God's Word comes from an entirely different orientation than that of our indulgent, authority-phobic culture. Solomon assumes that a godly parent knows God's Word (cf. Deut. 6:4–6). As such, he assumes that the parent knows better than his child. This being true, it is the parent's responsibility to point his child in a better way—which, candidly, is the parent's godly way, unless he is a fool or a superficial hypocrite.

SUMMARY of Proverbs 29:15a:

1. "The rod" is *emblematic,* standing for the parent's God-given power of discipline, leading up to and including corporal punishment.

2. The parent is to *use* the rod, to use the rod *with conviction*, and to use it *for his child's instruction.*

3. A parent who refuses to use the rod in love and wisdom *hates* his child, and is setting him up for disaster.

Now we shall dig into the second half of Line A: "…and reproof."

The Reproof

Opening Proposal

As *the rod* is emblematic of the parent's God-given power of discipline leading up to and including corporal punishment, so *reproof* is emblematic. It encompasses everything the parent does to teach, inform, evangelize, enlighten, instruct, guide, correct, reprove, rebuke, and encourage his child.

To understand what Solomon meant by this, it will be helpful to go back into the background in the Pentateuch (Genesis—Deuteronomy) that would have been informing him. *First*, we note…

Authoritative Parental Instruction Is Standard Operating Procedure

This is a pan-Biblical assumption that runs so deep it hardly needed to be legislated, per se. It is inherent in the creation mandate of Genesis 1:26–28. Since the purpose of having children was to assist in subduing the world under God, the authoritative instruction was a necessity. Because the pre-Fall portion of the Canon is so brief, we can only surmise what all this would have involved, but we are on firm ground in assuming that Adam would have been instructing his children.

As far as the text is concerned, Adam must have instructed Eve. When they had children, continuing instruction would be necessary. They would need to know who God was, why they existed, what their purpose was, how it was to be fulfilled, what had been done so far, and so on.

Then, later, in Genesis 18:19, God says this to Himself about Abraham:

> "Because I have known him, in order that he may command his sons and his house after him, and they will keep the way of Yahweh so as to do righteousness and judgment, in order that Yahweh will bring on Abraham what He spoke concerning him." (DJP)

God moved in Abram's life to effect his rearing of his children. As a result, Abram did not merely let his kids loose and hope that they would turn out all right. Nor did Abram simply set a good example, and hope they would decide to follow it. Rather, Abram would *command* his children to do God's will, and that in a comprehensive way.

Yahweh's assumption, then, is that Abraham (A) *knows* His way, specifically; that Abraham (B) will *teach* that way to his children after him; but not only will he teach, but Abraham (C) will *command* his children to walk in God's ways, making God's law the law of his house. Yahweh expects Abraham to teach authoritatively, because he has an authoritative model. God's ways to Abraham are not "Here's what I think, take it or leave it" options. They are "This is My way; walk it or be doomed" propositions.

Moving on to Exodus, we see legislated opportunities for authoritative parental instruction. For instance, in Exodus 13:8, 14–16 we read:

> "You shall tell your son on that day, 'It is because of what the LORD did for me when I came out of Egypt.' ...[14] And when in time to come your son asks you, 'What does this mean?' you shall say to him, 'By a strong hand the LORD brought us out of Egypt, from the house of slavery. [15] For when Pharaoh stubbornly refused to

let us go, the LORD killed all the firstborn in the land of Egypt, both the firstborn of man and the firstborn of animals. Therefore I sacrifice to the LORD all the males that first open the womb, but all the firstborn of my sons I redeem.' [16] It shall be as a mark on your hand or frontlets between your eyes, for by a strong hand the LORD brought us out of Egypt."

Perhaps we generally think of the Law as dealing only with things like "*Don't* do this [immoral thing,] and *do* do this [ritual], or this [righteous act]." We see here that God expressly commanded fathers to give their testimony to their sons (v. 8), and to teach them Bible history and Bible doctrine (vv. 14–16).

In this way, the Feast of Passover was turned (by law) into an instructional time for the child. Rather than saying, "I'll do a fresh miracle every year to instruct your children." Yahweh said in effect, "Keep alive the truth of My mighty deeds at Passover every year, using this Feast to instruct your children."[54]

Deuteronomy 4:9 says that an Israelite man should memorize the truths of God's Word, not only for his own benefit, but for his sons' benefit, and for his grandsons' benefit. The Word was to be retained and transmitted. Then 4:10 shows that Yahweh dealt with them, not only that they themselves might have a relationship with Him, but that their children might learn to fear Him as well, by parental instruction.

Then Deuteronomy 6:4–25 shows that my love for the true God (vv. 4, 5) will issue in personal fascination with the Word of God (v. 6), which in turn will issue in training my children in God's Word. We noted this previously; now, I point to Proverbs 1–9 as an example of such teaching. In that portion, we see the refrain of "My son...My son," and we note the range of topics treated:

- ✓ Choice of friends.
- ✓ Attitude toward the Word of God.
- ✓ Attitude toward God.
- ✓ "Church giving."
- ✓ Sexual morality—in great depth.
- ✓ Finances.
- ✓ Attitude toward work.

---

[54] Such references are found a number of times in Deuteronomy: see 4:9–10; 6:4–7; 6:20–25.

Not all Christian parents have received the lesson of this revealed wisdom. I have known more than one Christian who had been reared by believers, who said that their parents never taught them along these lines in any depth. Such parents are not only disobeying the pattern and commands of God; they are doing great disservice to their children.

Relation Between the Two Factors

We should not think of rod and reproof as either/or, but as both/and. Remember:

The rod

- Emblematic for punishment, imposition of limitations, strictures, and sanctions.
- It encompasses every form of punitive discipline extending up to corporal punishment.

Reproof

- Verbal instruction
- Includes correction, instruction, warning, explanation, encouragement, content-full communication.

Before a child is disciplined, he must be *instructed*. It is unjust and unfair and unwise for us to hold a child accountable for anything he could not have known. But discipline is not the end of the process, either. Early in our child-rearing together, my wife Valerie helped me see the importance of reinforcing a punishment by asking "Why were you sent to the corner [or whatever]?" Punishment without understanding and repentance simply means that the punishment will have to be repeated, to no gain for the child or the family (Prov. 17:10; 27:22).

Note next that reproof is issued for *correction*. The intent must never be about revenge, naked power, or convenience. The only divinely-sanctioned, fundamental motivation for discipline is love. See 3:11–12

> The discipline of Yahweh, my son, do not reject,
>   and do not loathe His reproof;
>
> [12] Because, whom Yahweh loves, He reproves,
>   even as a father *reproves* the son with whom he is pleased. (DJP)

It is very telling that this verse does not say that Yahweh refuses to discipline us, because He loves us. Nor does it assert that He disciplines in spite of the fact that He loves us, as if love and discipline were contraries. Rather, we learn that Yahweh in fact disciplines us precisely *because* He loves us. Love both motivates and necessitates His discipline.

As we have noted before, modern society, ever smarter and better than God (in its own eyes), sees the indulgent parent as the loving parent. By starkest contrast, God sees the wise disciplinarian as the loving parent, and He sees the indulgent parent as the hateful parent.

Mark the importance of reproof. Loving rebuke is seen as important *for the child* in a number of texts. For instance, in Proverbs 13:1 we read

> A wise son hears his father's instruction,
>   but a scoffer does not listen to rebuke.

At issue here is not whether the child permits his father to discipline him. That is taken for granted. The father does not need the child's permission. Not only does he have God's permission, but he is positively charged by God to dispense instruction. It is the father's right and responsibility.

What is at issue here is whether or not the child takes the discipline to heart. If he does, he is wise. If he does not... as Kidner well observes,

> The pairing of a *son*, under training, with a *scorner*, who is a fool in the last stages of folly (cf. 26:12), suggests that if you cannot stand home truths from your own father you are well on the way to becoming insufferable.[55]

"Insufferable" and, one might add, hopeless.

Parental training is not magic or automatically effective, any more than Biblical preaching is magically powerful. In a Bible-teaching fellowship, one is at least exposed to the teaching of the Word on a regular basis. However, simply sitting and allowing one's ear-drums to vibrate to the proclaimed Word makes no difference unless we take what we hear to heart in faith (cf. Heb. 4:2 NAS, NIV; and James 1:22–27).

---

[55] Derek Kidner, *Proverbs*, 95.

Again, note Proverbs 15:5—

> A dense man spurns the discipline of his father,
>> but he who keeps reproof acts shrewdly.

The presumption once again is that the father is doing his job. He is giving out wise, godly discipline. The dense son "shines it on," as the kids used to say. He rejects it. What sets the wise son apart from the dense son is that he keeps instruction, he hangs onto it, he takes it to heart and makes it his own.

Next we note the importance of reproof for the *parents*. The point is made in our theme-text, Proverbs 29:15—"The rod and reproof give wisdom, but a youth let loose shames his mother." If a mother indulges her child, if she imagines him an exception to God's Word and communicates that to him, it is a shame to her. Though her child will bear his sin and judgment, she will know that she failed him. She was to be his first evangelist, and she did not bring home the law and the Gospel.

Proverbs 29:17 adds yet a bit more light as to a parent's motivation:

> Discipline your son, that he may give you comfort,
>> and that he may give delights to your soul. (DJP)

As previously noted, a godly parent is like a farmer. He sows in hope. The harvest he hopes to reap is a godly son who brings him delight. The parent feels *literally* what the apostle John said *metaphorically:* "I have no greater joy than to hear that my children are walking in the truth" (3 John 4). The converse is also true. There may be no pain more bitter than what a parent feels when a child, knowing better, turns his back on walking with the Lord on the Lord's terms (John 14:15; 15:14; 1 John 5:3, etc.).

Since I mean to leave no major obstructive stone unpulverized, let us briefly ask and answer the question:

Did Pentecost Cancel Out this Command? (Eph. 6:4)

> And fathers, do not provoke your children to wrath, but *instead*
>> nourish them in the discipline and confrontation of the Lord. (DJP)

First, Paul writes, "do not provoke your children to wrath." How can this happen? This can occur as a result of criticism that is unfair and excessive, or not levied within a framework that is fundamentally loving and as encouraging as truth allows. It can also come from rules that are unreasonable, excessive, and oppressive.

This can also happen with a parent who does not take his parental responsibilities seriously, who sees parenthood as a popularity contest to meet his own ego needs, and so wouldn't dare cross the child's will for fear that the child might not like him anymore. As we have seen, the child needs graciously-strict, consistent discipline (even though he may not want it). When a parent fails to do his job, it is the same effect as a man who refuses to be a man to his wife: he reaps contempt and rage, to his own abiding bewilderment.

So much for the prohibition. Now we know what we should not do. What *should* we do, then?

Second, Paul goes on to pen the words, "but instead nourish them in the discipline and confrontation of the Lord." We must note right off what Paul does not say. The apostle does not write, "Do not provoke your children to wrath, but instead indulge them and let them find their own way and follow their hearts." Nor does Paul write, "Do not provoke your children to wrath by disciplining or confronting them." Nor does he say, "Do not provoke your children to wrath, but make sure that you are their best friends and number one playmate."

There is an important lesson for us here, a revolutionary and counter-cultural message from God to us. We must learn from this that, in the mind of God, the opposite of provoking children to wrath is not indulgence, but is consistent Biblical discipline. Instead of provoking them to wrath, Paul says, nurture them in the Lord's discipline and confrontation. The implication is that indulgence is in fact another way to provoke them to wrath.

Paul commands two activities: the *first* he commands is to nurture the child with discipline. The word he uses is *paideia*, which refers to the full-orbed education of a *pais*, a child. What would be the sourcebook for such *paideia*, such discipline and education?

Paul answers that question for us in 2 Timothy 3:16–17—

> All Scripture is God-breathed, and is beneficial for teaching, for reproof, for restoration, for training [*paideia*] which is in righteousness, [17]so that the man of God may be equipped, for every good work fully equipped. (DJP)

Both the noun and the corresponding verb *paideuō* occur repeatedly in Hebrews 12:5–11, where we learn that God disciplines us as a loving father must discipline his children.

This discipline corresponds to "the rod" in Proverbs 29:15. It accordingly includes a command that in our instruction we set limits, and that we enforce those limits with corporal punishment.

Second, Paul commands confrontation (*nouthesia*). The noun *nouthesia* is derived from combining two words: *nous* [mind] and *tithēmi* [put, place]. It means to admonish, to confront, to warn; to correct a problem in thought or behavior.

Though (strictly speaking) he may spill over a bit from strict etymology into pastoral preaching, I think Hermann Cremer's opening of the meaning of the corresponding verb *noutheteō* is instructive. Cremer says that the verb means

> **to put in mind, to work upon the mind of one**, with the accusative of the person, always with the idea of putting right, because some degree of opposition has to be encountered, and one wishes to subdue or remove it, not by punishment, but by influencing the [*nous* (mind)]… It is accordingly equivalent to, **with kindly purpose to admonish, to put right, to warn, to remind and advise**, *in order to guard against and ward off wrong,* etc. …Its fundamental idea is the well-intentioned seriousness with which one would influence the mind and disposition of another by advice, admonition, warning, putting right, according to circumstances.[56]

As we have seen, children have an innate problem. They *do* resist God's wisdom. They need discipline and instruction to correct that problem. The parent must get "up-close and personal" in bringing the Word of God to bear.

If the child grows up to walk with God, he will be grateful forever for being blessed with parents who lovingly disciplined and confronted him. If he does not, he may well despise his parents as he despises God—but he will have only himself to blame.

---

[56] Hermann Cremer, *Biblico-Theological Lexicon of New Testament Greek*, 4th ed. (Edinburgh: T. &. T. Clark: 1895), 441–442 (emphases in original).

A Critical Factor in the Rod and Reproof: Consistency

It is commonly said in both Christian and non-Christian books that "consistency" is an important factor in parenting. I have found to my alarm, however, that even wildly *inconsistent* parents will agree in principle with the importance of being consistent. Obviously, somewhere something is amiss.

One missing piece is lack of a precise definition. What is meant by "consistency"? A second lack is the failure to ground "consistency" directly in the Bible. For Christians, this is a critical defect.

We must ground any notion of *consistency* in Scripture. Toward that end, I propose this definition: "Consistency in parenting is saying only what you mean, and meaning everything that you say."

The Scriptural tie-in is located when we realize that inconsistency is a form of *lying*. Cast this way, it is easy to see that consistency is a crucial virtue for all, not only for parents.

Consider the following verses from Proverbs: 4:24; 6:16–19; 12:19; 12:22; 14:25; 21:6; 26:28; 30:8. All these verses open God's heart on the subject of lying, falsehood, and deception. God is crystal-clear on the subject of lying: He doesn't do it, and He doesn't want us to do it—ever. He *hates* it.

But is this really such a big deal? It is. Think about it: if you tell your child, "Don't _____," or "Do _____," no matter how trivial it is, you are saying in effect, "I, your father/mother, am exercising my God-given authority to give you the following order:..." Now, permit me a simple, direct question: Do you expect that order to be carried out? Will you see to it that it is carried out?

If you do not expect your orders to be carried out, then at least **four** truths follow:

1. You should not have given an order.

2. You simply must stop giving orders until you have a Biblical grasp of your God-given role, and are ready to give orders *and see them through*.

3. You are communicating several things to your child, intentionally or not:

   • "Johnny, you may safely ignore orders given by God-ordained authorities."

   • "Johnny, disobedience is safe and has no consequences."

- "Johnny, I do not take my responsibility very seriously, nor do you need to when you grow up."
- "Johnny, I just like to say things that I do not mean."

4. You should not be disappointed, and should never complain, when future orders are not carried out, and you are neither honored nor respected.

Anyone who is comfortable with the thought of giving children orders, though he has no intention of seeing them through, absolutely must reread his "job-description." He must reassess the situation. Then he must do some repenting and remodeling.

I saw a young boy behaving horridly once, in a public setting. He was abusing smaller boys and being a nuisance. When his father learned what he had been doing, he told the boy that was it, he was done, pack up, they were leaving. The boy threw a minor tantrum and tearfully refused to leave. I wondered if I was about to see why he was such a brat in the first place—but the father did not cave. He hung in there, and they left, just as Dad had said.

I thought "Good for you," and cancelled what I figured were my hasty judgments about why the boy had felt free to behave as he had.

That is, I cancelled them for about two minutes. That was how long they were gone. Then both father and son returned, and the sad picture became clear again.

Dad had *bluffed*. He'd said something he didn't mean. And his son knew it.

Remember, parent: if you do expect your orders to be carried out, then *you* are the one responsible for seeing to it that they are carried out.

Cast your mind far, far back to the Garden of Eden. Adam and Eve had eaten the fruit of the forbidden Tree, and now God was coming to call. The couple was in hiding.

Who did God look up? Whose name did He call? He had left Adam in charge, so He required that Adam give an account for himself and his responsibilities. It did not matter that Eve had disobeyed God. Adam was the man God had left in charge, and he must give an account for his stewardship.

You, father, are the man God left in charge of your family. The rod and reproof are the means that God has granted fathers and commanded them to use in leading our children.

Decades ago, I heard a lady call in on a radio psychologist's talk show, and told her, "I can't get my daughter to mind me!"

The psychologist—not a Christian, but remarkably savvy—asked the mother for her height and weight. Then she asked the child's height and weight.

After ascertaining the information, the psychologist said, "Yes, *you can* get your daughter to mind."

If you say, "If you _____,"[57] I will _____,"[58] and then you don't do what you said you would do, then you must face at least these *three* sad truths:

First, you are simply making and breaking a promise to your child; you are giving and breaking your word about the matter.

If you had no intention of doing what you said, then you deliberately lied to your child. You are not to be trusted, by your child or anyone else. You must now also expect your child not to trust you when you tell him about God's laws and discipline, or about Jesus, or about judgment and Hell.

If you intended to do what you said, but just allowed yourself to "forget," then you still broke a promise. In plainer words, you lied, even if it was unintentional. In this case, you have set an eloquent, and harmful, example of a person not being true to his word.

Second, you are again tacitly condoning disobedience, rebellion, sin; as da Vinci said, "He who does not punish evil, commands it to be done."[59]

Third, you need to repent, find God's forgiveness (and your child's), and make two binding personal resolutions:

1. *Never* to say anything that you do not really mean.

2. To strive to give your child reason to believe that you may be relied upon to do *ten out of ten* things that you say you will do, as far as humanly possible.

In closing, consider a self-test. Ask a friend, relative, or your pastor whether he sees you as consistent, under the definition given above. It must be someone who will be brutally honest with you. You must not punish that person if you do not get the answer you wanted.

---

[57] Fill in the blank: i.e. keep whining, hit your brother one more time, say that word again, grab for something in the store, leave the light on…

[58] Fill in the blank: slap your hand, stand you in the corner, take it away from you, make you write sentences, swat you, give you an unpleasant chore, make you sorry…

[59] Leonardo da Vinci, quoted without documentation by Charles Swindoll, *Growing Wise in Family Life* (Portland: Multnomah, 1988), 105.

A Final Warning: Proverbs 22:6

Start out a youth according to his own way—
  even should he grow old, he will not turn from it. (DJP)

This verse is commonly clung to as a "precious promise." However, it is not a promise, precious or otherwise. It is a consequence-proverb (B is what happens when you A). It is a threat, a warning, framed in terms of the most acid irony.[60]

Throughout the book, Solomon has warned many, many times where our natural tendency would take every one of us. He has told us that foolishness is natural to a child, inextricably interwoven in the fabric of his heart (22:15). Left to himself, a child will shame his mother (29:15). Why? Because, left to himself, he will have only his own heart to trust to—and that course leads inevitably away from wisdom and toward folly (28:26). It leaves him open to the wrong crowd (1:10ff.), to being influenced by his peers into greater and greater folly (13:20).

The sage sovereign has also repeatedly told us that there are only two ways. The way that "seems right" to us is the path that leads surely and inexorably toward destruction and death (14:12; 16:25; 18:17). But that way is the fool's chosen way. It is the way your child will choose, left to himself—and he will be doomed to eat the deadly fruit of that way (1:31; 14:14). But that way is what seems right to him, if he is started out "according to his own way" (cf. 12:15). In a universe of which he is the center, all of the ways such a one's corrupt heart chooses will seem pure and right to him (16:25).

Solomon warns that, if a parent runs a child-centered home; if he lets his child call the shots and shapes everything to the child's whims; if he molds the world of the family to suit the child, and never crosses the child's will—then he is setting that foolish, straying, rebellious heart in cement. He is confirming the inborn corruption of the child's nature. He is shielding his child from Law, resulting in a child feeling no need of Gospel or of the Savior it reveals.

The child will walk that selfish, doomed way as a child. He starts out on the way and grows accustomed to it. Even when he grows old, he will not depart from it. "Maturity" (counted on the calendar) does not deliver from this path, it only hardens one in it. There is no *natural* progression from the heart's own foolish way to God's way.

---

[60] This view is a minority view. I have focused here on expounding and applying the interpretation I favor. Thorough substantiation is provided in Appendix 3.

There is only a *supernatural* progression.

That is why Solomon thunderously proclaims, right from the start, that there simply *is* no knowledge or wisdom other than that which is based on repentant, submissive faith in the sovereign Yahweh (1:7; 9:10). The only counter to a child "following his own heart" to certain doom is the fear of Yahweh, bowing the knee before Him as Lord of all.

On that foundation, then, this is why Solomon again and again calls his son not to be wise in his own eyes, but to do the opposite: trust in Yahweh and walk in His way (Prov. 3:5–7). It is why he repeatedly urges the child to walk in God's ways, glorifies those ways, holds out God's way as the only way to walk and live and think (cf. 2:20; 3:6, 17; 4:11, 18; 6:6, 23; 8:20,32; 9:6; 10:17, 29; 11:5, 20; 12:28; 15:19, 24).

Do you wish to *doom* your child? Then start him out according to his own way. He will never leave it—barring a miracle.

Do you *love* God and your child? Then teach him the folly of his way. Teach him that he is not the center of the universe, but that the infinite-personal God of Scripture is. Show him how his way is under God's judgment and will lead to inevitable and sure death and doom. Show him his need of God's saving grace. Lead him to fear Yahweh and turn away from his own way. Use the rod and reproof to point him to God's ways, to show him that sin's fruits are bitter.

Show him to God's way.

Do not leave him to his own.

The Best Gift a Parent Can Give His Children

The parting thoughts I would leave you on this topic return us to the priorities mentioned at the chapter's opening. In fact, they take us all the way back to Proverbs' theme (1:7; 9:10; 31:30). The best methodology in the world is no substitute for what we are about to consider.

All loving parents are concerned that they leave something for their children. They want them to be taken care of, to have their needs met, to have their lives bettered, when they leave them through death. What is the best legacy, the best heritage, that a parent can leave his children?

Is it a *material* heritage? This certainly is a desirable and good goal. Proverbs is positive on the subject, as the following verses from Proverbs show:

A good man leaves an inheritance to his children's children,
>but the sinner's wealth is laid up for the righteous. (13:22 NAS)

House and wealth are inherited from fathers,
>but a prudent wife is from the LORD. (19:14 NAS)

Still, I am strongly impressed that these verses are a relative minority. There is a legacy that is a *twofold* blessing, which God sees as far surpassing a material heritage in value. What is that legacy?

First Blessing: the Legacy of God-Fearing Parents

I cannot think of a fancy way to put this: the best thing you can do for your children is to fear Yahweh consistently, yourself. I have seen far too many parents who see to their children's every material need, but who leave this one crucial, indispensable, all-important necessity neglected. A great many verses in Proverbs point to the blessedness of the children of righteous, God-fearing parents. "In the fear of Yahweh is strong confidence, And his sons will have a refuge" (Prov. 14:26 DJP). See also: Proverbs 3:33; 11:21; 12:3, 7, 12; 13:22; 14:1, 11, 26; 15:6, 25; 17:6; 19:14; 20:7; 24:3. Each of these verses is worth serious meditation by parents who would please God.

Another verse that perhaps strikes me resoundingly is Proverbs 20:7— "The righteous who walks in his integrity—blessed are his children after him!" *Three* truths stand revealed here:

First, who this loving parent is: he/she is a *righteous* person. In the Bible, living in a righteous manner[61] is a very specific concept. It does not mean merely being better than the lowest common denominator of godless society. "Nice" is not a synonym for "righteous." Nor does "does his best" describe the Biblical meaning of practical daily righteousness.

The best snapshot I know is found in God's description of Elizabeth and Zacharias, the parents of John the Baptist. God tells us that "they were both righteous before God, walking blamelessly in all the commandments and statutes of the Lord" (Luke 1:6).

---

[61] I take Solomon's emphasis to be practical righteousness, as we see in both Testaments. In terms of *forensic* righteousness, there is only one way to be perfectly righteous in God's eyes: through faith alone. Solomon would have known that (Gen. 15:6). We know that our only way to be right in God's eyes is through repentant faith in Jesus Christ, based on His person and work (Rom. 3:21–5:21).

Do you see it? Being "righteous before God" involves "walking blamelessly in all the commandments and statutes of the Lord." Righteousness is a lifestyle that specifically and consciously embraces the Word of God as the norm and guideline, and seeks to walk accordingly.

Does that describe you? Evaluate yourself by this list:

- Can your children see in you a driving desire to be righteous in the sight of God?

- Do your children ever see you work through issues by studying the Word of God, and seeking Biblical counsel?

- Have your children ever seen you apologize and/or change your ways, because you have been convicted by Scripture?

- Is the study of the Word something that is part of your family's regular endeavors?

- Do your family prayers reflect wording from Scripture, or just the tepid repetition of familiar family phrases?

- Have you selected for your family a church that stresses, not a profession of theoretical faith in the Bible, but a practice of teaching the Word of God, in service after service, in meeting after meeting?

In these terms, then, I ask again: are you a righteous person? If so, you are leaving your children a priceless legacy. If not, then I plead with you, for the sake of Christ, for your own sake, for your children's sake—repent.

Second, Proverbs 20:7 reveals that the righteous man walks in his *integrity*. This means more than walking by one's own personal moral code, whether Biblical or not. The Hebrew word *tōm* combines the ideas of integrity, wholeness, and commitment. The related term *tāmîm* pictures someone or something that has everything in proper place. It was used of sacrificial animals who were not missing any of their parts and had no defects (e.g., Lev. 21:21, 22). It was also used in Psalm 15:2 of a believer who rigorously applies God's standards to the details of his life, and who thus enjoys fellowship with God.

You cannot fool your children for long. Do your children see integrity in you? Is your righteousness a whole-hearted commitment, palpable through the week? Or does it only bloom on Sundays in public? Your children know, and your character will normally have a long-reaching impact on them for good or evil.

On that last note, it is sobering to note that the person, male or female, who refuses to walk with God *also* leaves a legacy. It is a bitter, sad, destructive legacy, too. Many verses in Proverbs sound this note of warning: 11:29; 14:1, 11; 15:25, 27; 17:13.

Again, I have been alarmed at the behavior of many professing Christians and have wondered if they could possibly have given any thought to the legacy that they are bequeathing to their children. They have rebelled against their parents, against pastoral leadership, against church discipline, against the Word itself. Yet they go on in lives of syrupy *faux* piety—and delude themselves that they love God and their children. The power of sin to create excuses and rationalizations is all too potent, a truth with which we are all intimately acquainted.

Third, we learn that the sons of this righteous man who walks in his integrity will be *blessed* after him. How will they be blessed? They will be blessed on many levels. Let us name just a few:

- They will have had a good example, in flesh and blood. This is of nearly infinite potential value, far surpassing the best manual or video.

- They may also have material blessings, since generally speaking the godly man works hard and well and knows the fruits of his labor (cf. 10:4; 13:22; 14:23).

- They will have a legacy of wisdom to live by and to pass on to their children (see next section as well).

So then, do you want to do something loving for your children? Then walk with God, all-out, "pedal to the metal." Establish a legacy of godliness. Work to make your family name a name that stands for God-honoring righteousness and integrity. In fact, it is important that your children know that you love God more than you love them (cf. Deut. 6:5f.; Luke 14:26).

Second Blessing: the Legacy of Godly Parental Teaching

Who is to teach your children? Your pastor? Yes, of course. Their Sunday School teachers? Hopefully so. But who is to be the *primary* instructor of your children, the person who gives them their first, their most comprehensive, and their most memorable instruction in the ways of God?

Mom, Dad—it is supposed to be *you*.

Study these verses from Proverbs: 1:8, 10, 15; 2:1; 3:1, 3:21; 4:1, 3, 10, 20; 5:1, 7–8, 20; 6:1, 3, 20; 7:1, 24; 13:1; 23:19, 26; 27:11; 29:17.

Now, that was only a *partial list*. If you have Bible software or an exhaustive concordance, you will see that Solomon repeatedly addresses his teaching to "My son." The whole book is framed as parental instruction, from father and mother to children.

And if you were to take the time to study out all of these instructions, you would see that father Solomon gave *absolutely comprehensive instruction* in the details of life. He instructs in the area of choosing friends, picking a mate, work, politics, religion, sexuality, finances, child-rearing—what we would call "the whole nine yards." Further, he says that in this he is only doing what his father did for him (cf. 4:1–4).

Let me be blunt. When your son or daughter comes to life-choices, you want him or her to be able to think of what *you* would say to do. Of course, you want your children to know the Bible, and you want them to be able to think for themselves; that should be a central part of your instruction. But you are the person whom God has put into your child's life to be a living, breathing example of how to live out the Word of God in action. So do it, be that for your child.

If you do not formally home-school, then be sure to spend time teaching your child. Do not merely give orders, but spend time teaching him about how to evaluate friends, how to view his responsibilities, how to talk to God, how to read the Bible, how to view work, and so on. If you do not, be sure that the world, the flesh, and the Devil will do so. Make no mistake: trashy tabloids, cheesy talk-shows, cheap friends, and hormonal drives will fill in every gap that you leave.

Why do so few professing Christian parents leave this legacy to their children? The answer is as simple as it is tragic: they do not leave them this legacy, because they do not have it to leave. They do not have enough knowledge of God, His Word and His ways to float a gnat. They bumble along, mouthing shallow prayers, living on religious vapors, attending churches that are high on *décor* and entertainment, and low on Biblical instruction—and the repercussions sound down through the decades.

In spite of its godly heritage in the receding past, our nation is reaping the dark, damaging legacy of lazy, flaccid, willfully ignorant "Christians." The vast majority profess to believe in the Bible, and yet they display utter ignorance of its contents.

These spiritual dwarfs leave no legacy of wisdom, quite simply because they have no such legacy to leave. Their children are the worse for it; and so is our nation.

Won't you be different, for the glory of God? Learn of Him; build up a storehouse of Divine wisdom. Give your child a legacy of godly, Biblical instruction, and you will leave him something that no thief, tragedy, or act of Congress can take away nor devalue. You will leave him something of literally eternal significance. Teach your children the ways of God.

Do note, however: the second blessing must flow from the first. If your children hear you telling them to honor you and your wife, while seeing you disgrace and dishonor your own parents; or talking about how important God is while living for possessions and never praying or studying the Word or involving yourself in a local church; or talking up marriage while treating each other as pagans would—they will have seen the form of religiosity, but none of its reality (cf. 2 Tim. 3:5). Your lips will be drowned out by your life.

Chapter Summary

1. Children are God-given arrows; parents are to aim them carefully at God's revealed target.

2. The means that God has given parents are twofold (Prov. 29:15):

   a. The **rod**, which is the symbol of the father's authority, standing for all discipline up to and including corporal punishment.

   b. The **rebuke**, which summarizes all the verbal instruction and warning which the parent gives from the Word of God.

3. Parents should apply the means that God has given with as much consistency as God gives the grace to muster—and then develop some more.

4. Over all, parents' *first* concern should be to leave their children the blessing of a godly legacy, from which everything else will flow.

Questions for Thought or Discussion

1. What are children, and what is their purpose, in God's eyes?

2. How was God's purpose for children to be carried out?

3. How is this design echoed and transformed in the New Testament?

4. How can a child benefit from a wise, godly upbringing?

5. How can parents benefit from children who have received a wise, godly upbringing?

6. How important is the Fifth Commandment, in Old and New Testaments? Be specific.

7. What are some of the terrible miseries awaiting the foolish child?

8. What is the center and goal of parental training?

9. Why is Proverbs 4:23 so crucial for parents?

10. What is the role of the Gospel in child-rearing?

11. What are the dangers of stressing obedience?

12. How do we counter those dangers?

13. Is the "Biblical method" guaranteed to produce wise, godly children?

14. What is the meaning of "the rod" in Proverbs 29:15?

15. What is the meaning of "reproof" in Proverbs 29:15?

16. What is the point of Proverbs 22:6?

17. What are the blessings of godly parents?

A Word to the Wise

When I write and when I preach, I always try to put myself in my audience's shoes. I don't want to be addressing an echo-chamber. I want to connect, help, make an impact, point to Christ.

So I envision that reading this book could be one of two very different kinds of experiences for people, broadly speaking.

First Reader

I can imagine an earnest person who started this study, eager to know about God's counsel for his or her life. He has dutifully labored through the chapters, and looked up all the verses. (Thank you!) He has felt the force and majesty of God's wisdom and been impressed with the fact that God's Lordship extends to absolutely every aspect of life. The Scriptures bore eloquent testimony, and he feels their force.

At the same time, the experience has been exhausting. No, more than exhausting, it has been disheartening, discouraging—in truth, it has been crushing.

This first reader has seen clearly that his life is not gripped by the fear of the Lord. He doubts that he has ever put together two consecutive seconds in his entire life, in which the glorious God of Scripture has truly been the very center of his thoughts and desires, believed and revered and loved with all his heart. He realizes now both that this is the fundamental building-block of wisdom, *and* that he is a complete stranger to it.

The more he reads and thinks, the worse it gets.

Since he is not gripped with the fear of God, his life has reflected little of God's wisdom. He has never sought God's counsel as heartily as Proverbs 2:1–5 bids. He has not handled his relationships as God's wisdom directs. Hurt and wrong and injuries, both given and received, litter the path of his life, perhaps including broken marriages and mishandled children.

Oh, and marriage! Children! In the area of sexuality, of relating, of child-rearing, how vastly he falls short. He can trace a sparkling moment here and there, perhaps; but they stand out as exceptions to the rule. And when he isn't misbehaving outwardly, his heart is full of bad desires and corruption—and he knows now that Yahweh sees his inside as clearly as his outside (Prov. 15:3; 20:27). God is judging his secrets (Eccl. 12:14; Rom. 2:16), and his secrets are *bad*.

All in all, reading the book of Proverbs has not proven to be the educational, uplifting, inspirational experience that he hoped it would be. It has laid yet another terribly heavy burden on his shoulders. It is a burden he now sees himself as utterly incapable of lifting. Against that standard, he falls hopelessly short. He is guilty and condemned, wholly unable to bring himself to the standard set out in this book.

Indeed, we have to ask in all candor: Who could? Whoever *could* embody all the ideals of Proverbs, let alone the rest of the Bible? What man, woman or child ever was utterly consumed with love for God, with dedication to God's glory? What human being ever had the breadth of mind (and purity of heart) to get his arms all the way around what Solomon wrote about, when even Solomon himself failed miserably to walk the way he sketched out?

What man ever turned from evil, gave himself utterly to righteousness; eschewed folly, and lived pure wisdom; lived a life of mercy, love, righteousness, justice, and wisdom? What child of this broken race ever exhibited the integrity, the whole-hearted commitment to the way of wisdom, the way of life, the way of God, that this book details with such bold colors?

No man ever did and was all that. No mere man, that is.

One man did.

One man, a great-great grandson of Solomon born of a human mother, walked the way of wisdom perfectly and wholly, from the womb to the tomb and beyond. Of Him it was prophesied—using a veritable catalogue of Solomon's wisdom-terms—

> There shall come forth a shoot from the stump of Jesse,
>> and a branch from his roots shall bear fruit.
>
> ² And the Spirit of the LORD shall rest upon him,
>> the Spirit of wisdom and understanding,
>> the Spirit of counsel and might,
>> the Spirit of knowledge and the fear of the LORD. (Isa. 11:1–2)

There it is! A descendant of David's father Jesse would be born, filled with the Spirit of Yahweh (as Lady Wisdom says she will do, in Prov. 1:23), filled with the Spirit of wisdom and understanding, filled with the Spirit of knowledge and the fear of Yahweh. This one, then, would heartily and absolutely embody and distill the ideal of the wisdom of Proverbs.

In distinction from a race of foolish men, this one would exemplify wisdom in its purest form. He would be a living, breathing, walking, talking incarnation of the fear of Yahweh.

And so it happened. Some seven hundred years after Isaiah's prophecy was delivered, nearly a millennium after Solomon put down his pen, God the Holy Spirit gave life to the womb of the virgin, Mary. The Child begotten in her was God incarnate, God with us, the Lord Jesus. Purely God as to His divine nature, yet purely man as to His human nature, Jesus lived the perfect and unswerving path of wisdom for every second of every minute of every hour of His life on earth. What is to us at best a goal and an ideal, was to Him His normal pace of life.

And then He gave Himself on the Cross.

Why? For what possible purpose? At first blush, such a miserable end would seem a flat contradiction of the rewards that Solomon promises to those who walk in the fear of Yahweh.

Solomon points to the answer in an angular fashion. It is where you'd never expect to see it: in Proverbs 17:15. Listen:

> He who justifies the wicked and he who condemns the righteous
>> are both alike an abomination to the LORD.

At first blush, there isn't an encouraging syllable in that verse. In fact, every pulse thunders condemnation to us. This verse asserts God's utterly righteous standard. He cannot pretend a guilty person to be righteous any more than He can imagine a righteous person to be guilty. To do so would shatter the foundation of His right to judge. It would be an abomination.

Yet the reader of the Old Testament recalls that *one* sinner was in fact declared righteous. He recalls father Abraham, back when he was still called "Abram." He recalls Genesis 15:6, where we read that Abram "believed the LORD, and he counted it to him as righteousness." Faith, mere faith—faith alone—counted to Abram as righteousness.

We see that is what we need. We need to be counted as righteous in God's eyes. But how could we ever get that righteousness? God cannot declare the wicked "righteous"—and we are wicked! How could we be judged to be right in His sight, without destroying the righteous foundation of His throne (cf. Psa. 89:14)?

If we have read the whole Old Testament, we know that Moses (who penned Genesis 15:6) was aware of the fundamental principle of Leviticus 17:11— "For the life of the flesh is in the blood, and I [Yahweh] have given it for you on the altar to make atonement for your souls, for it is the blood that makes atonement by the life." Moses knew that atonement for sin, for sins, for sins such as Abram's, can be made only by the shedding of blood. He knows that Yahweh Himself offered the first animal sacrifice, to cover the guilty shame of the couple who committed the first sin (Gen. 3:21). Moses knows that Abram had offered sacrifices (Gen. 12:7–8; 13:4, 18), and that Yahweh Himself had made bloody sacrifice on formalizing His covenant with Abram (Gen. 15).

Yet there is a tension within the OT itself on the subject of sacrifice. We saw it in Proverbs. For one thing, the sacrifices themselves had no transformative power. That is why many Biblical writers deride individuals who looked on sacrifices as if they were magical, box-checking, formalistic remedies for their unrepented moral crimes (Isa. 66:3; Jer. 11:15). Solomon himself brought scorching barrages to bear on anyone who viewed sacrifice as being externalistic whitewash for an unrepentant, unbelieving heart (Prov. 15:8; 21:27).

Even so, those sacrifices had to be repeated over and over again, signaling that they never truly and finally dealt with the sin-problem. Sacrifices were something like what IT professionals call a "workaround." They did not resolve the root problem, but they furnished a way to go on. They pointed the way, but were inadequate to solve our problem.

So we have both a partial solution, and a dilemma.

1. God *does in fact* declare the wicked righteous, and He forgives their sins (see Gen. 15:6; Leviticus).

2. He declares the wicked righteous through faith alone (Gen. 15:6).

3. He declares the wicked righteous on the basis of penal, substitutionary atonement that deals with their sins and His just wrath (Lev. 17:11)...

4. ...*But* the atonement provided within the OT itself was imperfect and insufficient.

Could this dilemma be solved?

Indeed, the Old Testament itself promised that it *could* be and it *would* be.

A major prophetic promise comes in a book which, ironically, begins (in part) by a thunderous and devastating denunciation of Israel's abuse of ritual and sacrifice to cover over her unbelieving lives (Isa. 1:10–15). I've long envisioned a contemporary of Isaiah's reading those words and thinking, "Wait—Yahweh doesn't want sacrifice? But that is what atones for our sins. They were His idea, His law. What does that leave us?"

Yahweh's ultimate and final answer is given in the jaw-dropping prophetic revelation of Isaiah 52:13–53:12. Though this isn't the place for a lengthy exposition, one can readily see the sacrificial imagery throughout this entire oracle.

Isaiah depicts this human being, this Servant of Yahweh—who clearly is not Israel, idealized or otherwise[1]—offering Himself up to bear the wrath of God for sins not His own, but His people's. This individual, Himself righteous (v. 11), dies as a penal, substitutionary sacrifice for the ungodly and wicked (cf. vv. 4–10).

The pivot, in connection with Proverbs 17:15, is found in Isaiah 53:11—

> Out of the anguish of his soul he shall see and be satisfied;
>> by his knowledge shall the righteous one, my servant,
>> make many to be accounted righteous,
>> and he shall bear their iniquities.

---

[1] Cf. v. 8, and the repeated contrasts of the one vs. the many, the *we* and the *Him*.

There it is:

- Many sinners...

- ...will be accounted righteous

- ...on the basis of the perfect and final penal, substitutionary atonement that the Servant of Yahweh would provide.

Now we are getting our answer. How can sinners be declared right in God's eyes? Through the penal, substitutionary, bodily death of the Servant of Yahweh as a sin-offering.

Fast-forward seven centuries and hear the apostle Paul laying it out plainly. Isaiah wrote prospectively, prophetically. Paul is able to write from the perspective of fulfillment, looking back at the death, burial, and resurrection of Jesus Christ:

> Now we know that whatever the law says it speaks to those who are under the law, so that every mouth may be stopped, and the whole world may be held accountable to God. [20] For by works of the law no human being will be justified in his sight, since through the law comes knowledge of sin. [21] But now the righteousness of God has been manifested apart from the law, although the Law and the Prophets bear witness to it—[22] the righteousness of God through faith in Jesus Christ for all who believe. For there is no distinction: [23] for all have sinned and fall short of the glory of God, [24] and are justified by his grace as a gift, through the redemption that is in Christ Jesus, [25] whom God put forward as a propitiation by his blood, to be received by faith. This was to show God's righteousness, because in his divine forbearance he had passed over former sins. [26] It was to show his righteousness at the present time, so that he might be just and the justifier of the one who has faith in Jesus. (Rom. 3:19–26)

The book of Proverbs, then, shuts our mouth and condemns us as guilty, fallen far short of God's standards. We are fools, every one of us—gullible, foolish, dense, stupid, perhaps even scoffers. We are unrighteous. There was a way that seemed right, and we took it. We were wise in our own eyes. We were sluggards, selfish, slackers.

Every aspect of our lives proclaims our inability to produce the wise life of integrity in righteousness that God rightly demands. *We* are the wicked, the crooked, the perverse, the dense, the stupid, the foolish, the evil, the scoffers whom He abominates. Our performance condemns us; our hearts condemn us. We are undone.

"But now," as Paul gloriously proclaims, God has revealed His righteousness in Christ. Jesus Christ is God's ἱλαστήριον [*hilastērion*, "propitiation," Rom. 3:25], the sacrifice that absorbs and deflects His just wrath. Jesus' blood deals with our sin; our sin is imputed to Him, and His righteousness is imputed to us. In this way, and in this way alone, God can be righteous *and* declare wicked Abram righteous through faith alone. God can be righteous *and* declare wicked Paul righteous through faith alone.

Here is the heart-stopping good news. God can be righteous, *and* declare wicked *you*, and wicked *me*, righteous through faith alone, by grace alone, on the basis of the sacrifice of Jesus Christ alone.

And so you see, the principle of Proverbs 17:15 is the key to the necessity of penal, substitutionary atonement.

1. If God, with no cause nor reason, pronounces guilty people righteous, then He violates His own principle of justice and un-Gods Himself. However,

2. If God imputes our sin to Christ, and imputes Christ's righteousness to us, with Christ making full atonement for our sin, then is He both just and the justifier of believers.

It was well that Thomas Watson called redemption "the masterpiece of divine wisdom." Watson envisions the counsels of eternity thus:

> God's mercy looked at us in our miserable and helpless estate, but how to do it without wronging the justice of God? It is a pity, says Mercy, that such a noble creature as man should be made to be undone; and yet God's justice must not be a loser. What way then shall be found out? Angels cannot satisfy for the wrong done to God's justice, nor is it fit that one nature should sin, and another nature suffer. What then? Shall man be for ever lost? Now, while Mercy was thus debating with itself, what to do for the recovery

of fallen man, the Wisdom of God stepped in; and thus the oracle spake:—Let God become man; let the Second Person in the Trinity be incarnate, and suffer; and so for fitness he shall be man, and for ability he shall be God; thus justice may be satisfied, and man saved. O the depth of the riches of the wisdom of God, thus to make justice and mercy to kiss each other![2]

Amen!

Remember that Solomon said,

> Like cold water to a thirsty soul,
>   so is good news from a far country. (Prov. 25:25)

That is precisely what this is. It is the very best of news from the very farthest of countries. It is the announcement of the Great King, that He has done a wondrous thing by His wisdom and His might. He has made pardon and reconciliation and perfect righteousness available to rebels, criminals, and outcasts. He now calls all in His kingdom to be reconciled to Him.

God calls us to do no more and no less than believe in Jesus Christ. In believing Christ, we turn from any hope of winning God's favor by our wisdom or our righteousness. We abandon all reliance on ourselves, cease to be wise in our own eyes, and turn to Him alone to save us. We leave the ways of folly and death, and flee to the ways of wisdom and life, in Him who is Himself the way, the truth, the life, and the wisdom of God (John 14:6; 1 Cor. 1:24).

God uses the instrument of that faith to "justify" us, to pronounce us perfectly righteous in Christ by grace alone, through faith alone, all credit and glory and thanks to Christ alone (cf. Rom. 3:24; 4:4–8).

And so it is *in and because of Christ* that we can approach God as righteous in His sight. It is *in Christ* that we can be accepted as righteous and upright.

Second Reader

Then Proverbs becomes a different book. The entire Bible becomes a different book. It seems to be transformed, because we have been transformed.

We no longer look to Proverbs to find out how to make ourselves acceptable before God, hoping to raise ourselves to His standards. We abandoned that false

---

2   Thomas Watson, *Body of Divinity* (Grand Rapids: Baker, 1979 [reprint of 1890 ed.]), 51.

hope at the Cross. Rather, we can (and must) learn from Proverbs the specifics for the kind of life that grows from the fear of Yahweh, the life that honors the God who has already accepted us as righteous in Christ.

Now, when we read Paul praying and asking that the Colossian Christians "may be filled with the knowledge of his will *in all spiritual wisdom and understanding*" (Col. 1:9), we realize that studying Proverbs is a means God will use to answer that prayer. When we read Paul's exhortation to the Ephesians, "Look carefully then how you walk, not as unwise but as wise, making the best use of the time, because the days are evil (Eph. 5:15–16), we know that Proverbs can teach us how to be wise, and how to make the best use of our time.

We now see Proverbs as part of that great body of literature God breathed out "for our instruction, that through endurance and through the encouragement of the Scriptures we might have hope" (Rom. 15:4). We accept it as part of our Father's book of instruction, which is "breathed out by God and profitable for teaching, for reproof, for correction, and for training in righteousness, that the man of God may be competent, equipped for every good work" (2 Tim. 3:16–17).

So we look to the wisdom and principles of Proverbs, never *in order that* we may become acceptable to God, but *because Christ has made us* acceptable to God. We do not turn to it to be saved, but because we have been saved. We turn to it for instruction in living lives skilled in godly living, that we might bring glory to our Father, whose Holy Spirit opened our eyes to the glories of Christ, and who has saved us in Him and made us His own forever.

Because in the final analysis, for the Christian, God is His Father, and in Proverbs we hear our Father's voice calling us to wise living that adorns our faith.

God grant us ears to hear, hearts to cherish and retain, and lives that show the difference, for Christ's glory.

Amen.

Questions for Thought or Discussion

1. What is a wrong way of reading this book?

2. What is the right way?

3. Which kind of reader are you?

4. Did Solomon fulfill his own ideal of wisdom?

5. Has anyone ever fulfilled Solomon's ideal of wisdom? Who?

6. What is the impact of the answer to #4 for us?

Who Wrote Proverbs, and What Difference Does It Make?

In this appendix, I will demonstrate two main truths:

1. We should take Proverbs 1:1, and all other notes of authorship in Proverbs, to mean exactly what they say.
2. Accepting these ascriptions as authoritative both guides and helps us in understanding and using Proverbs.

Authorship

The Book's Explicit Statements, and Why They Matter

Who wrote Proverbs? The identity of the main author is presented in the first verse (Prov. 1:1—"Proverbs of Solomon, son of David, king of Israel"), and is repeated again in 10:1a ("Proverbs of Solomon"). The next unambiguous note as to authorship is in 25:1 ("These also are proverbs of Solomon which the men of Hezekiah king of Judah copied"). Then, the final two chapters identify Agur (30:1) and King Lemuel (thanks to his mother; 31:1) as authors.

Thus, the only author named for chapters 1–29 is Solomon, son of David, king of Israel.

We must not hurry past 1:1. Those words surely seem to tell us who wrote the book, followed by an explanation of what he set out to do, and whom he was addressing. Those words matter. If we cannot trust and accept the words as truthful and clear, why should we trust anything else in the book? Why should we bother?

Further, if we want at least to attempt to work out what the author was meaning to say, rather than engaging in postmodern projection of our own notions into his words, it surely helps to know (A) who he was and (B) when he lived, so that we can know (C) what informed his own worldview.

One is accustomed to liberal writers, who do not hold to the authority and inerrancy of the text of Scripture, making sweeping dismissals of the wording of the text. For instance, Crawford H. Toy sniffs that "No OT. [sic] titles are in themselves authoritative," so none of the ascriptions to Solomon in Proverbs should determine our own thinking.[1] Nor did that attitude pass with the nineteenth century. Roland Murphy, a Roman Catholic writing for the reputedly evangelical Word Biblical Commentary series, portrays modern scholarship as monolithically ruling out Solomonic authorship.[2]

This attitude resembles that of the well-known professor at Fuller Theological Seminary with whom I had a conversation. He was explaining to me that Peter did not write 2 Peter. When I called attention to 1:1, he responded, "Well, that's beside the point, isn't it?"

Surprisingly, however, evangelical scholars who do respect the text of Scripture seem to find at least some of Proverbs' direct ascriptions of authorship "beside the point." For example, no less a defender of Biblical inerrancy than Edward J. Young stated flatly that "[d]uring the reign of Hezekiah, his scribes edited [chapters 10–24] and appended chapters 1–9, which were Solomonic."[3] How he concluded that Solomon did not himself write chapters 1–24 as we have them, Young did not explain.

At least Young allowed that chapters 1–9 were "Solomonic." Dillard and Longman, however, state that Proverbs 1:8–9:18 is "without an explicit

---

[1]   Toy, xix–xx.
[2]   Roland E. Murphy, *Proverbs*, Word Biblical Commentary (Waco: Nelson), xx.
[3]   Edward J. Young, *Introduction to the Old Testament* (Grand Rapids: Eerdmans, 1960), 312.

authorship attribution," asserting that the first seven verses serve as "an extended superscription and introduction to the book [and] connects authorship to Solomon, but does not claim it for the section itself."[4] Further, they conclude that "Following the information given by the captions, it is best to limit Solomon's contribution to 10:1–22:16 and 25:1–29:27."[5] But why follow "the information given by" the brief caption of 10:1, while brushing aside the lengthy ascription in 1:1? The conclusion is announced, not proven. Indeed, it is not even argued.

Derek Kidner held that the Solomonic proverbs were held off to chapter 10, because 10:1–22:16 needed an introduction, which some editor other than Solomon supplied.[6] But why a later editor? Why not take it that Solomon himself provided his own introduction? Kidner does not say directly, except to hint at differing styles among the sections.[7]

Evangelical authors Hill and Walton likewise refer to 10:1–22:16 as "Solomonic collections," but say that chapters 1–9 "probably combine Solomonic sayings with later wisdom teachings from anonymous sages."[8] Why? Again, though there is neither more nor less evidence of Solomon's authorship of one section over the other, Hill and Walton do not see a need to give any extended evidence for their conclusions. When John Drane sets about *Introducing the Old Testament*, and says that parts of Proverbs are said to have been composed by king Solomon, he cites only 10:1 and 25:1.[9] The first verse does not even merit a mention. Why not? We are not told.

Similarly Hubbard dismisses 1:1–6 as "an introductory statement of purpose,"[10] rather than a statement of *authorship and* purpose. Why? The closest Hubbard comes to a supporting argument is his assertion that "the writer of [chapters 1–9] is anonymous, since 1:1–6 probably refers to the entire book and

---

[4] Raymond B. Dillard and Tremper Longman III, *Introduction to the Old Testament* (Grand Rapids: Zondervan, 1994; used by permission), 236.

[5] Ibid.

[6] Kidner, 22.

[7] Ibid., 22–23.

[8] Andrew E. Hill and John H. Walton, *A Survey of the Old Testament*, 2nd ed. (Grand Rapids: Zondervan, 2000; used by permission), 357.

[9] John William Drane, *Introducing the Old Testament*, completely rev. and updated (Oxford: Lion Publishing plc, 2000), 106.

[10] David Allan Hubbard, article "Proverbs, Book of," in D. R. W. Wood and I. Howard Marshall, *New Bible Dictionary*, 3rd ed., (Leicester, England; Downers Grove, Ill.: InterVarsity Press, 1996), 977.

10:1 introduces a collection of proverbs which purport to be Solomonic."[11] How does a reference to the entire book rule out 1:1 as an exclusion of authorship?

One is simply left to wonder, What leads to such conclusions?

As we shall see, some point out that the style and contents of chapters 1–9 are very different from chapters 10–24. This seems to be a factor to Kidner, who says that chapters 25–29 have "Solomon's own touch" because of their "terse sayings."[12]

All are agreed that the two sections (1–9, 10–24) are distinct. Where we may part company, however, is in how we understand that difference, and what significance we find in it.

Distinct, or Divergent?

All one need do is read the first chapter of Proverbs, followed by the tenth. The difference is immediately apparent. Chapters 1–9 are in the form of a series of poems, or extended discourses, where a subject is brought up and developed at some length. For instance, 1:10 warns, "My son, if sinners entice you, do not consent." This warning is developed at length on up to verse 19. The same pattern generally continues on through the varied discourses of each following chapter, until the end of chapter 9.

Then, by contrast, chapters ten through 22:16 most commonly feature what we might call "two-liners." That is, the entire thought is expressed in two lines of poetry, as in 10:1b itself:

> A wise son gladdens *his* father,
>> but a stupid son is his mother's grief (DJP)

Those two lines form the complete thought. Unlike most passages of Scripture (and Proverbs 1–9), we can't read the verses before, or the verses after, to find a thought-flow such as would provide an interpretive context for interpretation. Most of Proverbs 10 and following are two-liners, with a few three-liners or more,[13] until the return of something like brief discourses in the final two chapters.

There is also some difference as to subject matter and tone between chapters 1–9 and 10–29, though I think that has been exaggerated.[14]

---

[11] Ibid.

[12] Kidner, 24.

[13] With chapter 22, the usual "two-liners" are joined by what we might call "four-liners" (i.e. 22:22 and 23, 24 and 25, etc.), "six-liners" (i.e. 24:11, 12), and even longer (i.e. 23:29–35; 31:10–31).

[14] Cf. Toy, vii; Raymond Van Leeuwen, "Proverbs," in *The New Interpreter's Bible* (Nashville:

For instance, chapters 1–9 are repeatedly voiced as a father addressing his son (e.g. 1:8, 10; 2:1; 3:1, etc.). Sometimes the father is joined by the mother (1:8; 6:20). This pattern is not as pronounced in the shorter proverbs that follow. However, the same speakers and audience are found (or presupposed) in the remainder of the explicitly Solomonic portion as well (cf. 19:27; 23:15, 19, 26; 24:13, 21; 27:11). It is hardly a major variance.

Again, chapters 2–7 dwell more on the specific dangers of immoral sex than we see in the following section. However, immorality is but a subcategory of unrighteousness and contempt for God's Word, which both are frequent topics through the rest of the book. Perhaps the opening stress reflects Solomon's awareness of the prevalence of sexual temptation for young men, and the eventuality that a collapse in this area often has a domino effect on the rest of one's character.[15] Solomon understood—and came to know all too well, in his own life—that a man who gives in to sexual temptation may leave the path of wisdom and righteousness for good.

If one accepts the text's ascription of common authorship as applying to the whole (1:1; 10:1), why would Solomon feel himself obliged to repeat in every chapter what he had already developed so poignantly in his opening discourses? In that case, critics might equally fault him for being repetitive; or "discover" a later editor trying to link the chapters back to 1–9 (or, equally, attempting to link 1–9 to later chapters). Abandon the text in exchange for speculation, and the sky is the limit.

Regardless, for reasons such as these, some have concluded that Solomon did not write the first nine chapters. It is common to see 1:1 as a general note, identifying Proverbs as a *Solomonic* collection, though Solomon did not himself write the first nine chapters. Or they call it "an editor's title of the whole book… although [Solomon's] own collection of proverbs will not be reached till chapter 10…"[16]

Abingdon, 1997), 23. Particularly cf. William McKane, *Proverbs: a New Approach* (Old Testament Library; Philadelphia: Westminster, 1970), 11ff. and 413ff. McKane actually rearranges the canonical text for his commentary, according to his theories of groupings.

[15] Additionally, such warnings are not absent from the larger portion: cf. 22:14; 23:26–28.

[16] Kidner, *Proverbs*, 22. (My disagreement with Kidner on this point does not detract from my admiration for his commentary as a whole.)

Chapters 1–9 Not "Proverbs"?

Writers sometimes also argue that the first nine chapters are not properly *proverbs*, which they say are more the terse, brief two-liners that we see in 10:1ff.[17] Instead, they are discourses. Real proverbs, it is asserted, start with 10:1.

At least two fatal flaws attend this way of thinking:

First fatal flaw: a "proverb" is not just a two-liner

This view takes too narrow a meaning of "proverb." A proverb (Hebrew מָשָׁל, *māšāl*) is not necessarily just a two-liner. It is employed in a wide variety of ways in Scripture.

Before Solomon's time, the word already enjoyed a wide application. For instance, seven times Balaam's poetic, prophetic discourses are called *māšāl* (Num. 23:7, 18; 24:3, 15, 20, 21, 23). How long is a *māšāl*, then, in these passages? The first use denotes a four-verse speech (23:7–10). The same word describes a seven-verse discourse in 23:18–24, another seven-verse prophecy (24:3–9), five verses (24:15–19), a pair of two-verse poems (24:21–22, 23–24), and a single one-liner (24:20).

Interestingly enough, then, the case with Balaam is parallel to that of Proverbs 1:1 and 10:1, in this way: *māšāl* equally describes two longer, seven-verse discourses (Num. 23:18–24; 24:3–9) and one terse, six-word oracle (Num. 24:20).

Job 27:1 and 29:1 indicate that all of chapters 26–31 could be styled a *māšāl*. In that case, so far from being limited to a single-verse one-liner, a *māšāl* takes up some 121 verses.

The dating of Psalm 49[18] depends on a number of factors. But if we take it as Davidic either in authorship or timeframe, it would be another pre-Solomonic use of *māšāl* to describe a longer work, in this case some 20 verses in the English text.

Asaph styles Psalm 78 as a *māšāl* (v. 2), and it runs 72 verses.

The use in Ecclesiastes 12:9 is problematic. If one takes Ecclesiastes to be authored by Solomon, as I do, then the question becomes whether the use in the

---

[17] An example would be Allen P. Ross' statement that the Hebrew term *mishlê* ("proverbs of") "does not describe any of the sayings in 1:8–9:18" ("Proverbs," in *Expositor's Bible Commentary*, ed. Frank E. Gaebelein [Grand Rapids: Zondervan, 1991; used by permission], 5:887. Ross' own conclusion is that 1:1–7 is an old introduction to part of the book, which was added last by the final editor; 1:8–9:18 may have come from Solomon's time, or as late as Hezekiah's time (5:888).

[18] Titled "A Psalm of the sons of Korah."

verse refers to Ecclesiastes itself. If it does, as seems likely, then Solomon himself is once again using *māšāl* of literature longer than single-verse sayings.

More evidence comes after Solomon's time. Isaiah's poetic "taunt" (*māšāl*) against Babylon takes up as many as 20 verses (14:4–23). Ezekiel's "parable" (*māšāl*; 17:2) extends from vv. 3–10; and a second "parable" runs from 24:3–17.

And so we see that the oft-heard insistence that a *māšāl* is by definition a brief saying, a two-liner,[19] simply cannot be sustained by the evidence. A *māšāl* might be quite lengthy. The misdefinition of *māšāl* cannot be thought to rule out the possibility that "Proverbs of Solomon" in Proverbs 1:1 applies equally to the first nine chapters.[20]

Second fatal flaw: How much clearer could 1:1 be?

This brings us to the *second* fatal objection. If the words "Proverbs of Solomon, son of David, king of Israel" (1:1) do not provide the title of the book and its author, then what words would? How could Solomon have expressed himself more clearly?[21] It is interesting to note that liberal writer J. Alberto Soggin at least acknowledged that, from 1:1, "it seems evident that the editors wanted to attribute the work to king Solomon."[22] Soggin does not accept that attribution as true, since he does not regard the Old Testament as the inerrant Word of God— but he at least does recognize the intent of the words. Evangelicals' unwillingness to acknowledge the same is hard to account for.

Several books, such as Mark and Job and Hebrews, contain no direct statement whatever about authorship. What student of the letter to the Hebrews would not

---

[19] This is reflected, for instance, in Allen's statement, quoted above, that *mišlê* "does not describe any of the sayings in 1:8–9:18" (5:887).

[20] In fact, does the reader not intuitively *assume* that the heading found in the first verse of a book will apply *at least* to the verses which come immediately after? Surely some specific statement would be required, if we were intended to take the words any other way. "The proverbs of Solomon—eventually. But first, a few lectures from an anonymous genius!"

[21] The reader might try to diagram the reasoning in this statement: "Since [Solomon] is mentioned again specifically as author of the collection which begins at 10:1, chs. 1–9 are probably the product of anonymous sages" (William Sanford La Sor, David Allan Hubbard, and Frederick William Bush, *Old Testament Survey* [Grand Rapids: Eerdmans, 1982], 551. On this reasoning, 10:1a ("Proverbs of Solomon") means that the following chapters *were* written by Solomon, and 1:1 ("Proverbs of Solomon") means that the following chapters *were not* written by Solomon. Yet the Hebrew text in both verses is identical, except that 1:1 is fuller. How can the same words bear the opposite meanings in two passages in the same book?

[22] *Introduction to the Old Testament*, translated by John Bowden (Philadelphia: Westminster, 1976), 382.

give his Greek flashcards for the equivalent of "The proverbs of Solomon" at the start of the text of the letter? The entire course of Hebrews studies would have been completely different had the opening words been (say) "Apollos, slave of Jesus Christ, to the faithful Jews in Rome."

Or again, what student of the Old Testament would not love to be able to "place" Job chronologically, with some identifiable claim to authorship or timeframe such as Proverbs 1:1? "In the days of Abraham, Elihu wrote the words of Job. And it came to pass that..."

Yet here in Proverbs 1:1 we have just exactly such information in plain Engl... well, in plain *Hebrew*, and yet some are all too willing to proceed as if those words were simply lacking.[23]

Third fatal flaw: If it fits, maybe it fits because it fits!

Commentator after commentator observes what a fitting introduction chapters 1–9 provides in relation to the rest of the book. In fact, Kidner says that chapters 10 and following positively needed just such an introduction. Why not acknowledge that the chapters form such an apropos introduction precisely because Solomon himself composed it for just such a purpose? After all, as the popular version of "Occam's razor" would suggest, sometimes the simplest and most obvious explanation is also the best explanation.

Other Indicators of Solomonic Authorship

There is good reason to affirm that Solomon wrote Proverbs 1–29. For one thing, as I have suggested, the *prima facie* meaning of the words should not be brushed aside. If "Proverbs of Solomon" does not indicate proverbs collected and/or written by Solomon, one has to wonder what words would convey that meaning.

---

[23] An example is the rather astonishing statement of Roland K. Harrison, in his magisterial *Introduction to the Old Testament* (Grand Rapids: Eerdmans, 1969). Harrison writes of "The first principal group of material attributed directly to King Solomon (10:1–22:16)..." (1017). If 10:1–22:16 is "The first principal group of material attributed directly to King Solomon," then what is 1:1? Harrison offers no explanation. No less puzzling are the words of Allen P. Ross, who says that the "heading in 10:1 clearly credits Solomon for the subsequent material" (887), yet the same author is unsure as to what *the identical words* mean in 1:1 (888). Dillard and Longman say that 10:1 and 25:1 "identify Solomon as the author of the proverbs found in these sections" (238), yet the same words in 1:1 having nothing to do with authorship of the first nine chapters (238)—indeed, dating 1–9 to Solomon's time is "dangerous" (239). The cause of all this reluctance and ambivalence is indeed difficult to ferret out.

Also, think about the very ascriptions of Proverbs 22:17a and 24:23a. The first begins, "Incline your ear, and hear the words of the wise," and the second reads, "These also are sayings of the wise." Many think that these introduce new collections by different authors, though I will set out a different view below. If some or all of Proverbs were sayings of various anonymous wise men, why designate two relatively small portions as originating with "wise men"? If we dismiss Solomon as author, then does that not make *all* of the remainder the sayings of anonymous wise men? How would these words distinguish these sections from the rest, unless Solomon is the direct author of the rest?

Similarly, the titles given in 30:1 and 31:1 favor a straightforward reading of 1:1 and 10:1.[24] That is, if 1:1 and/or 10:1 merely indicate that the proverbs are "Solomonic" (but not *Solomon's*), or if they are doffs of the cap to Solomon as "patron saint" of wisdom literature (who did not actually *write* any proverbs)—then what are 30:1 and 31:1? I am unaware of any great academic movement to interpret those verses as other than indications of authorship. No scholarly consensus calls for taking the otherwise-unknown Agur or Lemuel (and his mother) as patron-figures, leaving the subsequent proverbs as anonymous representatives, to be called "Agurian" and "Lemuelic." If 30:1 and 31:1 indicate authorship, on what basis can we say that 1:1 and 10:1 do not do so as well?

Similarly, the plain sense of 25:1 certainly indicates that "Hezekiah's men" thought the proverbs they transcribed, or copied, or moved, were actually proverbs of Solomon—not merely *Solomonic*. Their time was 250 years later; the memory of Solomon was doubtless as bittersweet as it was vivid. After all, the divided kingdom in which they lived traced its roots to Solomon's apostasy. So why attribute the proverbs to him, if they didn't think he had actually authored them?

If we grant that the intent of 25:1 is to indicate Solomon's authorship of the proverbs that follow, on what basis can we say that 1:1 and 10:1 are not written with the same meaning?

Further, 25:1 reads, "These *also* are the proverbs of Solomon," indicating that the writer affirmed the preceding to be equally traceable to the sagacious king. One wonders again: if the testimony of the text is to be accepted as to the Solomonic sourcing of chapters 25–29, what would be the factual basis for rejecting the textual testimony as to the preceding? And if "the preceding" include at least chapters 10–24, on what basis could chapters 1–9 be excluded, particularly

---

[24] The argument of this and the following paragraph is similar to Waltke, *Proverbs*, 1:31.

given the consensus that sees 1–9 as introductory (at least) to 10–22:16, if not all the way through 24?[25]

Given this straightforward textual assertion of authorship, one has to wonder why so many academics, evangelical as well as liberal, reject one or both ascriptions out of hand.[26] Is the reason scientific? Have deeper studies proven that chapters 1–9 (or 10–24) *cannot* be "the proverbs of Solomon"?

Old Testament scholar Bruce K. Waltke's answer is particularly pointed: "Denial of Solomonic authorship is based on the academic skepticism inherited from the historical criticism of the last century, not on *any* scientific data."[27] This observation is accurate. When Fox announces, "Historically, it is improbable that many—if any—of the proverbs were written by Solomon,"[28] he tips his hand. On what grounds can the ancient text itself be excluded from history? To define "historically" in a way that excludes the ancient text's explicit claims is to be driven by ideology, not evidence.

Thus Waltke correctly observes that the denial of Solomonic authorship of Proverbs "is the real fiction."[29] He laments the fact that "Some academics, including evangelicals, have not helped" in approaching Proverbs, in part because they "are skeptical about the book's claim to Solomonic authorship."[30]

---

[25] Another odd note in academic history is the view that chapters 1–9 are not from Solomon *specifically because* they introduce the chapters that follow. That reasoning is hard to graph. Chapter 1 of this book introduces all the chapters that follow. Does that mean that I did not write it? Indeed, Andrew E. Steinmann made a very strong case, on the basis of style and wording, that the person who wrote Proverbs 1–9 is the same person who also wrote the following chapters ("Proverbs 1–9 as a Solomonic Composition," vol. 43, *Journal of the Evangelical Theological Society* Volume 43, 4, 657–674 (Lynchburg, VA: The Evangelical Theological Society, 2000).

[26] Indeed, Longman does not even want to talk about authorship. The body of the text of *How to Read Proverbs* (Downers Grove: InterVarsity Press, 2002) contains no discussion of who wrote Proverbs. That topic is relegated to an unsatisfying glance in an appendix. Why ignore such basic questions until the last? Longman explains that he did it "because this is a book about how to read the book of Proverbs, and if we are quite honest, the authorship and date of the book have little or no impact on our interpretation of it" (159). For a professor of Old Testament literature to dismiss fundamental introductory matters as irrelevant—particularly in the face of such clear textual evidence—is remarkable indeed. Further, I shall attempt to demonstrate that how we understand authorship has a great and repeated impact on interpretation.

[27] "Proverbs, Theology of," in NIDOTTE, 4:1082.

[28] Fox, *Proverbs*, 1:56.

[29] Waltke, *Proverbs*, 1:31. Waltke adds, "No attribution of authorship within the Old Testament has been proved spurious" (ibid., 1:35).

[30] Ibid., 1:xxii.

The Implications of 1:1

The book we have is the book Jesus and the apostles had. It has been divided into thirty-one chapters by later editors. As written, it began with an ascription of authorship (1:1), a statement both of purpose and audience (1:2–6), a statement of the worldview-defining truth that is the foundation of all that follows (1:7), and an introduction of consequent truths on which the rest would stand (the remainders of chapters 1–9).

In the first lecture or discourse, Solomon's "son" is called to attend to his father and mother's wisdom and turn his back on the wrong crowd (1:8–19). Then Lady Wisdom appears as a street-preacher, powerfully summoning the simple to repent and enroll in her school (1:20–33).

Fast-forward to the end of the book, and the exact same themes occur in closing. A man and wife opened the book; a man (Agur; 30) and a queen-mother (31) close the book. Agur bids the reader to cling to the wisdom of God's Word (30:1–6), and calls to a humble, peaceful, contented life (30:7–33) that is the opposite of the wrong crowd's call in chapter 1. Then Lemuel's mother speaks, bidding him to reign wisely (31:1–9), and depicting a wife who is the flesh-and-blood embodiment of Lady Wisdom (31:10–31).

In all this, particularly note that the thematic foundation-statement of 1:7 is echoed in the closing poem, 31:30. Thus, the theme of the fear of Yahweh[31] forms an *inclusio*, a single bracketing idea to the book as a whole.[32] Solomon has structured the whole to emphasize that central theme.

The book's data, then, surely give the impression of a unity, with Solomon as the final editor. How to square this with the diversity in its pages? Let me approach this in the popular format of an FAQ list—a list of Frequently Asked Questions.

---

[31] As I explain more fully in Chapter 3, "Yahweh" is the covenant name of the God of Israel. It occurs some 6,823 times in the Old Testament, and lurks in the Hebrew text behind every occurrence of Lord or GOD in most standard English translations.

[32] In fact, Blocher suggests a sort of double-*inclusio*, seeing 9:10 as joining with 1:7 to bracket the first section (chapters 1–9), and 31:30 mirroring 1:7 in bracketing the whole (Henri Blocher, "The Fear of the Lord as the 'Principle' of Wisdom," *Tyndale Bulletin* 28 (1977): 4–5.

Authorship FAQ's

How Does 10:1 Relate to 1:1?

We have seen that it does not fit the facts to say that chapters 1–9 are not really proverbs, and that actual proverbs begin with 10:1. But if Solomon wrote the whole, why repeat the fact? Why not say, "These *also* are the proverbs of Solomon" (cf. 24:23; 25:1)?

First, this subtitle allows the reader to shift gears. We've seen that there are proverbs, and then there are proverbs. The book itself displays just this phenomenon: it has proverbs (longer discourses, 1–9), and it has proverbs (mostly two-liners, 10–29). The words of 10:1 signal the change in gear, like the traffic sign one sees at the sides of some California mountain roads: "Truckers use low gear."

Second, this format is similar to the wisdom literature of Solomon's day. Kenneth A. Kitchen made this case at length in a lecture given in 1976.[33] Kitchen argued persuasively that the shape of Proverbs 1–24 followed the pattern of what he called "*Type B*" literature, which featured "a formal title, a prologue, and then main text (sub-titles being optional)."[34] Kitchen took Proverbs 1:1 to be the formal title, the remainder of chapters 1–9 to be the prologue, 10:1 to be the briefer subtitle, followed by the proverbs of Solomon.

Duane Garrett confirms that "[s]ubtitles and titular interjections occur frequently in ancient Near Eastern wisdom texts and are by no means indications that the sections they head were once independent 'documents' from different sources."[35]

In sum, then, it is best to take at least chapters 1–24 as a unity in terms of authorship and design. Then 25:1 introduces the next portion (25–29) as from the same pen. This leaves only 30 and 31 as not coming directly from the hand (if not the mind) of King Solomon.

But What of 22:17 and 24:23?

Both of these verses are commonly taken to denote sub-collections within Proverbs. However, while it is true that both verses serve to highlight what follows,

---

[33] K. A. Kitchen, "Proverbs And Wisdom Books Of The Ancient Near East: The Factual History Of A Literary Form," *Tyndale Bulletin* 28, no. 1, (1977): 68–114.

[34] Kitchen, 73.

[35] Duane A. Garrett, *Proverbs, Ecclesiastes, Song of Songs* (Nashville: Broadmans, 1993), 44.

neither necessarily distinguishes the sub-section from the "proverbs of Solomon" (1:1; 10:1) in terms of authorship.

First, both notations are still framed in the first-person singular. That is, the writer of 22:17 speaks both of the "words of the wise" and of "my knowledge." He says "I have made them known to you" (v. 19), and "I" have "written for you" (v. 20). These are the words of a single author or editor. Who would that be? Should not 1:1 and 10:1 predispose us to identify the "I" as Solomon?

The same phenomenon follows 24:23, in the first-person narrative of 24:30–34—"I passed by the field of the sluggard…" In both cases we must ask: Who is the "I" of these passages? If the "I" is not still Solomon, then the speaker has not introduced himself. Waltke correctly notes that, if these passages are by other writers/editors, "then the 'I' who speaks in its prologue (22:17–21) has no antecedent."[36] In a book so scrupulous about identifying sources, this would be odd.

Second, the text itself has prepared us for these subsections. Solomon himself told us at the outset that he was going to present "the words of the wise and their enigmas" (1:6). If we accept the *prima facie* impact of the words, then 22:17ff. and 24:23ff. are simply Solomon delivering on his promise. He may have adapted foreign sources, and so the style may be different, but Solomon is still the responsible author.

What of Chapters 30 and 31?[37]

In Proverbs 30:1a, we certainly meet what could be called a "poser," because it poses a puzzling question. An apparent guest author named Agur steps forward and takes the stage. His opening words are capable of two very different translations. I would represent the traditional Hebrew text thus:

> The words of Agur, son of Jakeh, the oracle,[38]
> The declaration of the man to Ithiel,
>   To Ithiel and Ucal. (DJP)[39]

---

36 Waltke, in NIDOTTE, 4:1081.

37 It strikes me as a bit of perverse "reasoning" that Brevard S. Childs sees in chapters 30 and 31's claims to diverse authorship proof that 1:1 should not be taken too seriously (*Introduction to the Old Testament as* Scripture [Philadelphia: Fortress, 1979], 547–548; cf. 551). Why not rather see them as indicative of Solomon's concern to be clear as to who is writing what?

38 Or "burden."

39 My rendering is similar to the NAS. Both renderings take וְאֻכָל לְאִיתִיאֵל לְאִיתִיאֵל as proper nouns, and render them accordingly. This translation is also seen in the texts of the KJV,

However, with a very slight re-division of the consonants and a re-pointing of the vowels, we could read the text as Waltke does:

> The sayings of Agur son of Jakeh. An oracle
>   The inspired utterance of the man to Ithiel;
>   "I am weary, O God, but I can prevail."[40]

Either way, the writer is Agur. Were one to wade through commentaries, Old Testament introductions, and Bible dictionaries and encyclopedias, he still would not know who Agur is. Gleason L. Archer, Jr., summed it up nicely: "we have no information whatever as to Jakeh's [Agur's?] historical, geographical, or even ethnic background."[41]

In the absence of knowledge, one could speculate within bounds. Was Agur a converted friend or ally of Solomon's (or of Hezekiah's)? Was he a wise prophet in the court of Solomon (or Hezekiah)? Either is possible. Nothing in the section could not have been written in the time of Solomon. Nothing demands that we see Agur as a non-Israelite. If he is speaking to Ithiel, as the standard text indicates, the latter is an Israelite name (cf. Neh. 11:7). "Agur" could be a Jewish name meaning something like "gathered" or "collected," though the name is unexampled in the OT.

What do we know that is not sheer speculation?

First, we know that what Agur wrote was an "oracle" given by inspiration of God,[42] and that it is part of God's beneficial word to us (2 Tim. 3:16).

Second, we know that Agur revered the Word of God (30:5–6), and worshiped Yahweh devoutly (cf. 30:6). He was not a pagan philosopher. Agur was a devoted Yahwist, whose reasoning was built on the only true foundation (cf. 1:7).

ASV, RSV, NIV, NKJ, and CSB.

[40] Waltke, *Proverbs,* 2:454f. Cf. also, with variations, ESV, TNIV, New American Bible, New Living Translation, New Revised Standard Version, Young's Literal Translation; also the marginal readings of CSB and NIV.

[41] Gleason L. Archer, Jr., *A Survey of Old Testament Introduction,* 3rd ed. (Chicago: Moody, 1994), 518.

[42] Although it is capable of other translations, the word rendered "burden" is הַמַּשָּׂא (*hammaśśā*), which "appears twenty-seven times, only in prophetic contexts, with the exceptions of Prov 30:1; 31:1" (Walter Kaiser, TWOT, II:602). Kaiser says that the word means "a prophetical speech of a threatening...character" (ibid.). Similarly, the word translated "declaration" is נְאֻם (*n'um*). Leonard J. Coppes notes that this "noun occurs only as a formula...declaring the divine...origin and authority of the message so described" (TWOT, II:542). The preponderance of the 360 uses of *n'um* (of which 340 are in directly prophetic books) tip us in favor of seeing this too as a claim to prophetic inspiration (cf. Coppes, ibid.).

We possess about the same amount of information concerning King Lemuel, who recorded his mother's oracle, and evidently her "dating" advice as well, in chapter 31.[43]

> The words of Lemuel *the* king,
> The burden[44] with which his mother educated him. (DJP)

Who was Lemuel? Was King Lemuel a friend of King Solomon, a saved man with the gift of prophecy whom the king met and befriended at some Near Eastern King's Convention?[45] Was he one of the kings whom Solomon won to faith in Yahweh as a result of the international reputation that Solomon enjoyed as a supremely wise man (cf. 1 Kings 4:34)? Was "Lemuel" another nickname for Solomon (cf. 2 Sam. 12:25), or perhaps an alternate name of one of the other kings of Judah (cf. 2 Kings 24:17)?[46] We simply do not know.

But once again, we do know that what Lemuel had to say was a prophetic "burden," and forms part of the prophetic Scripture which the Holy Spirit produced for our good (cf. 1 Peter 1:10–12; 2 Peter 1:19–21).

Can Proverbs 30–31 Even *Possibly* Be Part of Solomon's Original Composition?

If it were not for chapters 25–29, I would with little hesitation conclude that the chapters are simply along the lines of "guest appendices," standing among the "words of the wise" promised in 1:6. As that element closes the introductory section of 1:1–6, these two chapters close the book as a whole.

However, Proverbs 25–29 as commonly interpreted do point away from seeing the final two chapters as coming from Solomon. Unless we have mistranslated a word… which is possible.

---

[43] Archer speculates that Lemuel may have been "a North Arabian prince, living possibly in an area not far from Uz, who still cherished a faith in the one true God" (518). Archer is evidently taking *maśśā'* as a place-name (see next footnote).

[44] Translating *maśśā'* as "burden" (i.e. prophetic burden, as often). This is how the Greek translation, the Septuagint (LXX) handles it. See also NKJV, NIV, NAS. It could equally well be a place-name, Massa—possibly an Arabian tribe (and so "Lemuel, king of Massa…"; cf. Gen. 25:14; so here the NIV footnote).

[45] Solomon had concourse with Gentile dignitaries (cf. 1 Kings 4:34; 10:1–10, 24). Did he find among them two converts, uniquely gifted to add to his work on wisdom? No Scripture rules out the possibility—Job, who may well have written much or all of his book (Job 31:40), was not an Israelite. Gentiles could prophesy on occasion. Balaam certainly did (Num. 22–24).

[46] Douglas Stuart says that it means "belonging to God" (art. "Lemuel," ISBE, 3:102).

Do Proverbs 25–29 Mean That Solomon's Original Work Ended With Chapter 24?

Possibly, but not necessarily.

Proverbs 25:1 is commonly translated as in the ESV: "These also are proverbs of Solomon which the men of Hezekiah king of Judah copied." The final word, "copied," renders the Hebrew word *he'tîqû* (הֶעְתִּיקוּ). There is little variance from the ESV's rendering in all major English translations.[47] Also, the old pre-Christian Greek translation of the Old Testament renders the verb as "they wrote out for themselves" (ἐξεγράψαντο, *exegrapsanto*).

However, look up the Hebrew verb, and lexical authorities give the verbal root form a meaning such as "move."[48] The verb was often used of moving around. Abram *moved* to the hill country east of Bethel (Gen. 12:8), Isaac *moved* away from quarrelsome cattlemen (Gen. 26:22), a rock *moves* from a toppling mountain (Job 14:18),[49] God *moves* a mountain from its location (9:5), and words are *moved away* from those who have been silenced in an argument (32:15).

Why not take the word in the same sense in Proverbs 25:1? Instead of assuming the words are copied to the end of a collection, after which two other works are appended to them, why not take it that the words were *moved* by Hezekiah's men from one location to another? Perhaps *transposed* would be a better translation than *transcribed*.[50]

Specifically, what if Solomon's original work were the present Proverbs 1–24 *and* 30–31, all written and edited by Solomon? What if Hezekiah's men knew of another Solomonic collection, and were guided by the Spirit of inspiration to *move* that collection into the existing book of Proverbs, to *insert* it between chapters 24 and 30? On that supposition, where else could they have "moved" this Solomonic material? Chapters 1–24 already existed as directly Solomonic work, and chapters 30–31 were the conclusion. It might well have seemed odd to have had 24 chapters of Solomon, two chapters of guest-writers… then five more chapters of Solomon. So, naturally enough, they inserted the Solomonic material after the existing body, and before the non-Solomonic writers.

---

[47] Cf. KJV, ASV, CSB, NAS ("transcribed"), NET, NIV, NKJ, NRS, RSV, TEV.

[48] So BDB, article עָתַק, and HALOT, article עתק.

[49] Of all the examples, only this is in the Qal stem; the others are in the Hiph'il, as is Proverbs 25:1.

[50] Though not arguing the position I am proposing, Fox notes that the root of the verb means to move or to "change place," and that its use in the Hiph'il stem means "to move from one place to another" (*Proverbs*, 2:777)—which accords very nicely with the sense I'm suggesting.

This reconstruction is, of course, speculative. However, it is *far less* speculative than many other reconstructions, particularly those that involve taking 1:1 and 10:1 in other than their *prima facie* sense.

What is more, in my reconstruction, 1:1 is allowed to retain its most natural force: the whole book does from Solomon *in exactly the sense stated*. Solomon himself either directly wrote, or edited, the whole. Thus the entire book is composed of Solomon's proverbs (excepting only 25:1), and of "the words of wise men and their enigmas" (1:6b DJP). In most cases, the "wise" whose sayings Solomon quotes or adapts are anonymous; in the cases of chapters 30 and 31, they are named. In those two "guest appendices," Solomon found what he regarded as the perfect capstone to his book.

Then, some 250 years later, Hezekiah's men were in possession of a block of Solomon's proverbs. It may well be that they edited those proverbs into a meaningful structure.[51] Hezekiah's men then "moved" the collection into the existing *opus*, inserting it between chapter 24 (the last proverbs from Solomon's own hand), and chapter 30 (the first of what I am calling the "guest appendices"). Then the process, and the book of Proverbs, was complete.

Is the Numeric Value of 1:1 and 10:1 Against Your Hypothesis?

This question rests on a bit of "inside baseball" for Hebrew readers, but I think we can note it relatively painlessly.

The letters of the Hebrew alphabet came to have numeric value, with the first letter having the value "1," and so on. That being the case, it has been noted that the Hebrew letters in 10:1a (translated "Proverbs of Solomon") would add up to 375, which is the number of proverbs found in 10:1–22:16.[52] What is more, all the letters of 1:1 would add up to 900, "which is close to the 934 lines of the present book."[53]

If we accept these numeric tallies as significant, then (A) 1:1 would suggest that whoever wrote that verse had the entire book before him, including chapters 25–29, which *must* have come in well after Solomon's time; and (B) 10:1 would seem to view 10:1–22:16 as a collection distinct from 22:17–24:34.

In response, I would offer three thoughts.

---

[51] Cf. Richard J. Clifford, *Proverbs*. The Old Testament Library. (Westminster John Knox Press, 1999), 219–220; and Waltke, *Proverbs*, 1:25.

[52] Clifford, 1. Cf. Waltke (*Proverbs*, 1:9), who adds that this "is too striking to be accidental."

[53] Clifford, 1, 5.

First, assuming that the counts are significant, 1:1 may be one of the only two verses composed and added by a later editor, the second being 25:1. The men of Hezekiah may have added that one collection of proverbs to the existing work, then as it were closed the book by composing 1:1, whose tally indicates the book's completion. The very existence (as well as the original form) of 1:1 as penned by Solomon would be a matter of sheer speculation.

Second, again assuming that the counts are significant, 10:1 may well single out 10:1–22:16, leaving out 22:17–24:34 only because they are "the words of the wise" promised in 1:6.

Third, however, there is no *directly textual* warrant for taking letters to represent numbers. That is, not one word in the entire Hebrew Old Testament either requires or depicts the practice. Further, there is simply no evidence for the use of Hebrew letters as numbers earlier than the second century BC, long after the time of both Solomon and the men of Hezekiah.[54]

What is more, if we are to find numeric significance to the titles 1:1 and 10:1, then why not also 25:1, 30:1, and 31:1, as well as the supposed subtitles of 22:17 and 24:23? I do not find the same authors who attribute import to the former consonants going on to argue for a hidden meaning in the latter.

While the correspondence between the numeric values of 1:1 and 10:1 is admittedly striking, it would be a poor basis for turning from a likelier plain reading of the semantic (rather than numeric) value of the words themselves. In other words, it strikes me as a poor deal to trade what the words actually say up-front for what they might dubiously hint at under the surface—particularly when the up-front sense makes perfectly good sense.

Conclusion as to 1:1

It is most natural to see 1:1 as giving the title and main author of the entire book: "Proverbs of Solomon, son of David, king of Israel." Solomon wrote (or edited) all of the proverbs from chapters 1–24, and edited chapters 30–31. Hezekiah's men inserted five more chapters of Solomon's proverbs between chapters 24 and 30.

Thus, these words form a preface for the book itself. They are followed immediately by an introduction (vv. 2–6), the foundational truth for the whole (1:7),

---

54 Waltke, *Proverbs*, 1:9–10. Cf. John J. Davis, "Biblical Numerics," *Grace Theological Journal*, Volume 5. Grace Seminary, 1984; 2002, 31.

and a series of proverbial poems or discourses,[55] written by Solomon (chapters 1–9).

Then the terse subtitle of 10:1 ("Proverbs of Solomon...") serves to give us a moment to shift literary gears for the main body of the book. We can thus pause to re-adjust our minds from reading the extended discourses of chapters 1–9, to reading the pithy, pointed two-liners which populate the following chapters.[56]

Gains

What does this understanding gain us? Let me just suggest four specifics:

1. In my opinion, it accords best with the kind of confidence in the canonical text that Jesus showed and taught.

2. It allows us to "place" Proverbs in a particular chronological point in the unfolding of revelation.

3. It enables us to identify which Scriptures would be informing Solomon's own understanding, giving us an interpretive "grid" to understand the intent of the author.

4. It gives us the ability to see what history or occurrences may have been in Solomon's mind, which he then compressed into proverbs.

None of these should be brushed by lightly. Treating Proverbs' own attributions will *ground* the interpreter in history and reality; each step away from them is a step into untethered speculation. In my 1983 thesis, I lamented that critical scholars do "not display an adequately self-critical consciousness of the veritable Fantasy Island onto which one of necessity steps when one casts aside the textual data, and begins to reconstruct history *de novo*."[57] Twenty-eight years later, James Hamilton notes the ongoing baleful effects of the same tendency.[58]

---

[55] Harrison nicely calls them "didactic poems" (1011).

[56] We can observe a similar phenomenon in 22:17–21. The preceding chapters (10:1–22:16) had featured "two-liners" almost exclusively. Now Solomon intends to bring out a series of four-liners and six-liners, as well as other variations. So the king stops the procession for a moment with the literary interlude of 22:17–21, before bringing out his collection of longer proverbs. Yet, as we noted, this pause does not signal a change in authorship; it is still "*my* knowledge" (v. 17), and "*I* have made them known to you [singular]" (v. 19), and "*I*" have "written for you [singular] thirty sayings" (v. 20).

[57] Daniel J. Phillips, *The Sovereignty of Yahweh in the Book of Proverbs: an Exercise in Theological Exegesis* (Master of Divinity thesis, Talbot Theological Seminary, May 1983), 20.

[58] Hamilton remarks that "the dichotomizing tendency of critical scholarship works like a reverse magnetic force, preventing" connections to the OT text itself, "while the broader context of ancient Near Eastern parallels can easily distract interpreters from the nearer context of the Old Testament canon" (290).

By contrast, when we credit the text, we anchor our thinking in the reality of Biblical history, and vistas of information and verification open up to us.

The rest of our studies provided a number of opportunities for me to demonstrate these gains.[59]

---

[59] For instance, see the study of Proverbs 22:4 in Chapter 3.

Words Related to Teaching in Proverbs

The whole of the Old Testament is concerned with the impartation of information. As the writer to the Hebrews masterfully summarizes the sweep of redemptive history, "…God spoke of old in many portions and in many manners to the fathers in the prophets" (Heb. 1:1 DJP). When He *spoke*, God imparted information — information about Himself, about man, about the world, and about His redemptive purposes and will. The *fathers* received that revelation, mediated through the *prophets* both *in many portions* (Πολυμερῶς) and *in many manners* (πολυτρόπως). The *fathers* then were responsible for transmitting that revelation to successive generations.

It is that transmission that is expressed by the major Hebrew terms for teaching and learning, many of which we encounter in Proverbs. This is a study of two major terms against their larger Biblical background.

An exhaustive study of every last Hebrew lexeme covering the syntactical range of teaching and learning would be exhausting and massive indeed. We will study only the terms יסר (*ysr*), and ירה (*yrh*). Verbal forms will be treated separately from their related noun forms.

יסר (*ysr*, Discipline, Chasten, Admonish)[1]

Uses of the verb

This verbal root occurs some forty-two times in the Old Testament, the *Tôrâ* (commonly spelled Torah). Beyond that observation, the subdivisions of its use seem to vary among authorities. According to Merrill, 74 percent of the instances are in the Pi'el stem.[2]

As to distribution, Merrill[3] finds the preponderance in poetic literature (fifteen occurrences, six in Wisdom books and nine in Psalms). The Prophets follow with thirteen instances, of which Jeremiah's seven constitute the lion's share. The remaining eight are found in the Pentateuch (five in Deuteronomy, three in Leviticus).

The semantic range includes *discipline, chasten, admonish,*[4] *chastise.*[5] The English Standard Version renders it "whip" in Deuteronomy 22:18,[6] a sense which seems to be echoed also in 1 Kings 12:11 and 14. There we find "My father disciplined you with whips" (ESV).[7] Other renderings in the ESV include "direct" (1 Chron. 15:22; NAS has "gave instruction"), "instructed" (Job 4:3), "be warned" (Psa. 2:10), "corrects" (Prov. 9:7), "take warning" (Ezek. 23:48), and "trained" (Hos. 7:15).

The parallelism in Proverbs 9:7 is instructive as to the impact of the verb: "Whoever corrects a scoffer gets himself abuse, and he who reproves a wicked man incurs injury." Here, the ESV renders the Qal participle יֹסֵר as "corrects," which the second stich parallels with מוֹכִיחַ, "reproves." Since no specific actor is identified, the statement is designedly general. The parallel participle of יכח

---

[1] This appendix is geared more to the student of the Hebrew Old Testament.

[2] Merrill identifies thirty-three Pi'el instances, plus two in Qal, five in Niphal, and one each in Nithpa'el and Hiph'il (E. H. Merrill, "יסר," in NIDOTTE, 2:479). However my own search, using BibleWorks software (version 6), yielded different results. I find five in the Qal (1 Chron. 15:22; Psa. 94:10; Prov. 9:7; and Hos. 10:10), five in Niph'al, thirty-one in the Pi'el, one in Nithpa'el, and one in Hiph'il. Similar results to mine are seen in BDB (article יסר). I do not know how to account for the variation.

[3] Merrill, NIDOTTE, 2:479.

[4] BDB, article יסַר.

[5] Lawrence O. Richards, *Expository Dictionary of Bible Words* (Grand Rapids: Zondervan, 1985; used by permission), 589.

[6] The footnote reads "Or *discipline.*"

[7] This is seen also in the parallel record of 2 Chronicles 12:11 and 14.

("reproves") indicates a corrective and specifically fault-finding communication, not merely colorless impartation of information; and any wise man could do it.

This parallel adds to our understanding of יסר. The verb "specifically relates not to formal education but to the instilling of values and norms of conduct by verbal (hortatory) means or, after the fact, by rebuke or even physical chastisement."[8] It brings home the content of the lesson in a forceful manner, particularly if there is initial resistance.

Who Is It Who Does the Disciplining/Chastening/Reproving?

Yahweh

By far, the preponderance of uses depict Yahweh as doling out the discipline, warning, instruction. Of the forty-two occurrences of the lemma, twenty-two have Yahweh as the actor, explicitly so in the majority of cases.[9] Most of these deal with Yahweh disciplining, or instructing, or warning the nation of Israel.[10] He does this verbally, in direct revelation, by speaking to them in His theophany at Mount Sinai (Deut. 4:36); or again verbally but by the mediated revelation of His *Tôrâ*. We see this latter sense, for instance, in Psalm 94:12, where the man is blessed whom Yahweh "disciplines" (אֲשֶׁר־תְּיַסְּרֶנּוּ) and "teaches" (תְלַמְּדֶנּוּ) out of His law.

Additionally, Yahweh disciplines providentially, through the imposition of covenantal disciplines and calamities (Lev. 26:18, 23, 28). In this, Israel is to know that "as a man disciplines his son, the LORD your God disciplines you" (Deut. 8:5). Even here, though, the framework for interpreting this providential discipline had already been laid down in the Law (cf., again, Lev. 26).

Providential discipline is seen again in Psalm 39:11, "When you discipline [יִסַּרְתָּ] a man with rebukes for sin, you consume like a moth what is dear to him; surely all mankind is a mere breath! Selah." In the context of the psalm,

---

8   Merrill, NIDOTTE, 2:479.

9   For instance, "Know then in your heart that, as a man disciplines (יְיַסֵּר) his son, the LORD your God disciplines you (מְיַסְּרֶךָ)" (Deut. 8:5), is explicit. By contrast, in Psalm 2:10 ("Now therefore, O kings, be wise; be warned [הִוָּסְרוּ], O rulers of the earth"), Yahweh is the implied Actor.

10   Once the object of Yahweh's יסר is said to be the nations: Psalm 94:10a — "He who disciplines [הֲיֹסֵר] the nations, does he not rebuke?" In struggling to catch the sense of this, the translations vary rather broadly. The LXX sticks with its customary use of *paideuō* (ὁ παιδεύων ἔθνη); the NAS has "chastens," the CSB has "instructs."

David in his sin has suffered under the hand of God, with God's plagues or strokes on him (v. 10). He prays for relief (vv. 12, 13).

David is echoed by the anonymous writer of Psalm 118:18, "The LORD has disciplined me severely [יַסֹּר יִסְּרַנִּי יָּהּ], but he has not given me over to death." Later Jeremiah, speaking either in his own person or as representing Israel, prays for God to moderate His discipline so as not to be overly severe (10:24—"Correct me [יַסְּרֵנִי], O LORD, but in justice; not in your anger, lest you bring me to nothing").

The end or goal of this disciplinary instruction is the restoration of God's people. God urges Israel to accept His יסר, so that He need not abandon them (Jer. 6:8). Indeed, Ephraim cries out, "You have disciplined me, and I was disciplined, like an untrained calf; bring me back that I may be restored, for you are the LORD my God" (Jer. 31:18b). Similarly Yahweh had earlier warned or instructed (וְיִסְּרֵנִי) Isaiah not to join the people in rebellion (Isa. 8:11). Merrill rightly observes that "Punishment is in this sense disciplinary, restorative, and purifying in its intents and results."[11]

Parents

The second-most frequent category is parental disciplinary instruction, found in five verses: Deuteronomy 8:5,[12] 21:18; Proverbs 19:18; 29:17; and 31:1. When the first cited verse states, "Know then in your heart that, as a man disciplines his son, the LORD your God disciplines you," the reader perhaps is first struck by the parental role Yahweh fulfills. At the same time, it must be noted that the text takes for granted that a father יְיַסֵּר—chastens, instructs, disciplines — his child. Instructive discipline is the proper province of a father. In this way, that fatherly role itself is a shadow of the Heavenly Father's disciplinary care of His children.

As Yahweh's discipline of the nation is restorative in intent, so is the father's discipline of his child. It is assumed that "Folly is bound up in the heart of a child"; this is why "the rod of discipline [מוּסָר, noun built from stem יסר]" is required to drive "it far from him" (Prov. 22:15). Hence, in every child there will be a resistance requiring the application of disciplinary instruction. Merely suggesting, explaining, opining, or setting a good example will not suffice.

---

[11] Merrill, NIDOTTE, 2:480.

[12] This verse is placed both in the Yahweh and parental categories, because it conceptually overlaps.

Clearly the intent of this parental instruction is the formation of the children's character. This is seen in Deuteronomy 21:18, which dictates that "If a man has a stubborn and rebellious son who will not obey the voice of his father or the voice of his mother, and, though they discipline [וְיִסְּרוּ] him, will not listen to them," the son is to be put to death (vv. 19-21). The יֹסֵר evidently was the son's opportunity to repent and reform. It would have put him on the right path, if he had heard/obeyed (יִשְׁמַע). Since he did not receive the discipline, his life was forfeited.

Proverbs reinforces this same impression and theme. Twice the parent is urged to discipline/chasten/instruct his son, once in the hopes of delivering him from death (19:18), and once in the hopes of producing a child who is a delight to the parent's heart (29:17). And finally we have the oracular instruction of King Lemuel's mother, with which she trained him (יִסְּרַתּוּ; 31:1).

Christian education authority Lawrence O. Richards well sums up the import of the word:

> *Yāsar* means "to discipline" or "to chastise." It indicates a word or act of correction that results in the education of a learner. The beneficial outcome marks such instruction as loving.[13]

These two themes — the educational discipline performed by Yahweh and the educational discipline performed by parents — well intersect in the ancient world. This will be developed further after the discussion of the noun *mûsār*.

מוּסָר (*mûsār*, Discipline, Correction, Instruction)

The noun מוּסָר occurs fifty-four times in the Old Testament.[14] Thirty-seven of these occurrences are in the Wisdom/Poetic Literature,[15] of which thirty (56%) are in Proverbs alone. One instance is found in Deuteronomy (11:2), and sixteen in the prophets: eight in Jeremiah, four in Isaiah, twice in Zephaniah, and once each in Ezekiel and Hosea.

---

13 Lawrence O. Richards, "Teaching/Learning," in *Expository Dictionary of Bible Words* (Grand Rapids: Zondervan, 1985; used by permission), 589.

14 Job (5x), Psalms (2x), Proverbs (30x). This count includes all occurrences of the lemma, four of which may be of a homograph meaning "bonds" (Job 12:18; Psa. 116:16; Isa. 28:22; 52:2); hence, Merrill finds fifty occurrences (NIDOTTE, 2:480).

15 Merrill says thirty-five (NIDOTTE, 2:481).

The noun "has to do with teaching/learning by exhortation and example, with warning as to the consequences of disobedience, and with the application of penalty following failure to adhere."[16] The semantic range includes discipline, chastisement, chastening, punishment. Lemaire suggests that "education" might be the way to translate *mûsār*.[17]

Who Doles Out the מוּסָר?

I find that eighteen times the discipline is clearly dealt out by Yahweh;[18] ten times it clearly issues from one or both parents — all in Proverbs.[19] In a number of verses, the source of the discipline is not stated; arguably it could either be Yahweh, parents, or Yahweh through one or both parents.[20] In still other verses, other persons impose the discipline.[21]

The *means* by which this education is enforced or applied varies. In a number of passages, it is *providential life-situations* that should discipline, or educate. For instance, in Isaiah 26 one of the themes is God's judgments on the nation (cf. vv. 5, 8-11, 14). The prophet says, "when your judgments are in the earth, the inhabitants of the world learn righteousness" (v. 9b). And so against this background comes verse 16: "O Lord, in distress they sought you; they poured out a whispered prayer when your discipline (מוּסָרְךָ) was upon them." That "discipline," then, was the providential imposition of God's judgments on them, intended to teach them and turn them.

Jeremiah sounds this note repeatedly. He quotes Yahweh as saying, "In vain have I struck your children; they took no correction [מוּסָר]; your own sword devoured your prophets like a ravening lion" (2:30). In 5:3, he himself says to Yahweh, "O Lord, do not your eyes look for truth? You have struck them down, but they felt no anguish; you have consumed them, but they refused to take correction [מוּסָר]. They have made their faces harder than rock; they have

---

[16] Merrill, NIDOTTE, 2:480-481.

[17] André Lemaire, "Education (Israel)," in *The Anchor Bible Dictionary*, ed. David Noel Freedman (New York: Doubleday, 1992), 2:305. Lemaire notes that the LXX regularly renders *mûsār* by *paideia* (ibid.).

[18] Deuteronomy 11:2; Job 5:17; 33:16; 36:10; Psalm 50:17; Proverbs 3:11; Isaiah 26:16; 53:5; Jeremiah 2:30; 5:3; 7:28; 17:23; 32:33; 35:13; Ezekiel 5:15; Hosea 5:2; Zephaniah 3:2, 7.

[19] Proverbs 1:8; 4:1; 6:23; 8:10; 13:1, 24; 15:5; 19:27; 22:15; 23:13.

[20] Cf. e.g., Proverbs 1:2, 3, 7; 4:13; 5:23; 7:22; 8:33; 10:17; 12:1; 13:18; 15:10, 32; 19:20, etc.

[21] Job 20:3; Proverbs 5:12; Jeremiah 30:14.

refused to repent." Their failure to accept corrected from this providential instruction became a damning indictment (7:28; 17:23; 32:33; cf. Zeph. 3:2, 7).

But the needed education also took *verbal* form. Children are appealed to thus: "Hear, my son, your father's instruction [מוּסַר], and forsake not your mother's teaching" (Prov. 1:8). This note is sounded again and again, both in direct appeal and in pronouncements of blessing on those who do hear, and of warnings to those who do not.[22] Children were urged to value and long for this disciplinary education, valuing it more than silver (8:10).

But even parents were not to rely on verbal warnings and instruction alone in imparting מוּסָר. As noted earlier, we read in Proverbs 22:15 that "Folly is bound up in the heart of a child, but the rod of discipline (מוּסָר) drives it far from him." A more idiomatic rendering of "rod of discipline" might be "disciplinary rod," or "rod that imparts discipline."

McKane's comments are apposite:

> There is more to education than making manifest what is already there or hastening the maturity of the seed which already contains all the possibilities of growth and nothing that would hinder it. The educator's task is both to tear down and to build up; he has to eradicate as well as to implant. There are elements of chaos in the mind of the youth and order has to be restored; his innate tendency is towards folly rather than wisdom, and only the šēbeṭ mûsär will put a distance between him and folly. This is not just a reference to corporal punishment, though it includes this. It is an indication of a theory of education which comes down strongly on the side of discipline, but the most important application of this is not corporal punishment. It is rather the emphasis on the intellectual authority of the teacher and the duty of unbroken attentiveness and unquestioning acceptance which is laid upon the pupil.[23]

It was the parents' God-given duty to be consistent and diligent in imposing מוּסָר on their children. Yahweh states categorically, through Solomon, that every father who loves his children will seek them early with discipline (שִׁחֲרוֹ מוּסָר;

---

[22] See Proverbs 4:1; 8:10; 13:1; 15:5; 19:27, etc.

[23] William McKane, *Proverbs: a New Approach*, The Old Testament Library (Philadelphia: Westminster, 1977).

Prov. 13:24). He is to regard it as a debt he owes his child, which he must not withhold from him (אַל־תִּמְנַע מִנַּעַר מוּסָר; 23:13). [24] The parental application of educational discipline is not one option among many, though it itself may be multiform. It is essential.

These texts have been examined from the perspective that the Hebrew terms for "father" and "son" in Proverbs retain their primary referents in the context of a family. This view is not universally held among scholars. As background, A. W. Morton first lays a comprehensive view of education in the ancient Near East thus:

> Educational systems had evolved as early as the 3rd millennium B.C.
> There are a number of school texts dating from about 2,500 B.C.
> From these documents we learn of numerous schools for scribes
> in ancient Sumer. In these schools literary works were copied and
> studied. The study was connected with the training for the needs
> of the Temple, palace courts and the administration of the empire.
> Education of this kind was voluntary and costly, and pupils were
> drawn from the upper class. Subjects studied were botany, zoology,
> geology, geography, mathematics, languages and other cultural
> studies. The schools were staffed by a professor and his assistants
> who gave regular classroom tuition. A teacher was referred to as
> "father" and he referred to his pupils as "sons."[25]

Then, on this basis, Morton asserts that the reader should "notice contact with the background of the ancient world in the reference to teachers as 'father' and the pupil as 'my son' (Prov 2:1, etc.)."[26]

I disagree with this assumption. *First,* while these are certainly various possible constructions to place on the words, they are by no means necessary, nor universally accepted. It is true that "father" can mean "teacher," and "son" can mean "student" (as is the probable meaning of the phrase "the sons of the

---

[24] Cf. the use of מנע in Proverbs 3:27 and 11:26.

[25] A. W. Morton, "Education in Biblical Times," ZPEB, 2:206-223.

[26] Ibid., 2:207. R. Alan Culpepper's position is similar, though it reveals a more direct departure from any concept of the authority of the text; he sees Proverbs 1:2-4 as reflecting the Sumerian sort of structure, dates it in the 4th or 3rd century BC, and casts all references to father and son into the supposed classroom milieu (R. Alan Culpepper, "Education," ISBE, 2:24).

prophets," as in 1 Kings 20:35, etc.). However, commonly "father" simply means "father," and "son" simply means "son."

This leads one to ask, *second*, what term might Solomon have better chosen if he had had literal parent and child in mind? There were other terms for teacher and pupil, and Solomon could have used them. Unless there is a compelling reason, we are not inclined to abandon the primary reference of the terms to the context of the family.

Third and perhaps most tellingly: if the "father" is the teacher, then what is the "mother" (1:8; 6:20, etc.)?

My position on this discipline and instruction of a son by his father is better represented in the words of J. L. Kelso, who observed,

> Ancient Jewish education was entirely religious education. In OT times there was no textbook except the Scriptures, and all education consisted of the reading and the study of them. There was no recognized office of teacher with a definite title. For the Jew, the real center of education was the home, and the responsibility of educating the child was laid on the parents (Deut 4:9, 10; 6:7, 20-25; 11:19; 32:46).[27]

Will Discipline Always Be Effective?

The usage reveals that the answer to this question is an emphatic "no." Eli may have failed his sons by withholding needed rebuke (כהה) from them (1 Sam. 3:13), but even a perfect parent may perfectly administer מוּסָר without the desired effect. This can be stated categorically. Yahweh Himself — the perfect Father — indeed disciplined His son Israel, yet Israel did not profit by it as they should have (cf. Jer. 7:28; 17:23; 32:33; Zeph. 3:2, 7).

What is the *sine qua non* of disciplinary education on the side of the recipient, the essential element without which it will be ineffective? He must acquire מוּסָר with the right attitude and eagerness, and make it his own. The student must *accept*, *keep hold* of, *buy, love, apply* his *heart* to, *love, purchase, take* or *receive* the discipline. He must *consider* it. One must not *belittle* it, *spurn* it, *hate* it, or *refuse* it.[28]

---

[27] J. L. Kelso, "Teacher," ZPEB, 5:606.

[28] Cf. "Instruction", in *Nelson's Expository Dictionary of the Old Testament*, eds. Merrill Unger and William White, Jr. (Nasville: Nelson, 1980), 201. Cf. also M. Sæbø, article יסר, in TLOT, 550.

If we were to study this out at length, we would see that *mûsār* must not be rejected (Job 5:17; Prov. 3:11), hated (Psa. 50:17; Prov. 5:12), belittled (Prov. 1:7; 3:11), neglected (Prov. 8:33), ignored (Prov. 13:18; 15:32), or spurned (Prov. 15:5). Instead, *mûsār* must be known (Prov. 1:2), received (Prov. 1:3; 8:10; 24:32; Jer. 2:30; 5:3; 7:28; 32:33; 35:13; Zeph. 3:2, 7), heard (Prov. 1:8; 4:1; 8:33; 13:1), kept hold of and guarded (Prov. 4:13), kept (Prov. 10:17), loved (Prov. 12:1), accepted (Prov. 19:20), made an object of an applied mind (Prov. 23:12), and purchased (Prov. 23:23).

As observed above, we see in these passages both the discipline of children by parents, and the discipline of the nation of Israel by Yahweh. These themes intersect in the ancient world. Of the occurrences of the verb, Merrill says that it is executed by Yahweh and is "usually of his own people and in the framework of covenant violation (Lev. 26:18, 28: Pss. 6:1; 38:1[2]; 39:11[12]; 94:10; 118:18; Hos. 10:10)."[29]

Further developing this, it has often been observed that the structure of Deuteronomy itself reflects the form of an ancient Near East suzerain/vassal treaty. In this vein, Paul Gilchrist makes this observation:

> The ancient treaties often refer to the suzerain king as a father and to the vassal as his son (cf. Mccarthy, CBQ 27: 144-47). In Moses' covenant hymn we read that Yahweh is referred to as Father (Deut 32:6; cf. Deut 1:31; Isa 1:2) of the covenant people (although Exo 4:22; Deut 1:31 teach the same concept). Hence, the theological basis for an earthly father's discipline over his son is in the covenant. He bears the image of his covenant Lord, and as such stands in parallel relationship over his children hastening, correcting, instructing, providing – which are expressions of an interpersonal relationship of love. So also the thirty usages in Prov and elsewhere, e.g. Prov 3:11-12 where *mûsār* and *tōkaḥat* "reproof, correction" are said to come from Yahweh "for whom the Lord loves ('āhab) he reproves (yākaḥ), even as a father the son in whom he delights." Hence, discipline gives assurance of sonship, for *mûsār* primarily points to a God-centered way of life, and only secondarily to ethical behavior. Proverbs 1:7 couples it with the "fear of Yahweh,"

---

[29] Merrill, NIDOTTE, 2:480.

and Prov 1:8 with *tôrâ* "instruction, teaching." Hence, also the pricelessness of *mûsār* (Prov 8:10) and the reason why fools despise it (Prov 15:5, 32). Proverbs and other wisdom literature speak of discipline with emphasis on instruction. It is tempting to see that the seemingly disparate notions of correction and instruction converge beautifully only in the covenant.[30]

ירה (*yrh*, Throw; Teach) and תורה (*twrh*, Law, Instruction)

In this section we shall consider together the verb ירה and its derivative noun תורה.

The verb *yārâ* is found forty-eight times in the Old Testament, of which eighteen times are in poetry and wisdom literature.[31] It means fundamentally to throw, to cast, to shoot (as of shooting arrows).[32] It then also has the meaning of pointing out, showing, as in Genesis 46:28—"He had sent Judah ahead of him to Joseph to show the way [לְהוֹרֹת] before him in Goshen, and they came into the land of Goshen."

Thence comes the idea of pointing out by way of teaching, as in Exodus 35:34, of Bezalel: "And he has inspired him to teach [וּלְהוֹרֹת נָתַן בְּלִבּוֹ], both him and Oholiab the son of Ahisamach of the tribe of Dan." As Merrill rightly observes even of the verb's description of teaching, "The semantic range is also broad, the general idea of teaching finding specific application in the mundane and the sacred worlds and with both divine and human subjects."[33]

What line of semantic development led (presumably) from "throw" to "teach"?[34] Unger and White think it developed from throwing or pointing to calling attention to facts or information.[35] Jefford adds that "The hiphil of *yārâ*

---

[30] Paul R. Gilchrist, "מוּסָר, יִסֹּר, יָסַר," in TWOT, 1:387.

[31] E. H. Merrill, "ירה," NIDOTTE, 2:538.

[32] Cf. BDB, article יָרָה.

[33] Merrill, NIDOTTE, 2:538

[34] Enns observes, "It is a debated point whether *tôrâ* is derived from *yrh* I, throw, shoot… or *yrh* III, instruct, teach… The latter appears more likely, although the matter is inconclusive" (Peter Enns, "Law of God," in NIDOTTE, 4:893).

[35] Merrill Unger and William White, Jr., "Teach," in *Nelson's Expository Dictionary of the Old Testament* (Nashville: Nelson, 1980), 420. Alternately, it may be a question of identical roots with different meanings (G. Liedke/C. Petersen, article תּוֹרָה, in TLOT, 1415; and Merrill, article יָרָה, in NIDOTTE, 2:537).

('throw,' 'shoot') focuses upon 'direction' in the course of instruction."[36]

The connection seems to be what Hartley calls "the strong sense of control by the subject."[37] He elaborates:

Lots were cast in regards to dividing the land among the various tribes (Josh 18:6). God cast the Egyptian army into the Red Sea (Exo 15:4; cf. Job 30:19). With stones it has the idea of placing them in a certain place; God laid the cornerstone of the world (Job 38:6) and Laban set up a heap of stones and a pillar as a witness between Jacob and himself to their covenant of peace (Gen 31:51).[38]

From the root ירה comes the noun תורה, which is found throughout the Old Testament. I find it in 29 of the 39 books of the Old Testament, according to the English Canon.[39] Enns details the distribution thus: fifty-four times in the Pentateuch (of which thirty-six are in Leviticus and Deuteronomy); sixty-three times in the historical books (twenty in Nehemiah alone); thirty-six times in Psalms (of which twenty-four are in Psa. 119); fourteen times in Wisdom Literature (thirteen of which are Proverbs); forty-six times in Prophetic Literature.[40]

The use of this term is far broader than what we would assume from the English word "law." True, many of the occurrences apply to "law" proper, in the sense of ritual and civil laws, dealing with sacrifices and the conduct of the life of the nation. But a great many uses are far different.

This is true of the majority of occurrences in Proverbs, the inspired textbook for the home school. Of the thirteen occurrences of the word therein, eight refer to the instruction of parents or other sage human sources (1:8; 3:1; 4:2; 6:20, 23; 7:2; 13:14; 31:26). The remaining five occurrences, arguably alluding to the law of God, are found in four verses (28:4, 7, 9; 29:18).

Lingering on the passages in Proverbs, we see that it is the parents who pass on the *tôrâ* to their children. The father calls on the son to hear and accept his *tôrâ* in 3:1; 4:2; 6:3; and 7:2. The mother as well is mentioned as a source of *tôrâ*, in 1:8; 6:20, and the excellent woman/wife of 31:26. As the tôrâ of Yahweh is to rule in the nation, the tôrâ of the parents is to rule subsidiarily in their home, and in their children's hearts.

---

[36] C. N. Jefford, "Teach," ISBE, 4:745.

[37] John E. Hartley, "תּוֹרָה, מוֹרֶה, מוֹרָה, יוֹרֶה, ירה," in TWOT, 1:403.

[38] Ibid.

[39] It is found in all books except Judges, Ruth, 1 Samuel, Esther, Ecclesiastes, Song of Solomon, Joel, Obadiah, Jonah, and Nahum.

[40] Peter Enns, "Law of God," in NIDOTTE, 4:893. (I have corrected his assignment of twelve

Clearly none of these Proverbs passages deals with sacrifices or ritual per se, in spite of what the English-text reader might assume for "law." Rather, we can glean from the book of Proverbs itself what the subjects of this parental *tôrâ* would include. They would range as broadly as the selection of friends (Prov. 1:10ff; 13:24), true femininity (12:4; 14:1; 31:10ff.), the value of hard work (18:9; 22:9), use of time (12:11), and a wide host of other details of life.

Gutbrod is right: "Not merely the cultus [worshiping community] but the whole of life stands under this Law. The claim of this God to dominion leaves no neutral zone."[41] It was authoritative instruction[42] that was meant to bring God's own perspective to bear on daily living.[43]

This process of transmission is depicted memorably in Psalm 78. In the first verse, Asaph issues this call: "Give ear, O my people, to my teaching [my *tôrâ*, תּוֹרָתִי]; incline your ears to the words of my mouth!" Thus, the entire psalm is characterized as תּוֹרָה, directive instruction. He goes on to locate his own transmission of *tôrâ* in a line stretching back as far as his fathers, coming down the generations through him, and continuing on to his generation's children (vv. 3-4).

Then comes this crucial passage:

> [Yahweh] established a testimony in Jacob and appointed a law [שָׂם וְתוֹרָה] in Israel, which he commanded our fathers to teach to their children, [6] that the next generation might know them, the children yet unborn, and arise and tell them to their children, [7] so that they should set their hope in God and not forget the works of God, but keep his commandments; [8] and that they should not be like their fathers, a stubborn and rebellious generation, a generation whose heart was not steadfast, whose spirit was not faithful to God. (vv. 5-8)

Yahweh appointed, set, a *tôrâ* in Israel; and He commanded the fathers to transmit that *tôrâ* to their children, who in turn would transmit it from generation

---

to Proverbs to the actual count, thirteen.)

[41] Walter Gutbrod, "The Law in the Old Testament," in TDNT, IV:1037.

[42] Lemaire notes that the main idea of *tôrâ* is "instruction," in spite of its frequently being translated by "law" (André Lemaire, "Education [Israel]," in *The Anchor Bible Dictionary*, ed. David Noel Freedman [New York: Doubleday, 1992], 2:305).

[43] "Essentially torah means 'teaching,' or 'instruction,' focusing on how one should conduct oneself in all of life's situations" (Lawrence O. Richards, "Teaching/Learning," in *Expository Dictionary of Bible Words* [Grand Rapids: Zondervan, 1985; used by permission], 589).

to generation. The effect of this trans-generational propagation of the *tôrâ* would result in the children setting their hope in God, remembering His works, keeping His commandments, and avoiding the sinful errors of the past generations (vv. 7, 8). This is how crucial the teaching responsibility of the parents would be to the very health and life of the nation of Israel.

The priestly office was to be another transmitter of *tôrâ*. The root occurs in two forms in 2 Chronicles 15:3, in the prophecy of Azariah: "For a long time Israel was without the true God, and without a teaching priest [כֹּהֵן מוֹרֶה] and without law [תּוֹרָה]." The Hiph'il participle מוֹרֶה, from ירה, is used adjectivally to characterize the kind of priest Israel had long lacked: a *teaching* priest. This is followed by the noun תּוֹרָה, the authoritative, divine instruction which the nation had long lacked.

Ezra appears in Israel's history as just such a *tôrâ*-loving and *tôrâ*-teaching priest. We read first that he is "a scribe skilled [מָהִיר, fast, adept] in the Law [תּוֹרָה] of Moses that the LORD the God of Israel had given" (Ezra 7:6). Then we find that he "had set his heart to study [לִדְרוֹשׁ, to seek] the Law of the LORD [אֶת־תּוֹרַת יְהוָה], and to do it and to teach [not ירה in this case, but לְלַמֵּד] his statutes and rules in Israel" (v. 10).

Finally in this connection, we have the fourfold use of תּוֹרָה in the four verses of Malachi 2:6-9, where Yahweh says speaks of the Levitical priesthood under the emblem of Levi:

> "True instruction [תּוֹרַת אֱמֶת] was in his mouth, and no wrong was found on his lips. He walked with me in peace and uprightness, and he turned many from iniquity. [7] For the lips of a priest should guard knowledge, and people should seek instruction [וְתוֹרָה יְבַקְשׁוּ] from his mouth, for he is the messenger of the LORD of hosts. [8] But you have turned aside from the way. You have caused many to stumble by your instruction [בַּתּוֹרָה]. You have corrupted the covenant of Levi, says the LORD of hosts, [9] and so I make you despised and abased before all the people, inasmuch as you do not keep my ways but show partiality in your instruction [בַּתּוֹרָה]."

Therefore, the priestly office was *meant* to be a reliable source of teaching, instruction, direction. It was to their shame, and Israel's lasting harm, that they were unfaithful in the discharging of this stewardship.

Conclusions and Application

We have studied the major Hebrew terms used in Proverbs for studying and learning. Whether the semantic focus is the impartation of information, or training, or the application of the pressure of discipline to drive the lesson home, the focus is always the same: the mind and word of God.

In the uses of יסר, we saw that instruction is to be *determined* and *effect-oriented*. When the instruction is based on the Word of God, the lessons are to be pressed home. God does so providentially, impressing His *mûsār* on the human soul by various means. Parents should use the rod in its various forms as needed, to supplement verbal instruction and impress the lessons they are teaching (Prov. 22:15).

But no matter how great the disciplinary instruction of parents or other teachers, it will not produce the slightest benefit in students who do not *accept* the discipline, take it to heart, personalize it and profit by it. Students must be taught to learn. They must be taught that the responsibility does not end with the teacher/parent's delivery of the lesson. The student himself must hear, receive, love, hold fast, personalize disciplinary instruction (Prov. 12:1; 13:1; Jer. 7:28; 17:23; 32:33).

The uses of ירה, and its corresponding noun תורה, point up the *directive* nature of instruction. The teacher must point out the right way authoritatively by his instruction, must provide the teaching that gives guidance and direction. The teaching must not be vague and merely theoretical, but detailed enough to provide real help and guidance.

In sum, then, God reaches out to teach His people His Word, using parents, prophets, priests and people in general. Whether in our homes or our institutions, this should be our focus as well. The great Reformer, Martin Luther, expressed a fear that proved prophetic: "I greatly fear that the universities are wide gates of hell, if they do not diligently teach the Holy Scriptures and impress them on the youth."[44]

So it has proven, to our day. God grant that the status quo will be changed, starting at home and in church, as more parents, teachers and pastors apply the discipline, direction, instruction, and training of God's Word.

---

[44] Martin Luther, "An Open Letter to the Christian Nobility of the German Nation concerning the Reform of the Christian Estate" (1520), from *Three Treatises* (Muhlenberg: 1960), 100; quoted by David J. Engelsma, *Reformed Education* (Grandville: Reformed Free Publishing Association, 2000), 21.

Proverbs 22:6 — Promise...or Threat?

The Tradition

In Chapter 8, I called Proverbs 22:6 a "warning." When I wrote that, in my mind I could hear some readers bursting out—

> "'Warning'? But...I love that verse! It's a precious promise. It means that, if I teach my child about God, and then he strays from God the moment he has the choice, he's still saved anyway, and will eventually come back to God. I even told little Bucky that. Are you saying that I was wrong?"

If that is your understanding of this verse, hang on to your hat. This, in my judgment, is one of the Bible's most frequently misused (and mistranslated) verses. But it is an important verse, given how deeply parents are invested in their children.

Hildebrandt nailed it: "This proverb has brought encouragement, hope, anxiety and guilt to countless parents who have faced the uncertainty and confusion of child-rearing."[1] The question I mean to pose and answer is: Is this verse a promise, or a warning?

Let us survey an array of translations of Proverbs 22:6—

> Train up a child in the way he should go;
>   and when he is old, he will not depart from it. (KJV)[2]

> Train children in the right way,
>   and when old, they will not stray. (NRSV)

> Train up a child in the way he should go,[3]
>   Even when he is old he will not depart from it. (NAS)

> Start children off on the way they should go,
>   and even when they are old they will not turn from it. (TNIV)

> Educate a child according to his life requirements;
>   even when he is old he will not veer from it. (MLB)

Though the versions display some variations, they are nearly unanimous in adding a modifier to "way" in Line A. That is, the translations take "way" as specifically the *right* way, the *morally obligatory* way—"the way he should go," or "the right road."

The Bare Bones

But now, by contrast, consider an extremely literal translation:

> Initiate for[4]-the-child on-the-mouth-of[5] his-way;
>   even-when he-is-old he-will-not-turn from-it.

Very different, isn't it? The terse wording bristles with questions. How does "initiate" mean "train"? Where did the "should go" go? It just says "his way," no modifier beyond the pronoun—no "good" or "right" or "should go." What kind of way is "*his* way"? Whose way? God's way? The child's way? I'm just a parent. What am I supposed to do? Help!

---

[1] "Proverbs 22:6a: Train Up a Child?" (*Grace Theological Journal* 9 [1988]), 3.
[2] So similarly ASV, ESV, RSV, NIV, CSB.
[3] Margin, "literally according to his way."
[4] Or *to*, or *with respect to*. See explanation below.
[5] An idiom meaning *according to, after the measure of*. See explanation below.

Traditionalism

As we begin our study, then, note the discerning words of Douglas Stuart: "The more well known a wording in the Bible is, the more hesitant modern translations are to depart from it."[6] Stuart is exactly right.

That said, let us commence our study, an examination which will illustrate the correctness of Stuart's point, particularly when it comes to the familiar words of Proverbs 22:6.[7]

TWO POPULAR VIEWS

The Majority View

The Meaning of the View

What must we parents do, according to this view? We must train up a child in the way he should go. What way is that? It is God's way, the way of wisdom and righteousness.

To get that meaning, we must take the Hebrew's literal wording "his way," and replace "his" with some sort of modifier such as "good" or "right" or "he should go."[8] Note that most of the translations listed above modify "way" very similarly. Specifically, notice how many translations feature some form of the phrase, "the way *he should go*."[9] Likewise, commentators assert that the reference must be to the right way, the proper way, the way of wisdom.[10]

---

[6] Douglas Stuart, *Old Testament Exegesis*, 2nd ed. (Philadelphia: Westminster, 1984), 52. Stuart is referring specifically to Proverbs 22:6, for which he favors the same translation and interpretation that I will commend.

[7] I have combed many commentaries, and have been surprised at how frequently the interpretation of this verse is simply asserted, with very little wrestling with the actual words of the Hebrew original. Waltke is a notable exception, though I disagree with his conclusions; Kitchen, Longman, and Clifford also interact more with the wording, with diverse results. Garrett manages both to note the Hebrew, and to be unhelpful.

[8] Longman sees some such insertion as an interpretive necessity here (commentary, 404–405).

[9] The Spanish-language LBA has "Enseña al niño el camino en que debe andar," "Teach the child the way in which he ought to walk."

[10] Cf. Sid S. Buzzell, in John F. Walvoord, Roy B. Zuck and Dallas Theological Seminary, *The Bible Knowledge Commentary : An Exposition of the Scriptures* (Wheaton, IL: Victor Books, 1983; Logos version). Cf. also Fox, *Proverbs*, 2:698. Donald Hustad wants to include good table manners, other Christian virtues—and music (article "A Spiritual Ministry of Music Part III: Music for Worship, Evangelism, and Christian Education," *Bibliotheca Sacra*, Volume 117, 468, 311 (Dallas, TX: Dallas Theological Seminary, 1960).

Absolute promise

What will happen if we translate and understand the verse in this way? To many Christians, Proverbs 22:6 gives us an ironclad promise.[11] Solomon here allegedly allows that our child may sow his wild oats in adolescence or early adulthood. Still, a godly parent is encouraged to cling to this verse's promise that the child will turn back one day. Perhaps it will happen when he is literally "old," in a deathbed-style conversion, or re-conversion. Though the lad might stray, he will one day return to his childhood teaching.[12] It's a "precious promise."[13]

Promising general principle

The absolutist form of this view is not easy to find in print, even among advocates of modifying "way" as suggested above. However, Waltke uses the language of promise: "In sum, the proverb promises the educator that his original, and early, moral initiative has a permanent effect on a person for good." However, Waltke adds, "But that is not the whole truth about religious education."[14]

Yet Waltke's exposition goes along the lines of presenting the proverb as an assured principle. He notes the word translated "even," and (contrary to the popular view) opines that it "probably aims to prevent the misinterpretation that there may be a moral lapse between the dedication and old age."[15]

Most commentators quite correctly point out the nature of Proverbs as presenting principles and aphorisms, not legal promises. For instance, John A. Kitchen favors modifying "way" as above.[16] But Kitchen then asks, "Does this dogmatically demand that, if proper parenting is employed, all children in the household will walk with God obediently?" Kitchen's response is sensitive and

---

[11] As noted in Chapter 8, Fugate speaks of this verse as a "guarantee" that proper parental training will be successful (http://www.foundationforbiblicalresearch.org/CT%20excerpt%203.htm/).

[12] So John P. and Judy V. Allison, "Parenting as Discipleship," vol. 29, *Ashland Theological Journal Volume 29*, 52 (Ashland, OH: Ashland Theological Seminary, 1997).

[13] Warren W. Wiersbe rightly observes that the verse does not promise a departure and return; but he says that it is a promise that if parents raise their children in God's ways, the children will not stray (*Be Skillful*, An Old Testament Study [Wheaton: Victor Books, 1996], 105. Then in a footnote later on the same page, Wiersbe adds that it is a principle, not an ironclad guarantee.

[14] Waltke, *Proverbs*, 2:206. He had earlier observed that "the proverb…must not be pushed to mean that the educator is ultimately responsible for the youth's entire moral education," and alluded to the fact that youths can still make disastrous choices in spite of their training (ibid.).

[15] Waltke, *Proverbs*, 2:205.

[16] Kitchen explains it as "the way one ought to go, the right way, the divine way, the wise and righteous way" (496).

pastoral, as he reminds both of the general-principle nature of proverbs and of the mystery of the interplay of God's sovereignty and human volition.[17]

Summary

The majority view sees Proverbs 22:6 as a promise that, if a parent will train a child well, that child will stay with that training. This is the dominant view, imbued with the force and tenacity of tradition and the seal of the beloved KJV. If truth were decided by majority vote, the "precious promise" interpretation would win hands-down.

However, there are significant and convincing reasons to reject the majority view.

The Problems with the Majority View

I see at least two major flaws in the majority view.

First: unwarranted additions

This flaw is nearly fatal, all by itself. It is simply this: *Solomon provided no modifier beyond the pronoun.* That's right. There is *nothing* in the Hebrew text— not one word, syllable, jot or tittle—that corresponds to or justifies the "should go" that most translations insert.[18] The only word that modifies "way" is the pronominal suffix meaning "his" (*darkô*). This is a simple fact of reading, not an interpretive assertion.[19]

"His way" = "God's way"? Whose way is "his" way? The original text provides nothing like a capital "h" to tell us whether it is "his way" (i.e., the child's way), or "His way" (i.e., God's way). Indeed, the Hebrew text has no capital letters, so such an indication is not even a possibility.[20] Therefore the Hebrew text does not and cannot indicate its meaning by font-variation.

---

[17] Kitchen, *Proverbs*, 496–497.

[18] In spite of this, the modifying phrase or some form of it is inserted by KJV, NKJV, ASV, RSV, ESV, CSB, NRSV, NAS, NIV, TNIV, and NEB, among many others. It is also seen in the translations by commentators Murphy (163), and McKane (245).

[19] Allen P. Ross makes this odd comment: "The way the verse has been translated shows that there is a standard of life to which he should go" ("Proverbs," in *The Expositor's Bible Commentary, Volume 5: Psalms, Proverbs, Ecclesiastes, Song of Songs*, ed. Frank E. Gaebelein, 1061 (Grand Rapids, MI: Zondervan Publishing House, 1991). Well, yes, that is what the *translation* suggests. But Ross (and I) are supposed to be basing our interpretation on the Hebrew text, not on a translation; and I shall show that the Hebrew text "shows" nothing of the kind.

[20] That is, "his" is not a separate word in Hebrew as it is in English. In Hebrew the personal pronoun (i.e., *his*) is commonly written as an appended consonant or two rather than a separate word. Here, it is indicated by the *-ô* of *darkô* ("*way-his*").

However, we must now ask: What in the wording of the verse itself would ever have suggested that "his way" meant God's way? Remember, these proverbs do not have context, per se. They stand alone. We cannot go to the preceding or following verses to find out whose way is "his way," as we might in an epistle or a narrative. We can consult the context of the larger book to see if a given interpretation clashes with the author's thinking, however.

Whose way? That said, does the proverb itself suggest a referent for "his"? Indeed it does. "The child" is the closest referent: start out *the child* according to *his* (i.e., the child's) way, Solomon writes. In terms of the verse itself, "his way" is neither difficult nor ambiguous. It is the lad's way that we have in view.

We can nail this down still more tightly. Faced with difficult interpretive choices, I invariably find it helpful to ask myself: How could each competing view have been better-said? If the Biblical writer had meant to say what this interpretation suggests—his *good* way, his *wise* way, his *godly* way—are these the best words in the best order? Or could he have said it more clearly and less ambiguously?

Longman, regrettably, brushes this principle aside. To begin with, his translation is odd, at best:

> "Train up youths [sic] in his [sic] path;
> Then when they [sic] age, they [sic] will not depart from it."[21]

In his comment, Longman notes that the verse "has some built-in ambiguities"—yet he goes on to say that translations are right to add modifiers such as "good," "right," or "should go"[22]—thus *removing* the designed ambiguity. Solomon was deliberately ambiguous, Longman says… but we'll fix that for him!

One must ask how firm the basis is for being more specific than Solomon, the inspired author, chose to be. Not firm at all, I think.

Let us ask, then: How might Solomon have more clearly stated the majority view? How could he have said "according to the way he should go," or "God's way," as this interpretation maintains?

---

21 Longman, commentary, 404. Without explanation, he pluralizes "youths," but retains the singular "his"; then again pluralizes the singular verbs in Line B, leaving "it" singular.
22 Longman, commentary, 404.

Second: clearer alternative Hebrew expressions available

Solomon could have expressed the majority view clearly in quite a few different ways. After the later analogy of Isaiah 48:17, Solomon could have added the verb *yēlēk* ("he will walk" or "should walk"), which would have communicated the meaning represented in the KJV and others.

> Thus says Yahweh, your Redeemer, the Holy One of Israel: "I am Yahweh, your God, the One who teaches you to make a profit, The one causing you to tread in the way *you should walk* [*madrîkᵃkā bᵉderek tēlēk*]." (DJP)[23]

Though that would have made the verse long for a proverb, it would not have been impossibly long.[24]

Or again, Solomon could have used the phrase his father used in Psalm 25:12 (emphasis added)—

> Who is the man who fears the LORD?
> Him will he instruct in the way *that he should choose* [*bᵉderek yibḥār*].

Yet again, Solomon could presumably have used the phrasing of these verses from Psalm 119[25] (emphases added)—

> In the way of *your testimonies* I delight
>   as much as in all riches. (119:14)

> Make me understand the way of *your precepts*,
>   and I will meditate on your wondrous works. (119:27)

> I have chosen the way of *faithfulness*;
>   I set your rules before me. (119:30)

> I will run in the way of *your commandments*
>   when you enlarge my heart! (119:32)

> Teach me, O LORD, the way of *your statutes*;
>   and I will keep it to the end. (119:33)

---

[23] The phrasing in Psalms 32:8 and 143:8 is very similar.

[24] Nine words as opposed to eight, counting the *maqqēf*-pairs as single words. The last verse in this chapter (Prov. 22:29) is a nine-word proverb.

[25] Assuming this psalm to be Davidic, or at least pre-Solomonic.

Clearer phrasings within Proverbs. Those are quite a few options, any one of which would have yielded the majority-view's meaning. But we need not stray from Proverbs itself to find alternate ways. Had he meant something other than the child's way, Solomon could have replaced the pronominal suffix with any of the following (emphases added):

> So you will walk in the way of *the good*
> and keep to the paths of the righteous. (2:20)

> I have taught you the way of *wisdom*;
> I have led you in the paths of uprightness. (4:11)

> For the commandment is a lamp and the teaching a light,
> and the reproofs of discipline are the way of *life*, (6:23)

> Leave your simple ways, and live,
> and walk in the way of *insight*. (9:6)

> The way of *the Lord* is a stronghold to the blameless,
> but destruction to evildoers. (10:29)

> A gray head is a crown of glory;
> It is found in the way of *righteousness* (16:31 NAS)

> One who wanders from the way of *good sense*
> will rest in the assembly of the dead. (21:16)

This is an impressive array. Solomon had a wide variety of options for making it clear that "the way" here is the good way, God's way—not the child's way. He used none of them. Instead, he spoke explicitly of "his way"—that is, the way of the innately foolish and sinful child.

Therefore, given that (A) the Hebrew does not include the words so many versions insert, and that (B) Solomon could have written that sense clearly had he wished to do so—why do so many versions include the words? Let us recall once more Stuart's sage observation: "The more well known a wording in the Bible is, the more hesitant modern translations are to depart from it"[26] Old habits die hard, even (especially?) for translation committees.

Nonetheless, we are about to see that the more deeply we examine the evidence, the less likely the traditional majority rendering appears.

---

[26] Douglas Stuart, *Old Testament Exegesis*, 2nd ed. (Philadelphia: Westminster: 1984), 52.

The Age-Appropriate View

This view is not as popular as the majority view, but it has its advocates. It acknowledges that the "way" is the child's way, which is an improvement on the majority view. If we grant that "his way" is "the child's way," what are the implications?

This view advocates the position that a child's upbringing should be age-sensitive.[27] Do not expect a teenager's capabilities in a toddler. Keep the child's level of understanding and ability in mind. The sense suggested is "according to the physical and mental abilities of the developing youth."[28] Garret advocates this view, but then sneaks in the previous option: "one should train a child using vocabulary, concepts, and illustrations a child can understand. ...one should begin instructing a child in elementary principles of right and wrong as soon as possible."[29]

No doubt, there is wisdom in this thought. But is it what Solomon meant? Probably not, for at least three reasons.

First, this interpretation simply does not make good sense of Line B. Think of the whole verse's resultant meaning: start out a child in a manner appropriate to his age; even when he becomes old, he will not depart from—from what? From the manner appropriate to his age? From his abilities? He will always be like a five-year-old, a seven-year-old, a twelve-year-old? And if that view makes sense, is it even worth saying? As Clifford tersely observes, this view "neglects the young/old distinction of the saying and is banal."[30]

Second, if it is insisted that the sense is, "he will not depart from his training" instead of "from his way," reaching back to an insufficiently warranted definition of the verb which starts the verse, my response would be threefold:

1. "From it" most naturally refers to "according to his way" at the end of Line A, not "Start out," at its beginning. The verse is not chiastic.

2. The verb simply means "Start out"; the notion of "training" is at best derivative and not emphasized. Thus even if we are willing to reach back to the start of the verse, it would have to mean "he will not depart from the start he was given."

---

[27] This is Garrett's view (*Proverbs, Ecclesiastes, Song of Songs*, electronic ed., Logos Library System; The New American Commentary [Nashville: Broadman & Holman Publishers, 2001], 187–88). So also Delitzsch, 2:86–87, and Lawrence O. Richards, *The Bible Reader's Companion*, electronic ed., 391 (Wheaton: Victor Books, 1991).

[28] Waltke, citing also Saadia, Malbim and Delitzsch (2:205).

[29] Garrett, 188.

[30] Clifford, 197.

3. This meaning (his age-abilities) does not suit the uses of "his way" in Proverbs, as I am about to show.

Third, this view is at variance with Solomon's other uses of "his way" in Proverbs. Let me explain and illustrate.

What is the meaning of "his way" in Proverbs?

One might wonder whether the translators were influenced by the manner in which Solomon uses "his way" in Proverbs. Perhaps there is some special nuance that indicates "his way" = "God's way," or "the right way"?

This exact form of the word, *darkô*,[31] occurs eight times in Proverbs.[32] In every one of those cases, it means exactly the same thing. There is no variation. The word *always* means "the way [the person] chooses," unless something nearby expressly indicates otherwise.

Here are all seven other occurrences (excluding 22:6):

> "The Lord possessed me at the beginning of his work [lit. "of His way,"
> i.e,. the way He chose to take],
> > the first of his acts of old." (8:22)

> The righteousness of the blameless keeps his way [i.e., his chosen
> lifestyle] straight,
> > but the wicked falls by his own wickedness. (11:5)

> The wisdom of the prudent is to discern his way [i.e., the way he
> will choose],
> > but the folly of fools is deceiving. (14:8)

> The heart of man plans his way [i.e., the way he will choose],
> > but the Lord establishes his steps. (16:9)

---

[31] I say "word"; *darkô* is *derek* ("way") plus the third-personal masculine suffix—*ô*: thus, "way-his").

[32] Proverbs 21:29 is a possible ninth, as some manuscripts and versions read "his way" in the place of "his ways" (cf. Waltke, *Proverbs*, 2:169). The plural represents the addition of the smallest letter in the Hebrew alphabet. If the original reading was singular, it would have the same meaning as all the rest: the way he chooses. Translations are divided, with the singular represented by KJV, Geneva, Darby, CSB, NAS, and NKJ, and the plural by ASV, NAB, NET, NIV, RSV, TNIV, and ESV.

The highway of the upright turns aside from evil;
> whoever guards his way [i.e., his path, his choices and actions]
> preserves his life. (16:17)

When a man's folly brings his way [i.e., the way he chooses] to ruin,
> his heart rages against the LORD. (19:3)

A man's steps are from the LORD;
> how then can man understand his way [i.e., the man's own way,
> course of life]? (20:24)

Note that every occurrence refers to the way chosen by the subject, with no moral/spiritual connotation inherent in the word itself. Note too, that in every case, with the sole formal exception of 16:17, "his" is specified by a substantive that is named in the very same line. In no case is the referent of "his" an actor not named in the verse—as we must suppose of 22:6 alone, if we take "his way" as meaning "Yahweh's way" or "God's way."

Resultant meaning of "his way"

All of this leads us to this conclusion: in all other uses, *darkô* means "the way [the person] chooses." Therefore, as a simple finding of exegesis, it is most likely that "train up a child according to his way" in 22:6 means "according to the way he chooses," as in all the other verses. Is the referent for "his" named in Line A? Indeed it is: "a child."

As the simplest reading, "Occam's razor" would favor this interpretation. Had Solomon wished to express another idea, we have seen that he could have done so unambiguously in any of a number of ways.

But... does that make sense?

The data as to "his way" are fairly clear. But now it seems that we have an interpretive problem. If "his way" means "the way the child chooses," the verse would seem to clash with the remainder of Proverbs. As we have seen (and will reiterate), Proverbs *uniformly discourages* giving a child his own way, warning against such indulgence fiercely. Letting children have their way is a recipe for disaster, on many levels. Yet here Solomon says, "Start out a child according to his own way." Is that not a contradiction?

Indeed, no, it is not a contradiction. But before we untangle the knot, let us look at one other view.

Adaptive Training View

What I am calling the "adaptive training" view is a variation of the "age-appropriate" view, above. What is the meaning of Proverbs 22:6 according to this interpretation?

The Explanation

The *verb* translated "train up" is explained as creating a taste or a thirst within a child.[33] It has been more specifically suggested that this Hebrew verb means that parents should give the child a sweet taste of the faith when they're young.[34]

The *preposition* "in" is explained by Swindoll in a way that seems to try to combine in keeping with, in co-öperation with, in accordance to, and so according to his way.[35]

The *noun* "his way" is explained at length as the child's own manner, mode, characteristics, temperament, vocation, individuality or even his bent.[36] Old Testament scholar J. Barton Payne said that the verse "is perhaps more accurately rendered, 'Train up a child according to his way [i.e., by methods that are adapted to his own special interests and capacities], and [then] even when he is old he will not depart from it."[37] Swindoll is emphatic that it is not the parent's way that should rule, it is the child's way, as he explains it.[38] Others insist that it is the parent's *duty* to fortify the child's individual interests, habits, abilities.[39]

---

[33] Cf. Charles Swindoll, *You and Your Child* (Nashville: Nelson, 1977), 19; and *Growing Wise in Family Life* (Portland, Multnomah: 1988), 90–91. Swindoll also tries to crowbar in the notion of bringing into submission (*You and Your Child*, 19). Swindoll bases this view on dubious etymology and usages never found in the Bible itself. As we shall see, the Bible simply employs the verb for inaugurating or dedicating something, starting it out.

[34] Jim Townsend, article "Grace In The Arts: Grace Abounding—In Great Literature," in vol. 3, *Journal of the Grace Evangelical Society* Volume 3, 2, 57 (Irving, TX: The Grace Evangelical Society, 1990).

[35] Swindoll, *You and Your Child*, 20. Cf. also Kidner, 139.

[36] *You and Your Child.*, 20–21; *Growing Wise in Family Life*, 90–92. Similarly Gene Getz, "The Christian Home Part II," *Bibliotheca Sacra*, Volume 126, 502, 112–13 (Dallas, TX: Dallas Theological Seminary, 1969). Getz simply asserts that this is the meaning of the verse, with no documentation or substantiation whatever.

[37] Article "Israel, Religion of," in Walter A. Elwell and Barry J. Beitzel, *Baker Encyclopedia of the Bible* (Grand Rapids, Mich.: Baker Book House, 1988), 1070.

[38] *You and Your Child*, 20; *Growing Wise in Family Life*, 91.

[39] Robert B. Hughes and J. Carl Laney, *Tyndale Concise Bible Commentary*, The Tyndale Reference

Here is what this view argues that God is telling parents: if you want your training to be godly and wise, then you must observe your child, be sensitive and alert so as to discover his way, and adapt your training accordingly.[40]

The Problems with the Adaptive Training View

There are, however, fatal problems with this interpretation.

As to the verb

For instance, this view's explanation of the verb translated "train up" is hopelessly muddled, further confused by throwing in meanings which are never found in Scriptural uses of the term. As I shall explain in a moment, etymology does not always determine a word's meaning. Nor is it valid to take a basket-full of senses and suggest that one use combines them all.[41]

Every one of the Biblical uses (apart from Proverbs 22:6) refers to the dedication of some building or other, as we shall see. The meaning is to start, to initiate, to inaugurate.

As to the noun

Reaching back to speculative etymology for a word (Hebrew *d-r-k*, "bend"), when the noun itself is never used that way, is an unsound way to approach interpretation.[42] One should always keep in mind: writers are communicators, not etymologists. They use words in the senses employed by their readers, not in line with some hypothetical origin in the dim, obscure past.

For instance, if it could be demonstrated that "cute" had a word-origin meaning "bow-legged," we still would have no grounds for saying that men who call young ladies "cute" are really saying that they are bow-legged. A word means what it is *employed* to mean, not what its root originally might have meant to long-dead generations.

Therefore, the rationale for seeing the straightforward, very common Hebrew word *derek* ("way") as meaning "bent" simply is not there. More specifically, as we have seen, "his way" in Proverbs always denotes the way the person chooses to go

---

Library (Wheaton, IL.: Tyndale House Publishers, 2001), 235

[40] . *You and Your Child*, 21

[41] . D. A. Carson memorably terms this error the "illegitimate totality transfer" (*Exegetical Fallacies* [Grand Rapids: Baker, 1984], 62).

[42] Carson refers to this as the "root fallacy (26–32).

or live. And Solomon uniformly counsels *against* giving a child his way. Verse after verse cautions *against* letting our homes become child-centered, child-led homes.

> The rod and reproof give wisdom,
>> but a child left to himself brings shame to his mother. (29:15)

> Folly is bound up in the heart of a child,
>> but the rod of discipline drives it far from him. (22:15)

> The way of a fool[43] is right in his own eyes,
>> but a wise man listens to advice. (12:15)

As to the notion

The idea of parents following a child's proclivities or abilities is simply not found in Proverbs. Longman correctly observes that the view "clearly would not be supported by the understanding of the rest of the book that it takes work, discipline, and even physical coercion to encourage a person to take the right direction in life."[44]

As to the summary

And then again, there is the problem that this view is hopelessly muddled. What exactly is a parent to do? Are parents supposed to key their upbringing to their child's temperament…so as to bring him into submission? But, if the child is determining what parents do, then who is submitting to whom? Thus, it is difficult for fathers or mothers to know exactly what this view is counseling.

Even more damaging, what will the result be? The verse says, Train up a child according to his way (meaning his temperament, his natural "bent," in this view), and even when he grows old, he will not depart from "it." If the child will not depart from *it*, then: what is "it"? If "his way" in the Line A means "his natural bent," then what is it that the child will not depart from in Line B?

Does this view suggest that the child will not depart from his temperament? If so, what sense does that make? What if the child's temperament is harmful? What if he is hot-tempered, or lazy, or impulsive? Aren't all of us born sinners, and thus

---

[43] The word for "fool" here (*ʾwîl*) is related to the "foolishness" (*ʾiwwelet*) that is "bound up" in the heart of a child (22:15). In other words, the fool *always* thinks that his way is right—and that kind of foolishness is in the heart of a child. This latter fact is why the child needs, not indulgence, but "the rod of discipline."

[44] Longman, Commentary, 404

born with temperaments that are problematic at best? Would this not mean that I am to harmonize my upbringing with a child's sinful, destructive temperament?

We are forced to conclude that the adaptive-training view does not really do justice to the wording of the verse or the context of Scripture; plus, it ends up not making good sense.

WARNING VIEW (PREFERRED)
Translation

Extremely literal: Initiate for[45] -the-child on-the-mouth-of his-way;
  Even-when he-is-old he-will-not-turn from-it.

Translated: Start out a youth according to his own way;
  even should he grow old, he will not turn from it.

Interpretive paraphrase: Start out a youth after his own chosen way
  —and he will never grow out of it.

Interpretation

Let's take this clause by clause:

"Start Out"

Meaning and usage

The verb translated "start out" is חֲנֹךְ (*ḥᵃnōḵ*). It means to *initiate,* to *inaugurate,* or to *dedicate* (in the sense of dedicating a house at its first use). It is used only five times in the Old Testament, always with some kind of building as the object—except in Proverbs 22:6.[46] Naudé correctly observes, "Although usually rendered *dedicate*, a more accurate translation is *begin, initiate,* or *inaugurate*."[47]

Deuteronomy 20:5 will give us a feel for the verb's customary canonical use.

> Then the officers shall speak to the people, saying, "Is there any man who has built a new house and has not dedicated it [*ḥᵃnāḵô*]? Let him go back to his house, lest he die in the battle and another man dedicate it [*yaḥᵃnᵉḵennû*]."

---

[45] . Or *to,* or *with respect to.*

[46] Jackie A. Naudé, article חנך, in NIDOTTE, 2:200.

[47] Ibid. The related noun חֲנֻכָּה (*ḥᵃnukkâ*) occurs eight times, always with reference to dedicating part or all of the Temple, putting it to its first use.

We will understand the verse better after we set it in its context. In verses 5–7 of Deuteronomy 20, there are three humanitarian categories of exemption from service in a war. Each involves something that a man has achieved, but not had the opportunity to "get going":

1. The first is a man who has built a new house, but has not yet lived in it and fitted it out (v. 5).

2. The second is a man who has planted a vineyard, but has not yet been able to make use of its fruit (v. 6).

3. The third is a man who has become engaged to be married, but has not yet consummated his marriage (v. 7).

In context, then, verse 5 should not make us think of a formal "dedication" ceremony, but of simply beginning to use the house.[48] This command constitutes a gracious offer of exemption to prospective soldiers who had built new homes, but who had not yet started to live in them. The idea is that they had not settled into these new homes, they hadn't gotten them started up, gotten them up and going as homes. Also, the men had not had an opportunity to make the houses fully fit and livable for their families.

Apart from Proverbs 22:6, the only other uses of this verb are 1 Kings 8:63 and 2 Chronicles 7:5. Both of these deal with Solomon's *dedication* or *inauguration* of the Temple, which he accomplished by offering a huge number of sacrifices. Clearly, the emphasis is not on a dedication ceremony per se, but on the fact that Solomon got the Temple going, he started it actually functioning in the service of Yahweh.

Fundamental idea of the verb

The verb, then, has the meaning of getting something going, starting it out, getting it functioning. There is nothing inherent suggesting ceremonies, let alone rubbing the palate with dates or continued training per se as some have suggested. Applied to Proverbs 22:6, it would mean simply starting a lad out, getting him going, getting him functioning, according to his own way.

---

[48] Cf. Peter C. Craigie, who points out that there "is no clear evidence…for the practice of dedicating a new house in ancient Israel," so that the "proper use of the verb seems to be: 'to initiate; to begin to use'" (*Deuteronomy*, New International Commentary on the Old Testament [Grand Rapids: Eerdmans, 1976], 272). Earl S. Kalland agrees, citing Rashi, Qunhi, O.S. Rankin, and S.C. Reif as forwarding the same view ("Deuteronomy," *Expositor's Bible*

"A Youth"[49]

The noun *na'ar* is used in more than 250 verses in the Old Testament. It simply is not possible to come up with a refined, precise meaning of the word. As Hildebrandt notes,

> ...the age span is so diverse that age cannot be the primary focus of the word. It is used of infancy: for a child yet unborn (Judg 13:5–12); one just born (1 Sam 4:21); an infant still unweaned (1 Sam 1:22); or a three month old baby (Exod 2:6). However, Joseph at 17— already a man in that culture—is also called a [*na'ar*] (Gen 37:2). When he is 30 years old—surely beyond childhood—he is still called a [*na'ar*] (Gen 41:12, 46). [50]

The noun *na'ar* is used seven other times in Proverbs.[51] Every occurrence depicts a child who is in need of instruction. In 1:4 and 7:7, it parallels "the gullible" (*p^{e}tayim*). In 20:11 the youth is a child who must reveal his character by his deeds. In 22:15 we see a child whose inborn denseness must be driven out by discipline. In 23:13, it is a child from whom a father must not withhold discipline. In 29:15, it is a child who shames his mother because he has been given his own way.

So we opt for "youth" as highlighting immaturity, without being too specific.

"According to"

The Hebrew phrase *'al-pî* very literally "upon the mouth of." It is of course an idiomatic expression, not to be taken any more literally than our phrase "tongue-in-cheek." Consider three common uses in Scriptures preceding Solomon:

Commentary [Grand Rapids: Zondervan, 1992; used by permission]), 129. Kalland favors translations such as "take up residence," "start to live" (ibid.).

49 The Hebrew is, too literally, "start out to-the-youth." The preposition rendered "to" simply marks the direct object of the verb (Waltke, *Proverbs*, 2:194 [citing his grammar book]). Waltke suggests that the definite article ("the") "may imply that he must be assessed individually to design personally the appropriate moral initiative" (*Proverbs*, 2:205). Adapting the assumed interpretation, I would suggest that it indicates the particular child: if the child is started out with indulgence, that child will not outgrow it.

50 Hildebrandt, 10. Hildebrandt himself argues for a specialized meaning in this verse of a young squire; as we shall see, that interpretation is no likelier than (say) "short-order cook."

51 Proverbs 1:4; 7:7; 20:11; 22:6, 15; 23:13; 29:15, 21. See further in Chapter 2, under the fourth benefit promised in Solomon's preface.

1. It refers to the standard, the measure and controlling factor,[52] with the idea of *after the measure of, according to* (Gen. 43:7; Exod. 34:27; Lev. 24:12; 27:8, 18; Deut. 17:10–11).

2. *According to the command of* (Gen. 45:21; Exod. 17:1; 38:21; Num. 3:16, 39, 51; 4:27; Josh. 19:50; 22:9).

3. *At the mouth of* (Josh. 10:27 [a cave]).

This phrase, then, answers the question, How to start this child out? Answer: after a particular measure or standard. Then we must ask, After which standard? The next word supplies the answer.

"His Own Way"

As we have noted at length, this translates the single word *darkô*, his way, the child's way, the way the lad chooses. That is the standard Solomon envisions.

But is this what Proverbs—let alone the rest of the Bible—promotes? Should children be allowed to choose their own way, their own values and operating principles, according to what is in their hearts? Is Hollywood right? Is "follow your heart" the real Gospel?

Not according to Proverbs, nor according to the rest of the Canon.

A child should be reared according to the standard of the Word of God (Deut. 6:5ff., Psa. 119:9, 11; among many others). As the expression of that standard, he should be reared in accord with the standard of parents who themselves have embraced and absorbed the Word of God (cf. Prov. 6:20–23).

But what is this verse apparently commending as the child's standard? Not God's way, but the child's own way.[53] And what way would that be? What does Scripture lead us to believe is the way that a child would naturally choose? Proverbs replies with one voice: he would choose the disastrous way of folly.[54]

Perhaps the reader is feeling dizzy at this point. Is this *true?* Is this a command—*in Scripture*—that we should start a child out according to his own standard? Not according to God's way, but according to his own way; his immature, foolish, sinful way?

The answer is a partial "yes." The verse indeed envisions letting the boy be and set his own standard, his own guidelines, so that he and not God (or the divine

---

[52] Cf. BDB, article פֶּה.
[53] See further discussion of that phrase below.
[54] Combine Proverbs 12:15, 22:15 and 29:15.

institution of parenthood) is the measure of his way. It means letting him concoct his own values, set his own pace, and formulate his own goals, using only his own human viewpoint as the measuring rod.

At this point, surely we feel like sputtering. How would this sort of "start" in life turn out? The modern, indulgent, New-Agey, child-centered notion is that the child's "higher nature" will win out, and he will properly find his own way within. Is that Solomon's view?

But we know that is not true. We know that the Biblical view is radically different. The Bible acknowledges the reality of inborn sin. We are all spiritually stillborn, brought forth dead in trespasses and sins, objects of God's wrath (Eph. 2:13). This is true of every one of Adam's natural descendants (Gen. 5:3; Rom. 5:12ff.).

How does that apply to child-training, in practical terms?

It means that our children *have* no "higher nature." Neither did their parents. Born of two sinners, by nature, folly is bound up with the child's mind (22:15). He will choose the self-willed way of destruction, which will invariably look good to him (12:15). His ultimate destination will be death (14:12)—*if* he is left to go "his own way."

Are you beginning to feel the tension? On the face of it, this verse is *terrible* advice! If we see in this verse an actual positive command—as so many have done—it is perhaps the worst child-rearing advice ever given. Why more expositors have not seen that is something of a mystery.

There is indeed a far better interpretation; but we will consider it after studying the rest of the terms.

"Even Should He Grow Old"

The phrase translated "Even should he grow old" considers a hypothetical situation.[55] It is not a "given" that he will live to older age, given Proverbs' many warnings against waywardness (cf. 1:24–32; 10:21; 11:19; 14:12; 15:10; 19:18).

---

[55] The sense of the כִּי in this case would be concessive (cf. HALOT), "Even though he grows old, he will not mature, he will not leave his indulgent ways." This answers Waltke's objection. Waltke says that taking this verse as sarcastic or ironic, while grammatically and rhetorically possible, "would then assume that the youth attained old age in his folly," which in Proverbs is a reward of the wise rather than of fools (Commentary, 2:205). However, the verse assumes no such thing. Solomon merely envisions a hypothetical: *even should he* attain old age, mere aging alone will not reverse this self-indulgent pattern. (Cf. also BDB, article גַּם.)

This child may or may not survive adolescence. He may never "become old." But Solomon concedes the possibility, only to say that, if he does age chronologically, the youth will not naturally turn from the start his indulgent parents gave him.

"He Will Not Turn From It"

The other views envision this as an assurance that the child will not forsake the good upbringing he had, the good and godly training his parents gave him. In fact, some seem to read Solomon as if he had written, "Even when he is old, he will turn back to it (i.e., the good way)," in suggesting a later return.[56]

So far, the actual wording has not been friendly to this view. This verb, at the close of Line B, is no more favorable than the preceding words.

The verb *sûr* is used some seventeen times in Proverbs. It is used both of turning from something evil and of turning from something good. The majority views assume that it is used in Proverbs 22:6 of turning from something good—that is, from the godly upbringing of one's parents. The lad "will not turn" from his good upbringing.

However, actual usage is opposed to this interpretation. Of the sixteen other uses of this verb, *fully thirteen of them* (81 percent) are clearly of turning from evil to good. Let me break it down:

- Turning from evil to good in some form: 3:7; 4:24; 4:27; 9:4 (the gullible turning to Lady Wisdom); 9:16 (the gullible turning to Lady Folly—from bad to worse); 13:14, 19; 14:16, 27; 15:24; 16:6, 17; 27:22.
- Of turning from good to evil in some form: 5:7; 11:22; 28:9.

Given that 81 percent of the other occurrences speak of turning from evil to good, what is the likelier meaning in this verse? Couple the usage statistics with the fact that the notion is of the old person turning from his childish way, and the fact that the child's own way is always foolish, what is the likelier meaning of *sûr* in this verse?

Solomon is saying that, when a child is started out after the measure of his own chosen, foolish, godless way, even if he should manage to grow old, he will not turn from the evil of that way to the good of God's way.

---

[56] Cf. hinted suggestions in Matthew Henry, *Matthew Henry's Commentary on the Whole Bible: Complete and Unabridged in One Volume*, Pr 22:6 (Peabody: Hendrickson, 1996); and John MacArthur, *The Fulfilled Family* (Chicago: Moody Press, 1997), np.

What Kind of "Command" Is This, Anyway?

Hopefully, one feels at this point the impossibility of seriously taking this verse as a positive command. The odds that Solomon is actually urging parents to start their children out accustomed always to getting their own way, and thus cemented into a pattern of self-absorbed godlessness, are nil. There must be a better way of seeing the verse.

Indeed there is a better way.

Not a Command at All

Proverbs 22:6 must be regarded as an *ironic imperative*. In form, an ironic imperative is a command, but it is an *ironic* command. It is meant to make a point, *not* to produce the commanded action.

In fact, the intent of an ironic imperative generally is to produce the opposite of the literal sense of the command. This is a command that is not meant to be carried out. Bullinger explains the figure of speech of *irony* thus:

> The figure is so called when the speaker intends to convey a sense contrary to the strict signification of the words employed: not with the intention of concealing his real meaning, but for the purpose of adding greater force to it.[57]

Watson also describes the use of irony in Hebrew poetry. Though he does not mention Proverbs 22:6, Watson describes *irony* as a case in which taking a statement literally yields the exact opposite of what the statement's meaning must be.[58] Watson suggests that the way to identify irony is when the only way to make sense of a statement is to reverse its *prima facie* meaning.[59] This applies directly to the interpretation of Proverbs 22:6, where the imperatival meaning is indeed "nonsensical."

It is difficult to over-stress the importance of detecting irony, when it is present. Particularly in the case of this verse, virtually every phrase cries out against the standard interpretation, rendering it banal nonsense that clashes with

---

[57] Ethelbert William Bullinger, *Figures of Speech Used in the Bible*, 807 (London; New York: Eyre & Spottiswoode; E. & J. B. Young & Co., 1898). Logos version.

[58] Wilfred G. E. Watson, *Classical Hebrew Poetry*, 2nd edition (Sheffield: JSOT Press, 1986), 306–307.

[59] Ibid., 307.

the rest of the book and, indeed, the rest of the Bible. Watson warns us that failure to detect irony can result in completely misunderstanding a text[60]—which, I am arguing, has been the case with Proverbs 22:6.

In sum, to take a text such as this as an ironic imperative is the rhetorical equivalent of our "Oh, right—you do that [disastrous thing]. And when you do, here's what will happen!"

"Ironic Imperative" Examples

The Bible contains numerous examples of ironic commands.

Judges 10:14. In Judges 10, we read that Israel "again did what was evil in the sight of the LORD and served the Baals and the Ashtaroth, the gods of Syria, the gods of Sidon, the gods of Moab, the gods of the Ammonites, and the gods of the Philistines," and that "they forsook the LORD and did not serve him" (verse 6). As a consequence, Yahweh abandoned them to their foes, who oppressed and crushed them (vv. 7–9). Israel was humbled and desperate, and we read that they "cried out to the LORD, saying, 'We have sinned against you, because we have forsaken our God and have served the Baals'" (v. 10).

How did Yahweh respond? He reminded them of His past blessings and their record of faithlessness, and said he would not save them (vv. 11–13). Moreover, He said this: "Go and cry out to the gods whom you have chosen; let them save you in the time of your distress" (v. 14).

What is this? Is Yahweh actually *commanding* them to worship and seek after pagan idols? Formally, yes. In grammatical terms, it is a straightforward command. Yet it is transparent that Yahweh means no such thing. Instead, He is convicting them of their sin by means of blistering sarcasm. They have left Him again and again for false gods; now, let those gods save them.

By this, Yahweh awoke them to the fact that those gods were no gods at all, and thus could not save. His irony brought them to humbled, broken repentance (vv. 15–16).

1 Kings 18:27. As a second example, we could consider Elijah's contest with the false prophets of Baal, in 1 Kings 18. The feat is to call on one's god(s), and "the God who answers by fire, he is God" (v. 24). First up are the 450 prophets of Baal, who are unable to bring fire from the false god by their performance.

---

[60] Ibid., 309.

Elijah mocks them.

> "Cry aloud, for he is a god. Either he is musing, or he is relieving himself, or he is on a journey, or perhaps he is asleep and must be awakened." (v. 27)

Is the prophet actually commending the worship of Baal? Grammatically, yes; in reality, of course not. His command is *ironic*. Elijah is mocking them. What he is telling them to do is the opposite of what they should do, as Elijah is there to prove—and they know it.

John 2:19. Now turn far ahead to John 2:18–22. In this passage, the Lord Jesus has just taken his handmade whip and cleared the Temple. Affronted, the leaders ask him, "What sign are You showing us, since You are doing these things?" (v. 18 DJP). Jesus' response was "You destroy this sanctuary, and in three days I will raise it up!" (v. 19 DJP).

In grammatical form, the words of verse 19 are a command: "Destroy this sanctuary," Jesus says, as if He were commanding them to do it. Is He, though? Is He commanding them to kill Him—so that it is not a sin, but obedience, when they betray and frame and condemn the Lord Jesus? When they stand before the judgment of God, will they be able to plead innocence, and insist that they were simply obeying Jesus' command?

Of course not. Though the *form* of the verb is an imperative, the *impact* of the words are not as a genuine command, or an expression of Christ's moral instruction to His hearers. The action (crucifying Him, an innocent Man) would be a horrendous sin. Clearly the Son of God is not ordering someone to sin.

But once again, we know this from the context and other considerations, rather than from the sheer grammatical form of the verb *lusate* ("destroy") itself.

What Jesus means, then, is "You go right ahead and do the horrendous sin of killing Me; but I shall resurrect Myself." It is a statement laced with acid irony.[61]

Proverbs 22:6 as ironic command

Let us plug this into Proverbs 22:6. This verse comes after chapter upon chapter warning of the need to discipline children, and to head them in God's

---

[61] Other instances of ironic (or sarcastic) commands include 1 Kings 2:22; 18:27; 22:15; Isaiah 2:10; Jeremiah 7:21; Ezekiel 20:39; and Amos 4:4–5.

way instead of their own. Solomon has shown us that children are born ignorant, gullible, vulnerable fools. He and his readers knew that they were unclean products of unclean parents (Job 14:4), conceived in iniquity (Psa. 51:5), in need of discipline (Prov. 13:24).

Now, leaving off the frontal approach, Solomon employs irony. Perhaps he hopes to wake up the reluctant, indulgent, lazy parents. "Go ahead," he shrugs, in effect. "Do it. Give that lad his start in life expecting to go his own way and get his own way. See how that turns out. Oh, and by the way… here is how it *will* turn out."

A tragic aside: "Baby Man"

Have you ever seen an infant in a man's body? Perhaps you have seen immature children—but nothing like the late William Windsor, known as "Baby Man."[62]

Windsor was a 54-year-old man who came into a nice inheritance, and used it to finance a lifestyle as a literal baby, 24 hours a day, 7 days a week. Though formerly a singer and actor, Windsor popped a pacifier into his mouth, and took to wearing (and using) diapers and a baby girl's clothes, complete with curly blond hair and earrings. He slept in a crib, sat in a huge high-chair, and paid people to feed him. Windsor's bizarre story had an unsurprisingly sad end, when his long-dead body was discovered in his apartment. He was 57.[63]

Windsor's story is shocking and sad, and it is extreme.

Maturity is not automatic

But many folks who are chronologically adult, and give no alarming signs such as Windsor did, have never grown to attain wisdom. The body has matured, but the heart, the mind, has not.

Maturity is not automatic. The wisdom of fearing Yahweh must be impressed by parents with loving insistence by means of the rod and reproof. Wisdom must be embraced by the child by his choosing it, seeking it, gaining it, acquiring it, and holding on to it.[64] If a child is started out "according to his own way," and

---

[62] "Baby Man," by Joe Watson, in the *Phoenix New Times News* (June 9, 2005; URL http://www. phoenixnewtimes.com/2005-06-09/news/baby-man/).

[63] "'Baby Man' William Windsor Found Dead in Home, Autopsy Underway," by Stephen Lemons, in the *Phoenix New Times News* (February 3, 2009; URL http://blogs.phoenixnewtimes.com/ bastard/2009/02/baby_man_william_windsor_found.php).

[64] Cf. Proverbs 2:1–5; 4:5–8; 16:16.

left to that way, the aged baby will not just naturally "evolve" into God's way. It is not enough to provide a "nurturing environment" (as I once heard it put *in church*, to my alarm) and let the child find his own way.

Remember: *Proverb*, Not Dissertation

We must keep in mind that this verse is a pithy proverb. Accordingly, Solomon naturally does not mention the possibility of a work of God's grace changing the grown child's heart. True to the genius of proverbs, this verse is simply laying out the way things would naturally be—"You do A [indulge a child], and B [lifelong selfish immaturity] will follow!"

Jay Adams correctly says that the passage

> Literally...reads, "train a child after the manner of his way," that is, after the standard or manner in which *he* wants to be trained. The verse stands not as a promise but as a warning to parents that if they allow a child to train himself after his own wishes (permissively) they should not expect him to want to change these patterns when he matures. Children are born sinners and when allowed to follow their own wishes will naturally develop sinful habit responses. The basic thought is that such habit patterns become deep-seated when they have been ingrained in the child from the earliest days. The corollary to this passage is found in Proverbs 19:18 where the writer exhorts the reader, "Discipline your son while there is hope; do not set your heart on his destruction."[65]

An Odd Twist

Sometimes we can gain insight by standing a law or a proverb on its head. If God warns against a certain behavior, we can learn what we should do, instead, from figuring out what the *opposite* of that behavior would be. For instance, the commandment *not* to steal implies a corollary commandment to be gainfully employed; the prohibitions of adultery and false witness commends marital faithfulness and truth, and so on.

---

[65] Jay Adams, *Competent to Counsel* (Grand Rapids: Baker, 1970), 158.

Accordingly, when we do that with this proverb, the meaning would be something like this:

1. If you start out a boy according to his own way, he will never grow out of it.

2. Therefore, do not start him out according to his own way; rather, start him out according to God's way.

So we see that, in a roundabout way, we are brought back to the doorstep of the Majority View. By discouraging us from starting out a child on his own way, Solomon implicitly directs us toward another way. That way would have to be *God's* way, the way of wisdom and uprightness. With this, many proverbs concur, including 4:11; 6:23; 9:6; 10:29; 12:28; 13:6; and 21:16.

I do not necessarily see a reverse promise that the child will not grow out of a godly upbringing, although it certainly is the grand hope of godly child-training. A consistently godly upbringing will confront the child with the whole counsel of God, and will provide the normal means used by the Spirit of God in our children's conversion and sanctification.

If a child so reared chooses the way of folly and of ungodliness, it will be in spite of his God-fearing parents' heartfelt prayers for grace, and their best, most earnest, and most insistent efforts to point him to the saving, sanctifying way of God. In the judgment, such a child will have no excuse.

Conclusion

The wise king wants to be sure he has reached us. Again and again he has modeled and stressed how we are all born fools, with no fear of Yahweh and no template for life. In our hearts are folly and the seeds of our own destruction.

Now Solomon lays aside the frontal approach and tries a new tack.

"You don't believe me?" he says, in effect. "You think your child is an exception? You think it best just to give him his lead, let him track his own course? Is it just too much trouble for you to love God, take in His Word, follow Him, and teach His ways to your child? Is it too hard to cross your child's will, to teach him, to reach out to his heart? Are you, after all, *not* wiser and *not* stronger than your child? Is it too hard to care, and work, and be consistent both in teaching and in discipline?

"Fine, then," Solomon continues. "Have it your way. Leave him be. Start him off thinking that there is no God to answer to, that there are no borders and no consequences, that there will be no day of judgment. Let him think it's safe to follow his own impulses, unjudged and unfiltered. Start him off following his own foolish heart, his own desires, his own drives. Start him off according to his own way.

"But I'll tell you this: even if he does make it to adulthood—which I can't guarantee—he'll never, ever turn from that evil way you started him on.

"Sound like fun?

"No?

"Then *don't do it.*"

Solomon says all that—but he does it in eight words.

Preaching and Teaching the Book of Proverbs

Purpose

The primary audience for this appendix is pastors and others involved in teaching or leading church Bible studies and fellowship groups. However, anyone involved in personal study, or in leading their children through Proverbs, should find helpful guidelines here as well.

I can only be brief and suggestive in dipping into a topic that itself would warrant part or all of the main body of a book. We shall consider some guiding principles in approaching Proverbs in a teaching/preaching context, as well as various ways of approaching the text.

Guiding Principles

Four truths should direct our approach to Proverbs.

First: Proverbs Is the *Word of God*

When our Lord asserted that Scripture could not be broken (John 10:35), He meant all of the Old Testament, and each part of the Old Testament. He meant Proverbs, as well as every other portion. And so, Christ's authorized representatives were guided by the Holy Spirit to quote from Proverbs, as we see when we compare the following:

- Proverbs 3:11–12 with Hebrews 12:5–6.
- Proverbs 3:34 with James 4:6 and 1 Peter 5:5.
- Proverbs 11:31 with 1 Peter 4:18.
- Proverbs 25:21–22 with Romans 12:20.
- Proverbs 26:11 with 2 Peter 2:22.

This being the case, we must treat Proverbs with as much reverence as any other portion of Scripture. It is not a mere book of maxims, such as portions of *Reader's Digest* or popular books of daily advice. Nor is Proverbs a collection of human-viewpoint, experiential observations. It is God's Word to us, written by authors who were carried along by the Holy Spirit (2 Peter 1:21).

Further, we must treat what Proverbs says about itself as befits a revelation of God. As I argued at length in Appendix 1, a student of Christ is not free to wave aside what the text of Proverbs says about its own composition, formation, and meaning. Rather, all those revealed and inscripturated facts are determinative for us.

An additional implication is that we mustn't dismiss any proverb as banal or trivial. Or, to put it positively, we must approach each verse with the conviction that it brims with revelation from God's heart to ours. When we approach the text itself in the fear of Yahweh (Prov. 1:7; 9:10; 31:30), we embrace the stance of students, not critics. If the text *seems* shallow or banal, what that means is that we have missed something. We must allow the text to challenge us, and never the reverse.

Second: Proverbs Has a Particular *Location* in the Unfolding of the Word of God

As we read in Hebrews 1:1, "God spoke of old in many *portions* ...to the fathers in the prophets" (DJP, emphasis added). Revelation unfolds, it develops—not, to be sure, in God's mind, to which all truth is simultaneously and intuitively apparent; but to our minds. God did not explain baptism nor church order to Adam... or, for that matter, to Abraham, or to Moses, or to Isaiah, or to Malachi. God unfolded His plan and His revelation stage by stage.

Our reading, preaching and teaching of the Word must respect that order. We must treat each portion of revelation as appropriate to the stage in which God set it. While (as I will argue in a moment) we mustn't forget later revelation, equally we must not try to jam Solomon into a Christian church pew or pulpit. The wise king lived under the law of Moses, in the context of its rules and rituals, its promises and threats. We should teach his proverbs in such a way that Solomon would own the gist of what we say. If an English-speaking Solomon were forced to exclaim, "I have no idea how you got *that* out of what I wrote," then we have misunderstood him.

And if we have misunderstood Solomon, we have misunderstood God.

So, to be precise, we should never forget what resource-library informed Solomon's faith and thought. We need to have a working idea of what books of the Bible Solomon might have possessed. It is likely that (for instance) the Pentateuch, Job, Joshua, Judges, Ruth, and the psalms of David were among Solomon's mental furniture. We go first to those books, both as to their ideas and as to their Hebrew vocabulary, to guide us in understanding Solomon. Nothing can be proven, exegetically, as to *Solomon's* meaning, by appeals to Isaiah, Ezekiel, or Paul.

Third: Proverbs Has a *Particular Shape* in the Word of God

Again, Hebrews 1:1 tells us that "God spoke of old ...in many *manners* to the fathers in the prophets" (Heb. 1:1 DJP, emphasis added). Scripture is not all stories, nor all sermons, nor all correspondence. It is not uniformly prose or poetry. As there are many kinds of flowers and birds, God laid open His heart through many styles of literature. We must recognize, understand and respect the significance of the shapes and forms He chose to use.

This merits emphasis. What would we think of a movie critic who panned a heartbreaking drama for not being funny? Or a food critic for dismissing a seafood dish as being worthless for driving nails? Or a music reviewer for slamming an album as producing poor gas mileage? We'd think each had lost his mind, and we'd have no use for their misguided meanderings.

The case is no different in a preacher or teacher who expounds Proverbs as if it were law or epistle or sermon. Proverbs was crafted in a distinctive genre by design. To ignore that fact and its implications is to fail to show sufficient respect to God, whose Spirit moved Solomon to select proverbic poetry over all the other colors available on his palette.

We should never forget this significance in our own study and preparation. But that is not all. Our audience most likely is not at all aware of the specific shape of Hebrew poetry in general, or of proverbs in particular. We must labor to ensure that they know what they are reading and hearing, so that they can receive this portion of revelation as God intended.

Fourth: Proverbs Must Be Understood in Light of the *Whole* Word of God

While Solomon had no idea what Jesus would preach, or what Paul would write, God did have that knowledge. We need not try to impress some *sensus plenior*[1] on the text in order to read it in the light of the whole.

For example: when Solomon wrote Proverbs 17:15 ("He who justifies the wicked and he who condemns the righteous / are both alike an abomination to the LORD"), did he have Romans 3 in mind, or the implications of his proverb for the doctrine of Christ's penal substitutionary atonement? Certainly not, and probably not, respectively. But *God* knew of those truths which He would later reveal more fully, and His Spirit moved Solomon to lay the stage and to write something which (viewed in the light of the whole) points forward to Christ. So while it is not legitimate to say that *Solomon consciously meant* some specifically Christ-centered point, it is valid to see Solomon's focus as crafted by God in such a way as ultimately to point to Christ.

Perhaps an analogy would help. Suppose a developer maps out a large plot of land and assigns building projects to a series of contractors. Each contractor builds houses and yards according to their own designs. Each plot is self-contained and complete.

Then after the project, the developer invites all the contractors to join him in a trip aboard his private jet. As they pass over the development, the contractors are amazed to see that all their houses together form a mosaic in the shape of the Statue of Liberty.

Now (in my analogy) each developer did exactly what he set out to do on the land assigned to him. Each house, each neighborhood makes sense in and of itself. They are real houses, which combine to form real neighborhoods.

Yet since each was contracted by a single developer with a single vision, each contributed to a picture grander than any part. It would be perfectly legitimate

---

[1] Latin "fuller sense," meaning the idea that Scripture is meant to convey meanings unknown, even unimaginable, to the original writers. It has been used essentially to brush aside serious grammatical, historical exegesis of Scripture in context, in favor of imposing meanings drawn from other contexts, or from the interpreter's own imagination.

to comment on what each house contributes to the whole portrait. We cannot assert that each contractor intended to be painting the Statue of Liberty, but we can investigate how the developer commissioned each of them with that grand vision in mind. There would be a real confluence, a real flowing-together, of the intents of the developer and those of the contractors.[2]

To see Proverbs thus, as a significant piece in a larger portrait, is simply to apply what Christ taught. Schooled by Christ, we expect to find all of Scripture pointing to Him in some way or other (Luke 24:27, 44–47). When Paul said that, even in his day, "the sacred writings" had abiding power to "make wise" unto salvation (2 Tim. 3:15), Proverbs would have been part of his referent.

This understanding bars us from isolating any proverb from the whole, and finding teachings at variance with the whole. Too many Christians have taught Proverbs as if it were a moralistic collection of ethical maxims or spiritual rules, by the keeping of which we can please God and secure a successful life (i.e., a life that goes the way we want it to). We can be rich, well-respected, and healthy—and have terrific kids!—if we only work the formula correctly.

Such a message not only is untrue to the genre and content of Proverbs, but it would jar hopelessly with the whole of Scripture, and with the truth as it is in Jesus.

The Challenge of Preaching or Teaching Proverbs

As I explained in Chapter 1, no master-outline of Proverbs has convinced me, beyond this rudimentary skeleton:

1. Introduction and Motto (Prov. 1:1–7)

2. Proverb Discourses (Prov. 1:7–9:18)

3. Classic Proverbs (Prov. 10–29)

4. Guest Appendices (Prov. 30–31)

Such an outline, I understand, is hardly a preacher's delight! The divisions do not start with the same letter, and they are hopelessly lopsided. The first is but seven verses long, followed by nearly nine full chapters, followed by twenty full chapters, followed by two.

---

[2]   A recent book arguing for the Messianic shape and import of the Old Testament, without forcing any alien interpretation on the writers' words, is Michael Rydelnik's *The Messianic Hope* (Nashville: B&H Publishing, 2010).

Of course it would be readily possible to make further subdivisions. Clearly, the discourses of the opening chapters subdivide into distinct sections, such as 1:8–19, 20–33, and so forth. But even within that section, there is no full unanimity among students of Proverbs as to where the divisions fall. The preacher must study and decide for himself.

Then when one reaches the tenth through twenty-ninth chapters, however, one abandons all hope of structure.[3] It is, as I've said, possible to find groupings within those chapters, but they are only such as can be explained by association in Solomon's mind.[4] There is no grand outline, however, tracing a flow of thought through every verse from the first to the last.[5]

This presents anyone with a challenge. It means that the vast bulk of the book defies division. How does one approach it? How can one break it down into preachable sections? Must one envision hundreds of sermons, devoted to a verse at a time? What do we find?

The answer is that, for the most part, one finds that Proverbs simply is not preached, not fully. It may well be that Proverbs is one of the least-preached books in the Canon—or, to be more precise, one of the least preached-through books.

While understandable, this isn't preferable, given that Proverbs no less than Romans is part of that whole of Scripture, which is God-breathed and profitable (2 Tim. 3:16–17).

What I mean to do in the remaining section is suggest several approaches to Proverbs that will allow the teacher in Christ's church to expose believers to the wisdom of God in Proverbs.

Approaches to *Teaching* Proverbs in Class/Group Settings

First, we consider approaches suitable for Bible studies, fellowships, and Sunday School classes. We will suggest treating Proverbs in *overview*, then in a series of *subject studies*, and finally as a study of the *whole book*.

---

3   That is, beyond the original proverbs of Solomon (10:1–24:34) and those inserted by the men of Hezekiah (25:1–29:27).

4   I envision that process as something like this: "Here is a proverb on the sovereignty of Yahweh. Oh—that reminds me of this one. And this one! And this! Okay, now one about laziness…"

5   The exception being the framing *inclusio* of 1:7 and 30:31, which teaches us that the dominant framing thought of the whole book is the fear of Yahweh. *All* verses must be read against that background, though they relate to it from widely divergent angles. See further in Chapter 1.

Overview

It is hard for me to imagine teaching Proverbs in less than one class, unless one were conducting a whirlwind Old Testament Survey series—which I've done. It would be possible, however, to teach Proverbs in overview, offering just enough to get folks' feet wet in the book, and spark their own individual studies. One might sketch out a three-part series at minimum, thus:

1. **Introduction to Proverbs.** This would cover authorship and date, principles for reading and understanding Hebrew poetry in general and Proverbs in particular, and a survey of major kinds of proverbs (evaluation, etc.).[6]

2. **The fear of Yahweh.** Rooting the concept in the entire Bible, and showing how the concept frames the entire book (1:7; 31:30).[7]

3. **Selected subject studies.** One could isolate the use of the tongue, marriage, or work. Survey the texts, show how to combine them to form a fuller picture.

Subject Study

With each of these major approaches, there will be repetition. But if one planned an extended series in Proverbs, he could select as many subjects as he wished, and develop them as fully as he thought profitable. Here is an example of just seven such classes:

1. **Who wrote Proverbs?** Introduce Solomon and expound God's gift of wisdom. Show how that wisdom blessed the kingdom he ruled, in practical ways. Expose how Solomon's wisdom failed him, and suggest its recovery in Ecclesiastes. Tie all this into the text of Proverbs.[8]

2. **The fear of Yahweh: its OT background.** Trace the many passages dealing with the fear of Yahweh in the Old Testament. Take time to show the doctrinal, religious, and intellectual meaning and implications of this central Biblical theme.[9]

---

[6] See Chapter 1.
[7] This is the emphasis of Chapter 3.
[8] Chapter 1 will provide useful background for this class.
[9] See Chapter 3 for material to use in teaching this and the next point.

3. **The fear of Yahweh in Proverbs and beyond.** Show how this concept frames the entire book (1:7; 31:30). Discuss what this means for the interpretation of the book. Then go into the New Testament to demonstrate its abiding relevance to believers today.

4. **Marriage: its meaning, potential, and hazards.** Develop the proverbs that warn of adultery and, in the process, define marriage. Lift out the blessed life of the woman of strength in Proverbs 31:10–31. Warn against the miseries of life with the foolish wife.[10]

5. **Mate-selection in Proverbs.** Sketch out the foolish man and woman, and apply the lesson to principles for evaluating prospective spouses.

6. **God's will in Proverbs.** Show God's sovereign control over everything, and His intent that we make our decisions freely, wisely, and responsibly within the bounds of His Word.

7. **Labor and employment in Proverbs.** Ground this in Genesis 1 and 3, and show Solomon's championing of hard work, discipline, and excellence.

Obviously, many other topics could be singled out and opened up. See the introductory section of Derek Kidner's commentary (31–56), the appendix to Longman's commentary (549–578), or the topical index in Ross' commentary (897–903).

Whole Book

Of course, this is a challenging approach. But done rightly, it could be a gateway to all of Scripture.

I would recommend *always* starting with introductory classes, dealing with authorship, poetry, principles of interpreting proverbs. Then simply dig into the text and don't come up until you've called for the excellent woman's works to praise her in the gates.

A men's fellowship I participated in once took the approach of going through a chapter a week, with a different man leading each time. Many of those attending were avid Bible students, and most weeks were rich times of fellowship and learning. I still carry marginal notes in my Bible program, sharp observations from "laymen," taken from this class.

---

10 Chapter 7 will help with this and the next topic.

This approach could work with single or multiple teachers. One could set a goal of a chapter a week and hit the highlights. Alternately, it would be possible to touch lightly on some verses, but "camp" on others.

If one were not afraid of a very, very long series, one could approach it this way:

1. Chapters 1–9: find the divisions that convince you, using the text and the commentaries, and teach each discourse as a single class.

2. Chapters 10–30: Do a verse or (if you see a theme) a collection of verses each class. Tie them in with *all* of Scripture. Charles Bridges' commentary will help particularly in finding illustrations in Scripture. In this way, Proverbs could serve as a sort of catalog for the whole Canon.

Now we move to the traditional Sunday service and the pulpit. Can Proverbs be preached? And if so, how?

Approaches to *Preaching* Proverbs in Worship Assembly

The Concept

I am here assuming the traditional understanding, in distinguishing classes from "worship" services. Of course, all teaching should preach, and all preaching should teach. A period of instruction in the Word that doesn't bring God before our hearers, that doesn't aim the hearers at repentance and humbled love for God, is a failure. Likewise, a sermon that isn't full of the truths of Scripture explained and applied is a wreck.

But the assumption I am making is that classes are less formal and geared for Christians and/or folks with some Biblical background and commitment. "Worship" services also should be geared to Christians, but will commonly (and wisely) cast the net a bit more broadly and will feature signposts held out to the unconverted, pointing them to Christ.

So how can Proverbs be brought into the pulpit?

A Must, Regardless

As I have already suggested: whichever approach one takes, one *must* preach at least one introductory sermon, which introduces Solomon and how to read Proverbs. Perhaps it would be better to devote a sermon to Solomon, aiming at his fitness to write Proverbs, followed by a sermon devoted to introducing Proverbs.

But it is essential to have "on the books" a sermon or two to which one can refer in coming weeks, which will frame one's approach to preaching the book.

Subject Studies

This can be patterned after the outlines suggested above. The difference will be in tone, voice, and overall "packaging." By that I mean that sermons tend to be more hortatory in tone, and laid out more simply and memorably.

For instance, I once preached a sermon called "Living in the Fear of the Lord," centered on Proverbs 1:7. I usually hand out outlines, with blanks for listeners to fill in. This is the sermon outline, with the CAPS indicating letters supplied to fill in the gaps in the distributed outline. Note that this sermon was preached as the close of a conference I had conducted in the book of Proverbs.[11]

Introduction

    1. Note this about the structure of Proverbs

        a. At the start: **1:7**—The **fear of the Lord** is the beginning of knowledge; fools despise wisdom and instruction.

        b. At the close: **31:30**—Charm is deceitful, and beauty is vain, but a **woman who fears the Lord** is to be praised.

        c. Explain *inclusio*

    2. You could say, then, that Proverbs is a book about **living in the fear of the Lord.**

    3. Solomon says it is the *best* thing:

        Better is a little with the fear of the Lord

            than great treasure and trouble with it (15:16)

    4. But what *is* it? Could you even *define* it, or *describe* it? Do you *have* it? Does it have you?

Transition: if God sees it as that important, we had better understand it. Let's!

I. The WHO of It

    A. The SUBject

        the subject is *me*, it's *you*; it's anybody, anywhere

---

[11] This sermon, and the entire conference, is currently available online, at http://www.sgbcaz.com/sermons/cat/SGBC%20Fall%20Conference/.

B. The OBJect: YAHWEH
   1. The God with a name
   2. The God of the Bible

II. The WHY of It
A. Because of His PRIMacy
   1. He is first as to the **universe**
   2. He is **first** as to **knowledge** and **wisdom**
   3. He should be first in our affections

B. Because of His ULTIMacy
   1. He is Lord of the most powerful
   2. He is Lord of the most random
   3. He is Lord of all
   4. He is Lord over my life

TRANSITION: How can we *not* fear such a God?

II I. The HOW of It
A. The Root Idea
   1. When you *fear* something, you see it as having the upper hand
   2. The accompanying emotion can be happy or not
   3. To *fear* God is to see His supremacy, His un–overridable, court-of-*last*-appeal, untamed sovereignty—and my corresponding smallness
   4. Should you be "afraid" of God? If you're not, you're a fool

B. The Fear of Yahweh Must Be LEARNED
   1. How did **Solomon** learn it?
      a. At home
      b. At work
   2. How are **others** to learn it?
      a. 2 Kings 17
      b. Psalm 119:38
   3. What is the **result**?
      a. A specific view of **God**
      b. A specific view **myself**
      c. A specific view of the **world**

  C. The Fear of Yahweh Must Be CHOSEN

    1:29 Because they hated knowledge

      and did not choose the fear of the LORD

  D. The Fear of Yahweh Must Be LIVED

    1. Character reveals beliefs, and walk reveals character (14:2)

    2. "All the day" (23:17)

IV. The Problem of It

 A. Whole Series Upshot

    The problem is—none of us walks in perfect wisdom!

 B. Jesus Christ

One could take this approach and use the subjects suggested above, to deliver a series of sermons on subjects in Proverbs. It could range anywhere from a four-week series to a six-month series. Proverbs easily provides God-honoring, edifying, challenging truth enough for any size and depth of a series.

Whole Book, in Periodic Bits

Because of the nature of the book of Proverbs, which is topical and diverse, it could easily be used to break up longer series. For instance, suppose a preacher were spending a year or two (or more) in Romans, Matthew, Revelation... or Ephesians! It might serve the congregation well to break up the series every 4–6 weeks with a single sermon from Proverbs.

The advantage this would provide would be to continue to deliver from the pulpit both practical and doctrinal instruction. Suppose one were in a very extended series on the doctrine of justification, or sin, or election, based in Romans or Ephesians. One's sheep would be served well to receive the occasional sermon from Proverbs on living out their faith by controlling their tongues, teaching their children, glorifying God at work, being a blessing to their city, or loving their spouses.

Since most of the verses in Proverbs are not woven into a larger flow, it does the book no harm—and could do Christians great good—if a preacher were to dip into it occasionally, breaking up more extended doctrinal series with a bit of Proverbs' pithy, pointed practicality.

Whole Book, Straight Through

Alternately, a hearty soul might take on himself to preach the entire book, verse by verse.

First, the elephant in the room: candidly, I have never known of this being done. I have never done it.

But that does not mean that it cannot be done. Proverbs is, after all, part of God's holy and profitable Word. There is a line from any verse to Christ, and the mind of God is unfolded in each verse, in one way or another.

Further, while most American churchgoers are accustomed to it, there is no rule in Scripture that each sermon must treat only one topic.

However, having said that, it does seem that most grow best in their understanding if not overwhelmed by too much input at one sitting. So a preacher could approach preaching the whole book thus (after beginning with the introductory material as laid out above):

1. Chapters 1–9: find the divisions that convince you, using the text and the commentaries, and preach each one as a single sermon.

   a. One sermon on 1:1, introducing "Solomon" and "proverbs."

   b. One sermon on 1:2–6, examining the purpose of the book.

   c. ...and so forth, perhaps devoting one sermon to each discourse.

2. Chapters 10–31: preach a verse or (if you see a theme) a collection of verses each sermon. Tie them in with *all* of Scripture. Bridges' commentary will help particularly in finding illustrations in Scripture. In this way, Proverbs could serve as a sort of catalog for the whole Canon. For instance:

   a. 10:1 (wise/foolish son)

   b. 10:2–5 (godly work)

   c. ...and so forth

Commentators Waltke and Garrett in particular are always looking for clusters and themes. They frequently seem to me to be "reaching" (particularly Garrett), but they also do point to clustered groups of verses.

Final Question: Is Proverbs a Christian Book, or a Jewish Book?

Many fault a certain approach to Proverbs as differing in no way from Jewish exposition. "A rabbi could teach it that way," is the criticism. Since Jesus showed that all Scripture points to Him (Luke 24:27, 44–47), many preachers feel driven to find Him everywhere, and to distinguish their preaching from rabbinic instruction.

Is this valid?

Yes, and no.

We must never forget that God "spoke *to the fathers* in the prophets" (Heb. 1:1). God did not speak to us Christians over the Israelites' heads, as they blinked in lost befuddlement. God's Word was intelligible to the first hearers. If we preach the Old Testament in such a way that the first hearers never could possibly have understood it, we are defying God's own word *about* His Word. It was a communication *to the fathers*, not a codebook.

Hence it is critical to apply the tools of grammatical, historical, theological exegesis, as sketched out at the beginning of this appendix. We must understand the Hebrew words and the Hebrew syntax; we must locate the text in the unfolding flow of revelation.

It would be illegitimate, then, to force Christ into the text in any way not intended by God. How do we know what God intended? By the words, grammatically, in their context. What the authors meant is what God meant.

However, having said that, at the same time we mustn't forget the end of the story. We mustn't forget that Christ fulfilled the law and the prophets in His person and work (Matt. 5:17), that He is the culmination of the law (Rom. 10:4). So Proverbs *does* legitimately point us to Christ.

How does Proverbs legitimately point to Christ? The answer to that could fill a book itself.[12] Let me just suggest a few ways:

1. Christ is the Wisdom of God (1 Cor. 1:24, 30), in whom are hid all the treasures of wisdom and understanding (Col. 2:3). Thus, only Christ embodies the ideal of the Wise Man of Proverbs. Otherwise,

---

[12] There is both helpful discussion and an instructive example with an initially unpromising verse (Prov. 15:27) in Dennis E. Johnson, *Him We Proclaim* (Nutley: Presbyterian & Reformed, 2007), 303–313. See also Anthony Selvaggio, *A Proverbs Driven Life* (Wapwallopen: Shepherd Press, 2008), 20–23.

they really are either banal maxims or unattainable ideals. Solomon's words, taken to their fullest meaning (as we do with the royal Psalms), form a glorious portrait, pointing us to the excellence of Christ. Only Jesus could perfectly balance Proverbs' virtues-in-tension, knowing (for instance) to be abrupt with the Rich Young Ruler, "teasing" with the Canaanite mother, and persistently patient with the Samaritan woman. We would have been lost at sea.

2. Christ is the way (John 14:6) and the life lived in believing union with Him is the way (Acts 9:2; 19:9, 23; 22:4; 24:14, 22). Proverbs constantly confronts us with *two ways*: the ways of wisdom and of folly, of death and of life, of cursing and of blessing, of joy and of sorrow. Taken in isolation, one might suppose that Solomon was a moralist, urging readers to cherish values and build a life on them. However, he tells us at the outset that everything hinges on fear of Yahweh (1:7), which he (or the final editor) reminds us of as we walk out the door (31:30). As we saw in Chapter 3, this fear of Yahweh is a contentful relationship. That relationship comes to full fruition in the incarnation of Yahweh in the person of Jesus Christ, who embodies both *the* way *and* those values which characterize it, such as truth and life (John 14:6). In this way, Proverbs points us to Christ, the very embodiment of the way of God, of wisdom, of life, of truth, of blessing and joy.

3. The wise and upright life in its perfection is unattainable by us because, as Solomon says, "there is no one who does not sin" (1 Kings 8:46). Taken as an expression of God's holy and lofty standards, the dictums and principles of Proverbs stand over against us, and they condemn us. We need more than sage advice and pithy observations. We need atonement, we need forgiveness, we need reconciliation with God, we need a wisdom and a righteousness we do not natively possess. We need a Savior. And so in this way, as with the Law of Moses, Proverbs points us to our need of Christ as our Savior.

4. Christ is the vindication of God's justice (Dan. 7:13–14, 22; John 5:22; Rom. 3:26). There is a tension throughout Proverbs, though it mostly simmers beneath the surface. By literary definition,

generally speaking the proverbs depict reality as black and white: there are wise people and fools; there are righteous people and wicked. The wise/righteous are blessed, the fools/wicked are cursed. However, none of this is universally true in the strict sense. By that, I mean no man in himself is perfectly righteous, and godly behavior is not always instantly and pleasantly rewarded. All of this ultimately is squared away in Christ, whose perfect righteousness is imputed to believers, who will perfectly and finally judge the living and the dead, and who will usher in a new world in which righteousness will be at home, justice will rule, and the knowledge of God will fill the earth as water fills the seas (Isa. 11:9; 2 Tim. 4:1; 2 Peter 3:13; Rev. 20–22). All the tensions in proverbs are fully and finally resolved in Christ, and in Christ alone.

5. Both Christ and His apostles call converted believers to be "wise as serpents" (Matt. 10:16), and to walk in a wise manner (Eph. 5:15; Col. 4:5). But what is wisdom? What is it to be a wise Christian? What is it, more specifically, to be a wise Christian husband, wife, father, child, employee, employer, citizen? Where can a Christian find details, principles, directions, instruction? We find this instruction in the Bible of Christ and the apostles: in the book of Proverbs.

The church today badly needs the fulsome, sage, bracing wisdom of Proverbs. It is my hope that these principles will bring Proverbs back into the life of the church, where God intends that it live.

Bibliography

Adams, Jay E. *Competent to Counsel.* Grand Rapids: Baker, 1970.

Alford, Henry. *Alford's Greek Testament: An Exegetical and Critical Commentary.* Bellingham, WA: Logos Research Systems, Inc., 2010.

Alter, Robert. *The Art of Biblical Poetry.* New York: Basic Books, 1985.

Archer, Gleason L., Jr. *A Survey of Old Testament Introduction.* 3rd ed. Chicago: Moody, 1994. (This is a must-have introduction to the Old Testament for Bible-believers who want substantial reading dealing with the facts of Old Testament introduction.)

Blocher, Henri. "The Fear of the Lord as the 'Principle' of Wisdom." *Tyndale Bulletin* Volume 28. Cambridge: Tyndale House, 1977: 3–28.

Bricker, Daniel P. "The Doctrine Of The 'Two Ways' In Proverbs." *Journal of the Evangelical Theological Society* 38, no 4 (1995): 501–517.

Bromiley, G. W., ed. *International Standard Bible Encyclopedia.* 4 vols. Grand Rapids: Eerdmans, 1988.

Brown, Francis, Samuel Rolles Driver, and Charles Augustus Briggs. *Enhanced Brown-Driver-Briggs Hebrew and English Lexicon.* Electronic ed. Oak Harbor, WA: Logos Research Systems, 2000. (Editors were theologically liberal, but this is still useful for any advancing student of Biblical Hebrew.)

Bullock, C. Hassell. *An Introduction to the Old Testament Poetic Books.* Chicago: Moody, 1988. (Conservative; basically good book.)

Carson, D. A. *Exegetical Fallacies.* Grand Rapids: Baker, 1984.

Childs, Brevard S. *Introduction to the Old Testament as Scripture.* Philadelphia: Fortress, 1979.

Cohen, Abraham. *Proverbs.* Soncino Books of the Bible. Brooklyn: Soncino, 1946.

Cremer, Hermann. *Biblico-Theological Lexicon of New Testament Greek.* 4th ed. Edinburgh: T. &. T. Clark: 1895.

Curtis, Edward M., and John J. Brugaletta. *Discovering the Way of Wisdom.* Grand Rapids: Kregel, 2004. (Ed Curtis has taught Old Testament classes at Biola University for decades. Written for earnest Christians looking to learn of spiritual growth from OT wisdom literature; built on good scholarship; adorned with illustration and application. Extended discussion of the NT concept of the Logos [cf. John 1:1], relating it to Wisdom.)

Delitzsch, Franz. *Proverbs, Ecclesiastes, Song of Solomon.* Vol. 6. *Commentary on the Old Testament in Ten Volumes.* Grand Rapids: Eerdmans, 1973 (reprint of 1872 edition). (Over a century old, but still a standard verse-by-verse commentary on the Hebrew text from a more conservative position.)

Dillard, Raymond B. and Tremper Longman III. *An Introduction to the Old Testament.* Grand Rapids: Zondervan, 1994.

Drane, John William. *Introducing the Old Testament.* Completely rev. and updated. Oxford: Lion Publishing plc, 2000.

Elwell, W. A., & B. J. Beitzel. *Baker Encyclopedia of the Bible.* Grand Rapids: Baker Book House, 1988.

Fox, Michael V. *Proverbs 1–9.* Vol. 18A. *The Anchor Bible.* New York: Doubleday, 2000.

———. *Proverbs 10–31.* Vol. 18B. *The Anchor Bible.* New York: Doubleday, 2009. (Jewish, theologically liberal, but full of much thoughtful, useful material.)

Garrett, Duane A. *Proverbs, Ecclesiastes, Song of Songs.* Nashville: Broadman Press, 1993. (Helpful and solid introduction, but frustrating and more often useless commentary. Garrett is more interested in discussing putative relations and groupings of verses than he is in opening the meaning of the verses themselves. I would say that 90% of the time I go to Garrett for help with a verse, I come away disappointed.)

Hamilton, James M. Jr. *God's Glory in Salvation through Judgment.* Wheaton: Crossway, 2010. (Terrifically insightful and readable Biblical theology, full of Hamilton's own creative insights and leads to other literature.)

Harris, R. Laird, Gleason L. Archer Jr., and Bruce K. Waltke, eds. *Theological Wordbook of the Old Testament.* Chicago: Moody, 1980.

Harrison, Everett F. *Jesus and His Contemporaries.* Grand Rapids: Baker, 1970 (reprint).

Harrison, Roland K. *Introduction to the Old Testament.* Grand Rapids: Eerdmans, 1969. (A tad less conservative than Archer, and more advanced reading level. Good book.)

Henry, Matthew. *Matthew Henry's Commentary on the Whole Bible : Complete and Unabridged in One Volume.* Peabody: Hendrickson, 1996.

Hildebrandt, Ted. "Proverbs 22:6a: Train Up a Child?" *Grace Theological Journal* Volume 9. Grace Seminary, 1988; 2002: 3–19.

Hill, Andrew E. and John H. Walton. 2nd ed. *A Survey of the Old Testament.* Grand Rapids: Zondervan, 2000.

Hunter, W. Bingham. *The God Who Hears*. Downers Grove: InterVarsity, 1986.

Jeffery, Steve, Michael Ovey, and Andrew Sach. *Pierced for Our Transgressions*. Wheaton: Crossway Books, 2007.

Jenni, Ernst, and Claus Westermann. *Theological Lexicon of the Old Testament*. Peabody, Mass.: Hendrickson Publishers, 1997.

Kidner, Derek. *Proverbs*. Tyndale Old Testament Commentaries. Downers Grove: InterVarsity Press, 1964. (Although Kidner does not comment on every verse, what he does say is always well worth considering. Very readable; Kidner has a wonderful style of writing, positively Proverbial in its pithy, well-considered terseness.)

―――. *Psalms 73–150*. Tyndale Old Testament Commentaries. Downers Grove: InterVarsity Press, 1975.

―――. *The Wisdom of Proverbs, Job & Ecclesiastes*. Downers Grove: InterVarsity Press, 1985.

Kitchen, John A. *Proverbs. Mentor Commentaries*. Ross-Shire: Christian Focus Publications, 2006. (Solid, reverent, unhurried verse-by-verse commentary. Recommended.)

Kitchen, K. A. "Proverbs And Wisdom Books Of The Ancient Near East: The Factual History Of A Literary Form." *Tyndale Bulletin* 28, no. 1, (1977).

Koehler, Ludwig, and Walter Baumgartner. *The Hebrew and Aramaic Lexicon of the Old Testament*. Edited by Johann Jakob Stam. Translated by M. E. J. Richardson. CD-ROM ed. Leiden: Brill, 1994. BibleWorks, v.8.

Kugel, James L. *How to Read the Bible*. New York: Free Press: 2007.

―――. *The Idea of Biblical Poetry*. Baltimore: Johns Hopkins, 1981. (Academic, knowledge of Hebrew assumed. Examines nature of Hebrew poetry, strongly opposing idea that "parallelism" means "line one is echoed in line two." Also argues that poetry is part of a continuum, rather than a precisely-distinct literary genre.)

La Sor, William Sanford, David Allan Hubbard, and Frederick William Bush. *Old Testament Survey*. Grand Rapids: Eerdmans, 1982. (Theologically more liberal than Harrison or Archer [or me]; still some thoughts and facts of value.)

Longman, Tremper III. *How to Read Proverbs*. Downers Grove: InterVarsity Press, 2002. (Readable and generally helpful. Deals with issues of interpretation and application, discussing the literary shape and genre of Proverbs and setting it in its context in the ancient Near East. Gives some development of the themes of money, sexuality, and use of words in Proverbs. The text is the New Living Translation paraphrase, an odd choice perhaps explained by Longman's involvement as senior translator for its wisdom books. Unfortunately, the reader must keep flipping back and forth from the text to the endnotes.)

―――. *Proverbs. Baker Commentary on the Old Testament Wisdom and Psalms.* Grand Rapids: Baker, 2006.

Longman III, Tremper and Peter Enns, eds. *Dictionary of the Old Testament: Wisdom, Poetry & Writings.* Downers Grove: InterVarsity, 2008.

Lucas, Ernest. *The Psalms and Wisdom Literature. Exploring the Old Testament.* Volume 3. London: SPCK, 2003.

Mc Kane, William. *Proverbs: a New Approach. Old Testament Library.* Philadelphia: Westminster, 1970. (Radically liberal; unless you're a writing academic, don't bother.)

Murphy, Roland E. *Proverbs.* Word Biblical Commentary. Waco: Word, 1998. (I cannot recommend the book to any but academics, and they won't find much help in it. Roman Catholic writer Murphy does not seem that interested in the text, whose ascriptions of authorship he does not take seriously. He is theologically tone-deaf, and often startlingly cursory, given the in-depth intent of the Word Biblical Commentary series in general. Disappointing.)

Noel, Cherie. *Wise Up! Wisdom in Proverbs.* Rocky Mount: Positive Action for Christ, 1992. (This is a study guide for children of junior-high age, available with a teacher's guide. It is really quite good; I recommend it. The publisher's address is P. O. Box 1948, 833 Falls Road, Rocky Mount, NC 27802-1948.)

Payne, J. Barton. *The Theology of the Older Testament.* Grand Rapids: Zondervan, 1962. (Good book; a bit heavy on the Covenant Theology here and there, but much valuable material.)

Petersen, David L., and Kent Harold Richards. *Interpreting Hebrew Poetry.* Minneapolis: Fortress, 1992.

Phillips, Daniel J. *The Sovereignty of Yahweh in the Book of Proverbs: an Exercise in Theological Exegesis.* Master of Divinity thesis, Talbot Theological Seminary, May 1983. (Available from the Biola University library in La Mirada, California; or online at http://faculty.gordon.edu/hu/bi/Ted_Hildebrandt/OTeSources/20-Proverbs/Text/Books/Phillips_YahwehInProv/Phillips_YhwhInProverbs.doc.)

―――. *The World-Tilting Gospel.* Grand Rapids: Kregel, 2011.

Ray, Bruce. *Withhold Not Correction.* Nutley: Presbyterian & Reformed, 1978.

Richards, Lawrence O. *Expository Dictionary of Bible Words..* Grand Rapids: Zondervan, 1985.

Ross, Allen P. "Proverbs," in vol. 5 of *Expositor's Bible Commentary*, Ed. Frank E. Gaebelein. Grand Rapids: Zondervan, 1991.

Rydelnik, Michael. *The Messianic Hope*. Nashville: B&H Publishing, 2010.

Ryken, Leland. *How to Read the Bible as Literature.*. Grand Rapids: Zondervan, 1984.

Scott, R. B. Y. *Proverbs, Ecclesiastes*. The Anchor Bible. New York: Doubleday, 1965. (Liberal; seldom very helpful.)

Selvaggio, Anthony. *A Proverbs Driven Life*. Wapwallopen: Shepherd Press, 2008. (Develops themes from Proverbs. Some good pastoral wisdom, particularly regarding marriage. However, virtually no interaction with the Hebrew text; and unfortunately the reader is forced to keep two bookmarks, in both text and endnotes. Wish I'd thought of the title first!)

Soggin, J. Alberto. *Introduction to the Old Testament*. Translated by John Bowden. Philadelphia: Westminster, 1976. (Museum-piece of unhinged liberalism.)

Spurgeon, C. H. *My Sermon Notes, Volumes 1 & 2: Genesis to Malachi*. Bellingham, WA: Logos Research Systems, Inc., 2009.

Steinmann, Andrew E. "Proverbs 1–9 as a Solomonic Composition." *Journal of the Evangelical Theological Society* Volume 43, 4, 657–674, 2000.

Stuart, Douglas. *Old Testament Exegesis*. 2nd ed. Philadelphia: Westminster, 1984.

Swindoll, Charles. *Growing Wise in Family Life*. Portland: Multnomah, 1988.

———. *You and Your Child*. Nashville: Nelson, 1977.

Tenney, Merrill C., ed. *Zondervan Pictorial Encyclopedia of the Bible*. 5 vols. Grand Rapids: Zondervan, 1975.

Toy, Crawford H. *A Critical and Exegetical Commentary on the Book of Proverbs*. International Critical Commentary. Edinburgh: T. & T. Clark, 1899. (Quite liberal; still, some material of use to the student of the Hebrew text.)

Tripp, Tedd. *Shepherding a Child's Heart*. Wapwallopen: Shepherd Press, 1995. (A seminar with Tedd Tripp, and this book, were extremely helpful to my wife and me. I would say that Tripp's highlighting of Proverbs 4:23 is one of the single most pivotal Biblical insights I've ever been exposed to as a parent.)

Unger, Merrill F., and William White, Jr. *Nelson's Expository Dictionary of the Old Testament*. Nasvhille: Nelson, 1980.

VanGemeren, Willem A. *New International Dictionary of Old Testament Theology and Exegesis*. 5 vols. Grand Rapids: Zondervan, 1997.

Virkler, Henry. *Hermeneutics: Principles and Processes of Biblical Interpretation*. Grand Rapids: Baker, 1981.

Waltke, Bruce K. *The Book Of Proverbs: Chapters 1–15*. Grand Rapids: Eerdmans, 2004.

———. *The Book of Proverbs: Chapters 15–31*. Grand Rapids: Eerdmans, 2005.

———. *Genesis: a Commentary*. Grand Rapids: Zondervan, 2001.

———. "Proverbs, Theology of." In Willem A. VanGemeren, *New International Dictionary of Old Testament Theology and Exegesis*, 4:1079–1094.

Walton, John H., and Andrew E Hill. *A Survey of the Old Testament*. 2nd edtion. Grand Rapids: Zondervan, 2000. (Unremarkable on Proverbs. Good section on poetry, pp. 307–326.)

Walvoord, John F., Roy B. Zuck, and Dallas Theological Seminary. *The Bible Knowledge Commentary : An Exposition of the Scriptures*. Wheaton, IL: Victor Books, 1983–.

Watson, Wilfred G. E. *Classical Hebrew Poetry*. 2nd edition. Sheffield: JSOT Press, 1986. (Very technical, academic, detailed analysis of Hebrew poetry, with comparison to Akkadian and Ugaritic poetry. Textbook style.)

Wenham, Gordon J. *Genesis 1–15*. Word Biblical Commentary. Waco: Word, 1987. (Deals with Hebrew text, doctrine; doesn't deal with Genesis as history. No help on Bible and science questions, no help on authorship.)

Wood, D. R. W. and I. Howard Marshall. *New Bible Dictionary*, 3rd ed. Leicester, England; Downers Grove, Ill.: InterVarsity Press, 1996.

Wright, H. Norman. *Making Peace With Your Partner*. Waco: Word, 1988. (Conflict resolution in marriage.)

Young, Edward J. *Introduction to the Old Testament*. Grand Rapids: Eerdmans, 1960.

Zöckler, Otto. "The Proverbs of Solomon." Translated and edited by Charles Aiken. In John Peter Lange's *Commentary on the Holy Scriptures*. Grand Rapids: Zondervan, 1978 (reprint).

Index of Major Subjects

Index of Scriptures

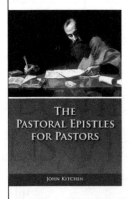

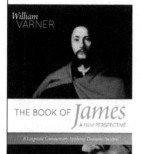

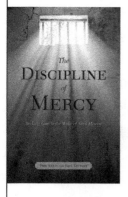

Expository Listening

Ken Ramey

Expository Listening is your handbook on biblical listening. It is designed to equip you not only to understand what true, biblical preaching sounds like, but also how to receive it, and ultimately, what to do about it

"Ken Ramey is a fine preacher and expositor himself with a shepherd's heart and a wonderful gift for teaching. I'm very grateful he has tackled this subject and given the church such an invaluable resource."

—John MacArthur

"The book is a valuable addition to the meager field of listening to sermons. I highly recommend it to every preacher, who would do himself and his congregation a huge favor by making it available. Get it today!"

—Jay Adams

978-1-934-952-09-2
Paperback, 144 pages

Available now at www.kressbiblical.com.

CPSIA information can be obtained
at www.ICGtesting.com
Printed in the USA
BVHW041409190420
577913BV00008B/542